Race, State, and Armed Forces in
Independence-Era Brazil

RACE, STATE, AND ARMED FORCES IN INDEPENDENCE-ERA BRAZIL

Bahia, 1790s–1840s

HENDRIK KRAAY

STANFORD UNIVERSITY PRESS

Stanford, California

Stanford University Press
Stanford, California
© 2001

Printed in the United States of America on acid-free,
archival-quality paper.

Library of Congress Cataloging-in-Publication Data
Kraay, Hendrik, 1964–
      Race, state, and armed forces in independence-era
   Brazil : Bahia, 1790's–1840's / Hendrik Kraay.
          p.   cm.
      Includes bibliographical references and index.
      ISBN 0-8047-4248-0 (alk. paper)
        1. Salvador (Brazil)—History—19th century.
   2. Salvador (Brazil)—Race relations.   3. Bahia (Brazil :
   State)—Militia—Recruiting, enlistment, etc.   4. Blacks—
   Brazil—Bahia (State)—History—19th century.   5. Social
   classes—Bahia (State)—History—19th century.   6. Civil-
   military relations—Brazil—Salvador.   7. Occupations
   and race.   I. Title.
   F2651.S1357 K73   2002
   306.2'7'098142—dc21   2001048429

Original printing 2001

Last figure below indicates year of this printing:
10   09   08   07   06   05   04   03   02   01

Typeset by Techbooks in 10.5/12.5 Minion

CONTENTS

LIST OF TABLES, FIGURES, AND MAPS

A Note on Currency, Military Ranks, Orthography, and Names

During the nineteenth century, the Brazilian currency was the mil-réis, 1,000 réis, written 1$000; 1,000 mil-réis, one *conto*, was written 1:000$000. The mil-réis declined considerably in value during the period covered by this book, from 72 English pence in 1808 to 28.7 pence in 1850. To compensate somewhat for this decline and to make possible comparisons of wealth among individuals whose estates were assessed at different times, I have used the exchange rate to convert currency figures in the tables and relevant discussions of officer wealth to "constant" 1822 mil-réis, when the currency was worth 49 pence.* Technically speaking, this is not a constant mil-réis, but it does make it possible to compensate partially for inflation.

Most eighteenth- and nineteenth-century Luso-Brazilian army ranks can be readily translated into English equivalents, except for *alferes* (an infantry and cavalry rank) and *segundo tenente* (the equivalent rank in the artillery and engineers), which I have both translated as second lieutenant; *tenente* (infantry and cavalry) and *primeiro tenente* (artillery and engineers), both translated as first lieutenant; and *furriel*, third sergeant.

Portuguese orthography has undergone a number of changes since the eighteenth century, and following convention, I have modernized the spelling of names in the text, retaining original orthography in the notes and bibliography.

---

*Exchange rate data is published in Mattoso, *Bahia: a cidade*, 243, n. 500.

Brazilian naming practices were maddeningly flexible. Individuals were often known by only a distinctive part of their given or last names and freely added or subtracted surnames during their lives. Thus Marshal Luiz Paulino de Oliveira Pinto da França was known as Marshal Luiz Paulino. Such usage of first names was and is common in Brazil, and implies no disrespect to the people in question. When it is known—as in Luiz Paulino's case—I refer to individuals by the name which they preferred (or which contemporary sources used); otherwise, I selected the portion of their name that would cause the least amount of confusion. Thus, for example, in Chapters 4 and 5, Lieutenant Colonel José Bruno Antunes Guimarães is referred to as Bruno, which is how he initialed documents, while Captain Joaquim José de Santana, who took Gomes as his surname in the early 1820s, is referred to in Chapters 4 and 8 as Gomes. I do not know whether he would have preferred this, but at least it distinguishes him from the other Joaquims, Josés, and Santanas that appear in this book (most notably his father, Lieutenant Colonel Joaquim José de Santana, who for lack of alternatives is referred to in Chapter 4 as Santana, but also their colleague, Colonel Joaquim de Santana Neves, who is referred to as Neves in Chapters 4 and 5). In the interest of clearly distinguishing Marshal Felisberto Caldeira Brant Pontes from his nephew, Colonel Felisberto Gomes Caldeira, I refer to the former as Brant (not the more common Caldeira Brant) and the latter as Caldeira. If readers find this confusing, they can take some comfort in the fact that I also do.

PREFACE

The author of a book that has been a decade in the making incurs numerous debts. Several institutions contributed research funding: the Social Sciences and Humanities Research Council of Canada, the Universities of Texas and Calgary, the Izaak Walton Killam Memorial Foundation (University of British Columbia), and the Associação Brasileira de Estudos Canadenses. My doctoral advisor, Richard Graham, provided years of guidance and support, not to mention the suggestion that resulted in this book. Roderick Barman, my postdoctoral advisor, pulled me in different directions, and likewise provided guidance and support. The research assistants who worked with me on this book deserve special thanks for their hard work: Lucineide dos Santos Vieira, Maria Cecília Ortolan Alves, Renato Soares dos Santos, Sonya Marie Scott, and Teresa dos Reis Lima. Elaine Ng drew the maps, graphs, and genealogies.

Numerous friends and colleagues exchanged ideas with me, called my attention to additional sources, and enriched the process of research and writing: Alexandra K. Brown, Avanete Pereira Souza, Bert J. Barickman, Célia Levy, Lt. Col. Celso Jaloto Avila Junior, Dale T. Graden, Erivaldo Fagundes Neves, Flávio dos Santos Gomes, Gladys Sabina Ribeiro, João José Reis, Kim D. Butler, Luís Henrique Dias Tavares, Luiz R. B. Mott, Marcus Joaquim Maciel de Carvalho, Maria Inês Côrtes de Oliveira, Mary Ann Mahony, Onildo Reis David, Peter M. Beattie, Sandra Lauderdale Graham, Ubiratan Castro de Araújo, and Walter Fraga Filho. I thank them all and hope that I have in some way reciprocated. Bert J. Barickman commented on early drafts of Chapters 3 and 4, and read the entire manuscript for Stanford University Press, as did Jeffrey Needell, who subjected it to his sharp and critical eye. The book is much the better for their assistance, but its flaws are of course solely my responsibility.

The Rotary Clubs of Kemptville (Ontario) and Volta Redonda-Leste (Rio de Janeiro), which sponsored and received me as an exchange student, set me on this path in 1982, although I did not know it then. Thanks to the Clinger, Galhardi, and Arbex families for their many lessons about Brazilian society. For their hospitality during my research trips, I especially thank Flávio Moura de Souza, Elom Moura de Souza, and Marcel and Denise Lavallée. Finally, I dedicate this book to my wife, Judith Elaine Clark, who did not proofread, edit, or otherwise contribute to it, but made the process more pleasant and worthwhile in numerous other ways.

Portions of Chapters 6 and 8 were originally published in " 'As Terrifying as Unexpected': The Bahian Sabinada, 1837–1838," *Hispanic American Historical Review* 72 (1992): 501–27. Portions of Chapters 3 and 7 were originally published in "Reconsidering Recruitment in Imperial Brazil," in *The Americas* 55 (July 1998): 1–33. Portions of Chapters 4, 5, and 8 originally appeared in "The Politics of Race in Independence-Era Bahia: The Black Militia Officers of Salvador, 1790–1840," in *Afro-Brazilian Culture and Politics: Bahia, 1790s–1990s,* ed. Hendrik Kraay, 30–56. Armonk, NY: M. E. Sharpe, 1998.

Race, State, and Armed Forces in
Independence-Era Brazil

Introduction

Armed forces lie at the center of modern states. This assertion, something of a truism in the historiography of early modern and modern Europe, whose multiple implications have been developed by scholars such as Charles Tilly and Brian Downing (among many others), has rarely been considered for Latin America, especially during the early years of ninteenth-century state formation.[1] The collapse of the colonial state and military apparati in the independence wars of the 1810s and early 1820s, followed by the scourges of caudillismo and political instability, have relegated military institutions to the historiographical back burner. Indeed, studies of immediate post-independence armed forces are almost as rare as works on the late-colonial militaries are common.[2] Yet armed forces often were a key issue in post-independence politics. Military institutions touched the lives of thousands of men and women, while their reform preoccupied liberals and conservatives alike.

This book examines the regular army and militias from the 1790s to the 1840s in the Brazilian city of Salvador, capital of the sugar-plantation captaincy and later province of Bahia, to trace the fundamental social and political changes that took place as the result of independence, which came to Brazil in 1822 but was only made effective in Bahia with the forcible expulsion of a Portuguese garrison in July 1823. Several themes run through this book. On one level, it is a study of state formation viewed from the periphery, rather than the center. Part of the imperial Portuguese and later Brazilian military, the Bahian army garrison was nevertheless organized locally until

1

the 1840s, when it was incorporated into the new national Brazilian army. Decisions taken in distant imperial capitals repeatedly affected the Bahian military in unexpected ways and the construction of a national Brazilian army entrained important changes. From direct control over the garrison through personal and familial ties to officers, the Bahian planter class's influence over the military gave way to indirect control through the Brazilian state, an ultimately more effective means of ensuring that the armed forces served their interests. Rather than the autonomous state that Raimundo Faoro and Eul-Soo Pang have seen as central to Luso-Brazilian history, this study underscores the close connections between state and dominant class.[3]

Not only do armed forces provide a well-documented trail through the evolution of the state apparatus, their influence also stretched deep into urban Brazilian society. In the late colonial period, the better part of the able-bodied free and freed adult male population served in a branch of the armed forces. No other sector of the state reached so far into society and a study of the military is thus a key contribution to the social history of urban Brazil that focuses on that large part of society who were neither slaves nor planters, the traditional categories of Brazilian historiography since at least the work of Gilberto Freyre in the 1930s.[4] In its various guises—regular army and militias—the military embodied, preserved, and elaborated the class and race hierarchies of colonial society. It constituted a key locus for struggles over the nature of postindependence society and was the constant object of liberal reform projects. To trace the evolution of military society and to follow the threads of military politics is thus to wrestle with the critical issues that Brazilians faced before and after independence.

At all levels, the Brazilian military was highly porous to civilian society. Certainly this was true for the militias and even more so for the civilian National Guard that replaced them in 1831. But it was also true for the army enlisted ranks and officer corps. Familiar concepts such as Erving Goffman's total institutions or Michel Foucault's "disciplinary society" have little relevance for the late colonial and early imperial Brazilian military, deeply embedded in urban society.[5] Rather, I seek to understand militaries as the product of usually conflictual social processes. Military discipline consisted of a complex interaction among soldiers, officers, and civilians, in which officers struggled with limited success to impose their views on enlisted men. Officers' concepts of professionalism left considerable latitude for the pursuit of nonmilitary interests. After independence, the Brazilian state and the emerging national army attempted (with some success) to shift the terms of this negotiation in the institution's favor.

In this light, states—and armed forces—are complex organizations through which individuals and groups pursue their interests, but they also constitute more abstract, potentially hegemonic forces that shape politics and even the culture of all groups in society.[6] They are fundamentally social institutions, the product of interactions among people who, while admittedly enjoying unequal power, struggle to shape their lives and in so doing affect state structures and shape state practices.[7] Colonial situations such as that of Bahia before independence (and the quasi-colonial one after independence) add the wrinkle of autonomy to the complex texture of the state. While much literature has demonstrated that Brazilian colonial interests played a key role in elaborating the reality of the colonial state, it is clear that the Portuguese state could and did sometimes pursue goals at odds with those of the Bahian planter class.[8] Much the same dynamic has been traced by José Murilo de Carvalho after independence, where within an overall context of close connections between imperial state and planter class, the imperial Brazilian government pursued certain policies notably at odds with the planter class, sometimes succeeding, sometimes failing.[9]

For many historians, Latin American independence was a nonevent as subjection to the imperial metropolis of Spain or Portugal was replaced by economic dependence on Great Britain. Slavery and latifundia endured; neither liberals' desires for legal equality nor their preference for small farms could overcome long-established social and economic patterns.[10] Such an emphasis on continuities is misplaced. Many years ago, Florestan Fernandes argued that, in fact, independence constituted "Brazil's first great social revolution" for it forced Brazilian planters to constitute themselves as a ruling class; the construction of a Brazilian state to replace the colonial regime centered in Lisbon thus marked an important stage in what this sociologist called his country's bourgeois revolution.[11] While few today accept Fernandes's overly teleological approach, a growing literature for Spanish America has demonstrated that the construction of a ruling class was no simple task. Not only did elites have to contend with competing regional economic interests and ideological differences, they also faced subordinate classes whose members actively contested elite projects, took liberal ideals to heart, and insisted on making their voices heard.[12] While there may not have been a profound shift in the locus of social and economic power after independence, politics would never be the same, even in Brazil, where the preservation of the monarchy and slavery mark important continuities with the colonial regime. Nevertheless, citizenship, constitutional precepts, and liberal discourse made it impossible to continue traditional practices unchanged.

The story of the Brazilian military that follows is thus one more chapter in the history of the "Age of Revolution" that swept the Atlantic World from the 1770s until well into the nineteenth century, and in countless ways, laid the foundations of the modern world.[13] To be sure, Brazil fits oddly into the Age of Revolution. With its peaceful transition to independence (at least in the misleading textbook interpretation), political unity of the former Portuguese colonies, and durable imperial regime so different from the ephemeral Mexican monarchies, Brazil can easily be mistaken for a continuation of the Old Regime, and both Peggy Liss and Lester D. Langley almost entirely ignore the country in their important surveys of the Americas in the Age of Revolution.[14] As we shall see, Brazilians of all classes could not escape the changes brought by the American, French, and Haitian Revolutions. Moreover, Bahia experienced bitter fighting comparable in intensity to that of many parts of Spanish America, dominated by the year-long siege of Salvador. Major rounds of social and political unrest in 1824, 1831–1833, and 1837–1838 involved the province's armed forces and constituted profound challenges to the political and social status quo. Furthermore, important changes in the social composition of the armed forces took place during these years, many of them the direct result of political and institutional changes in Brazil

This book's social- and political-history approach differs significantly from much Brazilian historiography in which independence is interpreted as the product of a structural crisis of the old colonial regime. By about 1800 or so, this system, resting on the triple pillars of political domination, a mercantilist commercial system, and forced labor (slavery) was under intense pressure from the rise of capitalism, to which its "primitive accumulation" had contributed. This in turn led to heightened consciousness of colonial exploitation in Brazil and British pressure to break colonial mercantilist restrictions. Out of this crisis grew Brazil's independence movements, which led in turn to the country's incorporation into a new system of dependency.[15] While the analysis of economic structures was a salutary antidote to superficial narratives of independence-era high politics that focused on Rio de Janeiro, it has led to an historiography that has had difficulty grasping the full range of social and political questions at stake throughout the Portuguese empire during this time. Not only is there evidence that the colonial system was not in profound crisis, but there are signs that, in Rio de Janeiro and Salvador, the late-colonial mercantile and plantation economy enjoyed significant autonomy from the Portuguese metropolitan economy.[16] And to see independence as the product of the old colonial regime's crisis can (perhaps inadvertently) turn it into a predetermined outcome, rather than the product of complex social and political struggles. While nationalist historians such as José Honório Rodrigues focus on Rio de Janeiro in their treatment of the independence period (and condemn provinces such as Bahia for not promptly falling in line with the eventual national capital), historiography emanating from outside of the Brazilian intellectual capitals of Rio de Janeiro and São Paulo has underscored that there was no single independence movement that produced "Brazil." The colonies (later provinces) or local *pátrias* (homelands) were central to "Brazilians' " identity and experience; the trajectories of the "independence movements" outside of Rio de Janeiro differed greatly and many did not see themselves as engaged in winning "Brazil's" freedom (in fact, few saw the choice as lying between that and colonial oppression).[17] Such was certainly the case in Bahia, and in the following pages I analyze the multiple issues at stake.

A central thread in this book is the relationship of individuals to the state, or citizenship. Many of the struggles of the Age of Revolution involved defining the relationship between property-holders and the state; citizenship was widely understood to be properly the preserve of those who had a material stake in society. As Luiz dos Santos Vilhena, a professor of Greek who resided in Salvador in the 1790s, put it, "what creates the citizen is property, and the fear of losing it is that which ties him to the *pátria*."[18] In this way exclusive at its origins, citizenship was nevertheless a powerful ideal, the narrower conceptions of it continually contested as those excluded from its benefits sought inclusion by adopting the rhetoric of equality among citizens so dear to liberals. As Bryan S. Turner has put it, "the critical factor in the emergence of citizenship is ... the overt and conscious struggle of social groups to achieve social participation," and Bahia offers much evidence to support this interpretation.[19]

When it came to military service, citizenship was doubly problematic. To fight and die for king, country, or community is of course the epitome of civic virtue in many societies, and the 1824 constitution obligated all Brazilians to take up arms in defence of their nation, much as the Portuguese monarchy expected all of its subjects to defend royal interests. Nevertheless, as Alan Forrest has put it for revolutionary France, a good number of citizens could not see citizenship's value if it required them to serve in the army rank and file.[20] Likewise in Brazil, where a host of race and class criteria regulated recruitment, military service constituted a conundrum for liberal reformers seeking to make citizenship meaningful. In this society, where exemptions from military service were well-established features of hierarchical patron–client relations, the notion of citizenship through military service threatened to reduce, rather than raise, individuals to equality, a paradox noted by Roberto DaMatta.[21]

Citizenship was one of the more visible and widely debated aspects of liberal reform after independence. Liberalism more generally, with its emphasis on universal rights, the need to eliminate privileges (which ancien-régime societies had understood as liberties), and belief in human capacity for betterment was, as Emília Viotti da Costa has stressed, the ideology of a European bourgeoisie. Nineteenth-century Brazil, as she and so many others have reminded us, lacked the social basis for the full flowering of liberalism, which was rather used selectively to advance the interests of the dominant classes and therefore fell far short of its professed ideals—property rights, for example, were more important than the rights of slaves.[22] Castigating Brazilian liberals for their failure to accomplish an idealized program, however, foreshortens our historical perspective, and some scholars have sought to make sense of Brazilian liberalism on its own terms to understand how intellectuals and politicians adopted and adapted this ideology.[23] Brazilian liberals implemented a host of reforms in the armed forces (and elsewhere), particularly during the years that they dominated Brazilian politics, from the late 1820s to the mid-1830s, and liberal ideals and language served as an important critique of the colonial and imperial order, resonating widely in the population.

Race figures prominently in this book's analysis of the Brazilian armed forces. It is, of course, a "social construction," which is not a new concept, as Stuart Schwartz has recently reminded us. Charles Wagley's classic study of "social race" first appeared in 1959, while Marvin Harris wrote a few years later about the "ingenious computation" by which "the genetic tracery of a million years of evolution [is] unraveled and each man assigned to his proper social box."[24] In other words, race is the social significance attributed to the natural variation among human beings. This does not make race any less "real" in its consequences, as Howard Winant has observed in commenting on Barbara Jeanne Fields' argument that race is a form of ideology.[25] If people define race as real, then it certainly has real consequences, and a generation of demographers has demonstrated the strong correlations between diminished life experiences and classification as *pardo* or *preto* in the modern Brazilian census.[26]

The armed forces are a particularly useful set of institutions in which to examine race and racial politics in Brazil. Race is made both by state apparati that find it useful to classify men and women according to such categories (and mandate the labels to be used) and through the actions of individuals who reproduce them. In Brazil, the colonial military upheld a tripartite racial hierarchy of *brancos*, pardos, and pretos; racial politics followed closely the differential experience of military personnel labeled white, brown, or black by the institution. After independence, liberal reforms gradually eliminated institutionalized racial discrimination in the military. In this new, ostensibly nonracial environment, racial politics assumed different, more binary forms, as most pardos and pretos were collapsed into generic "classes of color," while some pardos were absorbed into the category of branco. This book thus underscores the importance of the state in making and upholding race and shaping the patterns of racial politics, a point recently reiterated by Anthony Marx.[27]

Class too is a social construction, the product of a complex process through which people gain consciousness of their shared material interests.[28] Class and race, as the concept of "classes of color" suggests, have gone hand in hand in Brazilian society, as elsewhere. Privileging one category over the other or expecting class to supplant race as society "modernizes"—central premises in the race-versus-class debate—misrepresent the complexity of these categories which together have structured Brazilian social hierarchies and continue to do so.[29]

The focus on the single Portuguese captaincy and later Brazilian province of Bahia serves several purposes. Salvador was Brazil's second city, a major military center, and the locus of profound social and political conflicts after independence. Studying a single garrison makes possible the analysis of social ties that military men maintained with local society, connections difficult to perceive at the national level, on which, in any case, few military men acted. While regional political history is well established for nineteenth-century Mexico (and Peru),[30] it has found less favor in the historiography of the vaster, albeit less populous, Brazilian empire.[31] Still, the experience of imperial capitals cannot stand for entire countries and there is much to be learned from examining Brazil's formation from the perspective of one of its major constituent parts, all the more so when it is acknowledged that "Brazil" was not the necessary outcome of these years' struggles.

The period covered by this book—the 1790s to the 1840s—answers the call (often made but less often heeded) not to separate artificially the colonial, independence, and national periods in Latin American history.[32] In the Brazilian military institutions, where there was a good deal of organizational and personnel continuity during this period, postindependence practice and reform cannot be understood separately from the colonial period, nor can the changes wrought by the independence war in Bahia be comprehended without a thorough consideration of the late colonial period.

Chapter 1 presents the setting for this study—the city of Salvador—and analyzes its social structure. It also briefly surveys the salient political events from the 1790s to the 1840s that are subsequently analyzed in more depth insofar as they bear on the experience of the men (and women) in the armed forces. The following three chapters introduce the colonial army, focusing on its principal sectors of officers, enlisted men, and the militia. Together, these chapters analyze the colonial compact, the class alliances and racial structures that constituted the essence of the Portuguese imperial regime. Chapter 5 turns to the collapse of the colonial military in the five years from 1820 to 1825. The independence war produced numerous unexpected outcomes, breaking the alliance between officers and the planter class, darkening the enlisted ranks, and raising the stature of black and mulatto militiamen. Chapters 6 to 8 resume the sectoral approach to the armed forces; for officers, soldiers, and militiamen, these chapters examine the implications of the construction of the Brazilian state and the implementation of liberal reforms in a slave society that had embodied racial discrimination in its armed forces. The failures of recruitment and discipline reform exemplify the difficulties that liberals faced, while their ambivalence toward the racially discriminatory practices of the late colonial regime underscores their preference for maintaining these social hierarchies. By the 1840s, liberal reform was in rapid retreat in the armed forces and even the epitome of liberalism in military affairs—the National Guard—came to resemble the colonial militias in important ways.

Nevertheless, much was different, and the Conclusion assesses the significance of the changes that had taken place since the 1790s: racial discrimination was no longer legal in the armed forces; in replacing the militias, the National Guard removed them from the purview of the regular military; and the army officer corps increasingly looked to Rio de Janeiro, as careers focused on the national capital. Despite the darkening of the rank and file, corporal punishment was slowly being regulated out of existence. Forced recruitment continued but increasingly embarassed the civilian authorities charged with carrying it out. The nature of military professionalism evolved, leaving less room for officers' nonmilitary interests, while officers gained more control over enlisted men. Liberalism, so revolutionary from the 1790s to the 1830s, was finally tamed, although its revolutionary potential remained. The planter class increasingly ruled through the imperial state that administered the army in that class's larger interest, shared by its members throughout Brazil.

CHAPTER 1

Salvador: Race and Class In a Colonial Brazilian City

European travelers in most cases arrived at Salvador by sea. They invariably remarked on the city's exotic tropical beauty when viewed from shipboard; the sights, sounds, and smells of the bustling commercial lower city, where they landed, disappointed them, and most travelers quickly hired two slaves and a sedan chair in which to escape to the relative comforts of the breezy upper city, where the principal government buildings and elite residences were located.[1] Those travelers who paid attention to military matters reported favorably on the garrison or at least remarked that it was numerous. In 1764, Mrs. Nathaniel Kindersley could not help but notice the "extraordinary number" of militia who turned out to intimidate the unwelcome foreigners.[2] After the Portuguese crown opened Brazil's trade to friendly nations in 1808, travelers regularly stopped at Salvador and often described the impressively large and dapperly dressed militia, not to mention the thousands of men in the regulars. Black and mulatto militiamen sometimes caught their eye, while others surveyed the numerous forts, batteries, and barracks, concluding that the city could not be easily taken.[3] Such observations reveal that, in addition to its functions as one of the Atlantic World's great colonial commercial centers, the conduit for trade with its sugar-growing hinterland, and a center of colonial and ecclesiastical government, Salvador was also a major military base.

Founded in 1549 to serve as the site of Portuguese colonial government, Salvador had grown to about 50,000 people by the early 1800s, when it ranked among the largest cities of the Americas. With independence in

1822, the captaincy (colony) of Bahia, of which Salvador was the capital, became the imperial Brazilian province of the same name (Map 1.1). After border adjustments in the 1820s, Bahia's territory consisted of 563,000 km², about the size of France; its population of 336,000 in 1808 grew to 1,380,000 in 1872.[4]

Salvador was—and still is—a compelling city of contrasts, as Johann Baptist von Spix and Carl Friedrich Philippe von Martius discovered during their visit to the city in 1817–1818. Their host, Marshal Felisberto Caldeira Brant Pontes, the garrison's inspector general, was also one of Bahia's leading sugar planters and merchants. The Germans marveled at Salvador's ritual life, notably the religious processions in which lay brotherhoods exhibited "all the splendor of the old Roman [Catholic] faith," alongside Portuguese regulars with their "martial bearing" and the "pacific militia" of the city, surrounded by the "savage racket of rowdy blacks," and the "tumult of agile mulattoes." Grave European clerics, contrasting with the exhuberant baroque Catholicism of the lay brothers, rounded out this procession.[5] Despite their condescension toward blacks and mulattoes, Spix and Martius captured something of Salvador's social complexity and placed the military at the center of urban life. The product of its particular integration into the Atlantic World as an administrative and commercial center of the sugar plantation economy, Salvador's society exhibited distinct race and class structures. The state apparatus located in the city faced the issues typical of late-eighteenth-century and early-nineteenth-century American colonies, as it struggled to balance colonial and metropolitan (later regional and national) interests.

Salvador and Bahia

Salvador's growth from a hardscrabble outpost on the margins of Portugal's empire to a major colonial metropolis resulted from its ability to dominate the trade of the nearby sugar-growing district, the Recôncavo (Map 1.2). Beginning in the late sixteenth century, sugar plantations spread across the fertile lowlands surrounding the Bay of All Saints, and their slave laborers produced the principal export commodity on which rested the city's fortunes. The Recôncavo's plantations consumed African workers at a terrifying rate, and from the start of the slave trade in the mid-sixteenth century to its end, more than 300 years later, well over a million men and women suffered the middle passage to Salvador; between 1786 and 1856 alone, according to David Eltis's estimates, fully 409,000 Africans landed in

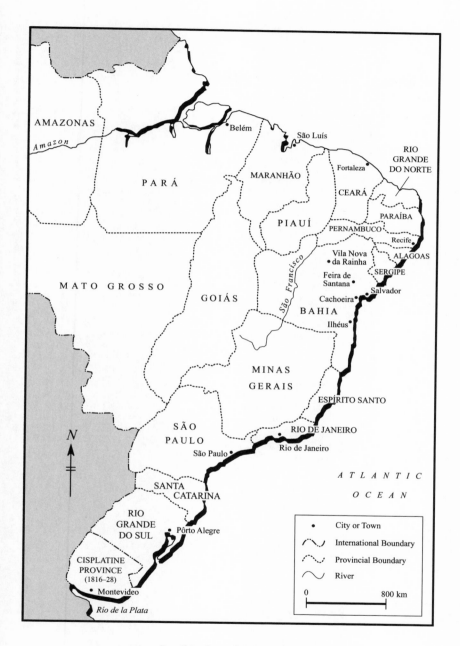

MAP 1.1 Brazil in the early nineteenth century.

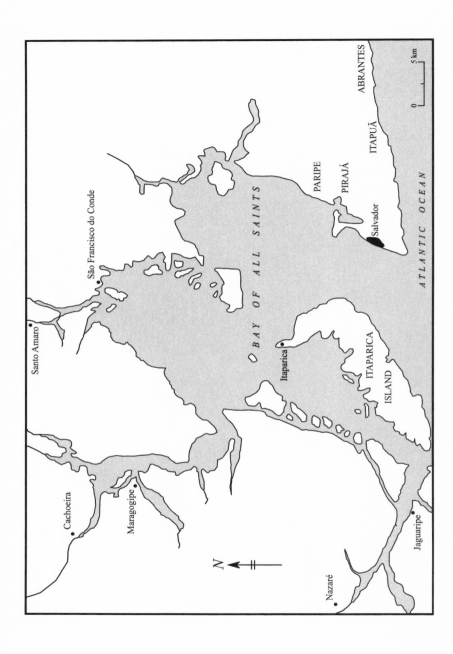

MAP 1.2 The Recôncavo.

SOURCE: "Plano Hydrographico da Bahia de Todos os Santos, Metrópoli do Estado do Brasil, Feito por Jozé Fernandes Portugal em Pernambuco no Anno de MDCCCIII," AHE/Mapas, M-5, G-5, no. 007.

the port. During this period, most of Bahia's slaves came from West Africa, especially the so-called Mina Coast, which arguably constituted another of Salvador's hinterlands.[6]

By the end of the eighteenth century, Recôncavo economy and society formed a complex mosaic, dominated to be sure by the *senhores de engenho* [lords of the (sugar) mill] but by no means limited to sugar plantations. Along the Recôncavo's southern and western margins, the districts of Maragogipe and Jaguaripe produced cassava or manioc, the staple food of slaves and the urban lower classes. West of Cachoeira, the Recôncavo's largest town, stretched a tobacco-growing region, whose crop found markets in Europe, played an important role in the African slave trade, and even turned up in the North American fur trade. Tobacco and cassava were generally small-farm crops; their producers employed but a few slaves rather than the scores who labored on a typical sugar plantation. Land remained plentiful in the region at this time, and free poor squatters could be found in many areas.[7]

Most of the eighteenth century had been a period of relative decline for the Bahian sugar economy, which struggled to compete with more efficient Caribbean producers on the international market and within Brazil against the lure of the precious metals discovered in the 1690s in Minas Gerais. The 1790s marked a dramatic shift in Bahia's fortunes, as the Haitian Revolution's destruction of what was then the world's greatest sugar producer led to a steep increase in prices. As B. J. Barickman has recently shown, the period from the 1790s to the mid-nineteenth century was the last era of prosperity for Bahia's plantation economy. The number of sugar mills soared from 221 to about 800, production also increased about fourfold, new strains of cane and new processing technologies increased efficiency, and a generally plentiful supply of slave labor compensated for the disruptions in trade occasioned by the political unrest of the 1820s and 1830s.[8]

Beyond the Recôncavo stretched the remote and arid *sertão*, whose cattle ranches supplied draft animals and beef on the hoof to sugar plantations and urban consumers. In some areas, cotton production gave this region an export commodity, but distance from markets and poor transportation combined to limit the spread of its cultivation; the discovery of diamonds in the 1840s led to a boom in the far interior. An often lawless frontier, the sertão remained largely beyond the control of government authorities, even as its share of Bahia's population increased significantly during the nineteenth century.[9] The south coast of Bahia, potentially fertile but still substantially under the control of hostile indigenous groups, was the repeated object of settlement schemes and roadbuilding projects, few of which bore fruit at this time.[10]

Bahia's economic networks converged on Salvador. Hundreds of launches and other small craft brought manioc and fresh fruit to the city every day. Along the Estrada das Boiadas (Cattle Drives' Highway) trudged some 20,000 head of cattle per year en route to the city's slaughterhouse.[11] Sugar was gathered in warehouses along the docks to await shipment to Lisbon and, after the opening of Brazil's ports to foreign trade in 1808, to other European cities, while tobacco piled up for shipment to Africa and Europe. Slave traders displayed newly arrived Africans to prospective buyers, shipping the rest of their human cargoes to consignees in the Recôncavo and elsewhere. Importers of wine, olive oil, dried cod, and other European commodities catered to the tastes of Portuguese immigrants, while textiles constituted the principal manufactured goods brought to the city. Wealthy Portuguese-born merchants controlled wholesale commerce but were often effectively rooted in the captaincy; by the 1780s, Salvador-based merchants controlled about half of the shipping to Portugal, and most of that engaged in the African trade. This impressive colonial mercantile establishment faced increasing competition from British, North American, and other European traders after 1808 and suffered rapid decline after independence. Beneath it, a much larger number of shopkeepers, peddlers, petty traders, and small-scale food-sellers engaged in buying and selling, supplying the needs of the city's population. Many were immigrants, and the gouging Portuguese shopkeeper became a staple of Brazilian lore, not to mention the frequent target of nativist wrath after independence. Lower yet in this commercial hierarchy were the African women—slave and freed—who dominated the petty food trade. Travelers frequently noted their existence, while residents of the city sometimes complained that they exercised an untoward monopoly over staple foods.[12]

The city also supported substantial service and artisan sectors. Slave porters not only ferried the well-to-do about the city in sedan chairs, but they carried almost all of the cargoes that passed through the city. Often working independently, remitting a fixed sum to their masters, such slaves-for-hire constructed a work culture that, at times in the nineteenth century, defied authorities' efforts to regulate it.[13] An elaborate hierarchy of trades and skill levels among artsians tended to exclude Afro-Brazilians from the most profitable lines of work. Slavery probably drove down tradesmen's wages, but the acquisition of a skill that improved earning capacity provided a route out of slavery for at least some men; slaves were, in fact, found in numerous trades.[14] And any discussion of the urban economy should not exclude domestic service, the single largest occupational category for both male and female slaves. No wealthy household could do without a large complement of domestic slaves, although as slavery declined, they were replaced by free dependents.[15] This was, nevertheless, a city whose economy could not employ all of its people; beggars and "vagrants" abounded, constituting a destitute mass whose members enjoyed freedom but preoccupied authorities.[16]

Salvador was a compelling city of contrasts. A rich baroque Catholicism flourished alongside vibrant Afro-Brazilian religions that can only be glimpsed when the authorities charged with repressing them deigned to record some details.[17] No spatial segregation existed among the city's main parishes; rather, rich and poor lived "promiscuously," sometimes in the same buildings, as well-off families rented upper story apartments while ground floors and basements were let to poor tenants and sometimes slaves.[18] In this disorderly urban space, military buildings abutted civilian properties. Commanding the heights of the peninsula that demarcates the north side of the Bay of All Saints, Salvador had originally been laid out on an easily defensible site. Forts and batteries constructed mostly in the seventeenth century encircled the old urban core and occupied several strategic points along the coast, but by 1800, the city had outgrown its defense works (Map 1.3). In the 1770s, the abbess of the Lapa Convent complained that a proposed military hospital would overlook the nuns' garden, fearing that the soldiers would threaten their decency. The construction of a new whale-rendering plant beside the small São Diogo fort in 1827 prompted concern that sparks might ignite the fort's powder magazine. Two decades later, blueprints for the expansion of Mouraria Barracks noted the need to demolish several encroaching private houses to make room for the new walls. In this respect, Salvador resembled the circum-Caribbean garrison towns of the Spanish empire.[19]

Salvador's society was similar to that of other urban centers in the plantation districts of the Americas. Extreme inequalities separated rich from poor and a complex racial hierarchy structured social relations. Masters and slaves struggled over the limits of exploitation; countless individual acts of defiance by slaves and several large rebellions between 1807 and 1835 demonstrate that slaves sought to shape their own lives.[20] Furthermore, beginning in 1798, free Bahians began to question publicly their relationship with the colonial state, initiating the half-century of social and

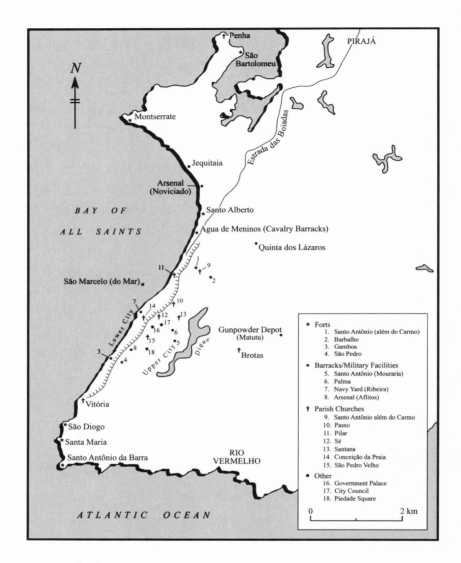

MAP 1.3 Salvador.

SOURCES: "Planta do Accampamento de Pirajá, Itapuan e mais Pontos occupados tanto pelo Exercito Imperial, como pelas Forças, rebeldes . . . executado pelo Capitão de Engenheiros Henrique de Beaurepaire Rohan," 5 July 1839, AHE/Mapas, M-13, BA-253; "Mappa topographica da Cidade de S. Salvador e seus suburbios levantada e dedicada a Illustre Assemblea Provincial por Carlos Augusto Weyll . . . ," c. 1840s, APEB/Mapas e Plantas, 32; "Planta da Cidade de São Salvador . . . ," c. 1889, AHE/Mapas, M-4, G-3, no. 025-c.

political unrest and change, institutional transformations, and restructuring of state–society relations that profoundly affected the armed forces.

Population and Society

Distinguished scholars have long wrestled with the incomplete and often contradictory surviving census data for Salvador before the first reasonably accurate count was completed in 1872.[21] Then the city boasted 108,000 people. Censuses in 1759, 1775, and 1780 each tallied about 40,000 people, while the governor reported 51,000 residents in 1807 on the basis of a census whose records have not survived. In 1848, the provincial president calculated a total free population of 54,652; if the proportion of slaves and freedpeople recorded in seven parishes during an incomplete 1855 census—31 percent (Table 1.1)—may be generalized for the city as a whole in 1848, then its mid-century population stood at slightly more than 70,000. Despite the problems of these sources, they generally concur that the city's population grew slowly, albeit perhaps at an accelerating rate during this period.

More important for understanding the city's society than the population's aggregate figures, however, are the categories used by census-takers. Most tallied the population along two axes, one of legal status (free, freed, or slave), and the other of what they called *qualidade* ("quality") or *cor* ("color"), usually read as "race" by modern scholars (Table 1.1). A third axis, less often counted by census-takers but sometimes implicit in the "racial" categories, was place of birth (Brazil, Europe, or Africa).[22] Status, "race," and place of birth mattered a great deal to contemporaries, and throughout this period, individuals' relationship to the state was affected by these categories, themselves in part the product of state action.

Until 1888, Brazil was a slave society. Free, freed, and enslaved lived under distinct legal regimes and faced different obligations toward the state. Several decades' worth of research has debunked the myth that Iberian slavery was milder than its Anglo-American counterpart; indeed, a central pillar of this argument—that slaves enjoyed legal rights—has crumbled under the weight of evidence that such "rights" sometimes did not even exist. Self-purchase, for instance, was but a widely accepted custom, not a legal right, and as Manuela Carneiro da Cunha has argued, the state judiciously avoided limiting masters' property rights until the 1870s, when it began to regulate abolition.[23] Despite its commitment to upholding masters' private power over slaves, the state's very presence as an institution introduced contradictions into the slave–master relationship, sometimes affording astute slaves

TABLE 1.1

Population of Salvador (in Percentages) by Race and Status,
1775–1855

Year and Source	Free	Freed	Slave	Total	Enumerated Population
1775 (Census, adults)					
Branco	32.7			32.7	
Pardo	12.5			12.5	
Preto forro		11.1		11.1	
Escravo			43.6	43.6	
Total	45.2	11.1	43.6	99.9	33,634
1807 (Census)					
Branco				28.4	
Pardo				22.1	
Preto				49.5	
Total				100.0	51,472
1848 (Census)					
Branco	36.6				
Pardo	36.6				
Preto	26.8				
Total	100.0				54,652
1855 (Scattered census manuscripts, seven parishes)					
Branco	32.4			32.4	
Pardo	22.7	0.3	1.5	24.5	
Cabra	3.1	0.1	1.3	4.5	
Crioulo	6.5	0.4	7.0	13.9	
Preto	4.2	2.8	17.6	24.6	
Total	68.9	3.6	27.4	99.9	7,334

SOURCES: "Mappa geral . . . ," 2 June 1775, in A. J. Costa, "População," following p. 274; Azevedo, *Povoamento*, 224, n. 282; "Quadro numerico da população livre . . . ," Pres., *Relatório* (1848); Nascimento, *Dez freguesias*, 95, 141.

leverage against masters. Such was especially the case in Brazilian cities, where slaves often labored on their own account and growing nineteenth-century police apparati took over the functions of the "absent overseer," becoming for slaves an alternative power source to masters.[24] Despite the slave trade, which continued in full force until the early 1850s, the proportion of slaves in the urban population declined significantly from 1775 to 1855 (Table 1.1).

Although the evidence is limited, the proportion of freedpeople in the population also fell dramatically, despite an apparently accelerating manumission rate for the remaining slaves.[25] Freedpeople lived under an ambiguous regime, halfway between freedom and slavery. Some were but conditionally freed, still owing masters the balance due on their freedom; others labored under the continued obligation to render deference to former owners (and failure to do so sometimes led to the revocation of manumissions). Under the terms of the Brazilian constitution of 1824, freedmen were barred from voting in the second-round elections. Because this qualification was the prerequisite for a host of civic and political offices, freedmen were effectively relegated to a second-class citizenship that institutionalized their inferior social standing.[26]

Place of birth also mattered a great deal to Brazilians. Most of Salvador's slaves were Africans; fully 64.9 percent of the 5,442 slaves recorded in 999 inventories between 1811 and 1850 had been imported into Brazil.[27] Most Africans remained slaves for the duration of their often short lives, while only a lucky few gained freedom. João José Reis has estimated that about 7 percent of Salvador's population consisted of freed Africans in 1835, but this figure is not borne out by the surviving 1855 census schedules, in which no more than 2.8 percent of the city's population are listed as freed Africans.[28] Concentrated at the lowest levels of society, their beliefs and culture denigrated as pagan by the dominant Christian society, their autonomous activities subject to police oversight, Africans also suffered under legal disabilities. Those few who gained freedom did not acceed to even the limited citizenship that freed Brazilians enjoyed under the 1824 constitutional regime; they remained stateless aliens. After the 1835 slave rebellion, the province of Bahia slapped additional legal disabilities on freed Africans, subjecting them to a poll tax intended to encourage their emigration (which probably contributed to their declining share in the population).[29]

Under the colonial regime, natives of Portugal enjoyed numerous privileges, dominating the top posts in government, the Church, and, to a lesser extent, the armed forces. Lisbon's commercial monopoly over the Portuguese colonial economy ensured that Salvador's merchants were primarily Portuguese; the personal and family networks so important to commerce at this time meant that clerks were usually natives of the mother country. Nevertheless, both Portuguese bureaucrats and merchants were easily absorbed into the mostly Brazilian-born planter elite as commercial, kinship, and patronage ties, not to mention a consciousness of shared economic interests, turned them into a reasonably cohesive class.[30] Not all Portuguese were wealthy and Luiz dos Santos Vilhena, a professor of Greek who left a detailed description of Salvador in the 1790s, scorned the indigent immigrants who in Portugal would have undertaken domestic service or agricultural labor but in Brazil refused even to take up artisan trades.[31] At independence, Portuguese-born residents automatically became Brazilian citizens (provided that they had not left the country or fought against independence), but an aggressive popular lusophobia attempted to limit Portuguese influence in the new state and introduced a new valorization of "Brazilian-ness" into politics and culture.[32]

Natives of Brazil rarely saw themselves as "Brazilians" in the late colonial period. The limited educational facilities and lack of a printing press before 1808 hampered the development of a "creole patriotism" among local notables comparable to that which David Brading has traced for Spanish America, although Brazilian elites likely shared some of their *criollo* counterparts' material grievances.[33] There are hints of pride in place of birth in colonial writings, but most focus on the captaincy or even smaller regions of it; in any case, few of these texts were published at that time. For Brazilians, their *pátria* ("homeland") was typically no larger than the captaincy, the largest meaningful unit of administration in Portuguese America. Certainly this was the case among the intellectuals of Minas Gerais involved in the 1789 conspiracy to make that captaincy independent.[34] Consciousness of being "Brazilian" emerged most strongly among those few of the late colonial elite who studied at Portugal's Coimbra University, interacting with fellow Brazilians and Portuguese students who sometimes disparaged their colonial origins.[35] By contrast, a small but significant number of Brazilians succeeded in pursuing empirewide military, bureaucratic, or ecclesiastic careers, forming a cohort of Luso-Brazilians who identified with the larger Portuguese empire.[36]

Qualidade or cor profoundly shaped Brazilian society and has rightly long been the object of scholarly work, much of which, however, focuses on the late nineteenth and twentieth centuries, when modern scientific racism began to affect Brazilian thinking about race.[37] Scholarship on late-colonial and early-nineteenth-century Brazilians' understandings and experience of race is rarer. Some of it has been hampered by an unwillingness to accept the full implications of race as a "social construction," particularly in the census manuscripts on the basis of which scholars have drawn numerous conclusions about Brazilian society. Census categories often say more about census-takers' vision of social organization than they do about the enumer-ated population and Kátia M. de Queirós Mattoso goes so far as to suggest that their "social impact" was "nil."[38] And it must be recognized that they recorded *qualidade*, a category that encompassed considerably more than the modern North American category of "race." To argue, for example, that "it is nothing short of extraordinary" that all married white men in the 1775 census had selected white women misses a key point: women likely acquired the *qualidade* of their husbands. For at least these census-takers, that was the most important criterion for determining women's "race."[39]

Several general conclusions can be drawn from the data in Table 1.1: The white (*branco*) population remained fairly constant during this time at about one-third of the population; the slave population declined as a share of the total between 1775 and 1855, while free and freed nonwhites increased their share. What these categories and their changing proportions meant for Bahians, however, is considerably more difficult to elucidate.

The social construction of whiteness, for example, has received little attention from scholars of Brazil.[40] Some of these "whites" were doubtlessly the so-called *brancos da Bahia*, whose African ancestry was frequently noted by foreign visitors. Those whose whiteness was accepted, however, could accede to all of the privileges of the dominant elite, or as Hippolyte Taunay and Ferdinand Dénis put it, be accepted "in good company."[41] Indeed, if they entered the regular army's officer corps, the state acknowledged their whiteness by not recording "racial" information on them. In this sense, then, whiteness was both an attribute of officership and a prerequisite for it.

The terms used to describe the nonwhite population in these four cen-suses pose complex problems of interpretation. *Pardo* ("brown") is usually read as synonymous to mulatto, while *preto* means "black". Thus, the 1807 and 1848 censuses indicate a triracial structure of whites, people of mixed race, and blacks. In the late-colonial militia—divided into preto, pardo, and branco units—this pattern also existed, and early postindependence censuses also often used these categories. This triracial structure, or the recognition of an intermediate group between black and white, is, of course, considered characteristic of race relations in Brazil and has figured promi-nently in scholarly analysis since at least the classic work of Carl Degler, who saw it as the key to understanding Brazilian racial dynamics.[42]

Many of the eighteenth- and early-nineteenth-century "racial" categor-ies, however, connoted more than just "race." Preto had strong associations with slavery and African ancestry. The 1775 census recorded all freedpeople as "freed *pretos*," underscoring that preto was a synonym for slave. Other scholars have frequently noted that preto signified African in nineteenth-century Bahia, and Ana Amélia Vieira do Nascimento observes that the 1855 preto population was "almost all African" [although the free pretos who accounted for 4.2 percent of the enumerated population could not have been African-born (Table 1.1)].[43] In 1855, most pretos were slaves, and most slaves were pretos. As the 1775 census suggests, pardo sometimes referred to all free-born nonwhites; in colonial and late nineteenth-century rural Rio de Janeiro, Hebe Maria Mattos de Castro and Sheila de Castro Faria have found pardo used in this way, but as B. J. Barickman has noted, this usage was not firmly established in nineteenth-century Bahia.[44] In 1855, there were some enslaved pardos, although most were free-born (Table 1.1). *Cabra*, as defined in the instructions for a 1781 census, was to be used for the children of a preto and a pardo; it is usually read as dark mulatto.[45] *Crioulo* ("creole") referred to place of birth, to people African descent born in Brazil. A final common "racial" term—*negro*—today roughly synonymous with the modern English "black," meant slave at this time and was rarely used in censuses.

Ultimately, censuses reveal more about the values that guided census-takers than they do about the people on whom the labels were applied. There is no way to verify the racial markers attributed to the population; in any case, Marvin Harris and his colleagues' recent controversial research that compares self-identification against researchers' measures of negritude smacks of phrenology.[46] Rather, at this remove, the census's racial labels approach the postmodern condition of free-floating signifiers that gain meaning only in relation to each other. More important, census categories tell us nothing about the identity of the individuals in question, their sense of self, and their relationships with others. And they impose a fixity on what were frequently flexible, ambiguous, and situational categories, as one lay brotherhood recognized when opening its membership to all those "known as *pardos*."[47]

In the following pages, therefore, I pay close attention to the uses of race by contemporaries, acknowledging a reciprocal relationship between the racial categories upheld and enforced by the state and individuals' experience of race. The military is an ideal institution in which to examine this dynamic, for its three sectors were structured racially, but in different ways. I have already noted the whiteness of officers; in the militia, segregated white, pardo, and preto battalions marked individuals' race in highly visible, public, and (after enlistment) immutable ways. Until 1837, the regulars excluded pretos, reluctantly accepted pardos, and preferred brancos. These discriminatory

cabra

patterns of recruitment profoundly shaped military men's experience and identity and influenced racial politics during these decades. As the empire abandoned the use of racial categories in the military during the 1820s and 1830s, racial politics in the armed forces (and often also in the larger society) assumed increasingly binary forms, as pardos and pretos were collapsed into "classes of color," discursively opposed to whites. The striking disappearance of a middle racial group in military politics after the state ceased to recognize it raises questions about just how meaningful the intermediate categories between black and white were in Brazilian society.[48]

This shift to a binary racial system was closely connected to the social and political turmoil of the Age of Revolution. The Haitian Revolution profoundly shook Brazilian planters' confidence; combined with the turmoil of the French Revolution and the wave of slave revolts in Brazil, it heralded a complete breakdown of ancien régime colonial certainties. In 1814, fearful Bahian merchants and planters recommended that the slave trade be ended and that white immigration be sponsored. A few years later, José da Silva Lisboa echoed these views, while Felisberto Caldeira Brant Pontes wrote of the urgent need to contract European mercenaries in 1824 to foster the "mixing of races": "tall, fair-skinned men" were essential, lest "the natives of the country [Brazil] be reduced to copper-colored dwarfs."[49] While none of these efforts slowed the slave trade or brought many European immigrants to Brazil, such thinking about race strikingly presaged the ideology of whitening that, three generations later, Brazilians produced in response to scientific racism.[50] More important, however, are the clear signs that the late-colonial elite could see race in binary terms.

Nevertheless, this was not the only approach to race in late-colonial Brazil. At the opposite extreme of those who set a large, undifferentiated, and dangerous black mass against a small white elite stood those who argued that, in fact, color was but an accidental quality and that good and evil could be found among blacks and whites alike. An anonymous pamphlet published in 1821 made this point, emphasizing the notable contributions that pretos such as Henrique Dias had made in the restoration of Pernambuco to Portuguese rule in the seventeenth century and presenting contemporary examples of distinguished preto clergymen and artisans. Only the servile condition of most pretos, argued the author, prevented the emergence of more such great men.[51] The worth of an individual, in short, did not depend on one's skin color and this view of race may have been widespread in popular thinking; certainly the Tailors' Conspiracy of 1798 provides evidence for this. And of course, such views meshed easily with liberal ideas about the equality of all men expressed by radical activists such as Cipriano José Barata de Almeida in the 1820s.[52] The advocates of such equality, however, rarely extended it to Africans (foreign-born and culturally different) or slaves.

Race alone cannot explain the dynamics of Brazilian society. Class, slavery, and Brazilians' belief in the value of social hierarchy tempered by patronage and kinship ties all shaped it as well. In the 1790s, Luiz dos Santos Vilhena divided the population into seven "classes" that betrayed strong influences of the society of estates: magistrates and fiscal officials, churchmen, military men, merchants, "noble" people, "mechanics," and slaves.[53] Few could fail to notice that Vilhena's first five categories constituted a tiny, if powerful, minority in society, while artisans, the free poor, and slaves constituted an overwhelming majority, and modern scholars have underscored the concentration of Bahia's wealth in the hands of a few.[54]

At the apex of late-eighteenth-century Bahian society stood an integrated class of landowning planters and merchants, most of whom resided in the city while managing their diverse economic interests. They or their representatives dominated municipal government, cultivated close ties with colonial authorities, led the local militias, and filled government posts before and after independence, supplying many of imperial Brazil's leading statesmen.[55] Genealogies "longer than those of the [biblical] Hebrews," in Vilhena's caustic phrase, served to legitimate their sometimes recent rise to wealth and prominence.[56] Elaborate marriage strategies sought to mitigate the community-property and equally partible inheritance provisions of Luso-Brazilian law that tended to dissipate fortunes. With few exceptions, property was held jointly by husbands and wives; upon the death of a spouse, half of the joint estate went to the surviving spouse, while two-thirds of the deceased's half was equally divided among his or her legitimate children (or in the absence of children, the ascendants of the deceased). The remainder (one-sixth of the total estate) could be allocated by testamentary provisions. Accordingly, elite families often limited marriages among their children, and marriages among cousins or between uncles and nieces were common, for they could reunite divided properties.[57]

Beneath this upper class, F. W. O. Morton has identified a small middle stratum, numbering perhaps 500 householders in the city, consisting of professionals, lower level civil servants, retail merchants, and cane farmers. Their sons dominated the ranks of the Bahians who matriculated at Coimbra and many would enjoy considerable social mobility through service to the state after independence. A far larger free lower class of petty shopkeepers, artisans, wage workers, and soldiers rounds out his model of Salvador's social structure. Mattoso divides Morton's second and third classes, differentiating slaves, beggars, and vagrants from the better established free poor. Such models of social structures, however, cannot capture the nature or quality of social relationships and, indeed, in her most recent work, Mattoso has abandoned the more mechanical formulations of her earlier studies.[58]

Slavery and the presence of a substantial African population lent a particular tone to social relationships in Salvador. Time and again, Brazilians made common cause against African-led slave rebellions, while the free of all classes could be relied upon to defend the social order of slavery. Indeed, widespread slaveholding—freedpeople and even slaves could and did own human property—ensured that support for the class interests of great slaveholders extended deep into society.[59]

Late-colonial and early-nineteenth-century authorities and elites profoundly believed in the value of social hierarchy. A contemporary praised Salvador's population in 1797, for being "docile in the extreme, and subordinate, great qualities for obtaining great things from them."[60] Others were less sanguine about the population's subordination. Vilhena lamented the laziness of freedpeople and proposed subjecting them to tutelage, while the governor complained about "uppity" pardos and struggled to formulate a policy by which they would be adequately rewarded but not "excessively equalized to the class of white men."[61] Nurtured in a slave society by an ethos of paternalism and patriarchalism, this concern for social hierarchy and deference to superiors infused all social relationships. Heads of households controlled the lives of their wives, children, servants, and slaves. Children dutifully asked their parents for blessings, while slaves as well traditionally requested the same favor of their masters.[62] Letters of liberty contain elaborate formulae that underscore slaves' loyal service to masters and stress their continued obligation to render deference.[63] The worst quality that witnesses recalled about João de Deus do Nascimento, the pardo tailor and leader of the 1798 conspiracy, was his "insolent and bold" character.[64] The lengthy and complex bureaucratic procedures that enmeshed officers seeking promotion underscored their position as supplicants to the crown, even as these men enjoyed considerably more liberty to express their views than did João de Deus.

The unequal, hierarchical patron–client relationships so important in recent analyses of Brazilian politics extended deep into the fabric of social life.[65] To be the customer (*freguês*) of a merchant, shopkeeper, or even a petty foodseller implied, as Mattoso has put it, close social ties as well, ranging from "loyalty and solidarity to more intimate relations of friendship and godparentage." Slaves, freedpeople, and free dependents constituted the clienteles of great landowners, over whom they maintained their power through both paternalistic gestures of munificence and resorting to violence when their power was threatened. The married freedman, Manoel dos Santos, who fell afoul of the planter on whose property he resided, learned of the nearly absolute power that such men enjoyed. Suspected of killing one of the planter's bulls after the planter had seized his plot of manioc, Manoel suffered the loss of his canoe and fishing nets and spent five days in the stocks in addition to receiving a beating. The planters' slaves, godchildren, and bastard brother, along with the "robust mulatto, André," who meted out the beating, did the planter's bidding and upheld his authority.[66]

Furthermore, family and kinship were essential to Brazilians' sense of self. While the majority of adult Bahians did not formalize their conjugal relationships through marriage in the Church and two-thirds of free births were to single mothers in nineteenth-century Salvador, legitimate marriage remained a social ideal.[67] Durable conjugal relations were, however, common, and fathers frequently recognized their "natural" children, defined as those born to parents who could have legally married as opposed to adulterine children. Godparentage extended kinship networks or created new ties and figured prominently in patron–client relations.[68] Family ties profoundly shaped social interaction. Extended elite families dominated rural and urban society and played central roles in politics and administration, adapting to and making use of the state apparatus that gradually strengthened during this period. To speak of a "middle class" in nineteenth-century Salvador may in fact be misleading, for many of its members were the poorer relations of planter families, which, according to Dain Borges, limited their identification with each other.[69] And family had profound importance to Africans. When a preto by the name of Firmino attempted to light the Forte do Mar's powder magazine during the 1833 revolt of political prisoners, he declared that he would do so for he "had no father, no mother, nor any relatives here." Lacking kin, he contemplated suicide with equanimity.[70] Both the elaborate kinship metaphors of Candomblé and the diligence with which freed Africans prepared wills underscore the importance of family for the men and women subjected to the "social death" of slavery.[71]

The brutal and stifling hierarchies of slavery, the extreme inequalities of wealth, and the deference and subordination expected of the free poor coexisted, according to Mattoso, with an "enormous capacity for assimilation" that permitted "great social mobility," miscegenation that blurred distinctions between white and black, and family and patronage ties that spanned class and race lines. Together they produced a hierarchical but, for many individuals, peculiarly open society.[72] Mattoso's remarks certainly exaggerate the openness of Bahian society; after all, the nonwhites who rose to prominence in colonial and imperial Brazil were men who accepted the larger exclusionary social and racial hierarchies.[73] Nevertheless, she points to the selective flexibility that, in the long run, served to maintain racial hierarchies and class structures.

Government and Politics

Late-colonial Salvador was an important government center. To be sure, it had lost the viceroyalty of Brazil to Rio de Janeiro in 1763, but it retained a high court (Relação) and the archbishopric. In any case, Rio de Janeiro's viceroys impinged but little on the day-to-day affairs of Bahian government; the governor in Salvador, like his counterparts in other northeastern captaincies, corresponded directly with Lisbon, while the colonial garrison, numbering some 2,000 men in the regulars and slightly more in the militia, was a predominantly local institution, as most officers and men spent their entire careers in Bahia.[74]

Foreign visitors struggled to comprehend Portuguese colonial government: Taunay and Dénis characterized it as a "bizarre mélange of military and judicial power."[75] These Frenchmen captured two important aspects of the late colonial state, its extreme militarization and the importance of the judiciary and the king's role as a fount of justice. Portugal's monarchs had long been great law-makers, and the *Ordenações Filipinas* of 1603, named after Felipe II (Philip III of Spain) served as Brazil's civil code until 1917. Royal authority manifested itself through the establishment of courts and the appointment of judges.[76] In the second half of the eighteenth century, colonial Brazil saw an increasing militarization of the state, with significant growth in the number of regular troops and the spread of militias to incorporate (at least in cities) virtually all free adult males. This militarization and its implications for state–society relations are a central concern of Chapters 2 to 4.

Historiography on the Portuguese colonial state has long demonstrated two competing traditions. In a classic work written in 1958, Raimundo Faoro stressed the state's autonomy and its ability to dominate Brazilian society through the actions of an administrative and bureaucratic caste, the power-holders (*donos do poder*) of his title. By contrast, a growing school of thought underscores the close linkages between state and society through patronage, the presence of planter–class representatives in the state apparatus, and the host of informal ties that connected the state's men to society.[77] While the armed forces (and especially the officer corps) are often seen as the exemplary autonomous sector of the state apparatus, they too were deeply embedded in society.

This approach to the state does not negate absolutely the possiblity of autonomous action by the state apparatus. Indeed, in a colonial situation such as that of Bahia before independence, and to a lesser extent, after as well, state interests almost inevitably diverge to some degree from those of the local elite. Repeatedly during this period, military policy formulated in Lisbon and Rio de Janeiro adversely affected Bahian elite interests. Nevertheless, this divergence should not be exaggerated and much of what passes for "autonomous" action is most effective when it conforms to the perceived interests of the dominant class. Thus, many of the eighteenth-century re- forms associated with the Marquis of Pombal, the enlightened but despotic statesman who dominated Portugal from 1750 to 1777, were welcomed when they benefitted colonial interests. The abolition of the fleet system in 1765 was popular, while the monopoly companies established to foster economic development in the north of Brazil faced opposition from those excluded.[78] The clumsy attempt to collect arrears in taxes on precious metals in Minas Gerais in the 1780s led to the 1789 conspiracy among local notables, demon- strating the limits of the state's ability to impose its will even when core fiscal interests were at stake.[79] Similarly, the military buildup of the 1810s relied heavily on the willingness of the planter class to support it; where crown and planters differed, notably over policy toward slavery, planter support for government initiatives melted away.

By the end of the eighteenth century, the Portuguese empire was an unwieldy structure. More than a few of the able statesmen who set policy for Queen Maria I (1777–1816), who descended into madness in the 1790s, and her indecisive son, João (prince regent from 1799 to 1816, King João VI thereafter), recognized that the reexport of Brazilian goods was all that maintained Portugal's positive balance of trade; the sugar boom (along with increased exports of tobacco, cotton, and rice) produced a substantial trade surplus in the 1790s. Given both the reality that Brazil was the economic center of the empire and the mother country's precarious position as Britain's ally on a continent dominated by Napoleonic France, proposals to move the monarchy's seat to Brazil surfaced at this time.[80] Eco- nomically weak and politically isolated, Portugal also faced internal threats to her colonial rule over Brazil. To be sure, the 1789 conspiracy in Minas Gerais had been precipitated by clumsy state action and the investigations into seditious talk in Rio de Janeiro in the mid-1790s turned up nothing, but authorities were clearly concerned that revolutionary ideals might spread to the overseas possessions.[81]

Historians of Brazil will be familiar with the events in Bahia from the 1790s to the 1840s that this book revisits. In 1798, colonial certainties crumbled with the discovery of what has become known as the Tailors' Conspiracy in Salvador. A group of mostly pardo soldiers and artisans, in touch with discussions about events in Europe among members of Bahia's educated elite, were discovered plotting to overthrow the colonial regime in favor of a "democratic" government. A lengthy and detailed investigation focused on the lower class plotters—the rest escaped with but token punishment—and demonstrated the dangerous appeal of revolutionary ideals among the *menu peuple* of the city (and incidentally affords an unusually rich view of late-colonial military life and the fissures of urban society). Worried authorities executed four scapegoats and exiled several more, maintaining a vigilant posture against subversion. In 1807, the first of the great African-led slave rebellions that regularly shook Bahia until 1835 took place, and slave unrest joined the concern about discontent among the free poor on the governor's agenda.

The 1808 arrival in Brazil of the monarch and her court, fleeing the French invasion of Portugal, transformed the colonial compact. Colonial ports were opened to free trade with friendly nations and, in 1815, Brazil was raised to the status of kingdom equal with Portugal, thereby satisfying many of the Brazilian planters' economic and political interests. A major military buildup in Salvador (and other cities) sought to defend the captaincy against foreign invasion by stiffening the alliance between crown and planter class. In 1817, the Bahian army demonstrated its loyalty and worth by helping to smash a republican revolt in Pernambuco.

Despite this triumph, the colonial compact rapidly unraveled in Bahia between 1820 and 1825. The 1820 liberal revolution in Porto produced a new regime in Lisbon that eventually recalled King João VI; he left his son, Pedro, behind in Rio de Janeiro as regent. By 1822, Pedro had turned himself into emperor of Brazil. Colonies distant from Rio de Janeiro, like Bahia, vacillated in their allegiance between the Brazilian capital and Lisbon. In Salvador, adherence to the liberal regime in Lisbon came in early 1821, and within a year, the city's government was completely dominated by recently arrived Portuguese troops who defeated the city's regiments in February 1822. Local patriots mobilized in the Recôncavo and besieged the city, forcing the Portuguese to evacuate in July 1823. In mid-1822, Recôncavo planters took charge of the mobilization, constituting an interim government and pledging loyalty to Pedro's government, in return for which he supplied military forces to aid in the siege.

As a legacy of these years' revolutionary militarization, the postwar garrison was involved in several rounds of seditions, social unrest, and political upheaval between 1824 and 1838. The first, the rebellion of the Periquitos Battalion in late 1824 constituted in effect a rising of the most radical sectors of the patriot army of 1822 and 1823. The second round of unrest from 1831 to 1833 was closely connected to Pedro I's abdication and the liberal and federalist reforms instituted during the early years of the regency (1831–1840). The last and greatest of these rebellions, the Sabinada (1837–1838), wove together many of the threads of postindependence military and political unrest into a movement that seized control of the city for four months.

Several themes run through the second half of this book, tying these diverse episodes together. The initially halting, but by the 1840s, accelerating construction of an effective Brazilian state apparatus, as measured by the creation of a national army, dominated the experience of soldiers and officers alike, whose careers increasingly carried them away from their home province; furthermore, it transformed the relationship between Bahian elites and the monarchy, as they sacrificed local autonomy in favor of a national state that could more effectively protect their class interests. In the struggle over liberal reform in the armed forces, Brazilians debated fundamental issues of social organization and wrestled with their colonial legacy. The National Guard—a civilian force of citizens—that replaced the colonial militias in 1831 embodied liberal aspirations but soon came to resemble its militia forebears. Finally, these years saw the emergence of a racialized politics that pitted "whites" against "blacks," closely connected to the state's abandonment of the colonial practice of upholding a triracial pattern of discrimination in the military. A liberal, color-blind military organization increased racial consciousness as it, inadvertently perhaps, revealed racial discrimination more clearly.

CHAPTER 2

Army Officers: The Alliance of State and Planters

In early February 1808, an Anglo-Portuguese fleet landed at Salvador, Bahia, carrying Queen Maria I, the prince regent (the future King João VI), and the rest of the court, refugees from the French occupation of Lisbon. Neither the queen nor her son cut particularly fine figures in Salvador; one of two Dutch naval officers interned in the city reported that news of her insanity spread quickly and that the prince regent was soon popularly known as "Dumb John."[1] Regardless of the royal family's flaws, its presence brought important sources of patronage, symbols of power, and centers of decision making within the colonial elite's grasp. Recognizing the value of hosting the court, Salvador's merchants and planters invited João to settle in the city, offering to build him a palace. For the monarch and his advisors, however, defence considerations, especially Salvador's exposed position at the mouth of a bay that could not be closed by artillery, militated against accepting this offer.[2]

Before the court set off for Rio de Janeiro, João left a detailed set of instructions for the defense of the captaincy and set up a committee to assist the governor on the implementation of military reforms. On paper, the Bahian garrison was already an impressive force composed of one artillery and two infantry regiments, some 2,200 men of all ranks, quartered in the capital, backed by a militia numbering slightly more (see the Appendix, Figures A.1–A.3). From the monarchy's perspective, these men were the first line of defense against the feared French invasion, as is clear from the instructions which mandated the raising of four cavalry companies, artillery practice against naval targets, and the acquisition of gunboats, all to forestall enemy landings.[3] As the debates over the military's role in the 1810s demonstrated, however, Bahia's merchants and planters were more concerned that the armed forces be available to protect them against slave revolts. Both crown and planter class, however, stood firmly together against the threat of revolution, a recognized possibility in the armed forces since the 1798 Tailors' Conspiracy.

This and the following two chapters examine the major sectors of the colonial armed forces—officers, enlisted men, and the militia—from the 1790s to the 1810s, or from about the Tailors' Conspiracy of 1798 to the end of the colonial period. For each sector of the military, the Tailors' Conspiracy constituted a deep crisis, but one that the colonial regime weathered successfully. Indeed, the resolution of the Tailors' Conspiracy demonstrates the colonial regime's strength, much of which was due to the alliance between the state and leading sectors of colonial society. This chapter analyzes one facet of that alliance—the connections between army officers and Bahian society. It begins with an examination of colonial officers' "military profession," their corporate identity, and the relationship to the monarch. Service to the crown was a core army officer value, but the concept stretched to encompass other social roles, notably that of property-holding patriarch.

Then this chapter turns to officers' relations with colonial society. Rather than constituting a closed caste, the officer corps strikingly reflected the Bahian class structure, with close ties binding senior officers to the dominant merchant, planter, and bureaucratic elites. The army's expansion in the 1810s, financed by planters and merchants, and the debate over the army's appropriate role in policing the captaincy demonstrate the importance that the colonial upper class placed on control over the armed forces.

To be sure, the officer corps was not immune to social tensions and political unrest, as the Tailors' Conspiracy revealed, yet it is striking how well the colonial regime coped with the threat of radical ideals in the corporation, the tensions between Portuguese and Brazilians whose origins many have seen in the late-colonial period, and the class and race fault lines that some have identified. Indeed, not until the cadetship reform of late 1820 and Bahia's adhesion to the Portuguese constitutional regime in February 1821 did the colonial officer corps change significantly. The final section of this chapter thus examines the mechanisms by which the colonial regime muted these conflicts.

Officers: Profession, Service, and Reward

"Every officer shall be reputed a gentleman and shall not exercise any type of employment other than the service of the king," declared the Count of Schaumburg-Lippe in the 1760s.[4] While Bahian officers fell short of the ideal of absolute commitment to crown and corporation espoused by this Anglo-German author of eighteenth-century Portugal's military legislation, this ideal expressed core values of the eighteenth-century military profession. Differing definitions of military professionalism have led historians to locate its origins in Brazil as early as the 1760s or as late as the 1870s and 1880s.[5] Rather than searching for the origins of professionalism, a task fraught with difficulties even in the case of the archetypal Prussian army, I prefer to view officership as a profession. Sociologists typically define professions as occupations which require the mastery of a body of knowledge and a certain moral commitment on the part of their practitioners. In addition, the members of a profession often enjoy privileges that allow them to regulate themselves and sometimes issue credentials to new entrants into their field.[6]

By these measures, officership constituted a profession in eighteenth-century Brazil. As was typical in contemporary European armies, formal education requirements for commissioning and promotion were most rigorous in the scientific arms (artillery and engineers) but even infantry and cavalry officers had to master a body of less formally structured knowledge for advancement. Lengthy careers and adherence to the criteria of promotion by merit and seniority (established in the 1760s) suggest a significant commitment to the profession of arms and the regular operation of its hierarchy on the part of most officers. Military law and court-martial proceedings ensured that officers would be judged by their peers for many offenses. While the monarch could commission whomever he desired and devout kings bestowed commissions (and salaries) on at least three images of Saint Anthony in eighteenth-century Bahia (in effect, army donations to the chapels that housed the saints),[7] commissioning usually followed recommendations from commanders who described the aspirants' qualifications. In the artillery, competitive examinations added an element of objectivity to evaluations for promotion.

Officers began their careers as either cadets or privates. Cadetship, established in the Portuguese army in 1757, was limited to the sons of nobles (relatively rare in Brazil), officers with the rank of major or higher in the regulars, and militia colonels.[8] The privileges granted to cadets—exemptions from corporal punishment and favored access to officers—as well as their more rapid promotion constitute a major obstacle to characterizing the colonial Bahian army as a professional corporation, for they contradict the principle of open admission to the officer corps on the basis of ability. Established in European services to preserve aristocratic dominaton of the officer corps by ensuring that young nobles gained expertise during formal training and military apprenticeships without having to serve as enlisted men, cadetship constituted a compromise between the need for technical skill and the desire to maintain aristocratic dominance.[9]

Brazilian cadets enjoyed numerous advantages over enlisted men. Luiz dos Santos Vilhena railed against the practice of commissioning boys too young to enlist as soldiers or lads with but eight months of experience, referring to the rapid promotion of some cadets.[10] Enlisting cadets at a young age allowed them to accumulate seniority, advantageous for later promotion, but some underage cadet commissions came with the express proviso that such service would not count toward promotion.[11] Available evidence suggests that the number of men commissioned in the Bahian garrison was divided about equally between cadets and noncadets: Twenty-five of 52 men in my sample of service records of men commissioned before 1819 had been cadets compared to 83 of 162 in data that Morton compiled from commission registry books. Morton argues that cadets were often much younger than sergeants when commissioned, reflecting the advantage that they enjoyed in their careers. The sixteen cadets for whom I could determine this information were on average 23.5 years of age at commissioning, while sixteen sergeants were on average 28.9 years of age.[12] Cadets thus likely had less experience than sergeants when commissioned. In late 1814, the governor faced a difficult choice for promotion to cavalry lieutenant: a cadet with five years of experience or a sergeant with eighteen years of service. In this case, his choice was simplified by the sergeant's death in July 1815.[13] Among those actually commissioned, the difference in length of service was about the same as the age difference. The 25 cadets had served an average of 7.3 years in contrast to the 27 noncadets, who had served for 13.5 years.

Since the 1760s, formal education requirements in the artillery service had distinguished this arm from the rest of the military. An 1810 manual stressed that artillery education should focus on military science to avoid "overloading" officers' minds with useless information and recommended that officers be given regular leaves for study. Under the guidance of senior officers, engineering (fortification) and artillery classes functioned in Salvador from the 1760s.[14] Thomas Lindley wrote favorably of Captain José Joaquim Veloso, educated in Salvador, whose "abilities were not merely professional," judging him a "well-informed man."[15] Officer education in the infantry and cavalry arms was less systematic than in the artillery and re-sembled an apprenticeship. Lieutenant Hermógenes Francisco de Aguilar, one of the conspirators of 1798, claimed that a seditious tract found in his house was actually a "General Essay on Tactics" by one M. Guibert, which he had been translating "for the sole purpose of advancing in the knowledge of his military profession." If this is a reference to the Comte de Guibert's *Essai générale de tactique* (1772), then Hermógenes was up to date in his studies; Guibert's work influenced, among others, Napoleon Bonaparte. The truth of Hermógenes's claim is of course less important than that he thought it a credible one in the context of the trial. A decade later, officers trying to sort out a squabble over precedence among captains emphasized that Hermógenes was the most intelligent and skilled, especially in contrast to another who suffered from "stupidity."[16] In retrospect, the credibility of Hermógenes's claim is enhanced—at least two French army manuals were translated and published by Bahians in the 1810s.[17]

A 1763 regulation established that promotions were to be "gradual and successive," that officers should pass through all of the ranks.[18] In this re-gard, promotions carefully followed the letter of the law; the length of time in each grade, however, varied considerably, notwithstanding the emphasis on seniority, for the practice of making supernumerary (*agregado*) and brevet (*graduado*) appointments allowed the monarchy to bypass the normal hi-erarchy. There was, according to the inspector general, little hope in 1813 that sergeants, cadets, and lieutenants in the cavalry would be promoted because of the "considerable number" of brevet and supernumerary offi-cers who claimed rights to the first vacancies in the higher ranks. No easy solution presented itself, and commenting on one case a few years later, the inspector observed that, while "justice" militated against further supernu-merary posts, "His Majesty's benevolence" argued in favor of them to rectify past preteritions (themselves quite possibly due to excessive supernumerary appointments).[19]

There was no way out of this vicious circle; with about 200 officers of all ranks (including retirees and those serving in nonline posts), Bahia was, as one put it, "a garrison in which all officers knew each other" and watched each other's careers closely. A favor granted to one soon became a right that all deserved; men whose careers had stalled were quick to allege violations of seniority.[20] When a second lieutenant was transferred into the Bahian Legion, its lieutenants seized upon an omission in the appointment papers to argue that the man should not take his post; in this way, they managed to prevent their being passed over for at least the time that it took the governor to obtain clarification from Rio de Janeiro.[21] Knowing their precise seniority in relation to fellow officers was thus essential. When the inspector general received his marshal's baton in 1819 and therefore had to count his seniority against all of the king's marshals, he dispatched letters to Rio de Janeiro to determine this information.[22]

A glance at recommendations for promotions reveals a complex balance of factors that superiors used to construct their image of an ideal officer. In 1788, the governor recommended that Captain José Gonçalves Galeão fill the vacant post of artillery major after he had successfully completed "an extended public examination" in which he demonstrated his "great knowledge of all aspects of artillery" science; Lieutenant Colonel Carlos Baltazar da Silveira, however, suffered from "quite limited knowledge" when it came to artillery, so the governor recommended him for retirement.[23] Artillery officers well knew what they needed to do for promotion. One long-serving second lieutenant requested transfer out of this regiment, lamenting that his "unfortunately limited understanding" precluded him from mastering geometry, thus dooming him to repeated preteritions.[24] With less emphasis on measurable book knowledge in the infantry, seniority figured more prominently. When forced to choose between two captains for promotion to major in the Second Regiment, the governor opted for the more senior one, despite his temperamental nature, instead of the junior one who was more knowledgeable and skilled in military matters. Ill health, of course, justified passing over an officer, as did the "innate laziness" of another.[25] To be sure, I cannot ascertain whether extramilitary considerations clouded such assessments but the private correspondence of the Marquis of Lavradio (governor from 1768 to 1769) contains indications of patronage appointments.[26] Nevertheless, it is clear that a discourse of professional accomplishment enveloped promotions.

Lengthy careers—a lifetime commitment to the military profession—characterized the colonial officer corps. Veterans with decades of service abounded in the officer corps; the longest serving officer that I know of, Francisco de Paula Miranda Chaves, rose from the rank of private in 1790 to that of colonel, at which he retired in 1852. Longevity ran in this officer's family; his father had retired as a lieutenant colonel after 41 years of service, as another veteran officer (with 53 years of service) noted when requesting similar pension benefits.[27] If the officer corps thus sometimes resembled a gerontocracy with all of its drawbacks (frequent ill health on the part of senior officers and slow promotion for junior officers), the long careers nevertheless can be seen as an accumulation of skill and experience in the officer corps.

Vilhena acerbically commented on officers' high opinion of themselves: "From second lieutenant to colonel, they judge themselves the *non plus ultra* of nobility . . . ," suggesting a corporate identity that appears in many aspects of officers' lives.[28] Rituals such as the serving of drinks (against regulations) on the night that a newly promoted captain mounted his first guard reinforced these loyalties.[29] In the first decade of the 1800s, officers collaborated to petition for the creation of a widows' fund (*montepio*) to finance pensions for their wives and dependents.[30] Brief references in inventories suggest that they assisted each other in handling money. Marshal Joaquim de Melo Leite Cogominho de Lacerda apparently acted as a regimental banker, holding onto 50$000 for a lieutenant and lending a cadet (the son of a colonel) 100$000 while they were in Lisbon.[31] The *foro militar*, the separate legal jurisdiction under which officers were judged by their peers for military crimes, gave the profession a certain degree of autonomous regulatory power.[32] While not as extensive as that of Spanish America, the foro was nevertheless an important mark that set officers off from civilians, and it may have contributed to their lack of respect for civilian justices, one more in Vilhena's long litany of complaints about military men.[33]

By the late eighteenth century, an identifiable army officer profession existed in Bahia. To be sure, Bahia's officers fell far short of modern standards of professionalism, but as Lieutenant Hermógenes demonstrated with his remarks about desiring to improve his knowledge of the "military profession," such a concept was known in eighteenth-century Bahia. Integral to officers' view of their profession, furthermore, were the twin concepts of service and reward that pervaded their discourse about their careers. Ever critical, Vilhena parodied officers' understanding of their profession:

> The sovereign is always their debtor; his minister never pays attention to the extent of their worthiness, failing to grant them justice. This is . . . the usual language of these heroes, whose services never exceed and never will exceed standing guard in the town square . . . , shouting a lot during drills, insulting unfortunate soldiers, serving as the governor's aide, and doing the rounds at sea when foreign ships dock here.

Elsewhere, he remarked that if all the young cadets "had the gall to live" to a ripe old age, there would be nothing left with which to reward them. Not only that, Bahia's officers spent more time petitioning than serving.[34]

In these remarks, Vilhena captured essential aspects of the relationship between officers and their monarch most clearly expressed in the petitions with which they showered the crown. To a large extent, petitions constitute what Natalie Zemon Davis has called "fiction in the archives."[35] Petitioners or the scribes who drafted these documents on behalf of officers carefully crafted them according to precise conventions. In contrast to my approach elsewhere, in which I attempt to peel away the fictional aspects of petitions to locate the historical fact—perhaps something as simple as that a given officer sought a promotion—here I examine the constructs that the officer used to frame his request. This language, in turn, reveals much about the ways in which officers thought about their profession, or better, the ways that the army hierarchy permitted them to express their thoughts about their careers.

Lieutenant colonel Alexandre Teotônio de Sousa petitioned in 1801 for promotion to colonel and command of the redoubts at Rio Vermelho, where he owned property (in effect, a dignified and well-paid retirement after 45 years of service). What justified this reward? The list of reasons was long: voluntary enlistment; "inveterately good conduct and obedience to superiors"; extraordinary services in the "remote continents" of Brazil's interior in which he risked his life and incurred "enormous expenses" as he arranged the transfer of prisoners destined for deportation to India; diligence in policing Salvador; two years in Rio de Janeiro in the 1770s; and to cap off his career, the well-executed mobilization of 130 of his slaves to ambush the participants in the 1798 Tailors' Conspiracy at their nighttime meeting outside of Salvador.[36] Another officer requested that his appointment to command the army arsenal in 1810 be made effective at once, noting his 37 years of service "performed for the royal crown, with that honor, zeal, selflessness, and fidelity with which a true loyal vassal must serve his royal sovereign."[37]

The discourse of service and reward suggests a reciprocal patron–client relationship between officers and the monarch whom they served, in which clients had the right to expect reward as much as the patron expected loyal service. Petitions also point to a patriarchal partnership between monarch and officer; through petitions, officers could speak directly to the monarch and boast of their personal contributions to his service. The permanence and quasi-noble features of officership reinforced this reciprocity, for the royal signature on his patent conferred nobility on the officer, a status virtually impossible to lose; once commissioned, no colonial officer that I know of resigned from the service.

As Vilhena's use of "debtor" suggests, service resembled a currency. Within certain degrees of consanguinity, Luso-Brazilian law permitted the transfer of accumulated services among the living. In 1806, a major added to his service record the nine years that his late son had served, and in 1798, a colonel donated to his son the services that he had inherited from his father.[38] Well into the nineteenth century, officers' wills contained clauses specifying which heirs would inherit the testator's services, and after independence, legislators could readily trade anecdotes about seventy-two-year-old officers with seventy-eight or eighty years of service.[39] Cadetship, granted on the basis of one's father's position, of course, also implied the heritability of service to the monarch and officers often cited their fathers' and grand-fathers' services when requesting promotions.[40]

However much officers' petitions may have exalted their service to the monarch, the concept of service stretched to encompass other social roles, particularly those of patriarch and property owner. Repeated leaves granted to officers who needed to run sugar plantations or manage other proper-ties acknowledged the foundations on which rested both Brazil's prosperity and that of its dominant class.[41] While the inspector general might insist, as he did in 1820, that a wealthy lieutenant should choose between the mil-itary and agricultural professions, most officers did not consider the two incompatible.[42] When transferred to the Goa Artillery, a Portuguese officer requested instead to be assigned to the Salvador garrison so that he could be "useful" to his widowed mother, who apparently resided in Bahia.[43] In this case, the officer's obligation to assume the role of family patriarch came before his military duties.

In short, through petitions, officers repeated and reinforced the values that underlay the patriarchal partnership that bound them to their monarch. This ideology of service and reward gave meaning to the military profession, exercised on behalf of the monarch. In important senses, it constituted a hegemonic ideal: A munificent monarch would reward his loyal servants with not only promotions, salaries, pensions, and decorations, but also tolerance for the extramilitary activities with which these men maintained themselves and reproduced their patriarchal power and class position.

The Social Composition of the Officer Corps

Officers' relations with the larger colonial society are a key aspect of state–society relations and characterizations of the officer corps as an au-tonomous caste parallel arguments about state autonomy in Brazil. Given the importance of cadetship and heritable service in the officer corps, some historians have perceived a caste of military families in the late colonial period,[44] but the evidence for this interpretation is unconvincing, particu-larly when all officers and their families are considered. As relatively small and readily identifiable groups for which basic biographical information is usually available, officer corps have often been studied using the meth-ods of prosopography or collective biography to determine their internal structure and degree of autonomy from society. For Brazil, four volumes of service-record data on officers who reached the rank of general officer (brigadier or higher) have constituted the principal source for work on the nineteenth-century officer corps.[45] To generalize from the experience of the most successful officers, however, may be misleading and I have endeavored to take into account all officers, that is, all men who held a commission in the regulars at the rank of at least second lieutenant (*alferes* or *segundo tenente*). By this method, the colonial officer corps emerges as a corporation in which career experiences were far more diverse than previously supposed, in which the wide range of social origins precluded the formation of an officer caste, and in which ties to the larger society and its class structure produced a corporation integrated into the colonial social hierarchy and strongly supportive of it.

To be sure, contemporaries sometimes spoke in terms of an officer caste: a private described the family of Lieutenant José Gomes de Oliveira as one whose members "were always employed in His Majesty's service in the regulars."[46] Military sources, with their emphasis on cadetship and service accumulated over generations, however, may be somewhat misleading in this regard for they rarely refer to the rest of the family in question. Not all boys who claimed cadet status pursued military careers, suggesting that the army was but one option of several. Lieutenant Hermógenes had a brother who, according to one witness in 1798, "was a cadet but today is a civilian."[47] Cadets Antônio and Sancho de Bitencourt Berenguer Cesar, whose family owned three sugar plantations, enjoyed the means to dabble in the army for a few years; in 1817, Antônio received a discharge to manage his property (which he sought to have entailed), and the following year, Sancho obtained leave to matriculate at Coimbra, claiming a militia colonelcy in his family's home district in the 1820s.[48] Rather than emphasizing the caste features of the officer corps, it is more fruitful to examine officers' ties to Bahian society and particularly the integration of senior officers into the planter, merchant, and bureaucratic elites.

The colonial army was overwhelmingly Bahian; almost three-fourths of those officers whose birthplace is known hailed from Bahia.[49] With the exception of a few Portuguese and Brazilians on an empirewide career track, officers served in the captaincy for the duration of their careers. Before 1817, no Portuguese units garrisoned Salvador, and the city's regiments could trace their institutional history back to the seventeenth century. But they could boast of no military exploits, for with the exception of a brief mobilization to garrison Rio de Janeiro in the 1770s, the eighteenth-century Luso-Spanish Wars had left Bahia untouched.[50] The captaincy's army administration reported, through the governor, directly to Lisbon, a pattern of colonial government that reinforced regional loyalties as officers built close ties to Bahian society, and one that hindered the establishment of links among Portugal's Brazilian captaincies.

At the top of the late colonial Bahian army hierarchy stood a small wealthy elite of general officers, men who successfully combined military careers with commerce and sugar planting. Portuguese, Bahians, and Brazilians, these men made their fortunes in the late colonial sugar boom and capitalized on the opening of Brazil's ports to establish far-flung trading networks. Professionally, they enjoyed rapid promotions, as the Bahian army grew significantly after the transfer of the court to Brazil in 1808. The names of three are familiar to students of Brazilian and Bahian history: Felisberto Caldeira Brant Pontes (later the Marquis of Barbacena); his wife's stepfather, José Inácio Aciavoli de Vasconcelos Brandão; and Luiz Paulino de Oliveira Pinto da França. While Brant and Luiz Paulino would make dramatically different political choices in the early 1820s, their colonial careers exemplify the experience of a Luso-Brazilian elite, at home in any part of the far-flung empire. Other general officers, not quite as successful as these three merchant/planter/marshals, nevertheless lived very comfortably, acquired land, and certainly belonged to the Bahian upper class.

Only one of the three, Luiz Paulino, was born into the Recôncavo planter class; his noble father had founded a sugar mill before returning to Portugal. The other two married into the merchant elite. Aciavoli hailed from Sergipe (then a part of Bahia) and Brant came from Minas Gerais.[51] Both Brant and Luiz Paulino received military educations in Portugal and served in the metropole's army before transferring back to Brazil in 1801 and 1813, respectively. As lieutenant colonels, they began their economic rise in 1801, when they married (respectively) the daughter and widow of an established merchant and received royal permission to engage in commerce on behalf of their wives.[52] In 1810, Aciavoli retired, presumably to devote himself full-time to commerce. On his death in 1826, he left a large plantation and distilling works on Itaparica Island, with 219 slaves. Judging by his inventory, he had retired from commerce to devote himself to planting and slaking Salvador's thirst for *cachaça* ("rum brandy").[53] Brant, appointed inspector general in 1811, successfully combined his military and business careers (and was elected to Salvador's town council three times between 1806 and 1813). His commercial correspondence from 1819 to 1821 reveals broad interests: a far-flung trading network with partners in Portugal, England, France, Hamburg, and Mozambique; sugar and cotton plantations in Bahia and Sergipe; and investments in army supply and steam navigation on the Bay of All Saints.[54]

Other officers employed similar strategies. Despite the governor's negative assessment of him, Dom Carlos Baltazar da Silveira reached the rank of
brigadier and married the daughter of a merchant (but he later had difficulty
gaining control of his father-in-law's estate). The Portuguese brigadier, José
Tomás Bocaciari, who arrived in Bahia in 1818 as Governor Palma's aide-de-
camp, obtained a land grant in southern Bahia in 1820. The future inspector
general, João Batista Vieira Godinho, married the daughter of a high court
judge in 1805, clearly linking him to the colonial bureaucracy.[55] In short, the
most successful of the top officers, if not directly drawn from the Bahian ruling class, quickly moved into it, regardless of national origin, in a pattern similar to the absorption of senior colonial bureaucrats into local elites throughout Latin America or the "Americanization" of the Spanish colonial forces.[56]

Generals lived well. On his death in 1818, Marshal Joaquim de Melo
Leite Cogominho de Lacerda owned twenty-five slaves (two of whom would
have carried him about Salvador in his sedan chairs), a multistory urban
residence, and a small farm which doubled as a summer retreat and source
of foodstuffs for the city household. As befitted his rank, he owned an
elaborately worked gold and silver rapier. Brant's son attended Coimbra
University in Portugal while his daughter learned to play harp and piano.[57]

Although these generals stood at the apex of their power in the 1810s,
the end of the late-colonial sugar boom (due to the recovery of Caribbean
sugar production and the expansion of beet sugar cultivation in Europe)
gradually undermined their position, as did the demands of their military
obligations, which robbed them of the time needed to manage their property. The assessors of Aciavoli's plantation noted that his mill and distilling
equipment needed repair and that his cane fields were "full of gaps and
poorly-tended."[58] Brant and Luiz Paulino's wife (who managed his plantation while he sat in the new Portuguese parliament) both lamented low sugar
prices.[59] The sugar boom which they had ridden to fortune was over and
their plantations were no longer highly profitable enterprises. Furthermore,
the difficulty of simultaneously managing property, which often required
their personal presence, and serving the monarch led to much frustration.
From Rio de Janeiro, Luiz Paulino wrote his brother-in-law in 1818, caution-
ing him not to begin the construction of a new mill until he could be there
to supervise the project himself.[60] A few years later, her patience exhausted
by unreliable overseers, his wife could only entrust the plantation's management to their son, Luiz, then a captain. While at the plantation, he in turn
chafed at his absence from Salvador, where disputes between Portuguese and
Brazilians were coming to a head. Furthermore, he could not afford leave

without pay to manage the unprofitable enterprise, for his family depended on his salary for out-of-pocket expenses.[61]

In comparison to the late-colonial generals, relatively little material is available on the lower ranking officers of the Bahian garrison. A few of these men were planter–generals at the early stages of their careers but others owned virtually no property at all. When the courts sequestered Lieutenant José Gomes de Oliveira's goods in 1798, the bailiff discovered that he owned only some changes of clothing; he even shared accommodations with a sergeant.[62] In addition to indicating the substantial class differences within the officer corps, such evidence bears out the repeated contemporary complaints that junior officers' salaries were insufficient to cover even minimal living expenses.[63] The widow of a lieutenant colonel declared that her husband had left no goods or patrimony other than his 38 years of service throughout the empire and even well-off officers such as Marshal Cogominho incurred debts when, "for a time, they did not pay salaries."[64] A few officers managed to combine modest ventures—as opposed to the noble business of sugar planting—with military service. The long-serving commander of Barbalho Fort operated, according to Lindley, a full-fledged "manufactory" on the premises, employing 24 gold- and silversmiths, a violation of Lippe's regulation that apparently brought him no disgrace.[65]

Officers of all ranks were familiar figures in urban society and scattered sources give indications of their daily lives. Their need for uniforms kept tailors employed but cash-strapped junior officers were not always prompt in their payment, as João de Deus do Nascimento complained in 1798; similarly, 7 of the 26 people who owed money to a tailor in 1832 were army officers. The arrival of a circus in Salvador allowed an officer to demonstrate his prowess in the bullring, which earned him the nickname of "Toureador." The fight between an officer and a sergeant over the attentions of Dona Rita Campela quickly became the subject of conversation among men involved in the Tailors' Conspiracy; one also knew that another officer frequented the house of a woman of ill repute. While interned in Salvador, Lindley glimpsed officers' respectable family life, including card games and singing *"en famille"* at the Forte do Mar, and at Barbalho Fort, a more stiffly formal courtesy visit from an officer, "his wife, daughter, and two sons, with a body of friends, slaves &c." Quirinus Mauritz Rudolph ver Huell, a Dutch prisoner-of-war, became familiar with a retired colonel who regularly took walks in the city and repeatedly warned of the evils of freemasonry.[66]

From wealthy sugar planters to poverty-stricken former enlisted men, the officer corps included men whose shared status as officers commissioned by the monarch only partially compensated for their class differences. Such distinctions inhibited the development of a true officer caste, for the wealthiest officers sought ties not with fellow officers but links to other members of the Bahian elite. Recognizing the importance of the officer corps and the desireability of links to the state apparatus, the colonial elite reciprocated this embrace, but in turn, demanded influence over the military, as became clear in the expansion of the colonial army in the 1810s.

Officers, Planters, and the State: Military Expansion and Slavery

The years after the transfer of the Portuguese court to Rio de Janeiro saw extensive reforms in the Bahian garrison and a vigorous debate over the appropriate role of the armed forces. Both raised important questions about the relationship of the Portuguese monarchy to the colonial planter and merchant upper classes. The reforms included the raising of four cavalry companies, the expansion of the militia, and the conversion of the Second Infantry Regiment into the larger and more mobile mixed infantry-cavalry legion. The 1810s thus saw considerable growth in the Bahian army, a militarization comparable to that of late-colonial Spanish America, where the size of the regular army establishment increased substantially.[67] Numbers alone suggest a roughly 40 percent increase in Bahia's garrison between 1808 and 1818, when it counted well over 3,000 men, although the latter figure included the 500 or so men of the Portuguese Twelfth Battalion, then stationed in the city (Figure A.1).[68]

This militarization counted on the local planter class to foot the bill. The decree that ordered the governor to create cavalry companies offered the captaincies to "those of my loyal vassals who, out of zeal for my service, resolve to raise the companies," and of course, pay for them. To ensure that these companies would not be led solely by amateurs, the lieutenants were to be regular officers named by the governor. By this time, candidates for the posts had already been lined up and the governor quickly selected four men. At least one captain of the new legion also offered to outfit his company's new recruits, but the inspector general later reported that the officer had not done so satisfactorily.[69]

While these men gained status from their association with the crown, a larger military proved costly, and reliance on direct contributions from Bahian planters and merchants soon proved inadequate. Despite the optimistic projections of the inspector general, by August 1810, a "voluntary" donation had raised only the modest sum of 16:709$000; the governing junta blamed the decline of trade for its failure to raise more funds.[70] A year later, the new governor, the Count of Arcos, complained of a "rapid change in the opinions of Bahia's greedy capitalists," who had become still more reluctant to contribute to further subscriptions for the purchase of weapons even as they financed public works such as the new library and the chamber of commerce building.[71] Apparently, Salvador's merchants did not agree with the government that Bahia faced a military threat from overseas.

Rather, the planter class saw slave revolt as the greatest threat to the captaincy; the most dramatic conflict between planters and the colonial government before independence concerned policy toward slaves. It affected the army, not only because of the inspector general's involvement, but also because it raised the question of the military's role. In a remarkable case of bureaucratic oversight, perhaps attributable to Inspector Godinho's age—he was by then 68 and would die in less than a year—the defense committee incorporated wholesale into its plans a proposal from 1776 that, in the event of alarm, all able-bodied male slaves be armed with lances and placed in the rear of their owners' regiments. Given the general fears prompted by the Haitian Revolution and the far more immediate examples of the 1807 and 1809 slave revolts in Bahia,[72] the measure drew a stiff rebuke from Rio de Janeiro. Godinho's defense—he argued that Bahia's slaves were "accustomed to the blindest obedience" and that one owner with a whip "causes the greatest terror among a hundred slaves"—was but a vain attempt to justify a serious lapse in judgment.[73]

Godinho's death in 1811 cleared the way for the appointment to the inspectorate of Brigadier Felisberto Caldeira Brant Pontes. Brant soon quarreled with Governor Arcos over slave policy. Noted for his reluctance to use force against slaves and for his tolerance of public manifestations of Afro-Brazilian culture—a paternalistic approach to controlling slaves—Arcos angered Bahian slaveowners who advocated harsh repression to counter continuing slave unrest. After a large revolt terrified planters in several Recôncavo districts in February 1816, Arcos convened a meeting of slaveowners in the town of São Francisco do Conde, under the chairmanship of a reluctant Brant. The inspector general, although an opponent of Arcos on slave policy, had no desire to involve himself in this assembly and complained to Rio de Janeiro. Amid "warm applause," the planters demanded the removal of Arcos, drafted a repressive slave code, and called for the establishment of an army constabulary of eight companies in the Recôncavo in addition to the troops based in the city. The governor refused to implement most of the measures; Brant traveled to Rio de Janeiro and obtained royal orders for a police crackdown on slaves. The inspector general was briefly imprisoned when he returned, until Arcos learned that he had been overruled on slave policy. In the end, both received severe rebukes from João VI and no regulars were stationed in the Recôncavo.[74]

The conflicts over slave policy and the difficulties that Arcos experienced in raising voluntary contributions for Bahia's defense point to disagreements over the appropriate role of the military in late colonial Bahia. Should the army act primarily as a police force or should it concentrate on preparing for defense against foreign enemies? As Arcos's problems in the 1810s reveal, maintaining a respectable force at its disposition was more to the Bahian elite's liking than paying for the defense of Salvador against the remote possibility of foreign invasion. In short, the state's interests in external defense collided with the security concerns of the local ruling class.

Tensions in the Officer Corps

Both state interests and those of the planter class, however, coincided in their opposition to revolution among the free. As the French Revolution and the Napoleonic Wars engulfed Europe and as news of revolutionary upheavals trickled into Bahia during the 1790s, authorities became increasingly concerned to maintain domestic security.[75] For the most part, Governor Fernando José de Portugal seemed unworried; in 1797, it came to his attention that some officers and civilians were discussing anti-Catholic ideas, but as one participant later recalled, he dismissed it as idle talk.[76] With the posting of a dozen or more seditious handbills in August 1798 and the subsequent discovery of what has become known as the Tailors' Conspiracy, the governor was disabused of his complacency. The handbills called for a "revolution" in Salvador to institute a regime of "liberty, equality, and fraternity," including racial equality, and claimed extensive support in the armed forces.[77]

Historians have analyzed numerous aspects of the conspiracy, focusing on the French Revolution's influence, seeing it as a (frustrated) social revolution, or interpreting it as evidence of the colonial regime's structural crisis. While most recognize that soldiers and officers were important participants, none have examined the particular elements of military life that shaped the conspiracy.[78] It remains unfortunately difficult to determine the extent of elite and army officer participation in the plot, perhaps due to the selectivity of authorities in choosing witnesses to screen participation by what one historian has called the "white gentry."[79] Indeed, the trial record reveals more about enlisted men than about officers or other members of the middle and upper classes. Lengthy and often self-incriminating depositions by artisans and soldiers contrast sharply with outright denials of complicity on the part of men such as Cipriano José Barata de Almeida, the white Coimbra-educated doctor (and future champion of radical liberalism), and his brother, José Raimundo. The former claimed that his comments on European politics had been "poorly understood by some of those *pardos*," while the latter insulted his accuser, Private Lucas Dantas de Amorim Torres, calling him a "half-breed [*cabra*], drunk, traitor, and insolent [fellow], concluding that . . . [his testimony] was a complete falsehood and the product of drunkeness."[80] The discourse of racial equality and fraternization expressed in the handbills did not last into the trial, when white prisoners invoked racial solidarity to secure favorable treatment.

Nevertheless, there are indications that some, perhaps many, army officers were involved in the sedition; one handbill claimed that 34 officers supported it and a participant twice testified to hearing from another conspirator that the revolution would take place on a day that the artillery did garrison duties, "for its officers were part of the same plot."[81] In the end, however, only two officers were arrested and interrogated (although a few others were mentioned as having participated in seditious gatherings): Lieutenant Hermógenes Francisco de Aguilar of the Second Infantry Regiment and Second Lieutenant José Gomes de Oliveira of the Artillery.[82] Neither of these two men left particularly enlightening testimony. Lieutenant José Gomes insisted that he was a loyal vassal and explained away his association with lower class conspirators: He had frequent contact with the tailor, João de Deus, only because the latter made his clothes; his familiarity with Lucas Dantas dated back to the day that the soldier had saved his life while they were arresting smugglers.[83] First Lieutenant Hermógenes too denied talking politics and claimed that seditious tracts were actually army manuals.[84] Witnesses nevertheless recalled his ostentatious irreligion, attributing it to the books that he read and shared with them.[85] One soldier recounted private conversations with Hermógenes while the two of them were patrolling the harbor. The private's ripped pants prompted the officer to

> lament . . . the miserable state of Portugal's troops, the low salary that privates receive, and the great subjection under which they live, which the French militia does not suffer, for each soldier receives a substantial salary, and they are only subject [to military law] when mobilized. At other times, they enjoy complete liberty and equality.[86]

Whether Hermógenes truly believed in equality between soldiers and officers is of course unknowable; that he and José Gomes broke the barrier between enlisted and commissioned ranks is significant and probably encouraged the soldiers to expect more from them. Unfortunately, the trial record does not allow historians to penetrate further. Both Hermógenes and José Gomes were sentenced to one year in prison; in 1812, Hermógenes was a captain while José Gomes does not appear in the city almanac.[87]

To the extent that it had penetrated the military and particularly the officer corps, the Tailors' Conspiracy constituted a profound threat to the colonial regime. Unable and unwilling to establish the sort of repressive apparatus that would have been necessary to secure the captaincy by force, the monarch opted for the exemplary public execution of a few lower class scapegoats, deportation to Africa for a few more, and brief penance and absolution for those higher class plotters whose participation could not be ignored. Portraying the conspiracy as a plot of lower class blacks and mulattoes and even an incipient slave rebellion underscored the class and race alliances necessary for the maintenance of the colonial regime. By and large, governors were strikingly successful in this regard after 1798 and no openly seditious acts were recorded in Bahia before 1821, although the governor did occasionally report the seizure of suspicious tracts. Indeed, in 1812, Salvador's *Idade de Ouro do Brazil* proclaimed that Brazil was the only "island of tranquility" in Europe and the Americas.[88]

Moreover, Bahian planters performed yeoman's service to the crown in their cooperation to suppress the 1817 republican revolt in Pernambuco. This revolt, generally interpreted as the response of a regional elite to the increasing centralization of power in Rio de Janeiro, reportedly had numerous sympathizers in Bahia.[89] Governor Arcos, however, effectively mobilized the Bahian army and planter class in defense of the crown; Brant personally arranged for substantial contributions from his merchant and planter colleagues to finance the expeditionary force.[90] Although Bahian troops embarked, according to an anonymous chronicler, "amid much crying and sadness among various families," such a reaction might be expected from the dependents of an army that had not mobilized in four decades and had not campaigned since the seventeenth century.[91] In any case, the Bahians acquitted themselves well, and in early 1818, the last of the expeditionary force returned to Salvador; most of the rebel leadership was imprisoned and tried in Salvador. While the revolt in Pernambuco was a relatively moderate affair—its planter and merchant leaders pledged to preserve private property, including slavery—it once again raised the possibility (muted since 1798) that radical liberalism might take hold in sectors of the colonial military. The 1817 rebellion had broken out in the barracks when authorities attempted to arrest officers denounced for the involvement in the plot; as would so often be the case in subsequent years, this type of revolt provided the occasion for the articulation of lower class radical demands.[92] Despite their convincing victory over the Pernambucans, Bahian regiments were the subject of secret investigations in late 1817 (although Governor Arcos did not pursue royal suspicions vigorously) and his successors received instructions that contemplated the possibility of a military revolt in Bahia, suggesting a significant loss of confidence on the government's part.[93]

While colonial authorities may have feared barracks conspiracy, they found little or no evidence of it in Salvador, and indeed, there are few contemporary signs of the tensions in the officer corps of the 1810s that historians have invoked to explain the leading role that officers eventually took in toppling the colonial regime in Bahia. Discrimination along the lines of class, race, and national origin are often cited to explain the prominence of younger officers in the political unrest of the early 1820s. Unfortunately, none of these three categories provides a satisfactory explanation for the revolutionary dynamics, in part because they do not take into account the significant personnel changes in the officer corps of the early 1820s. A glance at each, however, will help to underscore the novelty of the 1820s.

Because dramatic manifestations of lusophobia marked the independence war and the subsequent decades of Bahian history, historians have long assumed that, within the military, chronic differences long separated the natives of the colony from the metropole's officers. A Bahian textbook refers to the "shocking" treatment of Brazilian officers, "relegated to the inferior ranks," and one military historian claims that the Portuguese crown ceased to promote Brazilians past the rank of captain after 1817. Kátia M. de Queirós Mattoso's recent study of Bahians' wealth has added a further element to this discussion. In a sample of inventories, she found that junior officers' wealth at death exceeded that of their superiors, a pattern that she attributes to the domination of the upper ranks by poor Portuguese career officers who commanded wealthier natives of Bahia.[94] Thus, class and national differences allegedly combined to separate Bahian and Portuguese officers.

There is, however, precious little contemporary evidence for such divisions within the officer corps. Exaggerated assertions about the nonpromotion of Brazilians must be dismissed out of hand; promotions of Bahian-born captains both to army and militia majorships can easily be identified in the last years of the 1810s.[95] The Portuguese monarchy was far too sensitive to the potential dangers of discrimination to undertake such a policy. As far back as 1799, the queen had decreed that promotions within the colonial army must be given "in just proportion to the natives of the place, so that none have motives for complaint." In response to this decree, the commander of the garrison recommended that no more than one-third of the officers in each unit be Portuguese; at the time, only the Second Regiment approached that proportion.[96] While Morton has effectively documented the career advantages enjoyed by Portuguese officers, the known conflicts over violations of seniority do not break down along Portuguese-Brazilian lines. Morton cites the case of a Bahian-born major who publicly disobeyed two officers who were parachuted ahead of him into colonelcies in the First Regiment in 1801. A supernumerary lieutenant colonelcy briefly satisfied the major, but with the prospect of another advance for the man who had almost passed him over, the lieutenant colonel reminded the prince-regent of his seniority and sought a further promotion in 1805, which he received three years later.[97] This incident reveals, however, less the nativism of a Bahian officer than his strong adherence to the principle of seniority built up over generations. In any case, one of his rivals was a Brazilian, the future Inspector General Brant. The complexities of these career conflicts (and the difficulty of reducing them to manifestations of nativism) is revealed in an 1805 petition for redress from a Portuguese-born brevet colonel with four decades of service in Bahia because of the promotion of (then Colonel) Godinho, a Brazilian, who had recently been transferred from Goa into a supernumerary post in the Bahian artillery.[98]

In contrast to Mattoso's findings about the relationship between wealth, rank, and national origin, my data (from a larger number of inventories) suggest that, in the first half of the nineteenth century, wealth and rank correspond. At first sight, the figures in Table 2.1 appear to confirm the greater prosperity of the Bahians, but their advantage is due to the presence of two extremely wealthy officers, a colonel and a marshal. Excluding them would leave the remaining Bahians (a second and a first lieutenant, two captains, and a major) with an average wealth of little more than 4:117$000, far behind that of the Portuguese. Three of the five Bahians owned an average of 5.3 slaves each, again considerably less than the 18.6 slaves averaged by nine of the ten Portuguese. These ten (two majors, two lieutenant colonels, three brigadiers, and three marshals), on the whole, outranked the seven Bahians, and their wealth far exceeded that of those whom they outranked, a testament to the ability of these outsiders to penetrate the Bahian upper class.

Furthermore, the easy transfer from the regulars into paid posts in the militia, which would have appealed to Bahians who could then serve in their home districts, probably helped mute conflicts between natives and outsiders. While militia officerships have usually been portrayed as the exclusive

TABLE 2.1

Army Officers' Wealth and Slaveownership at Death by National and Provincial Origin, 1807–1850

	Average Wealth	Number	Number of Holding Slaves	Average Size of Holding
Portugal	14:754$965	10	9	18.6
Bahia	40:525$863	7	5	110.2
Other Brazil	957$951	2	2	4.0
Unknown	2:040$189	10	6	3.3
Total	15:639$603	29	22	33.9

NOTES: Constant 1822 mil-réis deflated by sterling exchange rate; includes slaves freed by testamentary provisions.

SOURCE: Twenty-nine invs. in APEB/SJ/IT.

preserve of the planter class,[99] this was only true for the unpaid commissions (which required no special training). It does not apply to the paid majorships and adjutancies, respectively filled by captains and sergeants drawn from the regulars. At the very least, the growth of the militia in the 1810s opened up new opportunities for officers whose careers in the line regiments did not look promising (see Chapter 4), thereby mitigating the effects of the disproportionate share of the army's upper ranks held by Portuguese. Officers who transferred to the militia retained their army seniority and pay; a Bahian-born infantry captain thus considered promotion to major of Salvador's Second Militia Regiment the best way to "speed his advance" in 1820.[100]

Because most non-Bahian officers arrived as individuals instead of as part of a foreign unit, they were absorbed rather easily into Bahian society, as both Brant and Godinho were, contracting advantageous marriages soon after arrival in Salvador.[101] Even the stationing of two Portuguese battalions in Salvador after the defeat of the revolt in Pernambuco did not dramatically change the context of army–society relations in Bahia. Morton has alleged that the captaincy, which had demonstrated its loyalty by mobilizing to suppress the republicans, now faced what looked suspiciously like an occupation.[102] Worries about rivalry between Portuguese and Brazilians cropped up in correspondence between Rio de Janeiro and Salvador but Governor Arcos received assurances that the battalions would soon be transferred.[103] The Second Battalion embarked for Pernambuco in

December 1817, and when the Twelfth Battalion finally departed to garrison Santa Catarina in 1819, an otherwise patriotic anonymous chronicler recorded "great sadness" in Salvador "because we had become familiar with them."[104] In May 1820, the Twelfth received orders to return to Salvador, and in the charged political environment of 1821 and 1822, their presence would become highly controversial.[105]

More generally, slow promotion, particularly for noncadets, probably introduced tensions into the officer corps. In 1798, Second Lieutenant Vicente Lopes was heard to complain "of the injustice that he had suffered: having served His Majesty for years in the regulars, only recently was he commissioned." Although expressed in the company of men then plotting the overthrow of the colonial government, Lopes's complaint was carefully couched in the language of service and reward and promotions for officers did not become a prominent issue in the plot, appearing only in passing in two of the handbills.[106] The army's expansion in the 1810s, as well as the growth of the militia, probably improved career prospects, but the average time from enlistment to commissioning (Lopes's complaint) remained constant at ten and a half years; this data, of course, cannot tell how many men who desired commissions never obtained them.[107]

Morton has suggested that many of the men like Lopes were blacks and mulattos and that racial grievances combined with career frustration to make them the most likely of Bahians to rebel in the early 1820s.[108] This assertion cuts to the heart of the problem posed by social construction of race; however likely it may be, Morton adduces no direct evidence for it. To avoid biologistic or determinist definitions of race, historians must accept what army documents imply by their absence of racial markers—that officers were white men. The complaints of the enlisted men in the Tailors' Conspiracy that pardos could look forward to no promotion would bear out this assertion; by contrast, however, Portuguese officers and foreign travelers were quick to detect traces of African ancestry in the officer corps (and in the Brazilian elite more generally).[109] Whiteness was clearly a malleable construct, and not all contemporaries agreed on its definition—somatic norms, to use Harmannus Hoetink's clumsy but familiar phrase, after all, differed.[110]

In this light, Private Luiz Gonzaga das Virgens e Veiga and Sergeant Joaquim Antônio da Silva provide an instructive contrast. Both men were arrested and tried for participation in the Tailors' Conspiracy, yet their fate was significantly different. By most measures, the "pardo" Luiz Gonzaga was sergeant and even officer material: Literate, he even knew a smattering of

Latin; something of a polymath, he knew the rudiments of pharmacy and bloodletting; he also kept up with military affairs by recording decrees in his notebooks.[111] His legitimate birth and these skills might well have allowed him to move into the officer corps and consequently the white racial category. Three desertions, a reputation for insubordination, and involvement in the 1798 conspiracy instead ensured that he remained a "pardo" in authorities' eyes and led him to the scaffold. The "white" Sergeant Joaquim Antônio, with whom Lieutenant José Gomes resided, appeared nervous and unsteady during his interrogation but managed to deny all the allegations against him and was acquitted. Officers later held no grudges against him, and a major who knew exactly what was at stake in promotions wrote on his behalf in 1803. He observed that the sergeant's greatest virtue was his "complete obedience to superiors" and refusal to "imitate the other noncommissioned officers and soldiers who fail to fulfill their obligations of respect, obedience, and subordination as they model their behavior according to current fashions, in which all are supposedly equal." Needless to say, Joaquim Antônio enjoyed a rapid and successful career: second lieutenant in 1804, first lieutenant in 1808, and militia major in 1811.[112]

The contrast between these two men also points to another important mechanism for maintaining the loyalty of the officer corps: Only those noncommissioned officers who demonstrated loyalty and subordination during their years in the ranks would be promoted. Given the dominance of the officer corps by cadets (the sons of senior officers or of the large planters who held the militia colonelcies) and carefully selected former enlisted men, the 1820 cadetship reform marked a profound change. Responding to "repeated petitions" for cadet status by men who merited consideration but did not fulfill the requirements of nobility set out in the 1750s, João VI created two additional cadet grades for the Brazilian army. The sons of lower ranking army and militia officers would henceforth be recognized as second cadets while those of men who merited "consideration" in civilian life, either through office holding or property ownership, could aspire to the rank of third cadet (*soldado particular*).[113] After this reform, most officers began their careers as cadets, enjoying exemptions from corporal punishment and privileged social access to officers. Thus, military service became much more attractive to those Bahians who had previously been deterred by the obligation to enlist as privates. In the early 1820s, numerous Bahians received cadet commissions; many found themselves catapulted into the officer corps during the independence war, before their qualifications—other than resolute patriotism—became known to their superiors.

The full impact of the cadet reform would, of course, not be felt until well into the 1820s, and through the 1810s, the surviving sources reveal a Bahian army strongly loyal to the crown and supportive of the colonial regime. The mechanisms of authority in the officer corps and the ties between officers and the Bahian elite generally ensured officers' loyalty to the crown. Officers' commitment to their profession and to the values of service to the monarchy—a concept flexible enough to accommodate important nonmilitary roles—combined with the integration of senior officers into the Bahian planter and merchant upper class (and bureaucratic elite) to make them a group strongly supportive of the colonial regime. With its wealthy, well-connected generals commanding less well-off lower ranking officers, the army's commissioned ranks strikingly paralleled the larger social structure.

To be sure, the alliance between state and planters was not without its tensions as the debate over the role of the armed forces in the 1810s demonstrates. The merchants and planters who quarreled with the crown over whether the armed forces should focus on internal security or external defense nevertheless stood firmly with their monarch against the threat of revolution among the free. While some officers were involved in the Tailors' Conspiracy, their commitment to revolutionary change was lukewarm at best, and when the plot was discovered, they distanced themselves from it. If anything, this conspiracy and its dénoument revealed the colonial regime's strength, as did the suppression of the 1817 rebellion in Pernambuco, notwithstanding the rumored sympathy for the rebels in Bahian military circles. Moreover, there is strikingly little evidence in late-colonial sources of the tensions between Brazilians and Portuguese that are the stuff of nationalist historiography. Brazilian-born officers were promoted to the highest ranks, wealth and rank largely corresponded, and promotion into the militia offered a respectable career path for many Bahian-born officers. And, given that whiteness was an attribute of officership, racial issues were silenced in the officer corps.

Almost all of this changed after news of the Portuguese Revolution reached Salvador in late October 1820. In the hothouse atmosphere that followed, tensions flourished, and over the next five years, the officer corps underwent a dramatic transformation as the colonial alliance between planters and monarchy in the officer corps shattered over the constitutional issues that destroyed Portuguese rule in Brazil. Nevertheless, officers' experience of the late-colonial years shaped their response to the changes that would come in the early 1820s.

CHAPTER 3

Slaves or Soldiers?
The Recruitment and Discipline
of Enlisted Men

That Brazilians were reluctant soldiers was a contemporary commonplace. Salvador's garrison commander remarked in 1800 that "all view the military profession . . . with horror" and complained of his inability to recruit effectively. As far as "fathers of families" were concerned, the "extortion of any of their sons" to serve as soldiers was an "intolerable attack" on their patriarchal authority, observed a commentator, who lamented that they forced their sons to take minor orders to avoid recruitment, which hurt population growth.[1] The men who ended up in the ranks, according to historians, were therefore mostly nonwhites recruited by force from among "criminal," "vagrant," and dangerous elements in the lowest classes of society. Treated little better than slaves—which many of these men had allegedly been—subject to corporal punishment and confinement to dank barracks, badly paid and poorly trained, viewed with disdain by the rest of society, the lot of soldiers was truly wretched, to which they responded by deserting frequently.[2] Many of these characterizations of the colonial army, however, merely repeat contemporary stereotypes—Luiz dos Santos Vilhena remarks that Salvador's soldiers were "exemplary" only in their "insubordination and insolence"[3]— and a careful reading of late-colonial sources suggests the need for a more nuanced view of the rank and file.

Admittedly, few desired to be impressed, but remarks about reluctance to serve notwithstanding, Salvador's garrison grew from 1,500 to 3,000 men from the 1790s to the 1810s, constituting a significant part of the urban population that numbered around 50,000 (see the Appendix, Figure A.1).

To be sure, state authorities' demands for military manpower were widely viewed as unwelcome impositions to be resisted whenever possible, and enlightened commentators such as Vilhena regularly condemned forced recruitment. This antirecruitment discourse was strikingly limited, however, for impressment was a well-established, and in practice, a widely accepted feature of patron–client relations. Criticisms of impressment often turn out to be complaints on the part of patrons that *their* loyal dependents had been summarily drafted. Recruitment pitted the government against local elites and local bosses against their clients in a triangular struggle whose outcome was a moderate and generally acceptable level of impressment that normally aroused little opposition, except from those unfortunate few actually pressed into service.

Like recruitment, the formally harsh and brutal military discipline in fact consisted of a complex interaction between social groups—in this case, soldiers, officers, and civilian society—whose outcome fell far short of the ideals sketched out in training manuals and the Articles of War. Each embodied a distinct model of military discipline but neither adequately accounts for the informal and ad hoc social processes that maintained a semblance of order in the ranks. The rejection of military authority by both large sectors of urban society and enlisted men forced officers to temper the most draconian features of military discipline. Indeed, the ease with which soldiers deserted marked the limits of officers' power as enlisted men reserved for themselves the right to quit the colors, leaving the corporation with few alternatives except periodically to pardon deserters.

Although frequently preceded by forcible recruitment from civilian society, soldiers' enlistment did not mark a complete break with their former lives, for many retained preenlistment social ties. Once in the army, they also built new solidarities, both vertically to officers and horizontally to their comrades and to members of the urban lower classes. Given that soldiers served for decades and that they were rarely posted outside the city of Salvador, the community of men and women centered on the regiments was a stable and well-established one. Within this barracks society, soldiers defined their identity as nonblack free men. Contrary to the impression left by North American historians, who have tended to write vaguely about a rank and file dominated by "free coloureds" or "African Brazilians,"[4] black men never served in the colonial rank and file, filled by whites and mulattoes (pardos); blacks (pretos) were, in fact, legally excluded. Enlisted men thus lived within a racially structured institution; for soldiers, their precarious status as free men nevertheless subject to corporal punishment provides a key to their identity. These experiences of soldiers furthermore fundamentally shaped the Conspiracy of 1798. After the eleven tailors who lent the plot its name, the nine enlisted men constituted the second-largest class of men arrested. They left an indelible stamp on the plot and the critique of colonial society that its participants articulated.

Recruitment

In determining that some men should serve in the armed forces and obliging them to do so, early modern states made one of their greatest demands on society. Too often seen simply as a powerful, arbitrary state's unwelcome imposition on a recalcitrant society that resolutely resisted such burdens,[5] recruitment evoked far more complex reactions in colonial Brazil. Vilhena, the professor of Greek, devotes several revealing pages of his treatise to discussing the colonial regime's recruitment problems. He considered the garrison too small, good for little more than policing the city, but wondered whether that were not due to deliberate policy; after all, a large standing force would be costly to maintain. He also attributed the lack of soldiers to recruiters' inability to find manpower. A large part of the white male population was engaged in commerce—essential to the colony's prosperity—and excessive rural recruitment would only hurt agriculture, the other basis of Bahian wealth.[6]

After thus laying out the considerations that guided (or ought to guide) recruitment—supplying an adequate number of soldiers at reasonable cost without unduly burdening the productive sectors of society—Vilhena condemned the press gangs occasionally let loose into Salvador, contrary to "both good order and reason." Such periodic manhunts, he claimed, failed to respect students attending the schools founded by royal charter; during recruitment drives, boys older than ten or eleven dared not show up for their lessons, fearing that press gangs were lying in wait outside classrooms. In one carefully planned razzia, a full regiment secretly infiltrated the city with orders to seize, "without exception, all the white men that they could find," excepting only those who were already soldiers or militiamen. Simultaneously leaping into action, the soldiers seized 445 men "of diverse qualities," including two priests. Scarcely 30 of them were enlisted, however, and most of these men soon discovered illnesses that excused them from service. While he condemned arbitrary recruitment, and especially that which undermined his status as a professor, Vilhena nevertheless lamented that he no longer enjoyed the power to recommend lazy and disrespectful students for enlistment so that they could "learn subordination."[7]

In these musings about recruitment, Vilhena exemplifies the contradictions of Brazilian impressment. He and government authorities agreed that recruitment was essential—they considered armies indispensable—but recognized that it was potentially disruptive of economy and society. Judiciously used, the power to recruit arbitrarily could be a mighty inducement to maintain order and respect for social hierarchy among those not impressed. Salvador's first printer, for example, solicited an extension of the exemption from recruitment that his employees enjoyed, arguing that this protection "makes them more diligent and attentive . . . promoting in all a useful emulation of work [habits]."[8] Forced recruitment is commonly identified in Latin American history as a tool of social control and instrument of labor coercion that sought to repress criminalized vagrancy.[9] Recklessly employed, however, the power to recruit threatened all social order and especially that of patrons whose authority over clients depended in part on their ability to protect the faithful from press gangs and have the disloyal recruited. Vilhena thus differed little from the rural landowners and militia commanders whom he denounced as worse than Nero in their exercise of recruitment powers. He did not mind packing off the occasional troublesome young Hellenist to the tender mercies of a drill sergeant but he objected vehemently to any recruiter who violated his pedagogical preserve.[10] As Vilhena unwittingly demonstrates, recruitment pitted the colonial state against local elites in a conflict over the free poor, who themselves were not passive actors in this struggle. Some avoided recruitment by linking themselves to patrons and gaining protection; others took matters into their own hands by hiding from recruiters. Still others played on the contradictions within the state apparatus to avoid recruitment.[11]

The colonial state struggled to keep control of the potentially disorderly process of impressment by producing a corpus of laws that carefully defined the population subject to forced recruitment and by exhorting authorities to follow these rules. As expressed in the most detailed set of colonial instructions, issued in 1816, single white and mulatto men ages sixteen to forty were the target of press gangs, but recruiters were to spare one son of each farmer, the cattle drivers who brought beef on the hoof to cities, master artisans, fishermen, slave drivers, clerks, and the men properly enrolled in the militias (who served the state in this capacity).[12] Censuses and militia rolls, compiled with increasing regularity in the late eighteenth century, were intended to provide local authorities with the means to identify men eligible for projected regular drafts (not surprisingly, many refused to co-operate with census-takers).[13] In practice, however, recruitment proceeded more haphazardly, with brief wartime surges followed by long periods of inactivity, much to the frustration of authorities in Lisbon, who wanted continual recruitment to compensate for the steady peacetime decline in regimental strength as death, desertion, discharge, and disease took their inevitable toll on soldiers.[14]

Recruitment drives occurred in the mid-1770s (in response to an invasion scare during the last Luso-Spanish War) and with greater frequency during the Napoleonic Wars. They followed standard patterns, with appeals for volunteers preceeding forced recruitment. Although the government enjoyed the means to recruit directly in Salvador, rural recruitment depended on cooperation from the local landowners who commanded the militia. Nominally the state's representatives in the interior, these men were, like Vilhena, often more interested in protecting their clients than in recruiting for Salvador's regiments, preferring to arrest individuals outside their patronage networks—the "patronless poor," to use Patricia Aufderheide's apt phrase. In 1810, for example, the sergeant major of Maragogipe found a navy deserter, two recent immigrants (a Portuguese man and an Italian wood-cutter), and an Indian; in 1797, his predecessor sent a vagrant who had abandoned his parents. Such outsiders, according to Vilhena, made poor soldiers, for they were likely to desert at the first opportunity.[15] From the perspective of local elites, however, the recruitment of such men served the dual purpose of maintaining order and upholding class rule, not to mention demonstrating their power to clients and their compliance with royal orders.

When pressure for recruits mounted in the 1770s and 1790s, so did social tensions in the countryside. From the manioc-growing districts of Maragogipe and Jaguaripe came impassioned appeals that the regions be spared because impressment would only hurt food production to the detriment of general military preparedness; Vilhena adds that rural recruitment raised the price of staple foods in Salvador, for fearful small farmers stopped bringing crops to market.[16] Authorities charged with impressment regularly reported that men subject to recruitment (and often all young men) were in hiding, reports that contained a substantial degree of truth, even as they probably exaggerated the dislocation to justify failure to recruit effectively; after all, local authorities usually desired to protect their clients before satisfying the demands of the state.[17] Furthermore, recruitment drives exposed the often bitter conflicts among local elite factions as rivals tried to impress each other's dependents, thereby sparing their own clients and labor force;

the territorial overlap of militia jurisdictions made such conflicts virtually inevitable.[18] Other authorities tried to satisfy state demands by impressing obviously ineligible men (who had perhaps naively counted on being safe from recruiters); hence, complaints about the enlistment of nine-year-old boys and fifty-year-old men abound.[19]

The objects of this struggle between the state and the planter class—the free poor—were not passive victims of recruitment. As recent literature has emphasized, the free poor were a highly differentiated, dynamic, and active social category, not simply a marginal class for whom Brazil's slave society left no social or economic space.[20] Faced with the threat of impressment, the men subject to recruitment took advantage of the conflicts among local authorities and manipulated the contradictions in the colonial state apparatus to escape enlistment. Some clung to their patrons, hoping to secure the protection due to loyal clients. Those who failed to elude press gangs and judged themselves exempt petitioned the monarch for discharges, seeking a restoration of the royal justice violated by arbitrary impressment. Factional divisions among local elites meant that there was often someone willing to testify to a recruit's legal exemption and the injustice of his impressment.[21] The vast majority of the 445 men impressed in the sweep described by Vilhena were thus quickly released. In short, a series of checks and balances operated in recruitment as the colonial state, local elites, and the free poor struggled over the execution of periodic recruitment orders. The outcome was a moderate and generally acceptable peacetime recruitment system that aroused little opposition except from the unlucky few actually impressed. Thomas Lindley, who witnessed a press gang at work in 1803, nicely captured this aspect of recruitment: Fifty soldiers swept through Salvador's port district in search of sailors to man a warship, acting "with all the brutality which such an infringement on the rights of humanity requires." "The surprise of capture threw" one seaman "into convulsions." As "he lay in extreme agony beating his head against the stones," passersby "offered no assistance; but, with a shrug, looked, and passed on," suggesting that they neither feared impressment nor objected to the man's arrest.[22]

Impressment probably did not weigh especially heavily on Bahian society for two additional reasons. Although quantitative evidence is not available, qualitative sources indicate that a number of soldiers were volunteers. For some, the army was a refuge from abject poverty; others enlisted to escape different obligations. Runaway slaves and boys seeking to break free from parental authority on occasion turned up in the ranks.[23] More important, long service terms meant that the garrison usually needed but few recruits each year. With a handful of temporary wartime exceptions, military service had no fixed term before 1808. The hardy souls who survived twenty-five years in the ranks could solicit retirement on full salary; thirty years earned a man the right to request retirement on salary and rations while thirty-five years earned him salary, rations, and uniform issues. A few petitions from men, especially noncommissioned officers, retired under these terms have survived.[24] In 1808, service terms shrank to sixteen years for conscripts and eight for volunteers. Men enlisted before 1808, however, continued to serve under the old terms; twenty of thirty-seven long-serving veterans discharged in 1835 had been in the ranks since at least 1808. The dean of this group, sixty-five-year-old Private Inácio José da Silva, had served since 1788.[25] All other things being equal, shorter service terms required more frequent recruitment, and as service terms contracted further in the 1820s, recruitment reform assumed importance as a major political issue (Chapter 7).

Notwithstanding the constant complaints about the garrison's small size and the difficulties of recruiting in the colony, Bahia maintained a growing number of men under arms from the 1790s to the 1810s. Viewed from this perspective, authorities' complaints appear somewhat misplaced, and their ability to raise the garrison's strength to almost 3,000 men demonstrates the effectiveness of the recruitment system. Moreover, in a city of some 50,000 inhabitants, the army employed as much as 10 percent of the male population, and a considerably larger proportion of the free adult males; soldiers thus constituted a large and highly visible proportion of the urban population.

Discipline

Upon enlistment, impressed men and volunteers were sworn in and came under the jurisdiction of the Articles of War, drafted in the 1760s by the Count of Schaumburg-Lippe, an Anglo-German military advisor who had reformed the Portuguese army during the Seven Years' War. For many historians, the Articles exemplify the crushing regime of discipline under which Brazilian soldiers served.[26] Read every five days, prior to the payment of salaries, the twenty-six articles that refer specifically to enlisted men threaten the death penalty fifteen times, for offenses ranging from desertion and mutiny to theft and sale of equipment. There are ten threats of prison terms (three including hard labor), three references to corporal punishment, four general threats of severe punishment, and a warning that drunkenness, rather than mitigating responsibility, would entail the doubling of punishment.[27] While the Articles of War sought to coerce obedience from soldiers, drill manuals exhorted officers to train their men so that they would internalize good military habits, beginning with marching in step without the aid of a drum beat, for "good order consists of perfect obedience."[28] An historian of Portuguese military legislation identifies in this literature the Enlightenment disciplinary project that, according to Michel Foucault, sought to control every aspect of soldiers' lives through regulation and surveillance, turning them into the disciplined cogs of a smoothly oiled machine.[29] From a very different sociobiological perspective, William H. McNeill has recently also underscored the importance of drill in armed forces, arguing that it builds a primordial solidarity among participants.[30]

On paper, the colonial army thus stood between two models of military discipline. The corporal punishments of the Articles of War have much in common with the Old Regime rituals of public torture, while drill manuals hint at the carceral institutions of the disciplinary society that, in Foucault's interpretation of Western culture, transformed eighteenth- and nineteenth-century Europe. Neither disciplinary regime, however, was effectively applied in the colonial garrison; instead, discipline can best be seen as, to use a currently fashionable metaphor, a constant process of "negotiation" with superiors over the very nature of military service.[31] Try as it might, the army failed to establish its hegemony over enlisted men; it convinced neither the rank and file nor substantial segments of Bahian society of the institutional order's legitimacy.

To be sure, enlisted men rarely voiced their discontent in public; those who returned from the campaign against the 1817 Pernambuco rebellion speaking "most ill" of their commanding officer were but a minority (unfortunately, the anonymous chronicler failed to indicate what had upset these men). Soldiers' private conversations, occasionally revealed in the Tailors' Conspiracy trial, indicate deep discontent. A harried Luiz Gonzaga das Virgens e Veiga unburdened his frustrations on fellow soldier Lucas Dantas de Amorim Torres: Unable to tolerate "the subjection under which I live, enduring corporals and little cadets [*cadetinhos*]," he confessed to his friend that he wished to die.[32] In deserting or going absent without leave (as Gonzaga did three times), however, many more silently expressed their rejection of the army's core disciplinary values.[33] The scale of soldiers' resistance to the army's minimum demand—that they be available for service—forced officers into policies of toleration that often turned the Articles of War into so much empty bluster. In short, soldiers (and their allies in civilian society) reshaped the army just as—to use an example more familiar to historians of Brazil—slaves' actions in their day-to-day relations with masters transformed slavery.[34]

The colonial army lacked the cardinal feature of both Michel Foucault's disciplinary society and American sociologists' "total institutions"—a clear separation between the corporation and civil society.[35] Quartered in forts and barracks that had once constituted the city's defensive perimeter but were being rapidly absorbed by the growing urban area, soldiers lived in the midst of the city (see Map 1.3 in Chapter 1). In 1825, a French engineer observed that Salvador's forts were "blockaded," not by enemy besiegers, but by the residents whom the redoubts ostensibly protected.[36] Vilhena, who fancied himself something of a military expert because of his service in Portugal, listed the garrison's additional failings. Officers rarely inspected the barracks at night, so they could not know whether their men were absent without leave; in any case, soldiers had no respect for curfews.[37]

Worse yet according to the professor, the army did not supply adequate rations to soldiers, who therefore had to "subsist on the loathsome meats that they buy from black women on the streets."[38] Such women, often overlooked by military historians most concerned to trace the development of formal institutions, in effect constituted the Bahian army's commissariat.[39] No regular procedure existed for supplying rations to enlisted men; in 1810, those on duty received one inadequate meal per day. That year, the inspector general recommended that soldiers supplement this meager fare by growing their own food around the barracks and on the forts' scarps; kitchen gardens were apparently planted in Palma Barracks.[40] That the army did not supply regular rations to enlisted men left soldiers vulnerable to the surge in basic food prices documented for the 1790s by Kátia M. de Queirós Mattoso, who identifies the failure of urban wages to keep pace with this inflation as one of the structural causes of the Tailors' Conspiracy.[41] No less than seven of the twelve surviving proclamations called for hefty increases in soldiers' wages and the conspirators had discussed a revised army salary scale.[42] A preoccupation with salaries and food prices led Luiz Gonzaga to calculate in 1795 that a fusilier's annual salary could buy him 52 *quartas* (471 liters) of manioc flour. Given that one-tenth of a quarta (.907 liters) constituted a traditional daily ration of this staple, a soldier would have to spend 70 percent of his salary on just this one item.[43] Further indications of the extent to which soldiers looked after their own meals can be gleaned from the investigations into the conflicts of February 1822 that marked the definitive rupture between Portuguese and Brazilians in the garrison. Private Miguel dos Anjos went home for dinner and thus missed the initial mutinous mobilization in the First Regiment. A corporal from this regiment who joined the patriots at Fort São Pedro recalled the "beans and beef" finally served to the men gathered there; little did he know how difficult it had been for officers to feed the multitude. There were no supplies on hand and most of the artillery regiment's petty cash fund had gone to pay officers' January salaries, which the Treasury had still not issued. Armed with what money the quartermaster sergeant could scrape together, several officers set out to buy meat and manioc flour; a sergeant was put out to sea to haggle with the masters of launches bringing supplies from the Recôncavo.[44]

Uniforms, whose importance for military discipline and cohesiveness has long been recognized by historians and social scientists alike,[45] failed to fulfill their purposes in Bahia. The market in used uniform pieces, to which soldiers often contributed illicitly,[46] meant that civilians might sport military attire, thus vitiating one purpose of uniforms—distinguishing soldiers from civilians. Furthermore, contemporary descriptions suggest that the haphazard system of army supply left many enlisted men ill-clad. In 1802, Lindley described the artillery regiment as

> the most beggarly set of beings that ever were honoured with the name of *soldiers*: they enter in an [sic] uniform consisting of a threadbare blue jacket (generally patched or torn), coarse white calico waistcoat, breeches of the same material, a white handkerchief and (a few only) with the remnant of a wretched shirt.

Ten years later, the inspector general concurred with this assessment, complaining of his "barefoot and ragged" subordinates. Such uniforms did not homogenize soldiers; rather, they provided fertile ground for their improvisations, as Lindley implied with his remarks about the variety of headgear that these men sported.[47]

In numerous other ways, the Bahian army was but a light taskmaster. Talk of extending leave to nine months and to as many soldiers as possible in 1799 and 1800, both as an economy measure and as a way to supply labor to agriculture, indicates that some were left to shift for themselves during part of the year. The decrees that created the legion in 1809 envisaged that each company would be at its full strength of 142 men for only three months of the year; during the remaining nine months, only 61 men would be in the barracks and the rest on leave.[48] While enjoying such a furlough in 1798, two artillery soldiers fell into the company of a civilian in Maragogipe; the three of them were accused of perpetrating a series of petty thefts. Many soldiers lived apart from their regiments even while on duty; among the enlisted men interrogated during the March 1822 investigations, no less than five mentioned that they had stopped at their houses during the previous month's disorders. According to the artillery commander, some sixty of his enlisted men could not reach the fort during the standoff, for they lived in parts of the city controlled by the Portuguese. All nine of the enlisted men charged in connection with the Tailors' Conspiracy lived on their own, as did Private José Antônio dos Santos, who resided in his *botequim* (tavern) in downtown Salvador. Lindley described soldiers' houses as "tiled cabins, open to the roof, with a single lattice window," comparable to the residences of the poorest free people and slaves. In 1817, the inspector general remarked that an artillery soldier's request for discharge after twenty-three years of service should not be granted: the 1808 provision of sixteen-year service terms did not apply to him, and in any case, he was only a musician, "which left him much free time."[49]

Soldiers drilled infrequently. In the late 1760s, Governor Lavradio found the garrison in woeful condition and instituted an intensive program of drill under his personal supervision; it is doubtful, however, that it survived the departure of this martinet (who claimed to derive great pleasure from overseeing drills).[50] In the 1790s, Vilhena remarked that the newly leveled Piedade Square was used for exercises,[51] but with so many soldiers on furlough and the rest employed in the various tasks necessary to maintaining functioning regiment, few had time for drill. As Lippe's regulations recommended, raw recruits went through some basic training and a sergeant was praised in 1803 for the "affectionate method" by which he made even the "most rustic" of them understand him; in 1814, the cavalry company had written instruction manuals for enlisted men.[52] After this stage in the soldier's career, drill and training became less frequent. The seven exercises in which veteran soldier Luiz Gonzaga participated in 1796 were sufficiently memorable (or burdensome) that he noted them in his diary. Private Romão Pinheiro recalled a live-fire drill in 1798; fatigued, he went home to rest instead of meeting with fellow conspirators.[53] In light of this evidence, the Foucaultian model of military discipline, although perhaps visible in training manuals, does but a poor job of explaining how the Bahian garrison actually functioned (McNeill's provocative interpretation of drill's significance cannot be assessed on the basis of historical evidence).

Given the constraints on discipline posed by the location of Salvador's barracks and the limited control that officers had over soldiers' lives, how did they obtain from enlisted men the subordination enjoined by military regulations? Until a substantial body of court-martial records is discovered and made available to researchers, key aspects of military discipline will remain obscure, but the surviving sources—mostly correspondence about discipline—suggest that the brutal punishments prescribed by the Articles were not regularly or consistently applied. Rather, military discipline emerges as a dynamic process. Although a relationship between two unequal parties, the weaker of which in this case had often been forcibly inducted into the army, soldiers and officers "negotiated" a more or less legitimate settlement that made service at least tolerable for the majority of enlisted men. To assume that, because surviving sources refer almost exclusively to disciplinary problems, most soldiers were either criminals or that they constantly resisted the army's demands are simplistic readings of the record. Indeed, one can surmise that most soldiers did their best to avoid falling afoul of army law, choosing rather to resist in subtle ways that eluded officers. Direct challenges to officers were surprisingly rare and the greatest threat to the army hierarchy between the 1798 conspiracy and the breakdown of relations between Portuguese and Brazilians in 1822—the 1808 murder of an officer by a soldier—demonstrates how discipline must be seen as a complex relationship among soldiers, officers, and society.

As a patrol marched to the Matatu gunpowder depot in 1808, a first lieutenant ordered a private to straighten his posture and weapon, touching the soldier with his sword to emphasize the order (another account more plausibly refers to several blows delivered by the officer). When the lieutenant turned his back and headed to the front of the column, the soldier fixed his bayonet and ran him through, instantly killing the thirty-three-year veteran officer. Two privates and a corporal received public beatings a few days later for praising the murderer. The governor took pains to ensure that the murderer's mother's appeal for clemency would be disregarded, insinuating that she had acted out of desperation on the advice of a cleric (who kept the soldier's sister as his mistress) when she requested that "scandalously false" articles be added to the trial transcript. Despite the governor's desire that the execution be carried out before the lieutenant's funeral, he submitted the court-martial to Rio de Janeiro for the required royal review. Almost a year passed before the murderer, tied to a stake, faced a firing squad in Piedade Square; the anonymous diarist, who probably witnessed the execution along with the rest of the garrison, tersely judged it "a cruel punishment." And cruel it was, according to Quirinus Mauritz Rudolph ver Huell's account. A first volley only wounded the murderer; screaming with pain, he faced a second volley which missed him entirely but fatally wounded a boy watching the proceedings from a nearby house. As civilian onlookers shouted for the executioners to stop, all decorum was lost; attending priests left the half-dead soldier to administer last rites to the boy. Only after the boy's body was removed could officers resume the execution. A bullet to the head from the third volley finally completed the work of royal justice.[54]

On the surface, the murder and the execution reveal an irremediable gulf separating soldiers and officers; they suggest a constant and brutal war within the corporation. Certainly the abusive treatment of enlisted men that prompted the violence against the officer was common. That the soldier should have received the death penalty is not surprising, for the "fragging," however unpremeditated, had literally been a stab in the back. The delay in carrying out the sentence, however, suggests that he had received due process, such as it was understood in 1808–1809. That some soldiers praised the murderer hints at the lieutenant's unpopularity among his subordinates and at their independent assessment of the crime. Together, the murder and the praise for it constituted a rare public articulation of the rank and file's views about officers. Needless to say, the army could not tolerate such a visible repudiation of its authority.

The public ritual of court-martial and execution that sought to restore that lost authority, however, almost failed to do so. The intercession of the accused's family highlights the larger society in which the Bahian army was deeply embedded, a society that often rejected the army's authority. While the botched execution and the boy's death may have resulted from the inaccuracy of early-nineteenth-century weapons, the inability of the firing squad to carry out its mission may also reflect sympathy for the murderer on the part of the soldiers detailed for the gruesome task. Ver Huell "clearly" observed gun barrels "swaying to and fro" after the squad had received the order to aim and attributed this to the soldiers' reluctance to kill "in cold blood."[55] Instead of being awed by the majesty of royal justice, spectators shouted for clemency and soldiers forgot their lessons in marksmanship.

Notwithstanding the promises of the Articles of War, such executions *pour encourager les autres* were extremely rare (which, according to Vilhena, only heightened soldiers' insolence[56]); corporal punishment was thus effectively the most severe exemplary disciplinary mechanism available to officers. Lippe's regulations gave officers the right to punish minor faults with "20, 30, or 50 blows of the *espada de prancha*," a flexible flat sword, short prison terms on bread-and-water rations, extra twenty-four-hour guard shifts, carrying several weapons for extended periods, or trussing up the soldier with two muskets, the *tornilho*.[57] Colonial Brazilian officers, like their British contemporaries, could not envision maintaining discipline without beating their men. One assured Lindley that "no duty could go on without" the use of his supplejack.[58] Michael C. McBeth has argued that officers—often themselves slaveowners—viewed their soldiers as little better than slaves.[59] Soldiers disagreed with this characterization. "For some time" before the discovery of the Tailors' Conspiracy, Lucas Dantas had tried to enlist the support of Private José Joaquim de Siqueira, "complaining to him about the slavery in which [we] live, subject to colonels and superiors, and the severity of punishments." The gauntlet that infantry Private Manoel de Santana ran in October 1797 for denying Mary's virginity (among other tenets of Catholicism) profoundly upset the garrison. Private Caetano Veloso Barreto recalled that artillery soldiers talked at length about the beating, with Lucas Dantas denouncing it as a "great inhumanity." The anonymous diarist also recorded a public beating of two soldiers who had aided in the escape of some prisoners, suggesting that it was a notable (and possibly rare) event. When reprimanded in 1815, Corporal José Ferreira da Rocha echoed Dantas's sentiments, emphasizing his status as a free man by declaring that the captain "could only order his blacks to shut up." In response to the captain's request that Rocha receive more than six days in prison (and one extra guard shift), the inspector general observed that the officer's well-known irascibility left him at least partly at fault for the corporal's insubordination.[60]

The inspector general's remark that the hot-tempered officer had contributed to the corporal's offense reveals that military discipline was a delicate construct which required moderation from officers as a way of maintaining their moral authority, that elusive ability to elicit obedience from enlisted men. Soldiers enjoyed the "right of petition," as it was sometimes called, a right to complain to superiors or, if the complaint involved an immediate superior, higher ranking officers.[61] To be sure, this was a risky strategy. As the governor explained in 1799, he never accepted soldiers' complaints at face value, for that would be contrary to the "good order of society and the respect due to public men." Nevertheless, good order sometimes required paying attention even to soldiers' complaints. In 1815, two privates appealed to the governor for redress after they had suffered a severe beating on the orders of the lieutenant commanding the guard post at which they arrived a bit late for their shift. When they complained orally—perhaps to their captain—they were told to file a petition. As he did in other such cases, the inspector general agreed that the protest was fully justified: to be sure, the men had been late but such tardiness only merited a brief stint in the stockade, not the beating that had left their backs purple with bruises.[62]

Elise K. Wirtschafter has suggested for the Imperial Russian army that such appeals to higher authority directed soldiers' grievances against individual officers and away from the hierarchy as a whole. Thus, the chastening of individual officers ultimately reinforced the institution's hegemony, for it demonstrated to soldiers that "justice" could be had within the corporation.[63] This Gramscian argument, however, exaggerates Brazilian officers' ideological domination. To be sure, soldiers' demands for respect from officers and no arbitrary punishment fall well within the army's official view of itself and suggest that soldiers accepted their place within the army. Their casual attitude toward desertion, however, contradicted the hierarchy in fundamental ways and marked the limits of officers' power.

Desertion

Because it constitutes a decisive repudiation of the army, desertion is the clearest indicator of soldiers' views about the corporation. In the first nine months of 1798, the garrison lost 110 of its 1,438 privates, an annual desertion rate of 10.2 percent; in the first half of 1813, the artillery posted an 11.8 percent annual desertion rate.[64] While these figures far exceed those of contemporary European armies (Wirtschafter, for example, estimates an early-nineteenth-century Russian army desertion rate of 0.6 percent), they compare surprisingly well with the rates posted by another American army: Between 1820 and 1860, the all-volunteer United States Army lost soldiers to desertion at an average annual rate of 14.8 percent.[65] Ultimately, desertion was a chronic problem in the Brazilian service for which officers found no satisfactory solution. With repression recognized as impossible, the army treated deserters indulgently, regularly pardoning them, as it sought to manage an uncontrollable problem.[66]

As regulated by an 1805 ordinance, peacetime absences of more than seven days constituted desertion. The law further distinguished between simple and aggravated desertion, the latter involving abandoning a post or theft of offensive weapons, and established a sliding scale of punishments ranging up to six and twelve years hard labor for, respectively, simple and aggravated third desertion. Voluntary return earned the deserter a reduced sentence. Three absences of three to eight days in one year counted as a first desertion, while the ordinance recommended punishment "at the discretion"of commanders for absences of less than three days.[67]

Deserters offered explanations for the crime that will be familiar to military historians.[68] One claimed to have deserted to avoid punishment for another fault, the loss of funds belonging to the regimental band, of which he was conductor. After he had recovered from his beating, the irreligious Manoel de Santana deserted in 1798, he said, out of shame at having run the gauntlet.[69] The protection that some labor-hungry rural landowners afforded deserters is a constant refrain in contemporary commentary.[70] Given such facilities, many a desertion was successful. Vilhena judged it a "very easy" crime to commit, and in 1803, Lindley witnessed the escape of a recaptured deserter who had "lived in every comfort" with his family in Sergipe; the man had confidently returned to Salvador to purchase supplies after three years of absence. In 1824, police in Salvador picked up a man whom the governor of arms recognized as a private who had deserted in 1817; another, who claimed that he had committed "only the crime of desertion," complained of languishing in jail for five months after his recapture; he had been absent for eight years.[71]

Officers offered few solutions to the problem of desertion. In 1769, Lavradio hoped that greater cooperation among governors to facilitate the return of recaptured deserters to their home garrisons would deter the crime, while the authors of the 1816 slave code noted that the proposed constabulary would capture deserters in addition to fugitive slaves.[72] Given the location of the barracks in the city and the considerable freedom that soldiers enjoyed, however, high desertion rates were inevitable. In response, the colonial government periodically pardoned the offenders. Between 1790 and 1819, Portuguese monarchs issued at least twenty-three general pardons for all those guilty of first and second simple desertion, at an average interval of about sixteen months. Deserters well understood this. The wayward conductor claimed that he did not leave the captaincy in 1816, for it was his "intention to return to his regiment by means of an indulgence or pardon." Another soldier stated that he planned to do the same in 1797 but a suspicious captain major nevertheless sent him under guard to Salvador.[73] Pardons brought in numerous deserters and cleared court-martial dockets, turning the barracks gate into a revolving door through which soldiers passed regularly. Three-time deserter Luiz Gonzaga enjoyed two pardons, one of which absolved him of two desertions. To be sure, unlucky deserters caught between pardons, such as the thirteen whose court-martial records were sent to Lisbon in 1805, received long sentences to the chain gangs but such individuals could still seek pardons directly from the monarch.[74]

Like recruitment, military discipline and desertion were complex social processes in which soldiers, officers, and members of civilian society struggled over the nature of enlisted men's experience. Just as the army fell far short of the ideal eighteenth-century disciplinary society, so the harsh penalties of the Old Regime Articles of War were tempered by the negotiation between officers and soldiers in which desertion functioned as enlisted men's ultimate weapon. The result was an at least tolerable existence for the majority of soldiers who did not desert and formed a community centered on the barracks.

Community

Notwithstanding the complaints about inadequate recruitment and the relatively high desertion rates, thousands of soldiers remained in the ranks (or if they did desert, eventually returned voluntarily or involuntarily). The nine soldiers of ten who did not desert each year formed a generally stable community of men linked not just to the corporation but also to the urban lower classes. Because of the lack of disability pensions, elderly and infirm soldiers had every incentive to remain in the ranks, hoping to become eligible for retirement. An 1812 inspection counted eighty-seven incapable enlisted men, twenty-five of whom suffered from "fatigue and old age"; another seven were simply "very old." The twenty-six soldiers retired in 1817 had each served for an average of thirty-six years and seven months.[75] While these men contributed little to military readiness, their presence (and that of more capable long-serving soldiers) stabilized the enlisted ranks. The fact that Bahian soldiers could expect to serve for the duration of their careers in Salvador encouraged and facilitated the establishment of wide social networks, both within and outside the army.

Well-established social connections are the dominant features of Quartermaster Sergeant Manoel José de Carvalho's 1815 will. Besides expressing his devotion to the Baroque Catholicism of the day with his invocation to "all the saints of the Celestial Court" and his request that fifty masses be said for his soul, the widowed Sergeant Manoel listed his property. He owned a house in which he did not reside (he indicated that he owed his landlord some months' worth of rent), some furniture, and four male slaves. In addition, the army owed him several uniform issues. Despite these assets, he was close to bankruptcy and he expected that most of his estate would be sold to settle debts totalling 1:270$000.[76] Although home and slave ownership distinguishes this sergeant from the typical enlisted man, his will reveals widespread social ties both within and outside the army, connections that many soldiers assiduously cultivated. Sergeant Manoel acknowledged debts to both civilians and officers; he had received a downpayment for the sale of his house from one of the latter. The debts that bound this sergeant to his creditors indicate more than merely an impecunious manager of company supplies; rather, they demonstrate that an enlisted man's place in military and civilian society depended as much on his social relationships with officers and people outside the army as it did on his formal rank.

Within the corporation, soldiers built ties to officers as a way of making service more tolerable and gaining advancement. Little favors, such as being excused from guard duty by an officer, were sufficiently important that Luiz Gonzaga noted them in his diary. Lucas Dantas, however, called Romão Pinheiro "stupid" for the effort that he put into "flattering officers so as to be relieved of guard duty." Soldiers from Lieutenant Hermógenes Francisco de Aguilar's company visited him at his home while he was sick.[77] Posts as orderlies may have involved demeaning personal service—a "most pernicious abuse," according to the inspector general in 1817—nevertheless, such assignments removed the soldier from barracks routine, a change that some avidly sought. One officer recommended that his brother pull a certain Manuel from the ranks to serve at his orders, for the soldier was "trustworthy and knew how to write very well and would be thankful for the favor, for he desired it very, very much." Selection as an orderly demonstrated officers' confidence in the soldier and crept into soldiers' petitions as evidence of their worthiness.[78] Others sought out congenial assignments within the corporation or attempted to combine service with other interests. An artillery soldier arranged a posting as nurse and apprentice surgeon in the military hospital in 1811, while a father sought his son's relief from regular duties as a cavalry soldier to continue his studies. Others tried to arrange transfers to units in which brothers or other relatives were serving and one demonstrated the importance of family by notarizing a bequest of his services to his natural son, thereby echoing officers' ideology of service and reward.[79]

Before the 1820 cadet reform that expanded this class of soldiers, passage through the enlisted ranks was a fairly common experience for officers. As noted in the last chapter, about half of the garrison's officers had begun their careers as privates. That these men did not rise as high or as fast in the hierarchy as their cadet colleagues is less important than the effect that their career prospects had on the enlisted ranks. A small but significant core of soldiers could expect promotion and avidly pursued it, as two petitions from corporals in the mid-1810s reveal. In this case, both had been acquitted by court-martial and complained of their exclusion from consideration for promotion to third sergeant.[80] In 1763, an ambitious volunteer solicited dispensation from regulations that required him to serve for a certain period of time before becoming eligible for promotion. Even some impressed men made lengthy careers of the army: Manoel José Vieira, forcibly recruited in 1806, rose up the enlisted ranks until 1819, when he was commissioned an infantry second lieutenant; he retired as a brevet major in 1837. Such advancement was perhaps easier in the artillery, where literate enlisted men could acquire professional training in the artillery and fortification (engineering) classes that had functioned in Salvador since the mid-eighteenth century. Indeed, one of the corporals seeking consideration for promotion noted that he had chosen the artillery over other arms because of its educational opportunities. Years later, Brevet Colonel José Pedro de Alcântara recalled his voluntary enlistment in 1806. He studied mathematics assiduously as he rose through the noncommissioned ranks, succesfully competing for promotion to second lieutenant in 1815.[81]

While the army became a career for some enlisted men, others sought discharges, perhaps continuing in this way their struggle to avoid enlistment in the first place. Discharge petitions provide further clues about the composition of the rank and file and point, again, to the importance of social ties both within the corporation and with Bahian society. Like officers, soldiers seeking releases from the service cited familial obligations. A carpenter and private noted simply in 1818 that "the interests of his house and family require his greater attention." Fathers' deaths, which required that sons assume the deceased's patriarchal roles, lay behind many a discharge petition. A soldier explained in 1811 that the death of his father in Sergipe left "helpless" his family, "consisting mostly of virgin daughters [i.e., the soldier's unmarried sisters]," who were now "subject to danger, or at least the censure of slanderers," and put at risk the family patrimony of "agricultural properties and livestock ranches."[82] These soldiers had never left the society from which they had been recruited.

The surest legal way for a soldier to quit the service was to present a substitute, as did the private noted above. While officers sometimes criticized the practice, arguing that replacing an experienced soldier with a raw recruit could only hurt the service, substitution was deeply embedded in army practice.[83] Arranging discharges, however, was a complicated process, one that took time, often cost money, and required assistance from officers. Greeting his discharge with relief, the anonymous diarist noted in 1809: "On June 31 [sic], a Monday, I received my discharge, for it pleased the Lord Our God." He recalled his difficulties—that his regiment did not accept the man whom he had first presented as a substitute and the substantial expenses that he had incurred (300$000)—and acknowledged the assistance that he received from a captain to secure his discharge papers. In 1818, an officer complained of the problems encountered in turning over such documents to a soldier, remarking somewhat acerbicly to his brother-in-law (who had interceded on behalf of the soldier): "Had it not been for you, I would not have done [it]."[84]

In addition to linking themselves to officers and retaining preenlistment family ties, soldiers also formed a community that reached out to the women and men of the urban lower classes. Soldiers apparently had clearly defined circles of friends: Lucas Dantas knew Félix Martins dos Santos but their "friendship" was only that "of one soldier with another . . . of the same regiment," not a close relationship. Luiz Gonzaga's ability to write made him a well-known figure in the garrison, as he drafted petitions on behalf of illiterate comrades.[85] Romão Pinheiro regularly visited the house of José Félix's master, for he and the slave had a "close friendship," while the husband of Gonzaga's late godmother sometimes fed him and let him sleep in the basement of his house.[86] For the most part, Brazilian officers did not concern themselves with soldiers' female companions, in contrast to European armies that had, since the seventeenth century, engaged in "a policy of restricting soldiers' copulations," as a German historian has put it.[87] Luso-Brazilian regulations required officers to permit the marriage of soldiers older than twenty-four as long as the woman was "respectable." Shortly after coming to Salvador from Alagoas, the poverty-stricken Caetano Veloso enlisted in the garrison and married the daughter of the First Regiment's fifer. Such ties probably discouraged desertion, and Palma Barracks had been designed with families in mind: it contained 108 separate lodgings; those for married soldiers opened directly onto the street, while single soldiers bunked together in quarters that faced the parade ground. Less likely to catch authorities' attention were the informal ties that soldiers maintained with women, unless they contravened other aspects of military discipline. Soldiers and food-sellers found grounds for a lucrative partnership, according to Vilhena, in which the men broke into butcher shops to steal meat which the women then prepared and sold, much to the detriment of poor civilians who were thus denied beef at official prices.[88]

Employment in nonmilitary occupations during their spare time brought soldiers into contact with the free and slave working classes, as they labored to supplement their salaries. A Portuguese-born private—highly praised by his superiors—declined promotion, and by 1820, was so successful in his unidentified business that he was able to pay other soldiers to do his guard shifts.[89] In 1798, Private Lucas Dantas lived in a small shop where he made canes and wooden chests and repaired furniture and soldiers' equipment.[90] Two of the men who denounced the Tailors' Conspiracy described the scene at João de Deus do Nascimento's shop in the late afternoon of 25 August 1798: Inácio da Silva Pimentel, a soldier in the Second Regiment, was stitching a waistcoat that belonged to a captain in the First Regiment. Described as a journeyman employee of João de Deus, he was working alongside a soldier from the Fourth Militia Regiment, a slave apprentice, and an unnamed private and journeyman tailor from the First Regiment. Such employment in artisan trades improved soldiers' standard of living at least somewhat. When the authorities raided Private Pimentel's house, they found some changes of clothing belonging to this tailor; in contrast, Private José Joaquim de Siqueira owned nothing that could be sequestered, "for he had no trade or means of gaining anything other than his salary."[91]

While military sources inevitably lead to a focus on soldiers' professional experience, civilian records such as those of the trials of the 1798 conspirators leave useful reminders that enlisted men were not just soldiers. Their lives revolved around more than just army routine and the daily struggle for survival that dominated the experience of Salvador's lower class, as is tantalizingly revealed by the casual reference to a dinner of stewed meat served by Private Lucas Dantas to celebrate the baptism of his daughter. Luiz Gonzaga and some of the other men implicated in the plot were there, but instead of discussing politics, the host recalled that they engaged in "carefree and relaxed conversation."[92]

Race, Status, and Identity

The apparent similarities between soldiers and slaves—forcible recruitment, lack of personal freedom, and subjection to corporal punishment—have caught historians' attention.[93] A glance at the recent social history of Brazilian slavery suggests other parallels. Like the urban *escravos de ganho*, who worked on their own account, Bahia's soldiers fended for themselves while on leave; both groups often lived independently. Like the rural slaves whose small plots constituted something of a "peasant breach" in slavery, soldiers grew some of their own food. Desertion has its counterpart in slave flight, and desertion pardons resemble the willingness of many slaveowners to forgive runaways if they returned voluntarily.[94] Just as most recent scholarship on slavery has demonstrated the ability of slaves to maintain a degree of autonomy, so officers could not fully control their subordinates' lives. Despite these structural similarities, however, important differences in race and status separated soldiers from slaves; soldiers, in fact, defined importants parts of their identity by distinguishing themselves from slaves.

How soldiers viewed their place in society varied greatly. Some identified themselves as sons or fathers before soldiers, seeing family ties as more important than service to the monarch, thereby sharing the ideology of patriarchy with which officers defined themselves as autonomous from the corporation. In their pursuit of military careers, others turned themselves into dutiful soldiers, earning the rewards available within the corporation. Rejecting the Articles of War and demonstrating a casual attitude toward desertion, still others negated the elements of their condition that threatened to reduce them to the status of slaves, corporal punishment and lack of free mobility. The gratuitous abuse that they heaped upon slaves—the weakest members of Bahian society—may indicate a rough and ready assertion of social superiority by soldiers who found it easy to bully bondsmen who were beyond the direct supervision of their masters.[95] The corporal's retort that the ill-tempered captain could only silence his blacks nicely encapsulates the importance of both race and status in soldiers' identity. Government policy tended to reinforce the distinctions between soldiers and slaves: by definition, soldiers were free men; by deliberate policy, they tended not to be black men.

Determining the "race" of enlisted men is a difficult task, given the complete absence of quantitative sources on the racial composition of the rank and file. Late colonial recruitment legislation, however, expressed clear racial preferences. "Single white men, and also freed pardos, whose color is not too dark [*fusca*]," were subject to impressment, according to the 1816 Instructions. The wording is curiously sloppy, for it suggests that free-born pardos were exempt from recruitment, an unlikely circumstance unless those who drafted it assumed that all pardos were slaves or had been at some point in their lives. Perhaps it merely recognized the ambiguity of the pardo category, which merged into white, and sought to stress that freed status was not an obstacle to recruitment. More important, this clause may indicate a movement in legislation away from officially limiting recruitment to white men, a process that would accelerate after 1820. Governors' complaints in the

1790s and early 1800s that it was impossible to recruit a sufficient number of soldiers given either the "lack of white men" or the predominance of "blacks and mulattoes" in the population reveal that these preferences existed, as does Vilhena's description of the recruitment razzia in which only white men were to be arrested.[96] The significance of this was not lost on astute foreign residents of Brazil. Henry Koster remarked on the privileged position of "negroes" who thus "escaped the persecutions under which the other castes suffer during the time of recruiting," and Johann Mauritz Rugendas concurred, adding that mulattoes were also excluded from the regulars.[97]

Surviving evidence suggests that authorities were generally able to maintain these racial preferences. Fully three-fourths of the soldiers residing off-base in two parishes in 1775 (admittedly not a representative sample of the rank and file) were described as white (branco) or the sons of white householders. A smattering of pardos and a single preto (the only black soldier that I have identified in the colonial period) round out this group (Table 3.1). There is also considerable qualitative evidence that pardos were admitted to the ranks. Vilhena reports that "those who remain longest in the regiments are the free mulattoes; since they are less dark[-skinned], there is little reluctance in enlisting them." Lindley concurs, describing the slovenly artillery soldiers as ranging "from an European white to the darkest shade of a Brasilian mulatto." In 1816, the inspector general exulted at finding a recruit "of excellent color," suggesting that it was normally hard to find such men.[98] The nine enlisted men arrested on suspicion of participation in the 1798 conspiracy (eight privates and one sergeant) included four whites and five mulattoes. Twenty-four enlisted men testified against them; they included seventeen whites, four pardos, and three men whose race was not recorded.[99] Like the soldiers enumerated in 1775, those mentioned in the Tailors' Conspiracy trials are not a representative sample, but all of the evidence points to the general exclusion of pretos, crioulos, or negros from the ranks.

This aspect of recruitment had important implications for army enlisted men's identity. As outlined in the previous chapter, officers were presumed to be white men, for whiteness was an attribute of officership. For enlisted men, "nonblackness" is the comparable criteria: soldiers were not negros, crioulos, or pretos. Vilhena's remarks about the lesser reluctance to enlist mulattoes and the 1816 ruling suggest the operation of a systematic preference expressed by the white authorities for those racially similar to them. Did, however, this ideal of whiteness extend to the rank-and-file soldiers, as Harmannus Hoetink's concept of a hegemonic racial ideal would have it?

TABLE 3.1
Race of Army Enlisted Men Residing Off-Base,
Penha and São Pedro Velho Parishes,
Salvador, 1775

	Parish		
	Penha	São Pedro	Total
Branco	7	21	28
Son of branco	15	1	16
Pardo	2	2	4
Son of pardo	2	0	2
Preto	0	1	1
Son of preto	1	0	1
Unknown	1	5	6
Total	28	30	58

SOURCES: "Mappa de todos os Moradores ... Penha ... ,"
30 Jan. 1775, Arquivo Histórico Ultramarino (Lisbon), caixa 85, doc.
8751; "Mapa exactissimo de todos os moradores ... S. Pedro ... ,"
18 Jan. 1775, in A. J. Costa, "População," 194–239.

No simple answer exists; unlike the colonial Mexican plebeians for whom, according to R. Douglas Cope, a common poverty shared by people of mixed Indian, African, and European descent muted the salience of race, racially discriminatory Brazilian enlistment practices marked soldiers as nonblack free men.[100] The corporal who talked back to his officer knew what he was not: a black slave (negro). On the other hand, there is plenty of evidence of social interaction that crossed racial lines and João de Deus's shop provides evidence to support Cope's view: A mulatto tailor employed free white and mulatto journeymen alongside an African slave apprentice, the sole black man arrested for participation in the plot. The two accusers who described that gathering do not mention the men's race (with the exception of the militia soldier from the Fourth Regiment), suggesting that race was less important to identifying these men than their status (slave or army and militia soldier) and occupation (apprentice or journeyman tailor). Indeed, these suspects' race can only be determined when they came into contact with authorities who identified them or required them to identify themselves by race.

It is, of course, impossible to establish individuals' sense of self on the basis of the racial markers sprinkled through the archives. Nevertheless, soldiers' experience as both members of a racially discriminatory military and as part of the city's artisan working classes left an indelible stamp on the Tailors' Conspiracy, making possible some inferences about soldiers' identity. Private Luiz Gonzaga was the likely author of the handbills that announced its existence on 12 August 1798 and the subsequent trial record contains traces of extensive discussions among soldiers about their condition. The concept of equality that figured so prominently in the conspirators' discourse addressed two closely related aspects of soldiers' experience. Their subjection to cadets and officers, which so upset Luiz Gonzaga that he wished to die, would disappear under the new regime in which men would live "in liberty and equality without subjection to others; and not subordinate and subject to superiors . . . and [to] the severity of . . . punishments . . . as the regulars live," as Lucas Dantas put it.[101] To this general notion of social equality, manifestly absent from the regulars, the conspirators added a demand for equal access to government posts for whites, pardos, and pretos. Mulattoes may have been admitted into the rank and file, but they were certainly not promoted further. Lucas Dantas repeatedly complained of pardos' exclusion from the higher ranks, as did Gonzaga. For Dantas, the solution was a "republic" which would offer "equality for all."[102] Gonzaga had, furthermore, made his discontent known to the governor in several petitions in which he sought either discharge or promotion to the post of adjutant in the mulatto militia regiment (the only commissioned post for which race would not be an obstacle to him). He knew that a 1773 *alvará* had declared freedmen to be eligible for "all offices and dignities" and did not hesitate to cite it to buttress his claims.[103] The petition was turned down, but the governor saved it, and the handwriting eventually betrayed Gonzaga.

Notwithstanding the emphasis on equality among whites, pardos, and blacks, the conspirators proved singularly unable to attract the support of blacks. Indeed, there are signs in the trial record that pardos looked down on pretos, a healthy rivalry as far as authorities were concerned and also an indication that perhaps the elite's racial hierarchy affected soldiers after all. Lucas Dantas, for example, spoke disparagingly of the black militia captain, Joaquim José de Santana, calling him a "*pretinho* [little *preto*]," even as he entertained hopes that the captain would join the plot.[104] Preto had strong, but not absolute, connotations with African birth and slave status, and black militia officers maintained close ties to both groups (Chapter 4). The issue here may have been less one of "race" than one of status and culture. That regular soldiers were neither slaves nor Africans is implicit in recruitment legislation and practice; as white men and free or freed pardos, they enjoyed a modicum of privilege, even though their subjection to corporal punishment threatened to reduce them to the status of slaves. Not surprisingly, then, the soldiers involved in the plot spoke little about freeing slaves. Gonzaga said nothing about it in the twelve handbills, while Inácio da Silva Pimentel recalled only a plan "to call up the captives," apparently a tactical measure to increase confusion in the city during the projected revolt.[105] Like the white Barata brothers, the pardo soldiers had difficulty implementing racial equality and envisaging equality with former slaves.

In short, while soldiers' day-to-day existence required continual inter-action among members of the racially diverse urban lower classes, whose members included slave, freed, and free, as exemplified in João de Deus's shop, where all were engaged in the struggle for survival, race and status mattered when it came to defining a new society. As nonblack free or freed-men, soldiers resisted anything that smacked of reducing them to the status of slaves and could not transform the personal ties that bound them to individual slaves into a project for abolition. At the same time, subject to officers, and in many cases, barred from promotion on racial grounds, they welcomed the liberal ideals that offered them equality with social super-iors. More than anything else, the conspirators' ambivalent attitude toward equality grew out of their place in the racially structured colonial army.

Forced recruitment looms large in historians' thinking about the late-colonial Brazilian armed forces, a legacy of the extensive anti-impressment discourse of imperial Brazil (Chapter 7). A careful examination of the late-colonial sources, however, suggests that impressment was a complex inter-action among military and state authorities, local elites, and the free poor, which usually resulted in an acceptable and moderate system of recruitment. Long service terms and the presence of volunteers furthermore limited the impact of impressment by reducing the garrison's need for new levies.

Like the officers who commanded them, late-colonial enlisted men were deeply rooted in Bahian society. Recruitment, however unwelcome it may have been for the individuals impressed, could not sever soldiers' ties to society. The barracks' location in Salvador, the army's inability to separate soldiers from society and to supply regular rations and uniforms, and its willingness to furlough enlisted men, not to mention the consequent lack of drill, meant that officers wielded few of the tools needed for effective discipline. Moreover, the violence recommended by the Articles of War against enlisted men—from summary corporal punishment to executions—had distinct limits, as it was often rejected by civilian society and might prompt soldiers to desert. Desertion, indeed, marked the limits of officers' authority, and desertion pardons publicly confessed it. Nevertheless, most soldiers did not desert. Some, in any case, were in the ranks voluntarily, as they saw the army as preferable to civilian life. Others made the best of a difficult situation, seeking discharges through legal means, while a significant group pursued careers in the army. All participated in a broad community that incorporated significant sectors of the urban lower class.

Several aspects of soldiers' condition shaped the Tailors' Conspiracy and highlight the fault lines in colonial society. Enlisted men's considerable freedom and employment in artisan trades was, of course, an essential prerequisite for the articulation of the plot. Racially discriminatory recruitment—the preference for white men, the exclusion of black men, and the reluctant admission of mulattoes—was a critical feature of soldiers' lives, as they thus experienced directly the social and racial hierarchies of the colonial regime. In response, the conspirators joined with members of Salvador's artisan classes to elaborate a vision of radical social reform, centered around the demand for legal and social equality. To be sure, the very structures of the colonial military—particularly racially discriminatory recruitment—rendered it difficult for these men to carry forward their radical program to its fullest extent and the governor reported with satisfaction that pretos and pardos had failed to make common cause. Here the importance of the state in shaping the patterns of racial politics is sharply revealed. Nevertheless, in linking racial discrimination, subjection to superiors, corporal punishment, and low pay, these enlisted men and artisans first articulated themes that would recur in the military unrest and high politics of the 1820s and 1830s as soldiers, officers, and statesmen struggled over the meaning of liberalism.

CHAPTER 4

Militia Officers: The Intersection of Race and Class

In his letters from Salvador, Luiz dos Santos Vilhena described the city's four militia regiments in the late 1790s: The First enrolled wholesale merchants and their clerks; the Second was "composed of artisans, shopkeepers, taverners, and other classes of white men"; "free *pardos* or mulattoes" served in the Fourth, an auxiliary artillery regiment; while "freed blacks [*pretos forros*]"—a misleading characterization—staffed the Third, known as the Henrique Dias Regiment (or more simply as the Henriques), after the black hero of the seventeenth-century wars against the Dutch in Pernambuco (see the Appendix, Figure A.3).[1] Vilhena's description of these regiments nicely encapsulates the intersection of race and class in the organization of the urban militia. His correspondent would, he presumes, know that merchants and clerks were Portuguese, so he does not mention race in connection with the First Regiment; artisans, shopkeepers, and taverners, however, were more racially ambiguous categories, and he stresses that the Second Regiment enrolled white men. Changing the numerical order of the city's regiments to correspond to the Brazilian racial hierarchy that ranked mulattoes above blacks, he discusses the Fourth Regiment before the Third; to Vilhena and to colonial authorities, these men's racial classification was more important than their occupation.

Racially segregated militias proliferated in eighteenth-century Latin America, a product both of the late colonial militarization of the Spanish and Portuguese empires and the Enlightenment penchant for ordering society and classifying its members. By establishing militias and expanding regular armed forces, Iberian monarchies sought to secure control over their colonies and to improve their ability to defend distant domains in an age of heightened imperial conflict. To be sure, militias often fell short of the model corporations envisaged by officials in Lisbon and Madrid; what is impressive about the Brazilian case, however, is the extent to which militias were effectively established in major centers such as Salvador and the large proportion of the free male population incorporated into these institutions.

Militia organization reflected and sought to impose race distinctions; black, mulatto, and white regiments epitomize the triracial structure that has been so important to analyses of Brazilian society. Recent literature has raised questions about the validity of this model, and the ambivalence in early-nineteenth-century Brazil, where the alleged distinctions between blacks and mulattoes were elided as both groups were collapsed into "classes of color," has already been noted. While significant differences and parallels can be identified between white and black officers—both groups important leaders in their respective communities—mulattoes occupied an ambiguous social and economic place in Salvador. Discrimination against black and mulatto officers clashed with the principle of equality among officers and proved a stumbling block to militia "professionalization," the appointment of regular officers to the paid positions of adjutant and major in each regiment. When no white officers willing to transfer to the black and mulatto militia could be found, the government established in 1802 a separate system of promotion by examination that allowed blacks and mulattoes to demonstrate their military qualifications and fill these posts. The segregated militia thus provided the institutional framework for the rise of a black military leadership that, in the 1820s and 1830s, played a prominent role in urban politics.

Regimenting Salvador: The Militia Project

In the second half of the eighteenth century, reform-minded Iberian monarchies sought to reinvigorate moribund colonial governments by binding elites to the crown through militia commissions that reinforced their authority and disciplining the lower classes through military drill and legal subjection to social superiors. While Lyle N. McAlister and others have argued that this program introduced a juridically autonomous militia hierarchy into colonial Spanish America—one that challenged local elites and ultimately destabilized society—the Brazilian experience most closely resembles that of Cuba as described by Allan J. Kuethe, in which militia expansion proceeded in the context of a firm alliance between crown and colonial elites.[2] Already visible in the creation of the legion and the post-1808 buildup of the regular army, the association between monarch and Bahian ruling class was crowned in 1811 with the creation of the grandly named Corpo de Artilharia Guarda Costa do Príncipe D. Pedro (Prince Pedro Coast Guard Artillery Corps). Its distinguishing feature was a special cavalry company, all of whose soldiers enjoyed the rank of second lieutenant. These men were not required to perform regular militia duties; rather, they took turns acting as the governor's adjutants. For the anonymous chronicler, this was "the Company of Nobles"; "richly uniformed," they lent lustre to the artillery's inaugural parade and allowed Salvador's elite to flaunt publicly the alliance with monarchy that constituted the essence of colonial government.[3] Pride in associating with the monarchy was, however, not limited to Salvador's white elite; a black officer detailed to escort an English visitor in 1800 "appeared not a little proud" of the "medal suspended from one of his button-holes," which he told his charges, "had been presented to him by the Prince of Brazil."[4]

The profusion of militias in eighteenth-century Brazil formed with the army a hierarchy of military corporations. At its apex stood the paid regulars, whose soldiers and officers were analyzed in the last chapters; next came the militia, which enrolled all healthy free adult males between the ages of eighteen and forty not serving in the regulars. Beneath the militia stood the *ordenanças*, a reserve militia that enrolled all remaining men. Two ordenanças regiments existed in Salvador but little is known about their functions, in contrast to the rural ordenanças that constituted frameworks for local government, providing services such as royal mail and forming press gangs.[5] Ideally, army, militia, and ordenanças together enrolled all free men in military institutions for the duration of their adult lives. Marcelino da Silva Torres, for example, served as an artillery soldier from 1779 to 1790 when he transferred to the militia. In 1796, he passed to the ordenanças as a sergeant, finally obtaining a full discharge in 1830. This man, a bank clerk in 1819, illustrates both the hierarchy among military institutions and the colonial government's regimentation of urban society.[6]

Militia officership expressed the hierarchical values of colonial society. Company-level officers, the captains and lieutenants who earned no salary, were expected to live honorably and to have the means to outfit themselves decently. Uniforms were costly, by far the most valuable item of clothing that they owned, and at least one contemporary critic lamented the fortunes wasted on lavish military attire.[7] Some officers also paid their companies' incidental expenses, as did the black captain, Manoel de Gouvea; all were required to have at least some military knowledge as well.[8] Promotion generally followed the principle of seniority so dear to regular officers—the militia was, after all, part of the army—but the need to promote men both competent and wealthy required that it be routinely breached.[9] In 1808, the commander of the Fourth Regiment recommended a lieutenant for promotion because he had "means and aptitude," but not a more senior one who "was very negligent of his obligations, confused [about them], and lacking in that discernment and vivacity [necessary] for the service." In 1821, a second lieutenant in the Third Regiment—the richest of its officers, "dextrous" in the service and "praiseworthy" in his conduct—went up for promotion ahead of other lieutenants who lacked the means to maintain themselves.[10] In the First Regiment, promotion lists carefully noted standing in the business community. Among the sergeants promoted to second lieutenant in 1814 were two "well-established registered merchants," one of whom had just successfully bid on a large tax farm, for which he "certainly deserve[d] some distinction"; the more senior sergeants not promoted included one whose establishment the commander dismissed as but a bar.[11] When the commander of the Second Regiment submitted a promotion list that followed seniority too literally, the inspector general struck a goldsmith on the grounds that he was too poor to hold a lieutenancy.[12] Only the most abject poverty or significant downward social mobility, however, justified removing an officer from his post. The destitution of a lieutenant in the Third Regiment prompted him to seek a full discharge in 1812, while the commander recommended that another, who gave up his trade as a tailor to serve in a judge's household, be reprimanded and cashiered in 1819.[13] In this case, the loss of independence rendered the man incapable of officership and command.

Promotion in the militia up to the rank of company captain thus obeyed a mix of professional and class criteria. Economic success was rewarded with promotion as the monarch conferred status on prosperous subjects, reinforcing other social hierarchies.[14] In the First Regiment (and in the Coast Guard Artillery), merchants commanded their clerks. As the clerks aged and assumed greater business responsibility, so they advanced up the noncommissioned ranks; by the time that they established themselves as independent merchants, they were ready to assume the responsibilities of officership.[15] Men who quit commerce to pursue different careers sometimes sought transfers to other regiments, as did Private Francisco Teixeira da Mata Bacellar after he took a job in a notary's office.[16] A similar pattern obtained in the other regiments when master artisans commanded journeymen employees, thereby reinforcing workplace hierarchies. Lieutenant Bonifácio Duarte Benfica, a Portuguese-born master tinsmith, left the tools of his shop to his journeyman, for whose child he had stood as godfather. It is not known, unfortunately, whether the journeyman was a soldier in Benfica's company but such an enlistment would only have further cemented their workplace relationship. Rare lists of militia soldiers and recruits reveal frequent artisan trades and it can be presumed that many of these men worked for officers.[17]

Much to the frustration of military planners, it often proved impossible to force society into the orderly hierarchy that they envisioned. Not only did the vagaries of the urban economy conflict with the principle of seniority in promotion, but individuals also demonstrated insufficient dedication to their military obligations. Young men arranged improper enlistments in the ordenanças to escape more onerous militia duties. Fear that a militia inspection in November 1809 was the prelude to a recruitment drive for the regulars prompted a wave of enlistments and promotions into the ordenanças, most of which were eventually declared null and void.[18] Men whose occupations required them to travel, such as peddlers, were the bane of authorities; the inspector general claimed in 1820 that such "gypsies" deliberately transferred from one regiment to another to escape duties altogether.[19] Militia service was an often unwelcome burden. Soldiers invoked the numerous legal provisions that allowed them to escape the Sunday drills and occasional guard shifts that constituted their principal obligations: pharmacists, workers at Salvador's printing press, men engaged in collecting alms for various crusades (vestiges of Portugal's wars with the Muslims), and pepper-growers (part of the monarchy's efforts to regain Portugal's long-lost place in the spice trade), to name just a few, enjoyed relief from duties.[20] Overwhelmed by petitions for exemptions that lacked legal foundation, the inspector general once muttered that nobody at all wanted to serve in the militia.[21] Nor did those actually enlisted always take their obligations seriously; according to Vilhena, the First Regiment mounted such slovenly guards that the monarchy would have been better served by not bothering to call them out.[22] Such lackadaisical attitudes were not confined to enlisted men. No less than fifty-one of the city's perhaps 120 militia officers in 1803 had failed to complete the paperwork (and pay the taxes) required for the issuance of their patents; repeated admonitions that they demonstrate more respect for bureaucratic procedure and the royal fisc failed to move them, and as late as 1830, the Brazilian government once again insisted that officers confirm their commissions on pain of losing their posts.[23] Since most militia

TABLE 4.1
The Size of Salvador's Militia Regiments, 1791–1812

	Regiments					
	First (White)	Second (White)	Third (Black)	Fourth (Mulatto)	Artillery (White)	Total
1791	419	733	655	712	—	2,519
1798	534	457	634	702	—	2,327
1808	427	349	452	514	—	1,762
1812	864	871	871	867	570	4,043

SOURCES: "Observação relativa aos corpos de auxiliares e orde-nanças...," Salvador, 11 June 1791, *ABN* 34 (1912), 220; Vilhena, *Re-copilação,* 1:260; "Mappa dos 4 Regim.tos de Milicias...," 2 Feb. 1808, BN/SM, II-33, 22, 62; "Mappa Mensal dos Regimentos Milicianos...," 12 Nov. 1812, BN/SM, II-33, 22, 65, doc. 10.

commissions carried no salary, officers had little pecuniary incentive to invest in the cumbersome process of "taking out" their patents, as it was called; others, particularly black officers such as Marcos Berlink, lacked the connections in Lisbon needed to handle the paperwork.[24]

Arguments about the burdensome nature of militia service, inadequate training, and slipshod performance of duties abound in studies of late-colonial militias, a literature that sometimes loses sight of the extent to which militia regiments nevertheless functioned in cities.[25] Salvador's militia enrolled thousands of men, peaking at more than 4,000 in 1812, a figure that, according to two travelers, was maintained in 1818 (Table 4.1).[26] This number probably represents very close to all of the city's able-bodied free adult males not serving in the regulars. In 1817, the government began raising a Fifth Regiment, to be composed of the same classes of men enrolled in the Second Regiment (Figure A.3).

Such numbers would have been difficult to attain had militia service not offered certain attractions to enlisted men. Like their officers, who gained status and power from their association with the monarchy, militia soldiers benefitted from dutiful service to officer-patrons. The clerks who served under their merchant-officers certainly gained from this. Enlistment in the militia, moreover, exempted men from recruitment into the regulars. In Pernambuco, Henry Koster noted that the close ties between officers and men in Recife's Henriques ensured that the latter "were less liable to be oppressed by any white man in office," and visitors to late-colonial Salvador singled out the city's Henriques for praise. For Maria Dundas Graham, they were "unquestionably the best trained, and most serviceable" of the regiments, while Ferdinand Dénis remarked on their "excellent appearance."[27] Indeed, a common argument in the extensive literature on black and mulatto militias in Spanish America is that those who served did so willingly, even eagerly, to acquire a status denied them in civilian society.[28]

Complaints about the militia notwithstanding, the regiments appear to have functioned fairly regularly. The newly appointed garrison commander told the governor in 1799 that he considered the city's militia at least as well trained as their counterparts in Portugal, although he held a much dimmer view of the rural regiments.[29] The very act of enlistment reminded men of the state's presence, a lesson reinforced in Sunday drills; according to the otherwise critical Vilhena, such exercises had some effect, for "all [militia soldiers] were sufficiently trained in weapons drill and marches."[30] After 1808, militia drills assumed the character of antirevolutionary rallies, as Quirinus Mauritz Rudolph ver Huell, mistaken for a "low, despicable Frenchman . . . unworthy of living," discovered when he narrowly escaped a lynching at the hands of a militia company on parade. Officers made no effort to stop the enthusiastic royalists until passersby confirmed the intended victim's identity as a paroled prisoner-of-war.[31] And the militia took turns at guarding public buildings, relieving the regulars from garrison duties, as evidenced by Vilhena's complaints about the sloppy soldiers of the First Regiment or the anonymous diarist's remark that soldiers from the Fourth Regiment were on duty at the hospital when two sick prisoners escaped in 1811.[32] In short, the militia was much more than a paper institution: It incorporated a substantial proportion of the free male population; militia soldiers were familiar sights on Salvador's streets while its commanders were prominent figures in urban society.

Militia Officership: Race, Class, and Community

The militia regimented Salvador's society in specifically racial ways. White, black, and mulatto regiments divided militiamen into the three great categories that colonial authorities perceived and sought to perpetuate. The militia also upheld class distinctions both within each regiment and among the white regiments; indeed, property holding was a prerequisite for officership. The parallel construction of what were in effect three separate class hierarchies raises the question of whether Brazil's three-tier structure of whites, mulattoes, and blacks reflected class differences among the three groups. Whether mulattoes occupied a position between whites and blacks remains a controversial issue. Social scientists working with twentieth-century census data argue that class differences between blacks and mulattoes are insignificant and that, in fact, the fundamental cleavage in Brazilian society lies (and has lain) between whites and nonwhites.[33]

Any comparison among groups must of course clearly define who belongs to each, a challenging requirement in the face of the notorious imprecision of socially constructed racial categories. Unlike in North America, where the modern consensus over the definition of black—any person with visible or known African ancestry—has resulted in unusually clear and impermeable lines between "black" and "white,"[34] Brazil's triracial structure combines ill-defined boundaries between groups with flexible racial definitions, in which class and occupation or status play a major role in attributing "race" to an individual. Historical research on eighteenth- and early-nineteenth-century censuses in São Paulo reveals considerable variation in individuals' classifications over several censuses, attributable only in part to changing census categories.[35] Salvador's militia was no exception to the phenomenon of racial variability. One chronicler notes that a second lieutenant, "although *pardo*, always served in the Henriques," while João de Deus do Nascimento, the tailor identified in the trials of the 1798 conspiracy as a pardo, nevertheless served as a corporal in the Second Militia Regiment.[36] There is, however, no evidence that officers transferred among white, black, or mulatto units, which suggests that, once commissioned, a man's "race" was fixed and immutable. Given the public nature of militia service, it was visible for all to see; as Ben Vinson III has noted for colonial Mexico, enlistment in a black or mulatto regiment precluded "passing" to white.[37] Designation of officers as "white," "black," or "mulatto" in this chapter, therefore, refers to the outcome of the contemporary social process of enlisting an individual in a segregated militia regiment, on which I have been unfortunately unable to locate any information. In Mexico, as Vinson has demonstrated, recruitment for the "free colored" units was a deeply conflictual process as individuals negotiated their "race" with authorities and it likely was in Brazil as well.[38]

In late 1809 and early 1810, Inspector General Felisberto Caldeira Brant Pontes ordered detailed reviews of Salvador's four militia regiments, which permit a comparison among white, mulatto, and black officers.

Commanders were instructed to assess officers' military qualifications and comment on their occupations. The colonel of the First Regiment listed no occupation information for his officers, perhaps because they were all merchants. Some 60 percent of all the officers in the other three regiments were artisans, but the proportion of artisans among those whose occupations are known varied significantly, from 43 percent of the white officers to 60 percent of the mulattoes and fully 83 percent of the blacks (Table 4.2), lending credence to Vilhena's observation that blacks were often artisans, mulattoes sometimes, and whites only rarely.[39] The rest of these men were engaged in a variety of other less clearly defined occupations in which white officers' domination of shopkeeping and civil service posts is the most notable feature.

Among the artisan trades, there are two important patterns: clear differences between white and black officers and the ambiguity of mulatto officers' position. Seven trades are represented more than once, allowing a comparison of the distribution of white, black, and mulatto officers among them. White men are found only in the prestigious metal-working trades and painting. At the other end of the racial hierarchy, black men labored only in lower status trades, as they filled the ranks of carpenters, tailors, coopers, and shoemakers.[40] Mulattoes, in turn, worked in both "white" and "black" trades, while no trade emerges as a distinctly mulatto occupation. In a careful study of mid-eighteenth-century Mexico City, Patricia Seed has argued that the different urban occupations dominated by Indians, blacks, and whites gave meaning to the *sistema de castas*, as its racial hierarchy was known; men and women whose professions did not correspond to those expected for their racial categories tended to have variable classifications.[41] A related proposition can be suggested for mulatto officers in Salvador. While they stood between blacks and whites, they occupied no distinct economic niche, a circumstance that has important implications for their failure to develop into a leadership group in the way that black officers did.

Twenty-two inventories of unpaid militia officers who died between 1803 and 1860 provide another means of approaching the class distinctions among white, mulatto, and black officers (Table 4.3). None of these officers was extremely wealthy and the average value of their estates (9:996$586) is but a modest figure; nor did they own impressive numbers of slaves. In part this is due to the heavy indebtedness of the First Regiment's merchant officers whose inventories I have located; others died long after independence, by which time foreign competition had eroded their fortunes.[42] The extreme poverty of the four black officers is striking; even excluding the

TABLE 4.2

Militia Officer Occupations (Captains and Lieutenants), 1809–1810

	Second Regiment (White)	Fourth Regiment (Mulatto)	Third Regiment (Black)	Total
Artisans				
Silver/goldsmiths	5	3		8
Painter	2	3		5
Tinsmith	2	1		3
Tailor		7	4	11
Cooper		1	2	3
Carpenter			5	5
Shoemaker			2	2
Leatherworker	1			1
Woodcarver		1		1
Gem-setter		1		1
Butcher		1		1
Stonemason			1	1
Silkworker			1	1
Total artisans	10	18	15	43
Other occupations				
Shopkeepers	8	2	1	11
Civil service	3	1		4
Procurator	1	2		3
Bookkeeping	1		1	2
Proprietor		1		1
Shipmaster		1		1
Miscellaneous Business (Agências)		4	1	5
Unknown		1		1
Illegible	5		13	18
Total	28	30	31	89

SOURCES: "Informação dos Off.es do 2.o Regim.to de Milicias . . . ," 1 Feb. 1810; "Informação dos officiaes do 4.o Regim.to de Milicias . . . "; "Informação dos Officiaes do 3.o Regimento de Milicias . . . ," 31 Dec. 1809, APEB, m. 247–6.

TABLE 4.3
Militia Officers' Average Wealth and Slaveownership
at Death, 1803–1860

	Average Wealth	Number	Number Holding Slaves	Average Size of Holding
White officers	13:867$274	12	9	12.1
Mulatto officers	8:789$099	6	6	7.0
Black officers	195$752	4	2	2.0
All officers	9:996$586	22	17	9.1

NOTES: Constant 1822 mil-réis deflated by sterling exchange rate; includes slaves freed by testamentary provisions.
SOURCE: Twenty-two invs., APEB/SJ/IT.

cabinet-maker who was effectively bankrupt—he died shortly after a period of enforced unemployment while imprisoned for participation in the Sabinada Rebellion of 1837–1838—does not significantly change these results. The average wealth of mulatto officers is skewed by the presence one rich individual—the third wealthiest of all twenty-two, a man who further confirms the point about the lack of a clearly defined economic role for mulatto officers. On his death in 1844, he was a successful building contractor and landlord who owned dozens of finished and unfinished houses. By then, thirteen years after the militia's formal abolition, he no longer used his militia rank in his business dealings, suggesting that he had distanced himself from his past as an officer in the mulatto regiment.[43] The remaining five mulatto officers left an average of 6.4 slaves each and estates averaging 2:964$948, a much more modest figure that places them closer to the black officers. Ultimately, however, this evidence is ambiguous and it can be read either to underscore the proximity of mulatto officers to black officers or to highlight their intermediate position.

As so many historians have reminded us, class is not simply a matter of occupation and wealth; it also involves culture and social relationships.[44] Just as white and black officers differed in their occupations and wealth, so they moved in distinct social milieux, as evidenced by the lay brotherhoods to which they belonged.[45] Five officers of the First Regiment referred to sodalities in their wills. Four of them belonged to the prestigious

Ordem Terceira da Nossa Senhora do Carmo and two were members of the Santa Casa da Misericórdia, the elite charity and brotherhood; a fifth officer left a large bequest for the Santa Casa's hospital. Colonel João Dias Coelho held office in the Carmo Third Order in 1827, while Lieutenant Colonel Inocêncio José da Costa's stern portrait still looks down at the tourists who visit the order's sachristy, evidence of his importance to this sodality.[46] Two of the Second Regiment's four officers who mentioned brotherhoods (the Portuguese tinsmith and a Portuguese shopkeeper and merchant) belonged to elite brotherhoods—the Carmo Third Order and the Santa Casa, respectively; both were also members of the Dominican Third Order, but neither mentioned holding office in any of these sodalities.[47] Only one of the two surviving mulatto-officer wills mentioned brotherhoods; three of the four to which Captain Manoel Pinto da Assunção belonged were traditionally mulatto sodalities.[48] Four black officers belonged to numerous black confraternities. Together, these men referred to fourteen different brotherhoods in their wills, mentioning five Rosário brotherhoods eight times and the black Saint Benedict three times. Like the white officers of the First Regiment, black officers held office in their brotherhoods, Captain Joaquim Félix de Santana in no less than three of the four to which he belonged.[49]

Judging by their wills, in which they frequently named each other as executors, black officers constituted a close-knit community not far removed from both slavery and African Bahia.[50] That they were officially known as the "*homens pretos* [black men]" does not necessarily imply African birth or previous or existing slave status (despite Vilhena's reference to them as "*pretos forros*"), for preto, so closely associated by historians with African birth and slave status, was a considerably more flexible term, especially when used as an adjective. At least two of the Henriques' officers, Lieutenant Colonel José Raimundo de Barros and Captain Joaquim Félix, were freed creoles and a third, Colonel Joaquim de Santana Neves, may also have been.[51] Others were certainly free-born.[52] While characterizing the Henriques as "composed of creoles," the early-twentieth-century historian of Afro-Bahia, Manoel Raimundo Querino, also identified four Africans among them. Neither of the two for whom he supplied a complete name, however, figure among the eighty-eight Henriques officers whom I have identified as active in Salvador from the 1790s to the 1830s, and a third was not a militia officer as is clear from the archival record on the incident whose oral history Querino recorded.[53] João José Reis has, however, identified two African-born enlisted men who served in the militia in the 1820s.[54]

Although no black officers can be identified as Africans, they were certainly very close to them and more generally to slaves. Captain Joaquim Félix and Colonel Joaquim de Santana Neves (both sons of African women) married Africans. Given the low rate of exogamous marriage among Africans that Maria Inês Cortes de Oliveira has found (only 3.4 percent of married African women had chosen creole partners), these unions were highly unusual.[55] The two black officers who fathered children by slaves did so by women who belonged to other masters, suggesting that the relationships were consensual. Colonel Manoel Pereira da Silva managed to acquire and free his daughter and sole heir, while Captain Joaquim Félix could only leave his estate to his still-enslaved daughter and mandate that his executors undertake to liberate her. The widowed Colonel Neves frequently stood as godfather to slave children, as he implied when leaving the balance of his estate to all of his female godchildren who had gained freedom. Three freedwomen still owed him the money that he had lent them to acquire freedom. Neves was a prominent black patriarch and would play a major role in the military politics of the 1820s.[56]

Close ties to Africans and slaves on the part of black officers, it should be added, did not imply a rejection of slavery, an institution deeply rooted in Brazilian society. Poverty explains the small number of slaves owned by these men (Table 4.3), in contrast to whites and mulattoes. To be sure, Colonel Neves bequeathed freedom to his two slaves but he had no children who would have been dispossessed by this generosity. In contrast, the freed Captain Joaquim Félix emerges from his will as a hard-nosed businessman who trained slaves in his trades of barber and musician, managing what must have been a profitable slave band. Having bought his own freedom, he was evidently in no mood to be generous to his slaves. At the time of writing his will, he had freed ten of them, all except an infant for cash; he subjected each to the additional obligation of paying for the recitation of fifty masses for his soul before they would receive their letters of liberty. Twelve more remained in bondage and would be inherited by his still-enslaved daughter.[57]

In short, black officers—all of whom were free or freed men born in Brazil—were nevertheless but a generation or so away from both slavery and African Bahia, maintaining close ties to members of these groups, especially relatives. The only white officer to have a long-standing relationship with an African woman, in contrast, did so from a position of power—she was his slave and had borne six of his children, one of whom he purchased from his brother (who had inherited the child).[58] Although the evidence is somewhat sketchy, none of the mulatto officers had the close relationships with African and slave women visible in black officers' wills and inventories.[59] Nor is there much evidence of nonmilitary ties among mulatto officers, with the exception of Captain Custódio Gomes de Almeida, the gem-setter, who owned a half interest in the brigantine of which Captain Inocêncio Marques de Santana was master and had stood as godfather to Major Leandro da Silva's son.[60]

White officers, especially the Portuguese merchants who dominated the First Regiment, maintained completely different social ties, as has already been suggested by the brotherhoods of which they were members. Lieutenant Colonel Inocêncio José da Costa, the commander of the First Regiment who died in 1805, epitomizes the well-connected Portuguese merchant and militia officer. His brother was a high court judge; close links to another judge in 1799 led to suspicions that he was a conduit for illegal commerce on the judiciary's part. His first wife belonged to a cadet branch of the Portuguese nobility; his second wife, a cousin of the planter-merchant-army officer José Inácio Aciavoli de Vasconcelos Brandão, was the daughter of a marshal.[61] Commerce and family reinforced each other. When Captain Manoel Ferreira da Silva's widow sought to become the tutor of her children, three registered merchants testified on her behalf, while a Portuguese captain financed his nephew's business ventures in Santo Amaro.[62]

The Antunes Guimarães family (Figure 4.1) exemplifies some of the familial and commercial patterns that structured the white militia. In 1841, João modestly described his father, the elder Inácio, as a man who "possessed some goods and fortune," while the younger Inácio described his family as one of the "most distinguished" of Salvador in the 1810s.[63] The children's failure to inventory their father's goods promptly in 1830 makes it difficult to assess his wealth, but he was certainly well connected: In 1810, the elder Inácio was a supernumerary lieutenant colonel in the First Regiment, and in 1811, he was named to command the Coast Guard Artillery; in 1817, he sat on Salvador's municipal council.[64] All three of Inácio's sons followed him into business. João served as chief clerk (without pay, as he later recalled) in his father's establishment from 1800 to 1813; in 1809, Bruno (as he was known) was importing calicoes and shipping sugar and cotton to Liverpool. Their sister married a man listed in 1824 as a forty-year-old merchant, Lieutenant Colonel Manoel José Freire de Carvalho. The elder Inácio, Bruno, João, and Manoel José jointly held a tax contract from 1818 to 1820. By the end of the 1810s, the younger Inácio had joined João to manage the whaling stations

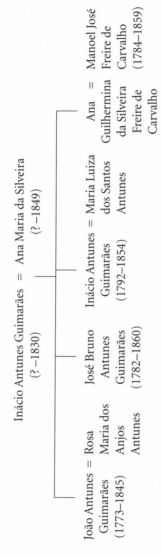

Inácio Antunes Guimarães = Ana Maria da Silveira
(?–1830)   (?–1849)

João Antunes = Rosa   José Bruno   Inácio Antunes = Maria Luiza   Ana   = Manoel José
Guimarães   Maria dos   Antunes   Guimarães   dos Santos   Guilhermina   Freire de
(1773–1845)   Anjos   Guimarães   (1792–1854)   Antunes   da Silveira   Carvalho
              Antunes   (1782–1860)   Freire de   (1784–1859)
                                                                                      Carvalho

FIGURE 4.1 The Antunes Guimarães Family.

SOURCES: Invs. in APEB/SJ/IT: Inácio Antunes Guimarães (father), 04/1668/2138/06, 04/1826/2297/11; José Bruno Antunes Guimarães, 05/2006/2477/11; Inácio Antunes Guimarães (son), 04/1681/2151/05; Manoel José Freire de Carvalho, 04/1580/2049/06; wills, I. A. Guimarães (son), APEB/SJ/IT, 05/2189/2658/43; João Antunes Guimarães, APEB/SJ/LRT, vol. 32, fols. 5r–9r; FOs, J. A. Guimarães, AHE/RQ, JJ-41-1136; I. A. Guimarães (son), BN/SM/DB, C.876.30; Bruno, BN/SM/DB, C.624.6.

that they owned at Itapuã, on the outskirts of Salvador, and on Itaparica Island, where they employed at least sixty slaves.[65]

João, Bruno, the younger Inácio, and Manoel José enjoyed successful militia careers. All three brothers enlisted in the First Regiment; within one and four years of enlisting, respectively, João and Bruno were commissioned. In 1811, Captain Bruno and Sergeant Inácio followed their father to the Coast Guard Artillery, with Inácio gaining the rank of second lieutenant by virtue of his service in the mounted company. João remained in the First Regiment, transferring to the suburban Torre militia in 1820, likely to be closer to the Itapuã whaling station. In 1817, Captain Manoel José requested a supernumerary lieutenant colonelcy, which rank he held in 1824.[66]

In their close integration of family, business, and militia service, the Antunes Guimarães clan was not unique. Colonel Caetano Maurício Machado's three daughters each married merchant officers, while his sole surviving son would eventually attain his father's grade of colonel in the First Regiment.[67] Like the planter/merchant/marshals analyzed in Chapter 2, the merchant–militia officers would face hard times in the 1820s and 1830s, as their prosperity of the first decades of the 1800s eroded under the shock of the independence war and the constant grind of ever more intense foreign competition.

To recapitulate this discussion of militia officers' socioeconomic positions, men in the black regiment were the poorest of all militia officers and tended to be artisans in low-status trades. Often they were but a generation removed from slavery; many maintained ties to Africans, slaves, and Afro-Brazilian Catholic religious institutions. Mulatto officers were somewhat better off than their black counterparts but they occupied no evident economic or cultural niche. Well-connected merchants, often but not always Portuguese, dominated the First Regiment while the Second Regiment contained a mix of Portuguese and Brazilian shopkeepers and artisans in the prestigious trades. In very different, yet strikingly parallel ways, white officers of the First Regiment and black officers of the Third constituted Luso-Brazilian and creole Afro-Brazilian elites. While mulattoes stood in an intermediate position between whites and blacks, their place in society was an ambiguous one, not conducive to the formation of a distinct mulatto social group; reforms that sought to professionalize the militia in the early 1800s perpetuated this ambiguity.

Professionalization and Racial Questions

Up to this point, I have examined the militia as a racially segmented status group, analyzing the economic and social criteria that the monarchy used in rewarding men with commissions and the social networks in which these men participated. At the same time, however, the militia was part of the military, which implied equality among the city's regiments and their officers, a point emphasized in the 1790s during a discussion of whether militia officers were entitled to wear red and blue ribbons, a privilege granted to the regulars by the queen. Legal experts concluded that no legislation denied the equality of militia and army officers.[68] Indeed, as early as the 1760s, the Portuguese government, then dominated by the Marquis of Pombal, had issued a series of decrees affirming the equality of black, mulatto, and white officers.[69] To be sure, Pombal's policy of breaking down racial barriers where they conflicted with other state interests such as maintaining a strong military provoked determined opposition from officials throughout Portugal's far-flung empire; nevertheless, this enlightened despot chipped the first cracks into the walls of institutionalized racial discrimination in the Luso-Brazilian world.[70] In the wake of Pombal's decrees, the discrimination suffered by black and mulatto militiamen was especially galling. Vilhena reports that the governor never entrusted the Fourth Regiment with the prestigious palace guard; he also twice witnessed the failure of regular officers to salute the mulatto regiment during the annual Corpus Christi parade. Black militiamen were frequently assigned to cleaning the moats and scarps of Salvador's forts; their officers' personnel files contain testimonials of good conduct and "zealous" service in the ditches, touching evidence of their lot.[71]

Vilhena also remarked that officers in the Fourth Regiment were especially offended at serving under a major not of their "quality" while the Henriques served under a "black colonel." This is the first reference to an issue that would drag on until the 1840s, exemplifying the complex racial politics of the transition from colonial regime to independent empire. On the death of the Fourth Regiment's colonel in 1796, command fell to José Luis Teixeira, a regular lieutenant promoted to militia major in 1787, and according to Vilhena, a man lacking the qualities that made for a good commander: "So pleased is he with his unexpected fortune . . . that he appears to have exceeded the bounds of fairness" in his treatment of subordinates. Whatever Teixeira's failings, his appointment was also an insult to the mulatto officers who, in contrast to their black colleagues, now did not serve under one of their own.[72] Teixeira's appointment was, in fact, part of a deliberate policy on the part of Governor Fernando José de Portugal, who had sought and received authorization to eliminate the mulatto colonels.[73]

That the Fourth Regiment was unhappy with its commander in 1798 was well known in Salvador. When the proclamations calling for equality among blacks, whites, and mulattoes appeared, heralding the existence of the Tailors' Conspiracy, popular opinion attributed them to mulatto militia soldiers and officers; authorities soon detained Second Lieutenant Domingos da Silva Lisboa, a Lisbon-born mulatto.[74] Lisboa turned out to be innocent and no other officers of the Fourth Regiment (or any other militia unit) were arrested, although one mulatto officer was later mentioned as a participant in seditious gatherings and the conspirators claimed the loyalty of fifty-four militia officers.[75]

As seen in the previous chapter, the core conspirators were mulatto artisans and regular soldiers like Luiz Gonzaga das Virgens e Veiga, the author of the handbills. They were well informed about the state of Salvador's militia in 1798. Lucas Dantas de Amorim Torres correctly calculated that there were more blacks and mulattoes than whites in the regiments and concluded from this that, if they allied, none could resist them (Table 4.1).[76] Dantas apparently encouraged the tailor and corporal in the second militia regiment, João de Deus, to approach the ambitious senior captain of the Henriques, a barber by the name of Joaquim José de Santana.[77] The captain was then assiduously studying military drill and spending time at the barracks, but as he remarked, he would certainly desist from his studies if the distressing rumors that a white man would be named regimental major proved true. João de Deus then invited Santana to join the plot, holding out the prospect of a colonelcy in the regulars under the new regime of promotion by merit alone. On the advice of one of his clients, a judge, Santana reported the conversation to the governor, who recommended that he receive the coveted majorship in reward for this service. Within a year or so, he obtained the post, which he considered "very little" when he sought further promotion in 1800.[78]

Although the conspirators of 1798 did not include any officers in the black and mulatto militia, the suspicions that first fell on the Fourth Regiment reveal authorities' worries, while the clumsy attempt to recruit Santana demonstrates that they were not entirely unfounded. In the lengthy debate over the nonwhite militia that followed, authorities hastened to emphasize the rivalry between blacks and mulattoes that they perceived in Santana's denunciation. That the mulatto captains continued to petition for the promotion of some of their number to colonel and lieutenant colonel and that one of them (a blacksmith) was dismissed in 1800 for writing a "disrespect-ful" letter to the major reinforced the widespread view that mulattoes were the most restive group in Brazil.[79] A royal bureaucrat bluntly declared that Pombal's policies and the creation of a mulatto regiment had been an "error" for they had only increased mulattoes' vanity, a frequent theme of late-colonial writings on Brazilian life.[80] For the minister of the navy and overseas dominions, the issue was quite simple, as he observed in com-menting on one of the mulatto officers' petitions: It was necessary "not to discourage *pardo* officers, who will serve with little zeal" without the prospect of promotion; on the other hand, they should "not be raised so high that they come to perturb public tranquility, given that, in all the colonies, these people have shown themselves to be the most restless," a veiled reference to the events of 1798.[81]

Implementing the minister's carefully calculated proposal, however, proved impossible, for the problem posed by promotion beyond the rank of captain in the black and mulatto regiments became inextricably linked to a policy of professionalizing or militarizing the militia.[82] In practice, this meant simply that the two adjutants and one major of each regiment, paid officers responsible for training and drill, would be selected from the regulars and that men with army experience would be named to command militia regiments. Majors tended to be lieutenants or captains transferred or temporarily assigned to the militia; adjutants were usually army sergeants promoted to lieutenant. For army officers, these were desirable postings. Militarization of the militia accelerated in the 1810s and a series of orders after the establishment of the Portuguese court in Rio de Janeiro insisted on regular drills, inspections, reports as well as the maintenance of troop registers; by October 1812, the inspector general could report considerable progress in these areas. To underscore the Coast Guard Artillery's obliga-tions, the governor had a special drill manual published for the new part-time artillerists.[83]

The most controversial aspect of this program was the policy of pro-moting men with regular experience to militia colonelcies, for in many regiments, adjutants and majors were the only officers who fulfilled this requirement. Militia colonelcies carried with them no salaries and the army officers promoted to militia colonel drew only the salary of their adjutant or major commissions. Insistence that militia commands go to the "most distinguished and wealthiest" men in the regiments, both because of the ex-penses inherent in the posts and because "poor men of low condition could not command the respect of their subordinates," indicates that it was not always possible to find militia officers who combined army experience with the social and economic requisites for militia commands.[84] In Salvador's First Regiment, command oscillated between merchants and professional officers after 1802, but not without controversy, as its officers protested the promotion of a regular officer to the command in 1806. This army captain of noble birth (he had enlisted as a cadet), who had transferred to the militia as a major in 1797, was succeeded in 1811 by a Portuguese merchant who had covered many company expenses during his long years of service. This man's retirement in 1816 provided the occasion to appoint a regular army major to head the regiment.[85] In 1817, the new Fifth Regiment received an army captain as its colonel.[86]

In the Third and Fourth Regiments, professionalizing the adjutants, majors, and colonels implied naming "white" regulars to train and command blacks and mulattoes. For more than a decade, the colonelcies of the Fourth Regiment remained vacant as officials on both sides of the Atlantic debated the wisdom of this policy. The government formally ruled on the issue in 1802, echoing Pombal's decrees by declaring emphatically that it considered blacks and mulattoes "worthy of all honors and military posts" and ordering that, in the Third and Fourth Regiments, preference be given "to officers of the same colors" as the men, thus reversing the governor's policy of the 1790s. While A. J. R. Russell-Wood has called it a "landmark in the history of race relations in colonial Brazil,"[87] the decision is nevertheless notable mostly for its ambiguity. The ruling modified its declaration of preference for blacks and mulattoes by noting that, since there were no black or mulatto regulars in Brazil, qualified men might not be found, in which case white officers might be promoted into the black and mulatto regiments after all. More generally, it firmly established the requirement that militia commanders, adjutants, and majors have either regular experience or demonstrate their qualifications through competitive examinations, opening up the possibility of promoting black and mulatto officers who lacked regular experience.[88]

The complex story of the 1802 ruling's implementation can best be examined separately for the Fourth and Third Regiments. As F. W. O. Morton has shown, a combination of bureaucratic oversight in Lisbon and opposition to promoting mulattoes on the part of Bahia's governors kept the posts of colonel and lieutenant colonel vacant in the Fourth Regiment until 1808.[89] The arrival of the court in Bahia prompted new petitions from mulatto officers requesting that their unit be placed on equal footing with the Henriques; both the inspector general and the governor agreed, and in short order, Major Teixeira was promoted to colonel. An army lieutenant with the apparently noble name of Antônio Manoel de Melo e Castro became lieutenant colonel and one of the adjutants, João Pereira Falcão, took the post of major.[90]

These promotions were not what the mulatto captains had been seeking but they were consistent with the policy of naming men with regular experience to the top posts in the militia. Although the 1802 ruling called for the promotion of mulatto officers, it did not require that majors and colonels be named from among the ranks of militia captains; rather, it only held this out as a possibility if no regular officers were willing to be transferred (and promoted) into the black and mulatto regiments. In the discussions leading up to the 1802 ruling, the Conselho Ultramarino (Overseas Council) had anticipated that the Bahian regulars would have a sufficient number of mulatto officers and sergeants from which to draw paid officers for the Fourth Regiment.[91] Keeping in mind the ambiguity of the socially constructed category of pardo, a closer look at the men promoted in 1808 suggests that the governor had, in fact, found officers whom he considered mulattoes for the posts, although they may not have been accepted as such by the Fourth Regiment's captains and were certainly not drawn from among their number. In 1824, one of Melo e Castro's slaves described his master as the "bastard *pardo* son" of the governor of Angola. After his arrival in Bahia in 1803, Melo e Castro married the daughter of the white militia officer and his African slave. Although he had enlisted as a cadet in Angola and served exactly two weeks at that rank before promotion to second lieutenant, illegitimate birth notwithstanding, he probably faced greater prejudice in Bahia, which obliged him to accept transfer and promotion to the much less prestigious Fourth Militia Regiment.[92] Little is known about Teixeira and Falcão but neither had enjoyed particularly successful careers in the regulars, which may have encouraged them to accept promotion into the mulatto militia.[93] In short, the 1808 promotions probably obeyed both the letter and the spirit of the 1802 ruling, at least in Melo e Castro's case, advancing both professionals and mulattoes; what they did not do, of course, was satisfy the mulatto militia captains' ambitions. In this regard, as in Vilhena's day, the officers of the Fourth Regiment stood on a very different footing from their colleagues in the Henriques.

In 1809, the Third Regiment had a full complement of black adjutants, majors, and colonels, none of whom had served in the regulars; after the regiment botched a firing drill, Inspector General Brant condemned these men's "profoundest ignorance" of all things military. In the inspection of later that year, he lambasted the major and adjutants as ignorant civilians and blacks among whom men capable of these posts could never be found. Accusing the second-in-command, now Lieutenant Colonel Joaquim José de Santana, of corruption, he further asserted that such malversation was not an individual failing but characteristic of all blacks, whose "bad breeding" left them bereft of "virtue and honor." Having thus disposed of Santana's eligibility to act as commander during the incapacitation of the colonel, the inspector recommended that white regular officers be appointed to run the regiment.[94]

Despite Brant's virulently racist diatribes against the officers of the Third Regiment, nothing came of his proposals to cashier them, and a few years later, he was dealing far more respectfully with even the allegedly venal Santana. On the death of the regiment's colonel in 1814, Santana took command after all and petitioned that his son, then a third sergeant, be commissioned. Brant opined that colonels' sons should indeed not remain enlisted men; because there were no provisions for naming cadets in the militia, Santana's son of the same name (who later added Gomes as his surname) was promoted to second lieutenant a few months later.[95] What had caused Brant's change of heart is not known; perhaps he reckoned it impossible to find regular officers willing to staff the Third Regiment. As a result of his perhaps grudging tolerance for black officers, a succession of black men moved through the examinations into adjutancies, later advancing to major and lieutenant colonel. None of them had regular army experience; rather, theirs was a separate career track in the military. Three would play prominent roles in the 1820s and 1830s: Adjutant Francisco Xavier Pereira (who later took Bigode as his surname) became major in 1813 and lieutenant colonel in 1820; behind him was Manoel Gonçalves da Silva, a silkworker who became adjutant in 1814 (and major in, probably, 1820). After these two men came the beneficiary of Brant's respect for the sons of senior officers and the only man to pass the 1820 adjutant examination, Joaquim José de Santana Gomes.[96] In short, what distinguished the Third from the First and Fourth Regiments was the uninterrupted promotion of company-level officers to command posts; in the 1810s, military and community leadership reinforced each other in the Third Regiment in ways much like the First Regiment and the Coast Guard Artillery.

In the Fourth Regiment, a similar but truncated process of gradual promotion from adjutant to colonel resumed after the 1808 promotions. By the end of the 1810s, Melo e Castro was colonel; a former adjutant, Pedro Inácio de Porciuncula, had reached the rank of lieutenant colonel; and his son, Adjutant José Maria Cirilo da Silva, was following in his footsteps. Neither of the latter two men had regular army experience and it finally appeared that the Fourth Regiment was falling into a pattern similar to that of the Third.[97] Nevertheless, in this regard, the Fourth Regiment was far behind the Third. The lack of a clear social, economic, and cultural space for mulattoes in Salvador and the hiatus in promotion of mulattoes into the paid posts in their regiment combined to prevent the emergence of a distinct mulatto military leadership. Independence sharply revealed these differences between blacks and mulattoes even as it raised the status of both relative to the white militia, whose signifcant contingent of Portuguese officers tended to side with the mother country during the conflict.

By the end of the 1810s, the militia continued to fulfill its purpose, and as two travelers put it, "contribute[d] much to the maintenance of order."[98] Like the regulars, militia regiments were subject to secret investigations in 1817 but there is no evidence that authorities discovered any seditious tendencies in them.[99] While complaints about the militia's ineffectiveness are common enough, there is also a significant evidence suggesting that the militia functioned relatively well. Indeed, the detailed documentation that made this chapter possible reveals the militia's efficiency and its importance to men who always used their ranks in civilian life.

The militia's regimentation of Salvador's society expressed a quintessentially Old Regime colonial vision of society, in which separate corporations, in this case, segregated by race, nevertheless bound all to the monarchy. More so than in the regular officer corps or enlisted ranks, in the militia the colonial state made race a central feature, publicly and visibly labeling men as whites, mulattoes, or blacks. Here race mattered, and to a remarkable degree, the segregated corporations also reflected class and cultural differences as the officers of the First and Third Regiments constituted, respectively, Luso-Brazilian merchant and Afro-Brazilian artisan elites. Pardo (mulatto) officers, by contrast, occupied no evident social or economic space in Salvador, a circumstance that had important implications for their political role at and after independence.

That black and mulatto officers were nominally equal to their white counterparts could not overcome the continued discrimination that they suffered. Royal affirmations of equality fell upon ears deafened by deeply ingrained attitudes. The colonial government's efforts to professionalize the militia through naming regular officers to key posts in the regiments fell afoul of these attitudes, obliging authorities to issue the peculiar compromise of the 1802 ruling. Establishing a segregated career path in the black and mulatto militias, it underwrote the status and position of a black military elite that would, in the 1820s and 1830s, play a key role in military politics.

The Tailors' Conspiracy, with its promise of equality among whites, mulattoes, and blacks, offered a liberal alternative to the colonial corporate society. That black and mulatto officers rejected the plotters' overtures likely reflected their (correct) calculation of the plot's limited prospect for success. It also demonstrated their support for the colonial regime of which they were beneficiaries. In the 1820s, with the independence struggle and the subsequent creation of a nominally liberal and constitutional regime, black and mulatto officers would face new and difficult challenges.

CHAPTER 5

Independence and Its Aftermath

Four days after news of the liberal revolution in Porto reached Salvador, on 27 October 1820, a worried Inspector General Felisberto Caldeira Brant Pontes observed that "the revolutionary pest seems to be the sickness of our century." Less than a month later, he recommended to the Count of Palmela (who would shortly assume the ministry of war and foreign affairs) that João VI take quick action to head off the all but inevitable Bahian adhesion to the liberal government in Portugal:

> "Any favor conceded before the revolution will be received with enthusiasm, and all good [men] will fall into His Majesty's arms. After the revolution everything [will] seem forced by events and God knows what character it will develop in a country with so many blacks and mulattoes".[1]

Two months later, his fear was borne out when a barracks revolt sparked Bahia's adherence to the liberal regime, conventionally considered the first step toward independence in Bahia. While F. W. O. Morton has described Bahia's subsequent experience as a "conservative revolution of independence,"[2] contemporaries such as Brant were far less sanguine about the final outcome: a stable, conservative and centralized constitutional monarchy in Rio de Janeiro, dominated by the planter class and generally governing in its members' interests through effectively functioning national Brazilian institutions. During the turbulent conflicts of these years, numerous challenges to this ultimately successful elite project emerged, and the independence era, like so many other revolutionary periods, burgeoned with alternative projects, as broad sectors of the population articulated demands and developed political programs.

Military affairs stood at the center of Bahian (and Brazilian) politics during these years. Not only did the province see the most extensive fighting of Brazil's war for independence (1822–1823), but the majority of free males—that class of the population so often enfranchised in some way during the liberal-democratic revolutions of the period—was connected to the armed forces in cities such as Salvador. As the most populous sector of the state apparatus, and the one that reached most deeply into everyday life, the military was a key locus for politics and debates over the nature of society; military reform, in turn, was an essential aspect of postindependence state building, reflecting fundamental political issues.

For each sector of the armed forces—regular officers, enlisted men, and the militia—these years brought sudden, wrenching changes. A revolutionary militarization broke the planter–officer alliance and flooded the officer corps with new entrants, many deeply politicized during the independence conflict. These men played a central role in the immediate post independence unrest that culminated in the so-called Periquitos' Revolt of 1824, and only afterward was a semblance of the colonial order restored, in brutal fashion, with the execution of two officers and wholesale purges of newly commissioned men. Wartime recruitment for the rank and file, which extended as far as the slave population, dramatically changed the composition of the enlisted ranks. In the atmosphere of heightened racially defined conflicts of the early 1820s, the recruitment of slaves during the independence war threatened soldiers' status as nonblack free men. Worried authorities firmly redrew the racially charged status line between slave and soldier by purging blacks and former slaves from the garrison in 1824 and 1825. The militia also demonstrates the extent to which independence constituted a social revolution in Salvador. Not only had black and mulatto patriots played a leading role in pushing Bahian planters to opt for independence, but they also dominated Salvador's postwar militia by sheer dint of numbers. How these men viewed the new state would thus become a fundamental question in political and military calculations. Generously rewarded for their services against the Portuguese, black and mulatto officers cast their lot with the new regime, seeing in it the possibility of a greater role for themselves; throughout the 1820s, these men were pillars of the monarchical order. Before turning to the separate experiences of officers, soldiers, and militiamen, this chapter first surveys the politics of independence in Bahia, analyzing the major issues at stake during these years.

The Politics of Independence in Bahia

Between late 1820 and early 1825, Bahians debated (and sometimes fought violently over) fundamental issues, including the nature of government (liberal and constitutional or absolutist, monarchical or republican), the province's place in larger polities (the trans-Atlantic Luso-Brazilian monarchy or the smaller, but still vast, Brazilian empire), the nature of society (on its simplest level, how liberal and constitutional principles would be applied to Brazilian society), and the place of foreigners (Africans and Portuguese) in the new Brazilian community. On a political level, it is important to recognize, as did contemporaries, that Brazil was plural. The Brazils were a series of Portuguese captaincies—Bahia one of the most important—that during these years stood between competing governments in Lisbon and Rio de Janeiro. While the Lisbon government and its parliament, the Cortes, were liberal and constitutional from 1820 to 1823, the regime of Pedro I in Rio de Janeiro was always perceived as lukewarm in its commitment to liberal constitutionalism. And, it bears repeating, the Bahia of the 1820s was a deeply divided society; Brant's fear of revolution among members of the "classes of color" was a very real component of these years' political calculations. Before analyzing these themes, however, a brief review of the salient events of 1820 to 1825 is in order.[3]

On 21 February 1821, scant months after Brant expressed his worries about the contagion of revolution, Bahia adhered to the Portuguese liberal regime after a rising led by Brazilian artillery officers. Brief clashes between constitutionalist and royalist troops marred the day, but peace was quickly restored and the victorious constitutionalists established a Provisional Junta, composed mostly of Portuguese bureaucrats, officers, and clergymen. The artillery's senior Bahian-born officer, Lieutenant Colonel Manoel Pedro de Freitas Guimarães, was promoted to brigadier, named commander of the garrison, and added to the Junta by popular acclamation.

After this auspicious beginning, relations between Bahia and Portugal deteriorated rapidly. While Roderick J. Barman has shown that the Cortes did not from the outset seek to return the Brazilian provinces to colonial status,[4] by the end of 1821 and early 1822, the Lisbon government was attempting to reduce the autonomy of the Rio de Janeiro government and impose more control over the other provinces. The Cortes ordered João VI to return to Lisbon; he complied in April, leaving his son, Pedro, as regent in Rio de Janeiro but he too soon received orders to sail for Portugal. In August, a substantial contingent of Portuguese troops, the Constitutional

Legion, arrived in Salvador from Lisbon. Originally invited by the Junta to defend the constitutional regime against reaction from Rio de Janeiro, these reinforcements eventually became perceived as an occupation army. In September, Bahia elected its eight deputies to the Cortes, all of whom were Brazilians. Among the merchants and planters who dominated the group was Marshal Luiz Paulino de Oliveira Pinto da França, the planter-general, but the representatives also included Cipriano José Barata de Almeida, implicated in the 1798 conspiracy. In late 1821 and early 1822, the Cortes undertook measures to reinstate Lisbon's commercial monopoly, appealing to the Portuguese mercantile community in Salvador, which had lost much ground to foreign competition. Increasingly it looked like "recolonization" was in the offing. In November, a group of Brazilian-born officers attempted to overthrow the Junta in Salvador. Arrested and sent to Lisbon, they were released on arrival and several returned to play leading roles in the events of mid-1822.

Bahians' loyalty to the Cortes was sorely tested by measures that subordinated Brazilian garrisons to Lisbon military authorities and the arrival on 11 February 1822 of orders to replace Brigadier Freitas Guimarães with Colonel Inácio Luiz Madeira de Melo, the Portuguese commander of the Twelfth Battalion, which had been posted back to Salvador in 1820. The municipal council refused to enact the formality of registering Madeira's patent; the Junta's attempt to conciliate the dispute failed and fighting broke out in Salvador on 19 February. The Portuguese troops carried the day. By the 21st, they had captured Freitas Guimarães, broken the Brazilian regular units, and secured Salvador. Many Bahian officers and soldiers escaped to the Recôncavo, joined by civilians who preferred to emigrate rather than remain in a city under military dictatorship.

Little is known of the next few months. A cautious Madeira bode his time in Salvador, perhaps seeing himself as victorious. In Rio de Janeiro, Pedro defied the Cortes by remaining in Brazil and gradually consolidated an alternative government to the Lisbon regime, receiving support from nearby provinces and promising in early June to convoke a constituent assembly. Later that month, the towns of the Recôncavo recognized Pedro as regent, establishing in September an Interim Council of Government dominated by sugar planters to coordinate military efforts against the Portuguese in Salvador. With support from Rio de Janeiro in the form of troops and a French officer to command them, Pierre (Pedro) Labatut, and aid from neighboring provinces, the Interim Council organized what it called the Exército Pacificador (Pacification Army); the very name hints at social unrest to be quelled as well as foreign troops to be expelled. A hodgepodge of Recôncavo militias, specially raised contingents, and reconstituted regular and militia regiments from Salvador, largely financed and supplied by Bahian planters, the Exército Pacificador besieged Salvador and starved the Portuguese troops out of the city. On the morning of 2 July 1823, they sailed for Portugal, leaving the victorious Brazilians to parade unopposed into Salvador that afternoon.

The peaceful occupation of Bahia's capital contrasted sharply with the troubled years that followed. Sporadic conflicts between Bahian and non-Bahian troops in late 1823 and scattered anti-Portuguese civilian violence culminated in a tumult when news of Pedro I's dissolution of the Brazilian Constituent Assembly reached Salvador in December. On the 17th, an act of the town council timidly expressed the Bahian elite's opposition to Pedro's illiberal actions, called on him to promulgate without delay the "doubly liberal" charter that he had promised, and attempted to satisfy the anti-Portuguese clamor by ordering the expulsion of those Portuguese who had failed to support independence. Recognizing the harm that such a measure would cause the economy, the provincial president (a chief executive appointed by the imperial government) delayed implementing it, and in April 1824, a group of Bahian officers, led by Major José Antônio da Silva Castro, formally protested the government's temporizing. The elaborate ritual affirmations of loyalty to the constitution granted by Pedro calmed the garrison in May, but the republican Confederação do Equador Rebellion centered in Pernambuco continued to offer an alternative vision of Brazilian development, at least until its defeat in September. In this, the other major northeastern plantation province, elites repeatedly rejected Pedro's nominations for president, thereby underscoring their commitment to local autonomy, even as they struggled to contain social unrest.[5]

On 25 October 1824, after Governor of Arms (garrison commander) Felisberto Gomes Caldeira had removed Major Castro, the popular commander of the Third Infantry Battalion [nicknamed the Periquitos (Parakeets) after the green and yellow trim of its uniform], in preparation for transferring the unit out of Bahia, some of its men shot Caldeira dead and acclaimed Castro as their commander. He reluctantly reassumed his post amid a tense standoff between troops loyal to the late governor and the mutineers. When attempts to conciliate the two factions failed, the loyalists retreated to the estates of a great planter family in nearby Abrantes. Caldeira's murder apparently unnerved the conspirators, for they loudly proclaimed their loyalty to the Emperor and the Third Battalion prepared for embarkation to

Pernambuco. In late November, the provincial government finally took refuge on a warship, thus escaping the rebels' clutches. The much-feared sack of Salvador did not take place (principally because the militia maintained order in late November), many of the soldiers and officers implicated in the mutinies fled of their own accord, and the loyalists from Abrantes reoccupied the city in early December. The execution of two officers, the court-martialing of the remaining rebels, and a significant purge of the rank and file removed troublemakers from the army but left many issues unresolved.

What was at stake in this frenetic blur of events? In March 1822, Madeira reported three parties active in Salvador: a Portuguese and constitutionalist one; a second, dominated by wealthy Bahians and linked to Rio de Janeiro, whose members desired "a constitution in which, like lords," they would be independent of Portugal; and a third, composed of less wealthy classes, who "desired a republican independence in which only natives of the country would figure." A month later, the captain major of Cachoeira also reported three parties in his district: a Brazilian, a European (Portuguese), and a black one, adding that the Brazilians were arming themselves.[6] Despite their simplification of complex alignments, these two reports touch on virtually all of the issues of these years, in which class, race, and an emerging sense of difference between Portuguese and Brazilians shaped debates over the nature of government, Bahia's place in larger polities, the role of liberalism in this slave society, and the place of foreigners in the nation.

Much of the debate of these years turned on the form of government to be adopted after independence. Few truly advocated a return to absolutism after 1821, but the more radical liberals were quick to suspect absolutist proclivities among those in power. Similarly, republicanism was a minority position—the monarchy was too deeply rooted in Brazilian society to be easily cast off—but authorities worried about "republican" agitators, often characterizing them as "anarchists," a multivalent term that often said more about authorities' fears than the "agitators'" program.[7] Rather, the core political conflict of these years concerned the nature of the constitutional monarchy. In December 1822, the Interim Council called for "a prudent and well-balanced division of powers" that respected both imperial prerogatives and "the sacrosanct [rights] of citizens." After Salvador's liberation, the municipal council clarified this elite vision of liberal and constitutional rule. The "sacred rights of individual security, prosperity, and immunity of citizens' domiciles" were the basis of constitutionalism, but for the sake of "harmony in all society," the council recommended that "each observe to the letter his duties," respect religion, venerate the emperor, and "give obedience to the government and its delegates."[8] These were the fervent desires of a slave-owning planter class that defined liberal constitutionalism narrowly, limiting its application (and the benefits of citizenship) to a minority. Inevitably, however, excluded groups sought the extension of liberal ideals and constitutional principles to them. For the elite, then, the central task was to ensure that the new ideals were properly understood, in other words, to establish and maintain an ideological hegemony that ensured, for instance, that slaves or the free poor subject to military recruitment recognized that guarantees of personal security or freedom from arbitrary arrest applied not to them.

Madeira's snide remark about the Bahian elite's desire to lord over a constitutional regime points to the appeal of local autonomy to the Bahian planter class. Subordination to a Lisbon parliamentary regime was no more to their liking than submission to a Rio de Janeiro monarch dogged by suspicions of absolutist pretensions.[9] Local autonomy and even federalism made sense to many, for whom the pátria (homeland) was Bahia, as Manoel Pedro de Freitas Guimarães declared in his first proclamation as garrison commander. Indeed, loyalty to the pátrias (the former captaincies, now provinces), rather than to Brazil, was widespread at this time, as Sérgio Buarque de Holanda noted long ago when he stressed that independence did not go hand in hand with Brazilian unity.[10] The degree of autonomy from the central government that Bahia would enjoy was an issue not resolved until the 1840s.

Equally important, however, was the maintenance of the "lords'" dominance of Bahian society. The vague but continual references to "anarchist" or "republican" factions whose members inadequately understood liberalism points to the profound politicization of these years and the threat that this posed to the planter class. Indeed, municipal councils used their acclamations of Pedro's regency to lament the "deplorable . . . ferment" in the Recôncavo and declare their opposition to those who would rouse the population into "anarchical excesses."[11] The elaborate militia parades that marked these adhesions were, as Iara Lis Carvalho Souza has observed, attempts to link the local social hierarchy (as institutionalized in the militia) to the new monarch.[12] From time to time, the Interim Council arrested radical patriots, such as the army surgeon, Francisco Sabino Alvares da Rocha Vieira, for fear that their presence in Cachoeira would be "contrary to good order." Official correspondence does not usually deign to record such men's aims but Labatut, complaining about Francisco Gê Acaíba Montezuma (the future Viscount of Jequitinonha, then still in the radical phase of his youth), declared that this "man without [good] birth and education" was spreading rumors that the emperor sought "to oppress the province and subject it to despotism." More often than contemporaries, historians comment that Sabino and Montezuma were mulattoes, suggesting that their actions reflected the ambitions of a nonwhite middle class.[13]

More broadly, the "black" party that concerned Cachoeira's captain major was, as João José Reis has argued, both a fearful elite's "ideological construction" and "absolutely real."[14] Slaves, freedpeople, and free nonwhites participated extensively in the conflicts of these years, seeking to influence the course of events and making their demands known. Slave revolt preoccupied observers and the patriot government, which held back troops to police plantation districts while accusing Madeira of fomenting rural slave revolts. Few uprisings actually took place during these years; rebellion against a well-armed master class was suicidal. Indeed, the May 1822 killing of 25 rebel slaves on Marshal José Inácio Aciavoli de Vasconcelos Brandão's plantation by the militia and Labatut's execution of 51 rebel Africans in December 1822 highlight an important point of agreement between the two rival parties: Slave rebellion had to be suppressed at all costs.[15] Nevertheless, slaves' attitudes changed in subtle but significant ways. Reports in 1822 that creoles and even long-resident Africans were demanding their freedom hint at the degree to which liberal ideals had penetrated Bahian society. For them, liberty from Portugal meant liberty from the master class, as the metaphors of slavery and freedom in elite public discourse (referring to Brazil's relationship with Portugal) gained deeper meanings.[16]

In popular discourse, political alignments furthermore assumed racial connotations, especially in the mutual and bitter recriminations between Portuguese and Brazilians. In August 1822, Portuguese constitutionalists analyzed the February conflicts in racial terms, asserting that not a single "individual who was not of white color" supported Madeira's appointment to command the garrison. They dismissed their opponents, the seditious soldiers of the regular artillery and militiamen of the Third and Fourth Regiments, as "men of color."[17] One Brazilian observer remarked with a wry understanding of the socially constructed nature of racial difference that Portuguese "judged that there was not one white in Brazil. They even called their own children blacks [*pretos*], half-breeds [*caboclos*], dark mulattoes [*pés de cabra*], Tupinambá [*Indians*], [and] cinnamon-colored [*canelas*]." In April 1822, the *Diário Constitucional* lamented that some Portuguese in Salvador were calling Brazilians "monkeys . . . from the coast of Africa."

Brazilians responded to these challenges by mocking Portuguese preten-sions: "whitewashed" (*caiado*) was a pejorative nickname for those born in the mother country while the European soldiery were nicknamed "sheep."[18] Such a racialization of politics was not solely a rhetorical device; while ex-aggerated, it reflected very real patterns in the armed forces and in the rest of society.

The conflicts of these years were crucibles of identity formation as patriots defined themselves in opposition to the Portuguese. Virulent anti-Portuguese discourse, not solely racial in content, marked a Brazilian and Bahian identity against the "Lusitanian rabble" or "uniformed wolves" who occupied Salvador.[19] During these years, lusophobia took deep root in the Bahian population and would color politics, especially radical liberal pol-itics, for decades. Less often explicit but nevertheless very real was the anti-African sentiment that demarcated the other side of the Brazilian na-tion. The residents of Jaguaripe who protested the recall of troops from their district in February 1823 worried that it left them "exposed to the *marotos* [Portuguese rogues], our enemies, concentrated here in large num-ber, and the African race whose malice" had often been demonstrated in the municipality.[20]

The conflicts over governance that that divided Portuguese, Bahians, and Brazilians in the early 1820s affected the military in sometimes surprising and unexpected ways. Time and again, the thousands of men who comprised Bahia's armed forces stood at the center of politics. Buffetted by the sudden changes of these years, they struggled to make sense of them, influence them, or simply adapt to them. Given the particular colonial structures of each sector of the armed forces, officers, enlisted men, and militiamen had distinct independence-era experiences.

The Transformation of the Officer Corps

Between 1820 and 1825, the colonial Bahian army disappeared, and along with this casualty of the independence struggle, the planter class's effective control over the armed forces evaporated. A decapitation of the institutional hierarchy eliminated the Luso-Brazilian general officers who had constituted the bridge to the Bahian elite. In its lower ranks, the offi-cer corps was flooded by new entrants, almost all Brazilians; many joined the army as cadets and quickly earned battlefield lieutenancies. Together, these changes transformed the dynamics of military authority, for the new junior officers, politicized in the struggle for independence, had less commitment to the army hierarchy than the cadets and long-serving non-commissioned officers promoted before 1820. The difficult relationship with the emerging Brazilian government in Rio de Janeiro, notably the conflict between the planter-led Interim Council in Cachoeira and Pedro Labatut, the French general appointed by Pedro I to command the Exército Pacificador, further hampered planters' ability to control Bahia's armed forces.

Army officers were central protagonists in the political changes that began with Bahia's adhesion to the still-unwritten Portuguese constitution on 10 February 1821, an episode that is poorly documented, particularly for the army officers who played a leading role in it. Contemporary or near-contemporary accounts all refer to constitutionalist clubs involving Cipriano José Barata de Almeida (the conspirator of 1798), Captain Manoel de São Boaventura Ferraz, and other artillery officers, influenced by the republican prisoners from the Pernambuco rising of 1817.[21] Morton has furthermore suggested that these educated officers, most of whom had risen through the ranks, faced the prospect of little further advance in their careers. In fact, five of the eleven mentioned by Inácio Acioli de Cerqueira e Silva had been cadets and only two are known with certainty to have begun their career as enlisted men.[22] Whatever their motives, this was no Brazilian nationalist rising: The officers hailed their "European brothers who [had] defeated despotism in Portugal" and railed against the "treason of Rio de Janeiro," where the King still opposed the constitution; indeed, one of the justifications for this rising was João's appointment of the archconservative Count of Vilaflor to govern the captaincy.[23] On the surface, then, the fighting pitted royalists against constitutionalists, as Inspector General Felisberto Caldeira Brant Pontes led troops from the legion and the First Regiment against the artillery. Among the casualties was Major Francisco Hermógenes de Aguilar; historians have remarked on the ironic demise in defense of absolutism of the most senior officer tried for involvment in the Tailors' Conspiracy.[24] Brant, whose horse had been shot out from under him, retreated to the palace, where he sought to have the Twelfth Battalion march on the constitutionalists. Marshal Luiz Paulino counseled compromise, and as groups of constitutionalists hailed the new regime throughout the city, the town council and leading citizens adhered to the new order, appointing a Provisional Junta. The new regime was apparently popular. In subsequent days, patriotic contributions flowed into government coffers (including more than 12:000$000 to be distributed among enlisted men), and numerous volunteers presented themselves to the regulars.[25]

Brant's political position may have been more complicated than simply that of defending the status quo. He had apparently been involved in some of the plotting and was subsequently accused of seeking to found a republican regime like that of the United States.[26] More likely, he had learned through his correspondence with the Count of Palmela of plans to separate an absolutist Brazil from a constitutionalist Portugal, quietly mooted in the court in early 1821. Just as in Rio de Janeiro, this was a highly unpopular proposal in Bahia, and Brant's call for a "new work of Brazilians" was poorly received at the town council meeting; several accounts refer to his narrow escape from physical harm at the hands of constitutionalists.[27] Defeated and politically marginalized, he shortly thereafter embarked for Rio de Janeiro. Only João's acceptance of the constitution later that month would make possible a Brazilian *and* constitutionalist position.

This episode also saw the acclamation of the deeply controversial Manoel Pedro de Freitas Guimarães as garrison commander. Unfortunately little is known about his early career. Born in Bahia, he enlisted as a navy cadet in 1796; commissioned in 1801, he transferred to the artillery as a supernumerary captain in 1805. Regular promotions followed, despite superiors' complaints that he was insufficiently attentive to his duties.[28] Lieutenant Colonel Freitas Guimarães's role in the plot made him a logical addition to the Junta, but he was only added to it (and promoted) after loud and insistent demands from the "people." Both of these ad hoc decisions received royal assent, but his many enemies were soon complaining about Freitas Guimarães's actions, either charitably calling them "ill-advised," or more bluntly, "idiocies."[29]

If the available sources suggest a significant degree of support for constitutional government in February 1821 and little animosity between Portuguese and Brazilians, either in the officer corps or in Bahian society at large, then the following year becomes a key period in defining political positions and social identities in Salvador's garrison.[30] By the end of 1821, brawling between Portuguese and Bahian troops was a regular occurrence, as Maria Dundas Graham reported in November.[31] The Junta later identified the source of this rivalry as the presence of a large core of soldiers and officers (the Twelfth Regiment and the Constitutional Legion that had arrived from Portugal in August) "whose profession, habits, and sojourner status in this country do not offer the . . . prospect of permanent relations with Bahians." The captaincy could absorb large numbers of individual Portuguese immigrants—officers, soldiers, and civilians alike—but it could not so easily assimilate regiments and legions whose members, as the town council put it, had "no ties that bound them to this country."[32]

In a poorly prepared coup attempt, a group of officers, including Lieutenant Colonel Felisberto Gomes Caldeira, attempted to overthrow the Junta on 3 November 1821. The coup's goals were unclear. The Junta blamed the plotters for seeking to separate Brazil from Portugal, but contemporaries recorded the protestors' "vivas" to the constitution and the Cortes.[33] To the extent that anti-Portuguese sentiment played a part in this plot, it did not translate into a desire for Brazilian independence. The coup's goal may have simply been home rule within a broader Luso-Brazilian constitutional framework, to which both the Junta and the Portuguese troops were the principal obstacles. In any case, this episode remains, as Morton notes, "obscure," but the role of Caldeira, an artillery officer who had enjoyed a highly successful career in the 1810s as aide-de-camp to his uncle, Inspector General Brant, and had extensive contacts among the Recôncavo planter class, suggests that there was broader support for a move toward local autonomy.[34]

Relations between Bahian and Portuguese troops continued to deteriorate, and by February 1822, when fighting broke out between Portuguese and Brazilian troops over the issue of Madeira's appointment to the garrison's command, each of the Brazilian regiments had a solid core of anti-Portuguese officers willing to lead their men in patriotic mutiny. In the Bahian legion, Second Lieutenant Manoel José de Carvalho reported having been threatened at knifepoint by Surgeon Sabino and Captain Caetano Maurício Machado, who demanded to know whether he was "on the side of the Europeans or the Bahians." Soldiers from the First Regiment heard officers calling on them "to defend the *pátria*" against "the *marotos* who wanted to become masters" of it. Subordination to superior officers fell by the wayside as patriots mobilized: Captain Machado declared "that Lieutenant-Colonel Dom Luiz [Baltazar da Silveira] should be given the boot [*ponta-pé*], for he was a great wimp [*muito mole*] and good for nothing."[35]

By this point, of course, all hope of unity in the transatlantic Portuguese nation was lost as both sides defined their identity in opposition to the other. There was no longer room for officers like Colonel Bento da França Pinto de Oliveira, who wrote plaintively to his father, Marshal Luiz Paulino: "I live in Brazil, belong to the army from over there [Portugal], [and] want the union of the provinces, for only in this way can Portugal be happy."[36] Nor was there room for neutrality and obedience to superiors, as Lieutenant Carvalho discovered. To the threats of his knife-wielding patriot comrades, he responded that he would dutifully "follow his unit wherever it were ordered." For him, this meant loyalty to Lisbon and evacuation to Portugal.[37]

Carvalho's experience highlights a key aspect of the period from 1821 to 1823: the rapid turnover in the officer corps, which was most unlike the stability of the late colonial period. The fighting during February 1822 dramatically split the officer corps. Many patriots fled to the Recôncavo while others, including Freitas Guimarães, were captured and interned for the duration of the conflict. During the war, scores of new men entered the officer corps, changing its social composition and reinforcing its lusophobia. In December 1823, the more radical patriots dealt with those who had displayed insufficient enthusiasm for their cause by pressuring Salvador's town council to call for the dismissal from the province's service of those who had fought against independence and the court-martialing of those who had remained in the city, a measure that the government was forced to accept. The result was, by the mid-1820s, a very different Bahian officer corps, one whose ties to the planter class were far less tight than those of the colonial army and one upon whose loyalty planters could consequently not rely.

The experience of the fifty-eight men proscribed in December 1823 reveals something of army politics' complexity during the previous years.[38] Families were deeply divided. Colonel Bento da França returned to Lisbon with Madeira; his brother, Captain Luiz, cast his lot with the patriots, while their father, Marshal Luiz Paulino, remained in the Cortes when the other Bahian deputies walked out and led an unsuccessful diplomatic mission to restore ties between Brazil and Portugal in 1823.[39] Captain Manoel de São Boaventura Ferraz, the constitutionalist conspirator of February 1821, remained in Salvador for the duration of the war; in his court-martial, he argued that, as manager of the Quinta dos Lázaros (a suburban hospital), he had performed invaluable services to the patriot cause as a spy, conduit for messages, and facilitator of emigrations. No witnesses testified against him and charges were dismissed.[40] The Portuguese-born secretary of the legion remained in Salvador and claimed in 1828 that he had been excluded in 1823 solely because of the antipathy toward natives of Portugal. To be sure, he had failed to emigrate but he had also not fought against the Brazilian cause, for he had spent the siege caring for his wife and seven children, who would have suffered in his absence, thus invoking the broader notions of service. In 1824, he proved his loyalty to Brazil by joining the anti-Periquitos forces at Abrantes, after which he served in the city's police, eventually retiring at the rank of captain.[41] By 1828, all but one of the officers who had failed to leave Salvador had been exonerated, and even he could make a case for having served the patriot cause by facilitating the emigration of artillery soldiers even as he commanded the remnants of this regiment that remained in Salvador. A sympathetic governor of arms observed that he had been included in the 1823 Act because he was the most senior artillery captain and therefore the first in line for promotion.[42]

Several features of this purge are striking. All but the most radical of patriot officers displayed a remarkable degree of legalism in dealing with comrades who had made what were in retrospect ill-advised decisions in 1822 and 1823. No one desired to establish precedents for stripping officers of their status and the patriots' purges were all submitted to Rio de Janeiro for review by the emperor, a recognition that only he could commission, promote, and dismiss officers. Furthermore, Portuguese-born officers were not excluded as a matter of course; rather, their actions were taken into account. Men who had been officers before 1821 were generally accepted in the postindependence army, provided that they had not fought against independence. In this way, the garrison maintained an important degree of continuity through the independence years.

This element of continuity, however, should not be exaggerated, for the officer corps also saw impressive personnel changes in this period. Not one of the planter-generals mentioned in Chapter 2 continued his career in Bahia after 1823.[43] José Tomás Bocaciari never enjoyed the land grant that he had obtained in 1820, for his alleged opposition to the Portuguese constitution earned him a summary expulsion from Salvador in November 1821; he committed suicide on arrival in Lisbon.[44] Brant fled to Rio de Janeiro after Bahia's adhesion to the Portuguese constitution and enjoyed a long career as diplomat, commander of the Brazilian forces in the Cisplatine War, and legislator, but he never again served in Bahia; in 1824, he complained that the war had devastated his properties, as patriot requisitions and Portuguese depredations exacted a severe toll.[45] And Luiz Paulino's loyalty to a transatlantic Portuguese nation has already been noted.

An influx of new men swelled the officer corps in the early 1820s, especially in its lower ranks. An incomplete list of Bahian officers in 1835 records the number of years of service of eighty-seven men.[46] Fully forty-one of them had begun their careers between 1821 and 1823. They were overwhelmingly Bahian by birth and twenty-three of them had not advanced past the rank of second lieutenant. Only two were colonels: Joaquim Pires de Carvalho e Albuquerque, the Viscount of Pirajá, a conservative but populist younger son of a leading planter family; and Antônio de Souza Lima, a

Portuguese-born merchant–planter with substantial holdings on Itaparica Island. Their army ranks reflected their services (and those of their dependents) during the war and their firm support of the planter regime after independence. Pirajá had led the first patriot besiegers of Salvador while Lima organized the anti-Portuguese forces on his home island, strategically located across the bay from Salvador.[47] Because they lacked the professional training of the colonial generals and only served sporadically in active capacities after independence, Pirajá and Lima represent but a partial continuation of the planter–general alliance that had characterized the late-colonial army. Moreover, not all of the new officers with close ties to land-owning families proved reliable defenders of the planter class. The controversial Major José Antônio da Silva Castro, commander of the Periquitos Battalion, the core of which he had raised in 1822, descended from a family highly influential in the sertão. Deeply involved in the conspiracy that resulted in the death of the governor of arms in 1824, he was spared punishment and returned to his land holdings.[48] If men like Pirajá, Lima, and Castro somewhat resembled the colonial planter-generals, there were certainly not enough of them in the postwar garrison, at least as far as Brant was concerned: He repeatedly called for the appointment of more officers from "the most respectable families."[49]

The cohort of junior officers who began their careers during the independence era was a new phenomenon in the Bahian army. Many had been recruited in 1821 and early 1822 by Freitas Guimarães, whom Madeira later accused of promoting and commissioning men "long known as famous advocates of independence."[50] Cadetship, whose requirements had been relaxed in late 1820 to the extent that it was now open to large segments of the Bahian "middle class," facilitated Freitas Guimarães's recruitment efforts as did the rising tide of Bahian patriotism. The need for officers during the independence war meant that many of these cadets would receive commissions before serving the apprenticeships that, in the colonial army, had permitted superiors to assess their worthiness. Joining the army as tensions between Bahians and Portuguese rose in 1821 declared support for greater autonomy from Portugal; it often also implied sympathy for the liberal cause. As did other regions of Latin America at this time, Bahia experienced a "revolutionary militarization" during these years, as military service became a favored way of expressing patriotism and the army a hothouse for radical politics.[51] João Primo, a petty merchant, proclaimed in 1823 that he had voluntarily enlisted as a cadet in 1821 "to encourage the Native Troops to reject the landing of Lusitanian Wolves [the

Constitutional Legion] and to demand the shipping to Portugal of the Twelfth Battalion"; in February 1822, Freitas Guimarães attempted to promote him to second lieutenant and one witness described Primo's "revolutionary spirit" as he denounced Madeira's appointment.[52] Patriotism notwithstanding, Primo probably found the army a far more congenial institution after the 1820 cadet reform, for he thus avoided demeaning service as an enlisted man.

New entrants into the officer corps also included two of the three officers elected by a volunteer company of forty-four students attached to the artillery after the proclamation of the constitution.[53] As Recôncavo elites took charge of the anti-Portuguese mobilization, they too assumed military ranks or sought to place sons and dependents in the officer corps. Cachoeira militia colonel Dom Brás Baltazar da Silveira outfitted a company of the Batalhão de Honra Imperial (Battalion of Imperial Honor) in late 1822 and insisted that his sons, Dom José and Dom Luiz, be commissioned captain and lieutenant, respectively. When the brothers claimed regular commissions in 1824, the governor of arms responded wearily that promotions in this unit (which had remained largely a paper force) were handed out "with that illegality with which everything was done at that time." Still, such services merited reward, and the brothers would be considered for promotion in due time.[54] Both eventually enjoyed long careers as officers (Chapter 6). Contemporary chroniclers recorded dozens of other patriots who raised volunteer units and sought to retain command of their men during the conflict.[55] Moreover, Pedro Labatut liberally promoted soldiers and officers, often without consulting their immediate superiors, especially after the Battle of Pirajá (8 November 1822).[56]

Not only did the war produce an unwelcome change in the officer corps's class composition, according to Brant, a "large part of the officers" serving in early 1824 were "mulattoes," including an artillery captain who had been merely an unlicensed lawyer (*requerente de papéis*) in Cachoeira before the war.[57] This is, significantly, the only explicit contemporary reference from a Brazilian (as opposed to a foreign) source for the darkening of the regular officer corps during these years [the presence of another nonwhite officer can be inferred from the transfer of a mulatto militia officer to the regulars (see below)]. That it came from the deeply racist Brant, whose antipathy toward black militia officers has already been noted, is not surprising, as is his emphasis on the presence of commissioned "mulattoes," not pretos; the latter remained outside of the officer corps. Unfortunately, little more can be said about race in the officer corps. After independence, whiteness remained an attribute of officership and the army kept no racial records on its commissioned ranks.

Besides contributing to the wartime upsetting of the army hierarchy through liberal promotions, Labatut also feuded bitterly with the Interim Council over the extent of his authority. Was he simply commander of the army besieging Salvador, as the council argued, or did he hold the post of military governor over the entire province? A Napoleonic officer of mysterious provenance, Labatut had been appointed (rather than a locally rooted officer) to impose the Rio de Janeiro government's control over the patriots, according to Luís Henrique Dias Tavares.[58] Many of Labatut's actions, borne of military necessity as he would later argue, therefore threatened (or appeared to threaten) the Bahian planter class. In December 1822, the Council compiled a long list of charges against the general, concluding that he had terrorized the "most important class of citizens, the class that acclaimed the Regency of His Imperial Majesty and that almost miraculously sustained for four months the acclamation that it had made, that is, the class of proprietors." Four months later, an embittered Labatut wrote that he did not desire to be captain general of the ill-fated province, suffering from enemy occupation and "the despicable pride of some of its inhabitants who judged that they should be governors or nothing."[59] Two different conceptions of military organization were at stake in this conflict. Labatut sought to create a disciplined force under his sole command and opposed the creation of volunteer companies; according to the council, this was impolitic, for the patriotic notables who had outfitted these units should not be simply cast aside.[60] Labatut thus demonstrated that the government in Rio de Janeiro might not be receptive to the Recôncavo planters' concerns, particularly their desire for local autonomy.

In May 1823, a well-executed conspiracy among the Exército Pacificador's officers resulted in Labatut's replacement with Colonel José Joaquim de Lima e Silva, the commander of the Rio de Janeiro troops. Little is known about the gestation of this plot, but a central figure was Colonel Felisberto Gomes Caldeira, removed from his command of the besieging army's Left Brigade on 19 May. Two days later, officers from the brigade arrested Labatut, and the Interim Council sanctioned the coup by naming Lima e Silva to replace the French general. In their public justifications, the officers repeated the by-then familiar litany of complaints about the imperious Labatut, suggesting a broad planter-class consensus that he had to go; Caldeira's role in the plot reinforces this interpretation.[61] Soon thereafter, Lima e Silva presided over the occupation of Salvador on 2 July 1823.

Demobilization of the Exército Pacificador proved a difficult and costly task. In September, the provincial government established a peacetime Bahian army of one cavalry squadron, one artillery battalion, and five infantry battalions (see the Appendix, Figure A.2). In the October reorganization of the provincial government, Caldeira became governor of arms, a measure shortly thereafter confirmed by Rio de Janeiro. Caldeira's position was an unenviable one. Not only were there far more officers (and aspirants to commissions) with patriot credentials than posts in the new units, but he brought considerable baggage to his command. Allegations that he had espoused "high republican" views during the war suggest that he had maintained an ambiguous political posture, formally distancing himself from the radical liberal group only after he became governor of arms.[62] Morton suggests that Caldeira's acceptance as garrison commander effectively coopted a "dangerous troublemaker," but this may exaggerate his erstwhile commitment to the radical cause; Manoel Correia Garcia suggests that Caldeira's politicking had a more base motive—winning himself command of the garrison.[63]

Caldeira moved quickly to rid himself of rivals and the most politicized officers. In late 1823, Manoel Pedro de Freitas Guimarães received an appointment as governor of arms of Mato Grosso, the province most distant from Salvador; increasingly evident insanity prevented the hero of 1821 from assuming the post, but some suspected that Caldeira was overhasty in having him interned in 1824.[64] From Caldeira's perspective, insanity made Freitas Guimarães easy to deal with in comparison to the numerous newly commissioned officers; the qualities that ensured these men commissions in 1822 and 1823 were not always welcome in the postwar army. He recommended in 1824 that six freshly minted second lieutenants be discharged: among them, João Francisco Paraguaçu and Francisco José da Rocha suffered from numerous vices; the former was "ardently anti-Portuguese" while the latter "promote[d] disorders among soldiers, turning them against the Portuguese."[65] As the officer corps had filled with new men, it became an increasingly politicized institution in which subordination to superiors was not assured. One chronicler described the conspirators of October 1824 as "young lads or irresponsible children" who suffered from "*politico-mania*" and the acting governor of arms explained that the leaders of the protests of April 1824 "were precisely those who came from the class of civilians. . . . Very few of those who followed the military hierarchy," he continued, had been involved, a view shared by at least one career officer.[66] Furthermore, several of the officers refused to obey orders to return to their barracks, declaring that "they were civilians"—some were dressed in mufti—while others insisted that "they were there as citizens and not as officers."[67]

The ideological positions of army-officer politics in the immediate postindependence period are difficult to elucidate. Lusophobia remained, as the December 1823 Act and the April 1824 protests revealed, a touchstone for a significant group of officers. The hostility toward the Rio de Janeiro and Pernambuco troops manifested in a series of incidents in the second half of 1823, reminiscent of the Portuguese–Bahian rivalries of 1821–1822, suggests a widespread desire to rid the pátria of "foreign" soldiers; the departure of these troops by the end of the year removed this source of conflict. Uncertainty over their future place in the army prompted officers to shower authorities with petitions in which they requested confirmation of their wartime commissions and assignment to regular posts, a concern seconded by the town council in December 1823.[68] No doubt personal antipathies and friendships borne of wartime experiences also shaped political and factional alignments. After his death in 1824, Governor of Arms Felisberto Gomes Caldeira was often (and conveniently) blamed for such partisanship.[69] A substantial group of mostly junior officers sympathized with republican elements in Pernambuco's Confederação do Equador; officers in the Third Battalion (the Periquitos), allegedly read rebel newpapers to their soldiers and taught them "modern" philosophy instead of imposing military discipline. Its commander, Major Castro, was known for his "republican and anarchist ideas," according to the French consul. Brant identified him as a principal source of disorder in the province, and he was reportedly in touch with Confederação do Equador government in May 1824.[70] Orders to have the Periquitos embarked for Pernambuco and Castro sent to Rio de Janeiro proved to be the spark that ignited what was, in effect, a rebellion of the radical wing of the old Exército Pacificador.

The timing of the revolt—it took place after the suppression of the Confederação do Equador—diminished its impact, and more important, Caldeira's unexpected (and brutal) murder unnerved the conspirators, who proved unwilling to pursue their more radical goals. Both of these factors ensured the rebellion's defeat. As the revolt wound down, the interim governor of arms recommended that a high-ranking officer with 1,000 soldiers from other provinces oversee the repression. The Brazilian government prudently chose not to occupy Salvador at this time and Brigadier José Egídio Gordilho de Barbuda, appointed governor of arms with extraordinary powers to try the officers implicated in the murder of his predecessor, arrived with only a token force of eighty artillery soldiers from Santa Catarina, a bodyguard nevertheless designated as a brigade.[71] The government did, however, create a police corps for the city [the Guarda Militar de Polícia (Military Police Guard)], selecting the most reliable enlisted men and placing them under the command of conservative officers.[72] A special military court headed by Barbuda took only twelve days to try and publicly execute Major Joaquim Sátiro da Cunha on 15 January 1825; Lieutenant Gaspar Lopes Vilasboas faced a firing squad a week later. The execution of officers was unheard of in Bahia and neither passed without incident. The hangman (himself a convicted murderer) refused to carry out Sátiro's sentence, requiring the use of a firing squad. Gaspar poisoned himself on the eve of his execution, which had to be delayed for seven hours until a priest could be prevailed upon to administer last rites to the dying man. The spectacle caused, according to the anonymous diarist, "great sorrow" among the populace.[73]

In all likelihood, Sátiro and Gaspar were scapegoats, but little is known about them. Gaspar was reportedly one of the enthusiastic patriots in February 1822, descending from his dignity as an officer to arm himself. Sátiro too had distinguished himself at this time, and both had been active in the independence war. That the former was probably related to the prominent Vilasboas planter family heightened the execution's impact; the *Grito da Razão* judged it a fate unworthy of a young man of "his birth."[74] Having made his point, Barbuda could afford magnanimity. Six more officers were sentenced to death but there was little chance of them facing the firing squad, for they had all fled. Another forty were imprisoned while their cases were heard by a regular court-martial and then the civilian justice system. By the end of 1828, most had finally been acquitted. The remainder received pardons in 1831, except for those who had gone into exile, whose fate the senate was still debating in 1836.[75] Not only were these punishments a stern warning to the radical officers of the Exército Pacificador, but the lengthy court-martial proceedings also ensured that troublemakers were safely distant from posts in Bahia's battalions.

The defeat of the Periquitos' Revolt and the crackdown that followed demonstrated to the planter class that the alliance with Rio de Janeiro could serve their interests. Not all of the representatives of the imperial government were "Labatuts," insensitive to local elite concerns. What remained to be seen, however, was how the new state would organize its army and what impact that would have in Bahia. The marginalization of the radical officers and the creation of a military police for Salvador produced, for a time, a garrison far more amenable to elite interests than the turbulent independence army of

1822 to 1824. Still, this garrison was very different from the colonial army: No locally rooted planter-generals commanded it; the new state's geopolitical interests and tentative army reforms would, in fact, often contradict planter interests until a new accommodation was found in the 1840s.

Recruiting and Disciplining the Exército Pacificador

Just as the independence war wrought significant changes in the officer corps, so it profoundly altered the enlisted ranks. Two closely related, and as far as contemporaries were concerned, often indistinguishable developments dominated discussions about wartime and postwar recruitment and discipline: the darkening of the enlisted ranks and the recruitment of slaves into the patriot forces.[76] In 1821 and 1822, the racially charged symbolism of slavery and freedom had proved a powerful rallying cry among enlisted men, who defined themselves as neither black nor slave and increasingly as not Portuguese either. Several patriot officers in the First Regiment mobilized their companies in February 1822 by asking the men whether they wanted to be slave or free, echoing the racially charged complaints of the soldiers involved in the 1798 plot. The soldiers unanimously declared that they wished to be free, after which their officers recommended that they prepare themselves to expel the Portuguese from Bahia.[77] Here the officers and soldiers were distinguishing themselves from both black slaves and white Portuguese, a theme that would emerge as a leitmotif of postindependence political discourse.

During the war, however, it became ever more difficult to maintain the boundary between soldiers and slaves both as the enlisted ranks came to include fewer whites and as slaves (and even a few Africans) entered the patriot forces. Widespread postwar worries about the dangers of a significantly nonwhite army and the institution of flogging as punishment for desertion and other military crimes underscore the changes that had taken place in 1822 and 1823; in the aftermath of the Periquitos' Rebellion, authorities whitened the garrison by removing black, African, and freed soldiers from the province. The treatment of these soldiers graphically demonstrates the Brazilian elite's fear of armed and sometimes rebellious "classes of color," while the changing social composition of the enlisted ranks rendered it more difficult for Brazilians to accept soldiers as part of the nation.

In July 1823, the victorious Exército Pacificador numbered 9,515 men of all ranks in Salvador (several thousand more remained under arms in the Recôncavo), the product of mobilization on a scale never before seen in Bahia.[78] For the first months of the war, patriot leaders avoided most of the excesses of impressment as they raised troops through appeals to citizens' patriotic sentiment or through patron–client ties. Hints that forced recruitment might be necessary appeared as early as December 1822, and in April 1823, the Interim Council recommended that captains major employ "moderate violence" against those still "insensitive to the *pátria's* call." It also proposed that parish priests compile rolls of young men to facilitate forced recuitment. As enthusiasm flagged, recruitment documentation came to resemble that of colonial impressment, with petitions for the release of impressed men occasionally appearing in the archives.[79]

Recruitment on the scale of 1822 and 1823 inevitably wrought changes in the composition of the rank and file. Scattered contemporary evidence suggests that the patriot enlisted ranks were notably darker than the colonial rank and file. An eyewitness described the garrison of a coastal fort as consisting of "whites, blacks, and mulattoes [*brancos, pretos e pardos*]," while an irregular company of volunteers consisted of thirty-one mulattoes (pardos), four whites (brancos), and two dark mulattoes (cabras), commanded, however, by three white officers.[80] Recruitment also reached into formerly exempt sectors of the population in mid-November 1822, when Labatut requested that the Council supply as many "freed *pardos* and blacks" as possible to fill a projected Batalhão de Libertos Constitucionais e Independentes do Imperador (Emperor's Battalion of Constitutional and Independent Freedmen). The Council responded that it would seek to recruit such men, but without coercion, for any resort to forced recruitment was "the most effective alarm to prompt the flight and dispersion of entire families into the forests, to the detriment of our cause and of agriculture," thus employing the well-worn explanation for failure to comply with recruitment orders.[81] At this point, Labatut was not contemplating slave recruitment; he was simply requesting that civilian authorities abandon their reluctance to recruit freedmen and especially black freedmen. A month later, however, the Council complained that he had undertaken the "appalling" measure of creating a "battalion of black slaves, creoles and Africans," whose soldiers were now undergoing training. Apparently, the general had confiscated and drafted the slaves of several absent Portuguese planters, and as a result, rumors spread that any slave who volunteered would be freed.[82]

With no end in sight to the siege of Salvador and manpower shortages looming, Labatut proposed in April 1823 that the Council arrange a voluntary contribution of slaves from Bahia's planters. The Council prevaricated, calling on Labatut to exercise more caution and recommending that municipal councils be consulted first, but Labatut insisted, sending two officers from his headquarters to Cachoeira to undertake this levy.[83] A week later, the municipal council of Jaguaripe advised, as might be expected, that Labatut's proposal was a great error. Not only were there few surplus slaves in the municipality, but slaves lacked the honor and disinterestedness of "worthy sons of Mars"; only the opportunity to sack enemy property would motivate them to fight. More important, concluded the council, the selection of slaves for military service would have disastrous results, as those not freed would join the slave soldiers in rebellion.[84] Apparently nothing came of this proposed levy and Labatut's overthrow in May 1823 put a stop to slave recruitment initiatives.

Amid Labatut's efforts to enlist slaves and the generalized wartime dislocation of 1822 and 1823, Bahia's slaves faced complex new opportunities. While slave rebellion was rare, flight increased significantly, which the *Idade d'Ouro do Brazil* blamed on patriot masters' bad example.[85] "Many slaves" gathered at the main Brazilian camp, recalled the future Viscount of Pirajá, where they were put to work on fortifications, while officers selected some of them as personal servants, so many that Lima e Silva issued orders to limit the number eligible to draw rations. Seeking to minimize the number of slaves actually enlisted in the army, he stressed that most of them were assigned to work as sappers or orderlies, traditional slave occupations of manual labor and personal service.[86]

For the Interim Council, Labatut's actions were deeply troubling, not only because of the threat that slave recruitment posed to property and the plantation economy but also because they touched on the delicate racial question. "It is an uncontestable truth," wrote the Council in mid-April 1823, "that the classes of color in Brazil have the greatest of jealousy because they do not enter equally into public employment." With the Portuguese hoping that a racial conflict on the Brazilian side would preserve their rule over Brazil, "it is not easy, nor in any way politic, to concede immediately that equality for men of color to obtain positions of the foremost [rank]. . . . [Therefore], it is most appropriate to be extremely cautious with the status of these classes, disarming them carefully and prudently." Labatut had instead acted rashly, insisted the Council, reviewing the general's efforts to enlist slaves and his refusal to heed its warnings. Most ominously, he had raised the issue of slave recruitment publicly; as a result, "*pardos, cabras,* and creoles speak of nothing else." Furthermore, the militia captain charged with recruiting slaves was himself a freedman and therefore far too interested in the measure's success: "He does not cease to talk with slaves, and is surrounded by them while in the streets" of Cachoeira.[87]

This exposition of the debate over slave enlistment in 1822 and 1823 raises several points. First, slave recruitment was an ad hoc expedient: Labatut apparently never issued a decree calling on slaves to join the patriots in return for freedom. That none of his many enemies ever accused the general of promising freedom to slaves strongly suggests that he did not do so informally either. Second, Labatut displayed considerable respect for Brazilian masters' property rights. He repeatedly consulted with the Council; the slaves enlisted in late 1822 belonged to absent Portuguese planters who apparently had no Brazilian heirs (where there were such heirs, the property was usually held in trust for them). On this level, the conflict between Labatut and the Council simply involved the disposition of valuable war booty. To be sure, the flight of slaves to the Brazilian camp blurred these finer distinctions of property rights—a runaway slave might look no different from a free poor man of color—but it is important to recognize the formal caution with which Labatut proceeded. Third, however much Labatut and the Interim Council may have disagreed over the wisdom of recruiting slaves, they shared one fundamental but unstated assumption: soldier and slave were two distinct categories (and therefore the enlistment of the latter implied a significant change in his status). Finally, the Council's concern about Labatut's advocacy of slave recruitment slid easily into worries about the "classes of color," that generalized fear of a white elite in an overwhelmingly nonwhite society.

After the war, victorious Bahian planters faced the difficult task of restoring their authority over a slave population that had heard and seen many novelties, over an army whose rank and file contained a significant number of slaves (whose status remained unresolved), and over "classes of color" who had gained a new sense of importance as a result of independence services. Restoring the boundary between slave and soldier was a fundamental first step. Once in control of Salvador, the Bahian government ordered local authorities to recapture vagrant slaves and return them to their owners.[88] The "large number" of slaves enlisted in the Exército Pacificador posed a more complex problem, as Lima e Silva explained: "I kept them" in the ranks "and always noted proofs of valor and heroism [among them], and a decided enthusiasm for the Cause of Brazilian Independence." Not only that, these "brothers-in-arms" had remained under discipline during the occupation of Salvador; therefore, "nothing would be more callous" than to return them to slavery.[89] Following this recommendation, the imperial government undertook to regularize their changed status by ordering the Bahian government to arrange for them to be freed. Fiscal concerns prompted the pious hope that the owners would willingly manumit their slaves; if not, the government would pay compensation, thereby protecting property rights.[90]

The imperial government's decision to ratify wartime slave recruitment and pursue it to its logical conclusion—that such slaves were officially free men—was probably in the interests of Bahian planters. After all, returning them to bondage was probably more impolitic than enlisting them in the first place. Many individual owners eventually accepted compensation and relinquished their property rights and "freed soldiers" occasionally surface in later documentation, including a Nagô (Yoruba) who testified at the trial of the 1835 slave rebellion.[91] Other owners fought their slaves' claims through the imperial bureaucracy and judiciary. In September 1825, the minister of justice instructed the president to persuade an unwilling owner to accept just compensation and free one Manoel Rufino Gomes, by then a sergeant.[92] From Itaparica Island, the merchant-planter and local military governor, Lieutenant Colonel Antônio de Souza Lima, wrote in 1825:

> Here no slave served during the campaign ... because there were no orders issued for this. Nor have I considered that this benefit [of freedom] should be extended beyond the battalion of freedmen created [by Labatut]. . . . Some slaves performed services here but they were those who fled from the city or those who, abandoned by their owners, wandered about the countryside, perpetrating robberies and disorders. They were returned to their owners as soon as they requisitioned them.[93]

By minimizing slaves' services and denying their status as soldiers, the planters who had opposed slave enlistment in the first place continued the struggle to protect their property. Some officers, in turn, defended their subordinates against masters' claims as both argued over the demarcation between slave and soldier, a line that all agreed ought to exist and ought to be clear. Indeed, the imperial government underscored this point in 1824, decreeing that men of color who volunteered had to prove their free status before enlisting.[94]

The worrisome blurring of distinctions between slave and soldier heralded a more general breakdown of order. Despite, or perhaps because of, their patriotic enthusiasm, the soldiers of the Exército Pacificador were a disorderly lot, at least as far as regular officers were concerned. One chronicler declared that "it was a rare day on which soldiers did not turn artillery pieces on their commanders or perpetrate [other] disorders," and the Interim Council later alluded to extensive problems with ill-disciplined enlisted men. José Antônio da Silva Castro's battalion, the core of the future Periquitos, earned a reputation for brutality as they sacked property during their August 1822 march through Nazaré and Jaguaripe.[95] Deserters from the patriot forces were recorded as early as September 1822, and the Interim Council instructed local authorities to maintain especial vigilance against them. Labatut ordered the execution of seven recaptured deserters, but arranged for them to be pardoned as they faced the firing squad. Cheers erupted from the battalion assembled to witness the execution, suggesting that the soldiers did not see desertion as a crime that merited the full rigor of military law.[96]

Wartime dislocation contributed to increased mobility among the Bahian lower classes as slave flight and banditry combined with desertion to presage a breakdown of social discipline. The United States consul noted in September 1823 that slaves and uniformed soldiers were plundering Portuguese property in Salvador, while his French counterpart reported endemic rural banditry, against which the government dared not send soldiers for fear that the men would desert.[97] In its December 1823 Act, the city council advised the governor of arms to "spare no occasion" for punishing soldiers, "keeping them occupied with frequent and intensive drill, the only way to rein in and contain them," but complaints about soldiers continued unabated.[98] In all likelihood, the social composition of the enlisted ranks had changed rapidly as the Exército Pacificador demobilized. Enlisted men with alternative employment or independent means probably mustered out as quickly as possible, leaving a garrison of proportionally more poor or marginal men, likely nonwhites, than the patriot army; furthermore, the former slaves had no incentive to seek discharges as long as their status was uncertain.

In response to the breakdown of military discipline, the Brazilian government decreed in 1823 that soldiers guilty of first and second simple desertion would summarily receive thirty and fifty lashes, a punishment doubled in 1824 and extended in 1825 to any form of disorder.[99] Instituting flogging as a punishment for desertion was a natural counterpart to the recruitment of slaves during the independence war. Former slave soldiers could only be controlled by the lash, or so military authorities thought. In Bahia, however, provincial authorities were still not satisfied. The president called for a "complete reform" of the troops in May 1824 emphasizing that "the blacks who comprise the battalions are inappropriate" for the rank and file of which, in his estimation, less than a tenth were whites and mulattoes. More graphically, Brant declared in February 1824 that "were it not for the uniforms," the barracks could be mistaken for "warehouses on the Mina Coast." Accordingly, he recommended a return to colonial recruitment practice—no black soldiers, only white noncommissioned officers—"and to neutralize the influence of *pardo* soldiers," 800 foreign mercenaries. While agreeing with the need for changes, Pedro prudently decided against stationing foreign troops in Salvador, but Brant, as minister to London, was instrumental in hiring the German and Irish mercenaries eventually sent to Rio de Janeiro.[100]

In the heat of the moment, both Brant and the president may have exaggerated the enlisted ranks' blackness. Other evidence suggests that a degree of segregation could still be found in the garrison of 1823–1824, as many of the former slaves ended up in the Periquitos Battalion, which one Inácio Acioli characterized as composed "in its majority of freedmen and other people from the heterogenous classes." The French consul distinguished among battalions when he described the Periquitos' Revolt as a standoff between white and black troops.[101] Perhaps this segregation reflected official government policy; it may also indicate a reluctance on the part of free men to serve alongside former slaves, an attitude clearly evident in the Sabinada Rebellion of 1837, when rebel soldiers refused to serve alongside the slaves enlisted by the rebel government (Chapter 6). Authorities reported deep animosity between the Periquitos and the soldiers of other battalions. They demonstrated little confidence in the loyalist troops, however, and soldier–officer relations were tense in the Abrantes camp; according to one chronicler, only incessant drill and repeated beatings maintained soldiers' subordination.[102]

In the aftermath of this rebellion, the Bahian and imperial governments expelled disorderly soldiers from Salvador's garrison and unequivocally demonstrated their determination to maintain order. A cadet who had attempted to kill his commanding officer in October 1824 ran a gauntlet of soldiers, an imposition of corporal punishment that violated cadet privileges; a soldier who had tried to do the same was executed.[103] The repression assumed racial connotations with the removal of black and ex-slave soldiers from Salvador. The departure of the Third Battalion from the province and the subsequent dispersion of its soldiers among other units banished what were then seen as the most troublesome men. Under the assumption that black soldiers would be less dangerous at sea than on land, the navy became the final destination for many. Even before the end of the revolt, the provincial government tried to transfer to the navy the freed soldiers not slated for the expedition to Pernambuco, a measure that the governor of arms then judged unwise, for it would only prompt them to desert. Others were later shipped to one of the Brazilian army's all-black units, the Tenth and Eleventh Battalions, stationed in safely remote Montevideo.[104] Imperial recruitment legislation reiterated the colonial exclusion of blacks from the army, an exclusion heeded in mid-1825, when the governor of arms declined a recruit because of his "black color."[105]

This was nothing less than a wholesale racial purge of the patriot army's remains. It was also strikingly effective: A list of 366 deserters from Bahian battalions during 27 months from 1825 to early 1827 records but 15 blacks among 275 pardos, 8 cabras, 4 caboclos, and 64 whites, a far cry from the 90 percent black rank and file of which the president had complained in 1824.[106] These numbers reveal the results of a deliberate effort to restore the distinction between mulattoes and blacks. Free or freed blacks might serve in the army, but they would have to endure "the delights of the cold in Montevideo," as one commentator dryly remarked on the fate of the Periquitos.[107] They would not serve in Salvador's garrison.

By the middle of the 1820s, the enlisted ranks retained many of their colonial features. Racial segregation continued, but soldiers found themselves in closer proximity to the status of slaves after the 1823 and 1824 decrees had mandated flogging as a punishment for desertion and other crimes. Amid the fears of disorderly soldiers and the post-Periquitos' Rebellion purge of the rank and file, an 1823 call for volunteers that emphasized the duty of "all citizens" to perform military service and recalled that in ancient Greece and Rome "all citizens were soldiers and all soldiers were citizens" stands out in stark contrast.[108] The liberal ideal of a soldier-citizen that would guide so much postwar military reform made little headway against fears of the armed "classes of color."

The Militia Counterpoint

The "classes of color" that so terrified contemporaries and figure prominently in the modern historiography of postindependence Brazil, however, were far from united. A significant sector of them—the officers and men of the black and mulatto militia—actually emerged as pillars of the post-independence imperial regime in Bahia, decisively contributing to the defeat of the 1824 Periquitos' Rebellion. Their ideology, vision of the state, and response to liberalism were essential aspects of these years' politics and hint at a possible conservative populist path that the Brazilian state did not pursue, comparable perhaps to Juan Manuel de Rosas's special relationship with Buenos Aires's Afro-Argentines.[109]

More so even than the regular officer corps, the militia split in 1821 and 1822. Virtually all of the First Regiment's merchant officers remained loyal to the Lisbon government; its commitment to restoring the Luso-Brazilian commercial system attracted men whose fortunes had suffered since the establishment of free trade in 1808. Indeed, in August 1822, supporters of the Lisbon government called for the return of the white militia to its traditional footing with merchant commanders (rather than the regular officers whom the colonial government had appointed in the 1810s), further recommending that only Portuguese be named militia officers.[110]

By contrast, the populist Manoel Pedro de Freitas Guimarães had mobilized considerable support among black and mulatto militiamen during his short stint as governor of arms. Among them was João do Prado Franco, a mulatto militia soldier and painter who volunteered for the regular artillery when "the Portuguese constitution was recognized" in Salvador. He served on the ship that carried Bahia's deputies to the Lisbon parliament; upon his return to Salvador, he obtained a discharge but resumed his military career as a gunner in the Exército Pacificador, notwithstanding a shipboard accident that had crippled his left arm.[111] In large numbers, mulatto and especially black militia officers and soldiers turned out to back the artillery in mid-February 1822; witnesses at the inquest often added that the patriots included armed barefoot blacks (slaves) as well.[112] The elderly black captain (and later colonel), Joaquim de Santana Neves, was in the thick of the skirmishing, personally breaking a Portuguese officer's arm. Artillery sergeants struggled unsuccessfully to restrain the militiamen, whose enthusiasm overcame their discipline as they fired on Portuguese troops without being ordered to do so.[113]

What these militiamen were fighting for is difficult to reconstruct. Only one witness in the March 1822 inquest left a few clues. This Brazilian-born army officer, who remained loyal to Portugal, confronted a soldier of the Fourth Militia Regiment speaking "great nonsense" while on guard at Piedade Square. When asked who had given him orders—an assertion of military authority on the part of the officer—the soldier responded "that he had gone there very much out of his own free will and that they were gathered there to defend their *pátria*." Not only that, the militiaman expressed great surprise at the question, declaring that, "if I were an honorable officer, I would be in the Fort." Militia officers came and went all afternoon, amid loud "vivas" to Freitas Guimarães.[114] Clearly the governor of arms had become the symbol and rallying point for those who sought to defend their homeland from the Portuguese.

After their defeat, patriot militiamen quit the city, followed by an exodus of officers and soldiers who had missed the fighting. In this way, the militia divided along roughly racial lines, with the Portuguese and some of the Brazilians in the white regiments remaining in Salvador, while most black and mulatto officers joined the patriots. The notable exceptions were Colonel Antônio Manoel de Melo e Castro and Lieutenant Colonel Pedro Inácio de Porciuncula of the mulatto regiment—whose limited connection to their men was analyzed in Chapter 4—who sided with Lisbon, for which they were ordered to face courts-martial in 1823.[115]

As patriots organized their forces in mid-1822, the officers and men of the Henriques came under the command of Major Manoel Gonçalves da Silva, promoted to lieutenant colonel in late 1822 or early 1823, while those of the Fourth Regiment, lacking senior officers, were distributed as reinforcements among other units, a decision also consistent with the racial preference in colonial recruitment: Mulattoes but not blacks could serve in the regulars.[116] An indecisive (or possibly sick) Lieutenant Colonel Francisco Xavier Bigode finally quit Salvador in December 1822, and although he brought with him the paraphernalia of his command—the regimental standard and troop registry—Brazilian commanders did not return him to his post at the head of the Henriques for, by then, Gonçalves "had heard the buzz of many bullets." Contemporaries hailed Gonçalves as "the new Henrique Dias" in their accounts of the victorious patriots' march into Salvador and effusively praised individual black officers. After a harrowing nighttime escape from Salvador in May 1823, the anonymous diarist was much relieved to surrender to "the admirable Captain Neves, a valiant man of much courage." "And [of] black color," he added as an afterthought.[117]

In September 1823, the Bahian government demobilized the Exército Pacificador and refounded the militia. Black officers and soldiers took pride of place as the First Battalion, followed by mulattoes in the Second Battalion; the four white militia units shrank to two and their commanders struggled to find soldiers (Figure A.3). The lieutenant colonel charged with assembling a militia artillery corps out of the remains of the Coast Guard Artillery could round up but eighty Brazilians and Portuguese "friendly to the cause of Brazil" from the rolls of the corps raised with so much fanfare in 1811. New enlistments increased its strength to a little over a hundred soldiers by early 1825. In contrast, Gonçalves reported his battalion close to full strength in November 1823 and formally requested that it receive its standards.[118] A year later, the black battalion enrolled 755 men and the mulattoes counted 745, while the white infantry only numbered 483 men of all ranks. A similar ratio prevailed among the militia officers who signed their battalions' oaths to the constitution in May 1824. Only thirteen artillery officers appeared, as well as twenty-nine white infantry officers, outnumbered by forty-eight black and forty-four mulatto officers.[119] In short, blacks and mulattoes outnumbered whites in the militia by a ratio of five to two after independence.

Command of the city's militia went to men with impeccable patriot credentials, while officers and sergeants who had received battlefield promotions led the companies.[120] Much to Bigode's chagrin, his seniority counted for little against Gonçalves's services in the war and the latter was formally appointed to head the First Battalion.[121] The Second Battalion came under the command of Antônio Lopes Tabira Bahiense, who may be the same man as the second lieutenant and painter, Antônio Lopes da Cunha, listed in the 1809 inspection (taking patriotic surnames was a common practice at the time), while the men of the Third served under a regular officer, Major Paulo Maria Nabuco de Araújo, who had distinguished himself during the war by raising a volunteer company.[122] The Antunes Guimarães clan had opted for independence but ill-health prevented Colonel Inácio from resuming his artillery command, so the thankless task of finding white soldiers for this unit fell to his son, Lieutenant Colonel Bruno, who now bore the patriotic surname of Guabiraba.[123]

Black and mulatto officers' views of their wartime experience is particularly revealing of the complexity of postindependence racial politics and the ambiguous legacy of the colonial regime. With their challenge to special corporate privileges and promise of equality, liberal ideals presented both an opportunity for black and mulatto officers—talk that any black man could reach the rank of general in independent Brazil's army was heard in 1824[124]—and a threat to their hard-won status under the colonial regime. Like Captain Joaquim José de Santana in 1798, most black and mulatto militia officers cast their lot with the imperial regime in the 1820s, but they did so in a conditional way, expecting to emerge as one of its pillars because of their prominent role in 1822 and 1823. In short, reward and recognition for services was their central demand. While hardly radical, the determination with which they pursued it reflects a newfound assertiveness on the part of a group of hitherto-marginalized men who now insisted on their importance, and through their domination of the militia, disposed of the means to back up their demands.

In petition after petition to the new emperor, mulatto and especially black officers articulated a version of the independence struggle in which they played a leading role. After a second lieutenant in the Henriques, Dionísio Ferreira de Santana, realized that the soldiers massing near his house were about to attack Brazilian units in February 1822, he donned his uniform and "rushed into the street amid those fierce Portuguese." With "pistol in hand" and "not the slightest fear that they might take his life," he joined the patriot forces who, defeated, dispersed into the countryside. That his postwar rhetoric reconstructed what was probably a furtive transit across the city into an heroic epic reveals the profound psychological break with the past that taking up arms against Portuguese troops represented. No less than twelve officers attested to his valor, military prowess, "patriotism, and support for the holy cause of Brazilian independence."[125]

Even as these petitions end with standard requests for promotion, decorations, and pensions, they implicitly call for black officers to fulfill a special role in the new state, a demand for which these men had no idiom other than the language of service and reward. One made explicit his aspirations. A cabinet-maker and black militia lieutenant who had moved to Rio de Janeiro in the 1810s, and therefore missed the fighting, offered in 1824 to raise a company of black Bahian swordsmen to defend the emperor's person and family against Portuguese attacks. Whether he commanded the necessary prestige among Bahian expatriates in the capital to mobilize such a black guard is not clear—the war ministry official who dutifully summarized the document did not think so—but this vision of a Brazil in which black volunteers would protect the Portuguese-born emperor from the Portuguese contrasts sharply with the plans to recruit European mercenaries then afoot at the highest levels of the state apparatus.[126] Nevertheless, Pedro remained a powerful symbol and the imagery of the black battalion as his protectors appeared in Bahia as well: A proclamation issued to the black battalion from outside Salvador during the 1824 Periquitos' standoff reminded the militiamen of their glories as "successors to Henrique Dias" and defenders "of the immortal Pedro I."[127]

Promotion into the new militia battalions satisfied some officers' ambitions. The pistol-toting Lieutenant Dionísio received a battlefield promotion in December 1822, and in the September 1823 reorganization of the Henriques, a captaincy and command of a company. Additional rewards granted to patriot leaders further confirmed the special place for black officers. A supernumerary lieutenant colonelcy in the First Battalion went to Captain Neves; eventually, he received a major's salary as well—in effect, a pension—in reward for his services and in compensation for the loss of his property which prevented him from resuming his trade. The imperial government, however, balked at declaring Neves a "Most Worthy Citizen [_Cidadão Benemerito_]" when the provincial president recommended him for this honorific title along with several paragons of the planter class, an early indication that there were limits to Brazil's willingness to accept black officers.[128]

The new militia faced its first and greatest test during the Periquitos' Rebellion. Within hours of Caldeira's murder, Gonçalves had mobilized 300 of his men, who joined the loyalist First Battalion. Rebel troops harassed black militia soldiers and officers; Gonçalves and some of his men eventually fled to the forces gathering on the outskirts of the city, where he was welcomed into loyalist councils as a senior officer.[129] Neves assumed command of the remaining Henriques stationed at Fort Santo Antônio além do Carmo, and when the provincial government finally retreated to a warship in the harbor, he was the highest ranking loyalist officer in the city. Amid fears that the rebels would sack the city before the regulars reoccupied it, the president appointed Neves to an autonomous command over all the city's militia; he mounted militia guards at the bank and other public buildings, handing the city over to loyalist forces two days later.[130]

Despite their notable services in November 1824, the black colonels played no part in the Periquitos' courts-martial. Twelve colonels and lieutenant colonels are known to have been named to these tribunals, no less than nine from the militia. Colonel Inácio Antunes Guimarães was too sick to accept his appointment to the special commission, but his son-in-law, Lieutenant Colonel Manoel José Freire de Carvalho, sat on the later permanent court-martial. No black officers sat in judgment over regular officers, but three pardo officers did: Tabira Bahiense, and more surprisingly, Melo e Castro and Porciuncula, both by then apparently exonerated of their failure to leave Salvador in 1822–1823.[131] Even as the Henriques demonstrated their loyalty to the new regime, it would not accept black colonels as truly equal to their counterparts from the rest of the militia.

Nevertheless, the Henriques were deeply committed both to the new empire and to the order that the planter class sought to restore. That a black (and perhaps freed) man, married to an African freedwoman, should have commanded the last line of defense against "anarchy" fomented by a battalion of freedmen should not surprise; a world of difference in class and status separated the slave-owning artisan Lieutenant Colonel Neves and the other officers and soldiers in the Henriques from the plebeian rank and file in the rebel Periquitos battalion. Militia officers needed stability to rebuild their lives. For some, this was an urgent task: A black captain and mason unsuccessfully requested as reward for independence services not further promotion but discharge from his military obligations to devote time to earning a living; having lost "absolutely everything that he owned," a lieutenant sought retirement in 1825, for his earnings as a goldsmith were insufficient to acquire a new uniform.[132] Others, particularly mulatto officers, hoped that independence services would lead to army commissions (and regular salaries), requests that the government repeatedly denied in the interest of retaining the regulars as a professional corps distinct from the militia.[133] To my knowledge, only one mulatto officer succeeded in obtaining a regular commission. Francisco de Paula Bahia (the son of Captain Domingos da Silva Lisboa, the man first suspected of having written the 1798 handbills) was promoted to second lieutenant in the Fourth Regiment during Freitas Guimarães's tenure as garrison commander; in 1829, he was a first lieutenant in an infantry battalion. That Bahia succeeded in obtaining this transfer is surprising, for even well connected white militia officers like Lieutenant Colonel Bruno failed to obtain regular commissions.[134]

On the surface, the years immediately after independence thus saw little change in the colonial resolution of racial issues in the militia. Segregated black, mulatto, and white battalions functioned side by side in Salvador, yet the militia's center of gravity had shifted toward the mulatto and especially the black battalions, for the independence war had destroyed the white merchant militia as a mainstay of the state. Black officers, with their close ties to African Bahia and their special status under colonial promotion rules, opted to support the planter-dominated monarchy, expecting to be recognized as one of the pillars of the new state. Many received reward for their independence services in the form of promotions and pensions, suggesting an incipient populist policy on the part of the new government. As statesmen refashioned the Brazilian state along liberal and constitutional lines, however, the segregated militia loomed as an ever more anomalous institution. By 1828, when Bigode regained his old command on Gonçalves's death, liberal reformers in Rio de Janeiro were aggressively challenging Brazil's colonial heritage, forcing black and mulatto officers to reconsider the support that they had so willing lent the imperial regime in 1824.

The independence war and its aftermath shook the colonial Bahian military to its very foundations, destroying the planter class's effective domination of it, but did not topple the edifice. It broke the planter–officer corps alliance, as none of the planter–generals weathered the storm to continue their careers in Bahia after independence. Even more important was the influx of new men into the officer corps, particularly individuals politicized and promoted during the war. From this cohort came most of the leadership of the Periquitos' Rebellion; the subsequent repression removed most of them from active roles in the garrison but they remained officers and many returned to play important roles in Bahian politics in the 1830s.

Wartime recruitment significantly changed the social and racial composition of the rank and file, as it brought significant numbers of blacks and slaves into the enlisted ranks, thereby blurring the late-colonial distinction between soldiers and slaves as well as weakening the racial preferences that had excluded blacks from the ranks. The disorderly soldiery of the Exército Pacificador and the immediate postindependence garrison thus heralded a profound challenge to racial hierarchies and to slavery. Reestablishing the demarcation between slave and soldier was accomplished by freeing slave–soldiers and removing them from Bahia, while the Periquitos' Rebellion provided the occasion for a racial purge of the rank and file. Both measures were highly successful in returning the army ranks to their colonial footing (excluding blacks), although the authorization of flogging remained a sore point, as it appeared to reduce soldiers to slave status.

As a result of the war, the militia's weight shifted substantially toward the black and mulatto battalions, and their officers and men saw themselves as defenders of the new regime which they had helped establish. Their political role after independence belies facile characterizations of homogenous and dangerous classes of color, and it underscores the important class differences among nonwhites. Black officers and militiamen were critical to the defeat of the radical elements of the Exército Pacificador in 1824 and expected to play a leading role in the new state. For a brief time in the mid-1820s they did so in Salvador, but the militia reforms of the late 1820s and early 1830s would push these men away from their support of the imperial order.

However much authorities and members of the planter class may have longed for a return to the stability of the colonial period, they could not turn the clock back. The next three decades would be dominated by nearly constant conflict over the nature of military institutions, as Bahians grappled with the social and ideological consequences of independence. The following chapters examine these developments from the perspective of the three main sectors of the Bahian garrison.

CHAPTER 6

Officers: From Bahian to Brazilian

In early October 1838, Salvador's theater announced the resumption of its programming with a performance of a "new and excellent overture entitled 'O Triunfo da Legalidade [The Triumph of Legality],'" especially composed for the occasion to commemorate the defeat of the Sabinada Rebellion in March of that year.[1] The functionaries and members of Salvador's merchant–planter elite who gathered for this victors' ritual had much to celebrate. The Sabinada had woven all of the threads of Bahia's postindependence social and political unrest into a five-month rebellion. Victory came at a high price—2,000 rebel dead and a similar number of deportations from the province—and those who attended the gala would have seen the effects of the three days of street fighting during which the rebellion was crushed, especially the burned-out buildings.

The late 1830s in Bahia punctuated by the Sabinada Rebellion, marked a turning point in Brazilian history. The 1820s had been marred by the disastrous Cisplatine War (1825–1828) and steadily deteriorating relations between Pedro I and parliament and regional elites; his abdication in 1831 ushered in a regency that implemented liberal and federalist reforms. In September 1837, the Regency took an abrupt conservative turn, the Regresso, and began strengthening the central state, rebuilding the army that the previous liberal regimes had substantially dismantled. This process, which laid the foundation for a national Brazilian army, was already well underway in October 1838, and in the 1840s brought significant changes to the experience of Bahia's army officers. Equally important, these developments marked a restructuring of the alliance that bound the Bahian planter class to the monarchy. The independence war had broken the informal but well-established social and familial ties that connected the Bahian elite to the officer corps, and no effective planter control over the army existed in the 1820s and early 1830s. Reliance on the imperial state to manage an army that would defend their interests was only possible after 1837, when post-Regresso governments took on this responsibility.

In the interim, Bahia (and much of the rest of Brazil) experienced a lengthy period of unrest in which the army garrison was often a central protagonist. Rather than recount in detail the events of these decades, this chapter begins with an analytical survey of the period from the mid-1820s to 1838. National politics—in reality, often simply events in Rio de Janeiro—profoundly affected developments in Bahia. Anti-Portuguese feeling, the ideologies of radical liberalism and federalism, racially defined conflicts, and the ever-present fear of slave revolt made for shifting alliances as Bahians fought over the nature of their newly independent state and society, struggles shaped at least in part by the terms of the 1824 constitution.

The remaining sections turn to the army, examining the two major models of military organization that competed during these years, a liberal-federalist one and an ultimately triumphant conservative-centralist one that produced a Brazilian national army in the 1840s. Buffeted by the political changes of the 1820s and 1830s, Bahia's officers were deeply affected by radical liberal politics in the 1830s. The Regresso and the Sabinada's defeat definitively eliminated radical officers from Bahian politics and brought abrupt changes in the officer profession that signaled the construction of the national army. Finally, this chapter examines the implications of these changes for individual officers and their families, tracing the officer corps's impoverishment and the final disappearance of the planter–general elite. By mid-century, Bahia's officers had ceased to be primarily Bahians; those who remained in the corporation were more likely to identify with the Brazilian state, their employer, which displayed little tolerance for the personal interests that the colonial regime had recognized.

Politics and Society: Brazil and Bahia, 1825–1838

The defeat of the Periquitos' Revolt and the reorganization of the military apparatus in Salvador in early 1825 brought a degree of peace and order to Bahia. The executions and the continuing labors of the permanent court-martial served as an unambiguous warning to those seeking to change the imperial order and conveniently kept troublesome officers away from the troops. In January 1826, Salvador hosted a visit by Pedro I. Amid elaborate rituals and ceremonies, members of the city's elite demonstrated their adherence to the monarch and he generously rewarded his loyal subjects, handing out decorations with regal munificence. All of the province's senior officers were rewarded with half a grade's worth of promotion (all brevet commissions were confirmed and the remaining officers received brevets in the next grade), while the most senior captains and lieutenants of each unit received similar reward.[2]

The middle years of the 1820s marked the apogee of Pedro's reign. The proclaimer of independence, he had successfully beaten back challenges to his authority and eliminated threats to the new state's political unity, winning international recognition for his regime from both Britain and Portugal in 1825. The honeymoon, however, was short. A rebellion in the Cisplatine Province (modern Uruguay) in late 1825 led to a declaration of war against Argentina, as Pedro continued to pursue the historic Luso-Brazilian aim of maintaining a border on the Río de la Plata. The campaign was unsuccessful, and in 1828, Brazil accepted the British-mediated peace that resulted in the creation of Uruguay.[3]

The Brazilian parliament first convened in May 1826, requiring Pedro to begin governing according to the terms of the charter that he had granted in 1824. While this constitution gave the emperor considerable authority, particularly the "moderating power" that allowed him to dissolve the legislature and name cabinets at will, it also contained notable liberal features, thus combining as one historian has put it, Pedro's "love of his personal power" and "some of the best . . . of the liberal revolution."[4] Voters included all free and freedmen ages twenty-five and older with an annual income of 100$000, but they could only cast ballots for electors (free-born men with double the income of voters), who in turn elected deputies (free-born men required to have an income of 400$000).[5] While historians often emphasize the restrictions placed on the franchise, the income requirement was actually quite low and Brazil had a broad electorate by the standards of the contemporary Atlantic world.[6] Moreover, the charter included an extensive bill of rights, largely lifted from the Declaration of the Rights of Man, including provisions for equal protection before the law and equal access to government posts on the basis of merit alone.[7] To be sure, none of this applied to slaves (almost entirely ignored in the document), and Emília Viotti da Costa has argued that the constitution meant little to most other Brazilians as well.[8] While this may be true, it misses the importance that the charter had in radical politics and in providing the language and grounds for a critique of Brazilian society that included broad sectors of the free population.

Parliament quickly became a focus for opponents of the monarch. Led by able liberal statesmen such as Bernardo Pereira de Vasconcelos, the opposition railed against Pedro's absolutist proclivities and worked to eliminate illiberal and unconstitutional elements from law, a process that had important, though sometimes ambiguous, implications for the armed forces. Major reforms to the country's judicial administration were passed during these years, including a new criminal code, and elected justices of the peace replaced appointed local magistrates. Personal scandals and Pedro's increasing interest in placing his daughter on the Portuguese throne soured relations with the Brazilian political class, while lack of success in the Cisplatine War and a disastrous mutiny of European mercenaries in Rio de Janeiro fueled opponents' criticisms.[9]

While no formal political parties existed at this time, loose groupings of Exaltados (radical liberals), Moderados (moderate liberals), and conservatives, known as Colunas or Caramurus, emerged by the end of the 1820s. Exaltados had little presence in the legislature, but few scruples about pursuing reforms by mobilizing the urban *menu peuple* and seeking allies among troops in Rio de Janeiro. As relations between Pedro and the legislature deteriorated, a loose Moderado–Exaltado alliance increased pressure on the monarch, and in March 1831, after his unsuccessful tour of Minas Gerais, violence broke out between supporters and opponents of the emperor. Unwilling to name a ministry amenable to the parliamentary Moderados, he abruptly abdicated on 7 April 1831, in favor of his five-year-old son, Pedro II.[10]

With the abdication, power suddenly fell into the hands of the erstwhile opposition. Moderados dominated the hastily-established regency government, breaking with Exaltados, for whom 7 April became, as Joaquim Nabuco put it, a *"journée des dupes."*[11] Exaltados took to the streets, seeking allies among disaffected military groups and the popular classes of Rio de Janeiro, whose mobilization had been crucial before 7 April. Moderados also faced opposition from restorationists, as Caramurus expounded the simple program of seeking Pedro I's return to the throne. A series of mutinies and popular protests in Rio de Janeiro (July 1831) almost succeeded in overthrowing the Moderado government dominated by Vasconcelos and Diogo Antônio Feijó, a priest from São Paulo just previously named minister of justice.[12] In this crisis climate, the government instituted a series of reforms, many of which had been mooted in liberal circles since the

1820s. Significant army cutbacks and the transfer of army battalions to their home provinces served the immediate purpose of ridding Rio de Janeiro of troublesome military men and achieved the liberal goal of reducing the corporation's size. The civilian National Guard (another of their aims) replaced the army-controlled militias and placed arms in the hands of Rio de Janeiro's property-holding citizens (Chapter 8).

Having weathered the crisis of 1831, Moderados carried forward the liberal reforms of the 1820s, producing a code of criminal procedure in 1832 which established trial by jury and a constitutional amendment, the Ato Adicional of 1834, which strengthened provincial governments by giving them responsibility for policing and the National Guard. Provincial legislatures with considerable autonomous power of taxation were established, but provincial chief executives, the presidents, remained imperial government appointees. That the Ato Adicional made an absolutist restoration more difficult facilitated its passage. Pedro's death changed the context of Brazilian politics, removing the possibility of a restoration and clearing the way for an eventual alliance between disillusioned Moderados and former restorationists, which produced the 1837 Regresso, or return to explicitly conservative policies. In the interim, however, the committed Moderado, Feijó, was narrowly elected sole regent in 1835; his resignation in 1837 marked the beginning of the Regresso.[13]

These national events impinged profoundly on Bahian politics.[14] The departure of the province's regular army units for the battlefields of the South in 1826 and 1827 removed one source of unrest. Bahia's troops returned only in mid-1831, playing a leading role in two major rounds of social unrest in Salvador (1831–1833 and 1837–1838). The first was closely connected to politics in the capital and the abdication. The March 1831 riots spilled over to Bahia in early April, when the city's militia commanders led officers and civilians in an occupation of Barbalho Fort. They called for the expulsion of all Portuguese-born officers, including the commander of arms. The president conceded most of the demands and resigned. Rumors that a Bahian merchant had been murdered by a Portuguese national sparked a vicious round of anti-Portuguese rioting on 13 April 1831, which soon spread to the towns of the Recôncavo. News of Pedro's abdication reached Salvador on 22 April, briefly lowering tensions, but in mid-May, a mutiny in the Twentieth Infantry provoked a new standoff between loyal and rebellious battalions, the latter again calling for the expulsion of Portuguese. A brief mutiny of artillery soldiers in Fort São Pedro on 1 September 1831, was quickly suppressed and the commander of arms discharged many of the

soldiers involved—thus satisfying their principal demand. Civilian municipal guards thwarted a federalist revolt in the Tenth Infantry shortly after
it broke out on 28 October. Many of its participants escaped to join the
federalist rebellion that briefly controlled the town of Cachoeira in February
1832. A series of alarms and minor incidents in Salvador culminated in a
rising of political prisoners in the Forte do Mar in late April 1833, who
proclaimed a federal system of government. After three days of artillery
exchanges between the prisoners in the fort (located in the harbor) and land
batteries, the rebels surrendered.

The last, and by far the greatest, of the rebellions, the Sabinada—named
after Francisco Sabino Álvares da Rocha Vieira, the substitute teacher at
Salvador's medical school and former army surgeon who dominated the
rebel government—began in November 1837 when the city's two army units
and the provincial police mutinied under the command of their majors and
junior officers. Completely without means to resist, the provincial government hastily retreated to warships in the harbor. As the rebels proclaimed,
after some hesitation, a temporary independence from Rio de Janeiro until
the majority of Pedro II and called for a more liberal regime, conservative planters in the Recôncavo mobilized their dependents and the National
Guard, besieged the city, and (with military support from other provinces
and Rio de Janeiro) took the city by storm in March 1838. The massacre of defenders, as well as the three years of purges that followed, concluded the cycle
of social and political unrest that began with the Tailors' Conspiracy of 1798.

The Bahian and Brazilian experience of considerable social and political
instability in the first decades after independence was not unique in Latin
America; most of the new states failed to establish workable governments
because deep social divisions and competing regional economic interests
prevented the emergence of a united ruling class strong enough to with-
stand challenges. The definition of new nations proved highly controversial,
given the deep racial and ethnic divisions that no amount of liberal emphasis
on equality could erase; much of the recent literature on postindependence
Spanish America is devoted to teasing out these lines of conflict.[15] Furthermore, the franchise was broad by contemporary standards and the proliferation of local-level elected offices such as justices of the peace and National
Guard posts, as well as the jury system, further expanded the political class.
The numerous newspapers—eighty-four titles were published in Salvador
between 1823 and 1837, most after 1831—made political debate accessible
to a much broader sector of the population; that some were designed to be
read aloud increased their impact.[16]

Several themes ran through the unrest in Bahia, including lusophobia, federalism, and radical liberalism. Continued Portuguese dominance
of retail commerce made natives of the former mother country unpopular among the city's lower classes. Given the postindependence economic
downturn and the flood of false copper currency that increased the hard-
ship of the city's lower classes, food riots figured prominently in the periods
of unrest; the anti-Portuguese clauses of rebel proclamations were probably their most popular and easily understood provisions. Although Brazil
never went so far as Mexico, which formally expelled large numbers of
Spaniards, lusophobia marked a fundamental step in defining the nation.
Indeed, many Brazilians received their first lessons in what it meant to be
Brazilian while hearing anti-Portuguese diatribes or participating in the
sack of a Portuguese shop.[17] In the army, lusophobia lent a patriotic justification to calls for the removal of Portuguese-born senior officers which,
in turn, would advance the Brazilians' careers. Nevertheless, politics cannot
be reduced to a struggle between Portuguese and Brazilians, and one historian has characterized it as a "tactical recourse" of liberals and especially
Exaltados.[18]

In contrast to lusophobia, an often dangerously lower class ideology, federalism had potentially broader appeal to Bahians increasingly disgruntled
with the domination exercised by Rio de Janeiro, sometimes characterized as
the internal metropole of Brazil.[19] A Salvador newspaper lamented in 1837
that Bahians were little more than "wretched colonized people and vassals
of the central court." Another hailed federalism in glowing terms: It would
"relieve the population of unjust tribute paid to tyrants ... protect agriculture and national commerce ... spread enlightenment and civilization
everywhere ... banish pomp and immorality in public affairs," and stop
the flow of taxes that only "fattened shameless courtiers." In more practical
terms, the *Nova Sentinela da Liberdade* explained in 1831 that "a unitary
government was not appropriate for a large state," while a federal regime
in which the provinces united to aid each other in defense would be more
responsive to regional interests.[20] Federalism could draw on Brazilians' association with their pátria and local notables' desire for autonomy; to a degree,
the 1834 Ato Adicional's devolution of powers to the provinces satisfied these
concerns.

Federalism's great weakness lay in its close association with radical
liberalism—radical in the context of Bahia's slave society—which sought
more profound reforms in Brazilian society than were acceptable to
Moderados. In one of its last proclamations, the Sabinada government called

for "liberty and social equality, the essential bases for prosperity," demanding that laws "be just and useful for the poor, the small, and the helpless, as well as for the rich, the great, and the powerful."[21] Radical liberal newspapers repeatedly expressed an ideal of government that rested on the consent of the governed, railing against Pedro I and the aristocracy. More pointedly, one of the Sabinada newspapers lashed out at the great planter families of the Recôncavo and their continued dominance of government posts despite the constitution's promise of equality of access to the public service on the basis of merit and virtue alone.[22] In so invoking the constitution, radical liberals focused on some of the charter's most progressive clauses, the extensive bill of citizens' rights, and used these liberal provisions to challenge the ethic of patronage on which rested so much of Brazilian politics and administration.[23]

A handbill that appeared not long after Pedro's visit to Salvador is a precious indication of the ways in which Bahian patriotism (with its implicit federalism), radical liberalism, and lusophobia merged in opposition to the emperor, seen as an illiberal ruler:

> Bahians! . . . Your homeland is reduced to a most horrible slavery, our rights will be banished, and our honor frustrated. Bahians! don't let yourself be deluded by the vandalous actions practiced by that monster Emperor, scourge of humanity. Fight for your holy rights, defend your liberty, and love your *pátria*. Remember that you have on the throne of Brazil a dragon, and not an Emperor . . . who only desires to see Bahians succumb. To arms! Throw from the soil of Brazil a tyrant who so oppresses us and install in your *pátria* a democratic government that guarantees our rights, honors the nation, and does not punish us without due process. Bahians! Attention, Attention! Overthrow without delay that little Portuguese rascal [*marotinho*].

The handbill concluded with a call for regicide and "vivas" to government by the people and to liberty.[24] The anonymity of this proclamation was perhaps its most worrisome feature to authorities, who repeatedly reported rumors of conspiracies fomented by what they called "anarchist" factions; proclamations like this one turned up with some regularity and the documentation left by the repression of the revolts hints at large numbers of sympathizers. Lusophobia, calls for federalism and more effective liberal reform, and a willingness to engage in extralegal political activity thus characterized radical liberal politics in Bahia, just as it did the similar Exaltado politics of Rio de Janeiro.

Radicals had to deal with two additional issues, both of which are crucial to understanding Bahia's military politics of the 1830s: the place of slaves and Africans in Brazilian society and racial questions. They tended to define the nation as Brazilian, that is, composed of men who were neither Portuguese nor Africans. The *Nova Sentinela da Liberdade* struck at both of these enemies when it accused Portuguese nationals of fomenting Nagô (Yoruba) slave revolts in 1831 and lambasted a Portuguese-born judge for equating Brazilians and "blacks from the coast of Africa" when he referred to one Elesbão, an African sedan-chair porter, as a citizen. *O Sete de Novembro* angrily denied accusations that the Sabinada government was recruiting Africans: "The simple fact that we are Bahians, and free Bahians," according to the newspaper, belied the imputation.[25] The rebel government rather recruited only Brazilian-born slaves for its army in the last months of the rebellion, making clear its rejection of Africans.[26] Bound up with efforts to secure Brazil's place in a world dominated by Europeans and reflecting a well-founded fear of slave revolt (generally led by Africans at this time), the rejection of Africa marked the Brazilian nation's limits.[27]

The Sabinada's resort to slave recruitment deeply worried authorities, who along with foreign observers had long expressed fears that slaves would take advantage of the divisions in the free population to stage their own rebellions.[28] Certainly many slaves took advantage of the disorder of the revolts to run away or to join in the looting of Portuguese property. A few self-consciously joined the rebellions as individuals: one creole fled his master in the Recôncavo, stole some cartridges, and reported to the Sabinada's front lines in January 1838.[29] Slave revolts, the largest of which—an African Muslim rebellion—shook Salvador in January 1835, however, rarely connected to those of the free; as it had during the independence war, the free population always submerged its differences to cooperate in controlling slaves, just as they could agree on excluding Africans from the nation. Indeed, the Sabinada's free soldiers refused to serve alongside the newly freed recruits.[30]

The Exaltado ranks included a significant number of nonwhites; the majority of those charged for complicity in the Bahian federalist revolts of the 1830s were recorded as pardos and radical liberals' enemies regularly blamed "people of color" for disorder. "No lack of insults on the part of blacks and mulattoes," characterized life in Salvador during the Sabinada, according to one observer, while a conservative deputy reported that the rebellion's forces consisted of "the meanest rabble, almost all [men] of color" who proclaimed a "war against the 'Caiados,' " or "whitewashed," a pejorative nickname for whites.[31] They also sought to link Exaltados to slave revolt. In late April 1831, Cipriano José Barata de Almeida was arrested and accused of fomenting a "republican revolt with blacks from the Mina Coast and slaves"; the *Nova Sentinela da Liberdade* sprang to his defense and published evidence that revealed a conspiracy to discredit the radical liberal champion by associating him with slave revolt.[32] Barata's enemies played on these widely shared fears as they defined Brazilian society in dichotomous terms, with a small white elite living precariously among a large, undifferentiated, and often dangerous nonwhite mass that included many slaves and Africans. In this sense, race (sometimes conflated with fear of slave revolt and disdain for Africans) was an issue that usually belonged to conservatives, not to liberals.

This tendency to use racial rhetoric against Exaltados makes it difficult to assess the discussions of race in Bahia's few surviving radical newspapers. Thomas Flory has argued that the "mulatto press" of Rio de Janeiro reflected political party competition, rather than explicit appeals by or on behalf of men of color, but there is little evidence for this in Salvador.[33] As in the capital, Bahia's radical liberal newspapers often condemned Portuguese racism, such as that of a navy officer who contrasted "Brazilians and people of color." In response, radical liberals often expressed a broad and inclusive understanding of the Brazilian nation in racial terms. After his arrest in 1831, Barata wrote of the April riots in Salvador, during which the "people" had sought to acclaim him president: "These views of the multitude, whites, *pardos*, freed creole blacks, and *cabras*, all good patriots and our brothers, struck fear into the government." He of course excluded Africans, slaves, and Portuguese from his patriotic brothers, but included essentially everyone else.[34] Barata and other radical liberals sometimes appropriated racial slurs, as did the *Nova Sentinela da Liberdade* when it proclaimed that "all of us native-born Brazilians" were "*cabras* and *melaços* [honey-colored]"; similarly, a broadsheet proclaimed in 1830 that the blond and blue-eyed but indubitably Brazilian-born heir apparent was "*cabra* just like us."[35]

Some spoke out explicitly on behalf of nonwhites. Antônio Pereira Rebouças, son of a Portuguese man and a freedwoman, elected deputy for Bahia in 1830, 1837, and 1843, was later remembered as "always speaking in the name of the 'mulatto population,' " but his position toward racial politics was ambiguous. Flory argues that Rebouças used race as a metaphor for other conventional political issues; more important, as a successful,

upwardly mobile self-taught lawyer, his commitment to radical politics had
strict limits: He rejected the Sabinada's resort to armed struggle, for which
the rebels roundly criticized him.[36] Although no newspapers with explicitly racial titles appeared in Salvador (another contrast to Rio de Janeiro),
isolated surviving newspapers reveal that claims were made on behalf of
"men of color." In 1836, *O Defensor do Povo* carried articles that recalled the
central role of "men of color" in the independence struggle; it condemned
the *Diario da Bahia* for arguing that their lack in public employment was
due to their fathers' failure to send them to law school. Pointing out that
higher education was not needed for most government jobs, it invoked the
constitution's provision that the law must be equal for all, asserting that
racism lay behind nonwhites' absence.[37]

The limited development of a racially based politics, despite evident
racial discrimination, points to the strength of racial hierarchies in Brazilian
society and the capacity of patronage structures to defuse racial conflict
by defining race flexibly for individuals and opening up opportunities to
small numbers of nonwhites such as Rebouças.[38] Those who made collective
claims were accused of fomenting dangerous intrigues: In response to an
article similar to that of *O Defensor*, another newspaper argued in 1831 that
there were already numerous men of color in the legislature and in civil and
military posts, adding that those who raised racial issues were enemies of
"order."[39] Only the Sabinada Rebellion expressed a clear and unambiguous
racial ideology, most closely connected with the black militia officers, a
group of men for whom whitening or absorption into the elite was not an
option (Chapter 8). Not surprisingly, this failure of social control could only
be remedied through violence, and the massacre of Sabinada supporters was
the inevitable response to the rebellion.

Federalism, radical liberalism, slave unrest, talk of legal and social equality, and racially based claims, not to mention a dangerously active political
underground, all combined to challenge the hegemony of Bahia's planter
class, particularly in the early 1830s. This threat to their dominance was
all the more severe given the lack of reliable military institutions. While
changes in the local garrison associated with the Brazilian empire's initial
efforts to build a national army served the Bahian elite well enough in the
1820s, the Moderado governments of the early 1830s undid this work, significantly weakening the Bahian garrison; both these army reforms and the
political context of these years reinvigorated the army-officer radicalism that
culminated in the Sabinada.

Army Politics, 1826–1838

During the 1820s and 1830s, Brazilian army organization underwent several abrupt changes. The new empire inherited an unwieldy complex of military institutions from the colonial regime—army, militia, and ordenanças—for which it lacked a central administrative apparatus. The war ministry struggled to gain control of these forces, seeking to create what can best be termed a "national army," a corporation loyal to the central government and effectively under its control. Deeply suspicious of regular armies as the agents of absolutism, liberal reformers by contrast worked to diminish the army's role. As opponents of Pedro I gained legislative ascendancy in the last years of his reign, they cut the army's size, and after the abdication, Moderados dismantled much of the corporation. In keeping with their federalist goals, they decentralized it as well. Recognizing these very different conceptions of military organization, Joaquim Nabuco concluded that Pedro I was the army's "best friend," while the legislature opposed the corporation's development.[40] Only in the late 1830s, with the Regresso, did Brazil abandon the liberal and federalist model of military organization, creating by the 1840s an effective national army.

In the 1820s, the new imperial government struggled to gain administrative control over its far-flung army. The establishment of a war ministry in Rio de Janeiro in 1808 had not significantly altered the regional basis of army administration, especially in northeastern provinces such as Bahia. Insistent demands that provincial authorities supply information about local garrisons testify to the war ministry's difficulty in managing the army. Not even Saint Anthony, often invoked by Brazilians to help find lost items, could have made sense of the data on provincial garrisons submitted to the legislature in 1826, according to the deputy and brigadier, Raimundo José da Cunha Matos. By the end of the 1820s, legislators no longer made light of this problem, routinely suspecting executive foot-dragging on constitutional obligations to provide parliament with sufficient information on which to legislate the army's strength.[41]

While the ministry worked to centralize control over the army, little help came from the legislature, and most significant measures came by executive decree or administrative decision. A Brazil-wide renumeration of battalions in late 1824 marked each unit with a national stamp. Efforts to standardize drill in the mid-1820s brought selected junior officers and sergeants from each garrison to Rio de Janeiro. In 1829, the ministry attempted to compile information on all officers' seniority, presumably a prelude to the institution of armywide promotions (under the terms of an 1822 law, officers were to compete for promotion only against colleagues from the provincial garrison in which they served, much as they had done under the colonial regime).[42] Little came of this measure, but the war ministry badly needed detailed information on promotions carried out in the provinces. Complaints over preteritions, rare before 1822, reached epidemic proportions in the 1820s; a brief debate over a promotions bill quickly degenerated into accusations of corruption, patronage, and nepotism in promotions.[43]

Petitions from Bahia reveal the extent to which the independence conflicts had upset the army hierarchy. In 1828, First Lieutenant José Vicente de Amorim Bezerra submitted a long petition in which he complained of having been passed over. He contrasted his education and regular promotions with the irregular advance of several officers who had made captain in the 1826 promotion, which had excluded the forty or so officers facing charges in connection with the Periquitos' Revolt and men like Bezerra, who were absent (he had received leave to study in France). As an artillery cadet, he had passed the qualifying examination in December 1821 and had received his second lieutenant's commission in late 1822 from Pedro Labatut. One of the captains who had advanced ahead of Bezerra in 1826, however, had obtained his lieutenancy in 1821 by popular acclaim from patriotic students—"a mere verbal nomination from some fellows who organized the unit called Minerva." Two other captains had only held brevet second lieutenancies during the war; in any case, one had spent the conflict imprisoned by the Portuguese and neither had obtained formal royal confirmation of their commissions.[44] Bezerra's observations about his superiors' seniority also illustrates the avidity with which officers watched each other's progress and underlines the legal status of promotions: They were as much a right as a reward for good service.[45] Piecemeal rectifications of individual preteritions, such as Bezerra's promotion to captain in 1828, however, could not restore the army hierarchy. Such promotions often bore the qualification, "without prejudice to those who have greater seniority," a red flag that frequently prompted new complaints.[46]

The Cisplatine War and the ensuing growth of the army to 25,742 men nationally (a figure reported for 1 January 1828)[47] further demonstrated the weakness of Brazil's administrative capacity, which no doubt contributed to the imperial forces' poor showing. The soldiers and officers who had failed to accomplish Pedro's goal of keeping the Cisplatine Province suffered badly during the conflict, and in 1829, opposition deputies and newspapers were condemning salary arrears of eighteen months or longer.[48] Nevertheless, this conflict had important implications for the imperial government's efforts to gain control over its army, as most regular troops were removed from their home provinces. By mid-1827, only the Minas Gerais Militia Battalion and the Fifteenth Infantry remained in Salvador; the latter embarked sometime in 1828. This wartime separation of the Bahian army from Salvador not only put a definitive end to the military revolts of the early 1820s, as F. W. O. Morton has noted,[49] but it also provided the occasion for a significant redeployment of troops after the conflict. Rather than returning the Bahian battalions to Salvador in 1829, the government chose to garrison the city with units from southern Brazil, finally implementing the recommendations of 1824 for the occupation of Salvador with non-Bahian troops. By early 1831, only the cavalry squadron had returned to Bahia, and Salvador was garrisoned by four battalions raised in other provinces (see the Appendix, Figure A.2). With radical Bahian officers thus at a safe distance in Rio de Janeiro, military rebelliousness had been contained; more important, this deployment suggests that the government of Pedro I was seeking to break army units' ties to their home provinces.

During the 1820s, the imperial government lacked a free hand to undertake military reforms. Liberals, both Exaltados and Moderados, doubted the utility of regular armed forces and worried that they might be used as instruments of absolutism.[50] The 1826 decision to reintegrate foreign-born (Portuguese) officers expelled by provincial decrees such as the December 1823 Act of Salvador's town council, a measure logical enough from the standpoint of an army hierarchy seeking to restore orderly promotions, drew a rebuke from the legislature in 1828, with some deputies calling for the execution of such traitors.[51] The increasingly emboldened liberal group in the chamber of deputies legislated major force reductions in 1830, setting the army's strength at 12,000 enlisted men for 1831–1832; dissolved the battalions of European mercenaries raised by Pedro I; and imposed significant budget cuts.[52] Outside parliament, liberal newspapers repeatedly condemned the corporation. Salvador's *Sentinela da Liberdade* expressed an extreme liberal suspicion of officers in commenting on the appointment of a general to the presidency of Minas Gerais: Such men, "raised with [the ideals of] military despotism . . . and corporate spirit" would reduce that province to "the time of tyrannical colonial absolutism." Warming to his topic, editor Cipriano Barata lambasted officers as men who "barely know how to read, write, and count"; a good number of these "mustachioed werewolves" were "Portuguese and foreign" to boot.[53]

In this environment, the Moderado regency government faced difficult choices. Their immediate concern was with the troops in Rio de Janeiro. Moderados supported army cutbacks in principle and disbanded units in early May to comply with the 1830 law that set the army's strength at 12,000 as of 1 July 1831.[54] This in turn alienated the Exaltado junior officers who had played a key role in forcing the abdication. At the same time, senior officers, many of them closely tied to Pedro I, some also Portuguese, appeared to be plotting a restoration. With the Rio de Janeiro garrison thus divided, and the city facing the threat of social revolution, Moderados drew sufficient support from officers (organized into a separate battalion) to bring the July 1831 Exaltado rebellions under control. This victory cleared the way for Moderados' military reforms. Besides disbanding additional army units, they removed policing from the army's purview, first by creating a corps of civilian municipal guards for Rio de Janeiro and Brazil's other major cities and then by authorizing provinces to raise civilian militarized police forces.[55] The National Guard replaced the old militias and made property-holding citizens responsible for their collective security (Chapter 8). In keeping with liberals' preference for decentralized government, the Moderado government adopted a policy of extreme federalism in army affairs, removing almost all of the regular forces from the capital and returning units to their provinces of origin. While reversing the deployment policy of the late 1820s secured Rio de Janeiro, it foisted military disorder onto the provinces.[56]

The Regency thus invigorated the radical liberals in Bahia and the 1831 troop movements help make sense of the events in Salvador. The protests of early April were led not by army officers but by the commanders of Salvador's militia; by and large, the non-Bahian regulars remained loyal to the government in 1831. The decision to embark them and the return to Bahia of locally raised battalions, however, changed the context of Salvador's politics. While the Franciscan friars sang a *Te Deum* for the safe return of "our troops," an anonymous denunciation warned in August that the "enemies of order" were waiting for the Second Battalion (a unit raised in Rio de Janeiro) to leave before "bringing upon this capital disorder, vengeance, death, and civil war." The arrival of Bahian battalions, it said, boded ill for future peace and the conspirators could already count on the recently returned Thirteenth and part of the Fourteenth Battalions as well as the cavalry.[57] The revolt of November 1831 bears out, at least in part, the denunciation of a broad conspiracy. Several civilians arrived at the Tenth (formerly Fourteenth) Battalion's post and called upon officers to "fulfill their promises" and lead their soldiers in the defense of "endangered liberty."[58] The president had

been warned of the plot and civilian municipal guards surrounded the barracks, preventing the rebels from leaving while arresting civilian supporters
who had gathered elsewhere. The government then disbanded the Tenth
and discharged numerous soldiers. Many of those involved fled to São Félix
and Cachoeira, where they joined the federalist revolt of early 1832.[59]

Not only did the Regency return officers to Bahia, where they had
connections and political interests, but the reduction of the army and the
elimination of the central government's role in providing police forces contradicted the immediate interests of the Bahian planter class, whose spokes-
men regularly called for a larger repressive state apparatus in the 1820s
and early 1830s, with an eye to improving policing in the Recôncavo.[60]
Neither the establishment of a provincial constabulary nor the empower-
ment of local elites in the National Guard compensated for the reduction of
Salvador's army garrison. Whereas, in early 1831, one artillery and three infantry battalions, the Guarda Militar de Polícia, and a cavalry squadron had
garrisoned the city, by late 1832, only two battalions remained. The president briefly held up orders to disband the cavalry because he judged them
loyal and felt it necessary to maintain a mobile force at his disposition.[61]
In the mid-1830s, the provincial government regularly complained to Rio
de Janeiro that the reduction of the province's garrison had left it unable
to suppress disorder, arguing that the January 1835 slave revolt demonstrated the need for more troops in Bahia.[62] Matters worsened in 1836 and
1837, when small expeditionary forces were sent to Rio Grande do Sul and
Maranhão.

Just as the Bahian elite would have to make do with both a smaller army
and the untried liberal institutions, so Bahia's officers were forced to adapt to
a very different army in the 1830s. After having served in Rio de Janeiro and
the South for half a decade, almost all of these men were ordered to Salvador;
only a handful were assigned to other provinces.[63] The cutbacks had resulted
in a surplus of officers, exacerbated by the return to the regulars of officers
who had served in paid militia posts. Some took advantage of generous
provisions that allowed them to accumulate seniority while on leave without
pay; a few retired; but most remained in the army, where they reverted
to the class of *avulso* (excess) officers to await vacancies in the remaining
battalions. For several years, the government halted promotions, although
by the middle of the decade, a shortage of trained artillery and engineering
officers prompted the legislature to authorize promotions in these arms if
no qualified avulsos could be found. In 1836, the legislature authorized the
government to promote officers who had distinguished themselves against

the rebellions in Pará and Rio Grande do Sul.[64] Neither of these exceptions, however, affected the majority of avulsos.

Worries about the excessive number of avulso officers, nationally estimated to number 910 in 1835, pervaded the commander of arms's correspondence in the early 1830s, as he noted that they were worthy of reward for their loyalty, lamented the lack of service opportunities for senior officers (for whom there would never be sufficient vacancies in regular battalions), and requested permission to employ them as supernumeraries in the remaining battalions.[65] In 1837, mere weeks before the Sabinada, the president warned that the suspension of promotions had undermined the reciprocal relationship implied by the values of service and reward, advising the war minister to hold a general promotion in the province, for it would "inspire them to remain contentedly in the honorable career to which they have dedicated themselves, maintaining . . . the order and tranquility of this province."[66] War ministers needed little reminding of this, but had found it impossible to wrench authorization for general promotions out of a reluctant legislature.[67]

For officers, these were trying times. One complained that he had become a "worthless individual, a burden to his family," and confessed to having contemplated suicide.[68] Relegation to the class of avulsos meant a substantial pay cut, for actively serving officers received supplements that augmented their base pay (the *soldo de patente*) by as much as 50 percent.[69] The high cost of living prompted calls for salary increases, even from quarters not evidently connected to the army.[70] Officers scrambled to secure appointments as National Guard instructors, posts in the police, or sinecures such as the command of disarmed forts to supplement their pay. The suspension of promotions stalled careers and deprived officers of their principal nonmonetary compensation. By 1837, the typical Bahian officer had held the same rank for more than ten years, in contrast to the four years which he had served in his previous grade.[71]

In response to these wrenching changes in their profession, Bahia's officers turned to politics for redress. A small but vocal and highly visible cohort of junior officers embroiled themselves in radical liberal politics, while a larger group, a majority of the garrison's officers, articulated a corporate ideology that defended their professional and personal interests. These two strands fused in the Sabinada Rebellion, which demonstrated the limits of army-officer politics.

In late 1832, Salvador's officers founded a short-lived Sociedade Militar (Officers' Club), as did their colleagues in other provinces. In its heyday, the Sociedade published a newspaper, *O Militar* (1833–1834), of which only one issue has survived, and repeatedly met to declare officers' loyalty during unrest.[72] It successfully lobbied for the payment of salaries in metal rather than in devalued paper currency.[73] In 1833, the Sociedade also advocated enlisted men's voting rights, correctly arguing that their salary and rations put them just above the minimum income level required to participate in elections. No doubt company captains or battalion commanders hoped to become barracks ward bosses, wielding blocks of soldiers' votes, but justices of the peace reluctantly permitted only a handful of enlisted men to cast ballots as individuals.[74]

The Sociedade's members rallied around the standard of opposition to the Regency's military reforms. *O Militar* declared in 1833 that the entire history of the Brazilian army in the previous two years amounted to a sorry tale of annihilation "at the hands of compatriots whose rights and liberties" the army had defended. Both this issue and a petition to the provincial legislature signed by 124 officers two years later enumerated virtually identical grievances: the reduction and consolidation of provincial army administration—General Troop Treasuries, for example, were reduced to Paymasters' Offices—the elimination of commands of arms in small provinces, the dilapidation of fortresses, the raising of better paid provincial police forces, their apparently permanent condition of unemployment, the abolition of the militia, and the creation of what they considered a useless National Guard. In short, virtually every measure of the Regency came under fire from Bahian officers, and in the Sabinada, rebel officers would reverse most of them.[75]

Corporate loyalty, however, only partially overcame the political differences in the officer corps. Liberal newspapers condemned the Sociedades as conclaves of absolutists and restorationists and this served as a justification for closing Rio de Janeiro's Sociedade Militar in 1833. Bahia's Sociedade, however, was itself deeply divided over political issues and one officer described "heated discussions" during meetings, complaining that a colleague had discredited the club by expressing his discontent at the abdication.[76]

While the Sociedade Militar addressed national issues, given that the objectionable measures had been undertaken by the government in Rio de Janeiro, it was organized as a provincial institution and reinforced ties among Bahia's officers. The vast majority of them had been born in the province (88 percent of the sixty-seven signatories to the 1835 petition whose birthplace is known), and had strong local loyalties. Most had, of course, fought for independence and had family and economic interests in the province. Not surprisingly, none are known to have complained about their transfers back to Salvador in 1831. A provincial patriotism and an interest in local history can be inferred from the thirty-one officers who contributed to the publication of Second Lieutenant Ladislau dos Santos Titara's epic poem about Bahian independence, *Paraguaçu* (1835–1837), and the twenty-nine who subscribed to the four volumes of Inácio Acioli de Cerqueira e Silva's *Memórias históricas e políticas da província da Bahia* (*Historical and Political Memoirs of the Province of Bahia*), published before 1837.[77] For these men, federalism had strong attractions.

A small but highly vocal core of officers remained squarely within the radical liberal camp. Many of these forty or so men (about a fifth of the garrison's officers) had histories of involvement in radical politics dating to the independence years. As officers, they shared the corporate interests of their colleagues, and tension between their roles as army officers and their liberal politics ultimately limited their radicalism, as a brief look at Lieutenant Daniel Gomes de Freitas, the quintessential junior officer rebel, demonstrates. One of Manoel Pedro de Freitas Guimarães's recruits in 1821, recognized as a second cadet that same year, he reported to the Recôncavo patriot camp in July 1822, and after the Battle of Pirajá, obtained a second lieutenant's commission.[78] Involvement in conspiracies and rebellions, interspersed with attempts to resume his army career, dominated the next 22 years of Freitas's life. Arrested for complicity in the Periquitos' Revolt, he remained in prison until his acquittal in early 1828. Upon his release, he sought retroactive inclusion in the 1826 Bahia-wide promotion on the grounds that he had been unjustly imprisoned in 1824, backing up his request with eight testimonials of service during the independence war.[79] He received no promotion, but in 1830, he was assigned to the Seventh Artillery, a Bahian unit then stationed in Rio de Janeiro.

The Regency returned Freitas and the artillery to Salvador and offered him new hope for advancement as it investigated the preteritions and involuntary retirements of the previous regime; on 1 September 1831, the special commission charged with this task ruled that he, in fact, deserved a promotion with retroactive seniority back to 1826. Ironically, on that very day, he was arrested for complicity in the mutiny of artillery soldiers, putting a stop to his promotion but not his conspiring; in early 1832, he faced charges in connection with the abortive October 1831 federalist revolt. He spent the next three years in prison, from which he led the 1833 Forte do Mar revolt. Another acquittal—typical of the legal system of that time—sent Freitas back to his military career. By this time, he was probably the most senior of

Bahia's second lieutenants but his reputation cost him another preterition in 1835, when a vacancy in the Third Artillery went to a more junior second lieutenant. The army's policy of employing avulso officers on the basis of seniority and his acquittals eventually stood Freitas in good stead for, in 1836, the commander of arms finally assigned him to the Third Artillery.[80]

From this vantage point, Freitas played a leading role in the Sabinada rebellion; he finally received his coveted promotion (to lieutenant colonel) and sat in the rebel cabinet as minister of war. Despite his prominence, he escaped the defeat and remained in hiding until the 1840 amnesty pardoned all of the rebels in prison or still at large. Ordered to reside in São Paulo by the terms of the amnesty, Freitas again tried to resume his army career, requesting back pay for the time that he had been in hiding. In 1842, he took part in the brief liberal revolt in São Paulo, after which he disappeared amid speculation that he had joined the remnants of the Farroupilha Rebellion in Rio Grande do Sul.[81]

While in hiding, Freitas wrote an account of the Sabinada; unfortunately, he was not given to introspection and does not attempt to justify his actions in the revolt. Rather, as Paulo Cesar Souza has observed, the narrative resembles the report of a "zealous functionary," a civil servant concerned with smooth administration; it also emphasizes his defense of private property and his opposition to the enlistment of slaves.[82] Perhaps Freitas considered the narrative a draft for an eventual legal defense; if so, the emphasis on his reluctance to enroll slaves in his army and his protection of buildings from arsonists' torches may have been self-serving. More likely, however, the narrative simply reflects the caution of so many Exaltados: men like Freitas sought a greater role in society, rather than an overthrow of the social order, especially if that would involve equality with former slaves.

Freitas's commitment to his military career reveals a further contradiction of army-officer radicalism that helps to explain its limitations. Radical officers needed the command of troops to further their program; to retain their position in the corporation, they needed to defend its hierarchical principles and the permanence of officership. Here radical officers found surprising allies. No government established provisions for the discharge of officers (although the Regency did consider buying out avulsos' commissions); in fact, the constitution prohibited cashiering them except through due process, which came to mean court-martial conviction.[83] Fellow officers, mindful of the need to protect their own careers, steadfastly refused to vote for the expulsion of their colleagues, and men such as Freitas remained in the corporation. Thus, the war ministry recommended in 1832 that all officers who adhered to "restorationist or anarchist factions" be employed only in positions that kept them away from troops; it had no means of removing them from the corporation.[84] In short, the profession's corporate autonomy protected radical officers while limiting their demands for change.

The Sabinada addressed accumulated officer grievances and marked the last effort to implement the radical liberal program by force in Bahia. Rebel officers reminded their colleagues of the insults suffered by the army since 1831, warning them not to join the "enemies of your class" in the Recôncavo.[85] Despite this emphasis on corporate loyalty, the Sabinada revealed the same divisions in the officer corps that the Sociedade Militar had been unable to overcome. The rebels immediately redressed corporate grievances, awarding themselves two grades' worth of promotion, raising their salaries, abolishing the National Guard, and restoring the old militias, while scarcely lamenting the quick defection of the police who had initially supported the revolt.[86] While the rebels included officers of all ranks, the core of rebel support lay in the junior officer ranks, particularly among the cohort of officers active in radical politics since the early 1820s. In a moment of lucidity, Manoel Pedro de Freitas Guimarães, the controversial garrison commander of 1821–1822, sat in the rebel cabinet. Manoel de São Boaventura Ferraz, around whom constitutionalist plotters had gathered in 1820–1821, joined the revolt, as did several men implicated in the Periquitos' Rebellion, like Freitas.

Once in power, these men proved remarkably hesitant to implement the radical liberal and federalist program. They proclaimed Bahia independent of Rio de Janeiro, but quickly modified the declaration of independence to limit it to the duration of Pedro II's minority status, a decision that reveals the durability of the monarchical symbol and perhaps also the hope that he would reverse the Regresso when he came to power. While the rebels talked much about legal and social equality, they proved cautious reformers, stressing their "love of order" and determination to preserve private property, slavery, the law, and the monarchy.[87] Moreover, these cautious leaders soon lost control of the movement as lower class anti-Portuguese violence, slave resistance, and a racial discourse associated with black militia officers came to dominate the rebellion. As the Sabinada evolved from a relatively moderate movement for political reform and redress of military grievances, it rapidly lost elite support and its embattled and isolated leaders struggled to contain both social unrest in the city and maintain their defences against a strengthening reaction in the Recôncavo.

Large-scale purges in the Bahian army followed the Sabinada's defeat in March 1838. The two battalions were formally disbanded and large numbers of rebel soldiers were deported from Bahia and enlisted in other battalions. The government reorganized the two units, employing officers who had remained loyal and hastily commissioning nineteen new second lieutenants from among the loyalist ranks. It sent the two units to opposite ends of the empire, the artillery to Maranhão in 1839 and the infantry to Rio Grande do Sul the following year; both would have their hands full repressing rebellions. Rebel officers, amnestied in 1840, were ordered to reside in distant provinces. For a few years, Salvador's garrison stood at only a few hundred men, mostly invalids, artisans, and a small number of soldiers attached to a new recruitment depot (Figures A.1 and A.2), but a cavalry squadron was raised in 1839, giving the president a mobile force.[88]

In this sense, the post-Sabinada repression resembled that of the mid-1820s, as deportations from the province removed the most troublesome men, and service outside of Bahia separated battalions from the province. More important, in the late 1830s and early 1840s, Regresso governments began building a national Brazilian army, one that ultimately served the Bahian upper class far better than the contentious Bahian army of the 1820s and 1830s had ever done, a process that had precedents in the immediate post-Cisplatine War period.

Imposing Order: The National Army

In the middle of the 1830s, a conservative reaction to liberal reformism gathered strength. Bernardo Pereira de Vasconcelos's oft-quoted but possibly apocryphal justification for his break with the Moderados and his alliance with conservatives that propelled him to leadership of the Regresso bears repeating. While he had been a liberal in the 1820s and early 1830s, liberalism at that time was new and needed to be implemented in law and practice. By the late 1830s, Brazil's condition was different: "Democratic principles had triumphed and compromised much; society which then ran the risk of [absolute] power, now is in danger of anarchical disorganization."[89] In other words, liberal reforms had undermined authority and now threatened social order; the succession of regional rebellions that broke out in 1835 (in Pará and Rio Grande do Sul), 1838 (the Sabinada in Bahia), and 1839 (in Maranhão) confirmed these fears.[90]

While the Regresso was far from a homogenous movement and the cabinet most closely associated with it lasted little more than a year, the complex national politics from 1837 to the mid-1840s did not impinge upon Bahia's military in the way that the national politics of the 1830s did. While opponents of the Regresso engineered something of a coup in 1840, proclaiming Pedro II's premature accession, their position soon eroded, and a more conservative administration completed the major Regresso reforms in the early 1840s, namely a judicial reform that reduced the role of the justice of the peace and juries in favor of a centralized judicial police system and an interpretation of the Ato Adicional that weakened provincial governments. In the 1840s, Liberal and Conservative parties gradually consolidated themselves, and extreme polarization between them led to brief Liberal revolts in São Paulo and Minas Gerais in 1842, when it appeared that they were to be ousted from power. The emperor permitted Liberals to return to government in the mid-1840s, but their ministries innovated little, apparently accepting the basic Regresso reforms.[91] These developments had relatively little direct impact on Bahia, in part because the province lagged behind the rest of Brazil in the establishment of organized party politics.[92]

While the Regresso's institutional and judicial reforms, as well as its efforts to put down regional rebellions, are relatively well known, its efforts to rebuild the Brazilian army are less familiar.[93] As far back as 1835, it was a concern of Bahian deputy Francisco Ramiro de Assis Coelho, who argued that Brazilians were insufficiently enlightened to "uphold the law" and that the country, with its "vast territory [and] mixed population of slaves," demanded a powerful army, rigorously disciplined with suitable rewards for officers and certain punishment for crimes.[94] Regresso ministries reorganized the officer corps, increased the army's size, and consolidated army administration in Rio de Janeiro. The establishment of a policy of rotating battalions among provinces and officers among battalions broke the provincial career orientation of line officers and forced those who wished to advance into national careers. For the Bahian upper class, the new army provided welcome relief from the disorderly soldiery of the 1820s and 1830s. Indeed, through the Regresso, Bahian planters gained security; however, it cost them political autonomy.

The first Regresso ministry boldly bid to seize control of the army during the 1838 legislative session. Promotions had largely been suspended since 1831 and vacancies in army units went, in order of seniority, to avulso officers. Given the institutional commitment to these men's careers and the professional autonomy of the officer corps, the administration had no control over the corporation and could not prevent the gradual advance into battalion posts of even chronic troublemakers such as Daniel Gomes de Freitas. To cut through this Gordian knot, the war minister proposed two measures. The first extended the authority to promote officers who had performed notable services in the supression of revolts in Rio Grande do Sul and Pará to all who distinguished themselves in "the restoration of public order" anywhere in Brazil. The second measure, contained in the annual bill to set the army's size, gave the minister the authority to retire (with pay) surplus officers, even those who had not completed the minimum of twenty years of service required for the receipt of pensions.[95]

These two seemingly innocuous proposals roused a storm of protest in the legislature. Liberal opposition deputies lambasted the government for attempting to create a "party-line army" by making promotion dependent on support for the government and arrogating for itself the right to cashier officers without due process.[96] Even though the retirement proposal died in committee, one deputy condemned it as "one of the corollaries of the policies of terror" by which the conservative administration sought to remain in power. Rather than such arbitrary measures, he called on the minister to produce a bill for the reform of the army.[97] Marshal José Joaquim de Lima e Silva (the former commander of the Exército Pacificador), while not rising to the rhetorical heights of his civilian colleagues, forcefully defended the restoration of regular promotions based on the old principles of merit and seniority.[98]

More important, Lima e Silva reminded the chamber that a bill to organize active and retired lists as a preliminary to the resumption of promotions had languished in the Senate since 1836.[99] Indeed, the most significant result of the Regresso government's attempt to seize control of the officer corps was the impetus that it gave to the bill that authorized the reorganization of the officer corps. Here the government found consensus in the legislature and quickly passed a law that required it to identify those officers "who, because of their age, constitution, training, and conduct, are worthy of serving." The rest were to be summarily retired.[100] Although some deputies argued that this measure still gave the government too much power and introduced amendments to spell out the criteria by which officers were to be assessed, the enabling legislation was a model of simplicity. The most senior officers in each province were charged with assessing their subordinates' qualifications, presumably using generally accepted criteria to judge training and conduct.[101] In Bahia, this board retired numerous unreliable—especially those involved in the Sabinada—and incapacitated officers. Many officers vehemently protested their enforced retirements and deputies charged that numerous officers had been inappropriately retired; the imperial government eventually reversed some of the commission's recommendations.[102] In 1842, work on this project was finally complete and the ministry classified 893 officers as capable of active service; sixty-one were either unaccounted for or facing courts-martial. Given that the army then required 1,346 officers, the backlog of avulsos had finally been cleared up.[103] To publicize its work, the army produced a directory listing all of its officers by rank and seniority, the *Almanac* of 1844.[104]

The most significant result of the effort to compile active and retired lists was that it put order into the system of promotions upset during the independence period, restoring the old principles of gradual promotion within each arm, based on merit and seniority, putting them on a national footing. Until all officers' seniority vis à vis their colleagues was clearly established, promotions would inevitably upset the hierarchy, all the more so if they were granted for vaguely defined services in defense of order. With the publication of the 1844 *Almanac*, officers could be sure of their seniority. Those few who still felt aggrieved were quick to cite the new publication to buttress their claims for redress in the form of compensatory promotions.[105]

The significance of the 1838 debate was not lost on legislators. The war minister angrily but disingenuously denied accusations that he sought to create a ministerial rather than a national army.[106] Whereas his early proposals would have created an army dependent on the government of the day, the bill that passed respected the army's professional autonomy. Promotions resumed in the 1840s, necessitated by the expansion of the army in 1839 and the shortage of qualified officers.[107] Indeed, the 1850 promotion law, often presented as an innovation, and the reorganization of the officer corps that followed it, built on the work of the early 1840s by perfecting the procedures for maintaining information on officers.[108]

Not only did Brazil construct a central administrative and bureaucratic apparatus to manage its officers' careers in the 1840s, it also began to separate them from their home provinces, essential to the Regresso's program of building a national army. The justification for this policy was quite simple: Local secession movements were unlikely to gain adherents among battalions not from the province in question.[109] This policy can easily be traced for Bahia's army units. When reconstituted out of loyalists after the Sabinada, the two battalions retained their homegrown complexion.[110] In 1839, Bahia's infantry and artillery battalions departed to campaign against rebels in, respectively, southern and northern Brazil. When the artillery battalion (redesignated as the Fourth Foot Artillery) briefly returned to Salvador later in the decade, seventeen of its thirty-two officers hailed from provinces other than

Bahia, a reflection of the new policy of rotating line units among provinces and officers among line units.[111] Furthermore, anything that smacked of local patriotism was anathema to the new army and the war minister rebuked Bahia's president for authorizing the payment of passage to Rio de Janeiro for a delegation of the garrison's officers to attend Pedro II's coronation in 1841.[112]

Service records reveal an abrupt shift in career patterns around 1840, as line officers began rotating among battalions. Lieutenant Martinho Batista Ferreira Tamarindo, one of the numerous officers commissioned during the independence war, served in Bahian battalions during the 1820s; rendered avulso in 1832, he briefly served in Salvador's police and embarked with a small army contingent for the South just before the Sabinada. Promotions to captain and major followed in 1838 and 1839; in 1842, he was promoted again and received command of a battalion in Rio Grande do Sul. A member of Tamarindo's cohort, Second Lieutenant Isidoro José Rocha do Brasil joined the Third Artillery in 1833 after a brief stint as an avulso. Absent from Salvador during the Sabinada, he embarked with the artillery to Maranhão in 1839, receiving quick promotions (first lieutenant in 1839 and captain in 1842). In the 1840s, he saw service in four provinces in addition to his native Bahia. Manoel Luciano da Câmara Guaraná, who belonged to a much younger generation of officers, demonstrates the same career pattern. He volunteered for Bahia's infantry in 1832 and rose up the noncommissioned hierarchy before his commissioning in 1842. His promotion entailed a transfer to another unit; five more transfers followed in the next thirteen years, as Guaraná rose to the rank of captain. Transfers among units and redeployments of units within Brazil resulted in nine interprovincial moves for Guaraná between 1837 and 1855 and gave him service experience in six different provinces.[113]

Army education was similarly nationalized. Late-colonial officer training had consisted primarily of mathematics classes conducted in the artillery regiments and less formal apprenticeships for infantry and cavalry officers. The departure of Bahia's artillery during the Cisplatine War put an end to these classes, leaving some officers without the required theoretical training for promotion.[114] With the return of Bahia's units in the 1830s, classes resumed in Salvador; while not in prison, Daniel Gomes de Freitas attended them.[115] Through the 1830s, officer education thus remained a local affair, and as late as 1838, only 4 of the 130 students in Rio de Janeiro's military academy hailed from Bahia.[116] In the 1840s, the imperial government took firm control of artillery education, consolidating it in the capital. More and more Bahians enrolled in the academy, judging by requests for passage to Rio de Janeiro. Semestral reports from the Fourth Foot Artillery reveal the rapid progress made in educating its officers by 1847. Thirteen of its 32 officers had completed all or part of the Rio academy's artillery course; only 8 had no formal education whatsoever and the commander recommended that they be transferred to other branches. A dozen of the unit's 31 cadets were enrolled in the academy.[117] As this battalion lost its Bahian complexion, its officers and cadets gained the common experience of education in Rio de Janeiro, which, like the imperial law schools, trained a national elite.[118] To be sure, infantry and cavalry education lagged behind that of the artillery and continued to resemble the apprenticeships of the colonial years; nevertheless, the transfer of officers among battalions and the rotation of battalions among garrisons affected the infantry and cavalry in the same way that it did the artillery.

For Bahia's officers, the Regresso initiated a complete overhaul of their professional lives. In the 1840s, promotions resumed in orderly fashion, careers took them away from Salvador, and transfers of officers among battalions sapped units' provincial ties. For artillery officers, Rio de Janeiro emerged as the center of military education. These changes had important implications for both officers' personal lives and state–society relations in Bahia.

Officers and Society

In 1839, Bahia's commander of arms received orders to raise a new cavalry squadron to replace the unit disbanded earlier in the decade. It proved to be a difficult task and he lamented "the repugnance of the best people of this country" for service as army officers.[119] Thirty years earlier, members of the planter class had competed for the privilege of outfitting such units. In the interim, profound changes had taken place in both the relationship of the planter class to the officer corps (and the state more generally) and in the social composition of the officer corps. The construction of a national army made military service a far less attractive career for members of the Bahian elite, for lengthy absences from the provinces hindered their management of property and prevented them from dominating local affairs.

The disappearance of elite families from the officer corps had implications beyond the difficulties experienced in raising a prestigious cavalry company. Postmortem inventories reveal a significant impoverishment of officers. Although the data is somewhat skewed by the Baron of Maragogipe (an army officer who had transferred to command the militia cavalry in his native Maragogipe sometime during the 1820s), who left three plantations and 316 slaves in 1850, accounting for almost half of the value of all the property left by thirty-seven officers between 1835 and 1864, officers' wealth at death declined significantly in the nineteenth century. The twenty-nine officers who died before 1851 left estates valued on average at 15:639$603 (8:879$780 excluding the baron) while forty-seven officers who passed away in the second half of the century held property worth only 4:896$881. Their slave holding demonstrates a similar pattern: The twenty-two of twenty-nine who held slaves before 1851 owned an average of 33.9 (20.5 excluding the baron), while the twenty-four slave-owners among forty-six officers held an average of 6.7 slaves each after mid-century. When distributed by decade, the data reveal a steep decline early in the century, followed by mid-century stability and a collapse late in the century (Figure 6.1). A small number of wealthy officers prevented a more marked mid-century decline, and the Baron of Maragogipe significantly changes the results for 1845–1854.

This data suggests, and individual inventories confirm, that officers became increasingly "middle class," enjoying but a modest standard of living and depending heavily on their salaries and the state that paid them. My definition of middle class, which focuses on wealth and culture, differs from that of Nelson Werneck Sodré, whose classic study identified ninteenth-century officers as allies of a rising bourgeoisie and consequently a revolutionary force. As Celso Castro has noted, officers' standard of living (and their literacy) placed them far above the vast majority of the population; in many ways, they remained a privileged elite.[120] Officers were, however, a declining elite whose members adopted several strategies in response to the changing demands of their career. Wealthy families withdrew from the officer corps shortly after independence, and as the commander of arms discovered in 1839, none of their members could be induced to lead a new cavalry company. Less prosperous families persisted longer in the service, while the most durable officer families tended to be the poorest of those that I could trace during this period. For lack of alternatives, they remained in the corporation, a strategy that at best slowed downward social mobility.

The successors to the planter–generals who had dominated the late colonial Bahian army were men of modest means. Eight generals died in Bahia in the late 1860s and 1870, and at least five received funerals at government expense, an indication of their poverty.[121] A complete inventory of only one, a brigadier, has survived: In 1867, he left some furniture, a one-story house in Salvador, and a month's unpaid salary, together worth only 1:159$028. Another left his family only his "proverbial honor . . . and the relevant services rendered to his country."[122] Only two of these men, Marshal Alexandre Gomes de Argolo Ferrão (the Baron of Cajaíba) and his illegitimate son of the same name and rank (the Viscount of Itaparica), can be counted as

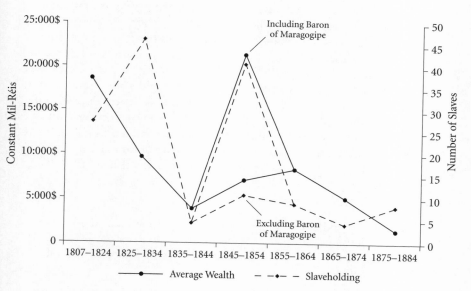

FIGURE 6.1 Officers' wealth and slaveholding at death, 1807–1884.
SOURCE: Seventy-five invs. in APEB/SJ/IT.

members of the Bahian planter class. Both died in 1870—Cajaíba after a long retirement to his plantation and Itaparica shortly after distinguishing himself in the Paraguayan War (1865–1870).[123] The other six generals include two born in Portugal and four Bahians. The Portuguese had both made clear their loyalty to Brazil at independence and suffered no handicap in their careers. Indeed, perhaps because their fathers had been generals, they rose rapidly after their enlistment as cadets in the 1810s.[124] But so did the four Bahians, three of whom served as privates before obtaining commissions.[125] All six reached superior officer rank in the 1820s, just in time to see their careers stall in the 1830s. Nevertheless, they retained a strong commitment to their profession, while more well-off fellow officers sought leaves or retired, often citing the need to manage plantations.[126] As these men were gaining influence within the army, it was losing its importance within the state apparatus in Bahia, and army decision making moved to Rio de Janeiro. In short, they had little to offer the Bahian elite, which turned its attention to filling the rapidly growing judiciary and the new National Guard. Furthermore, by the 1840s, their careers would take most of them away from Salvador for extended periods. As full-time and only moderately influential government employees, the Bahian generals had little opportunity for enrichment.

While a handful of officers maintained a comfortable standard of living, will after will proclaims officers' poverty. Major Cipriano Xavier de Jesus, for example, advised his heirs in 1831:

> "I do not have, and therefore do not leave, money of any kind, nor gold, nor silver, nor [precious] stones . . . for I live solely from my salary which, only through [my] thrift, suffices to cover my expenses. . . . I have not given my wife anything of value".[127]

Four decades later, his son, Second Lieutenant João Antônio Xavier, left his widow and six children only a house on the verge of collapse in Salvador's suburbs.[128] Inventories of poor officers abound. Some are little more than the formality required by the paymaster for heirs to collect a few weeks' worth of unpaid salary, the deceased's only asset. Early in the century, poorer officers might still own a domestic slave or two; later, they were more likely to keep small sums in bonds or bank accounts. They usually owned some furniture; at best, one or two pieces of jewelry (sometimes pawned); and occasionally a one-story house or a small farm in Salvador's suburbs. Settling accounts with shopkeepers, doctors, pharmacists, and other creditors usually ate up most of the estate, obliging heirs to sell slaves or real estate.[129]

Economic strategies of poor officers focused on the state, the source of their livelihood. Second Lieutenant Xavier unsuccessfully requested retirement in the next grade in 1840 on the grounds of ill health. Like many other retired officers, he later sought another government job to supplement his pension, which he judged inadequate to support his large family.[130] A retired first lieutenant declared in 1851 that he supported his nine illegitimate children on his pension and salary as doorman at the paymaster's office.[131] When there were insufficient sinecures for poverty-stricken officers, the army let them reside in the spare rooms of Salvador's numerous forts.[132] A few went into business. One put a slave to work in his *botequim*, the food and drink stands still ubiquitous along Salvador's streets.[133] Recognizing that he could not expect further advance in 1833, a first lieutenant cast about for alternatives. He tried his hand at brewing beer, considered distilling, went prospecting when he heard rumors of gold in Salvador's suburbs, and finally settled down as a bookbinder.[134]

Rich and poor officers alike, however, were not isolated individuals—only a handful died without any heirs or relatives—and they must be seen in the context of their families; indeed, the army recognized the importance of family ties in the institution of cadetship. Because it only mentions sons who followed their fathers into the military, however, the documentation left by cadetship has led many historians to refer to military families; one even posits the emergence of a "general (and perhaps officer) caste" by the second half of the nineteenth century.[135] This issue has already been examined for the late colonial period (Chapter 2); because the changes in officer duties as the corporation became a national one seem tailor-made for the creation of an officer caste, the question must be revisited.

There are actually few signs to indicate that officers constituted a caste. Cadetship was but a weak predictor of future commissioning as an officer. The proliferation of cadets after the 1820 reform turned them into a privileged class of enlisted men rather than officers in training. Once recognized, either concurrently with enlistment or sometime thereafter, cadets merely enjoyed preferential treatment as soldiers. Despite their insignia, social access to officers, and exemption from corporal punishment and onerous duties, cadets remained soldiers. So many men had been recognized as cadets in the cavalry squadron in 1841 that insufficient privates remained to guard and clean the stables.[136] The obligation of first cadets' fathers to support their sons with an allowance of 130$000 per year reinforced cadets' distinction from enlisted men and sometimes burdened parents. One father solved the problem of maintaining a cadet in Alagoas by sending a slave to accompany his son.[137] Cadetship was, however, often a poor investment. The 1820 reform produced far more cadets than could be commissioned and the rank quickly lost the attributes of nobility that it had in the colonial period. Cadets and sergeants alike competed for entry into the military academy and for recommendation for promotion. Certainly cadets were more likely to be promoted to second lieutenant than noncommissioned officers; in the 1855 national promotion, for example, sixty-six cadets and only fourteen sergeants were commissioned second lieutenant.[138] Cadets' social origins rendered it more likely that they would be literate and have the social skills that smoothed their advance. Nonetheless, enlisted men like Manoel Luciano da Câmara Guaraná could aspire to promotion far up the officer hierarchy. Despite these advantages, many— probably most—cadets failed to reach the rank of second lieutenant. Some chose other careers. Others proved incompetent. A lieutenant colonel's son twice failed the Military Academy's first-year course and returned to Bahia to serve out his enlistment in 1848. In 1847, a cadet gave his commander "little hope" for the future because he "loved his creature comforts" (*é amigo de seu cômodo*); another performed his duties so sloppily that he was "a perfect distraction" to his commanders.[139] In short, cadetship offered no guarantee of a commission, as the many cadets who served for decades without obtaining a lieutenancy discovered.[140] To the extent that it attracted men into the army who might otherwise not have enlisted (given the low status of service in the ranks), cadetship permitted the army to select its officers from a wider pool of candidates who had proved themselves as enlisted men.

Few families can be characterized as truly "military" for more than a generation or two. Rather, they entered and left the corporation in response to the decline of the army's importance in the state apparatus and the changing demands of the officer career. Marriage ties among officers were rare: just five of sixty-one adult daughters of officers mentioned in seventy-six inventories had married their fathers' colleagues (of the other fifty-six daughters, twenty-eight were married to civilians, twenty-seven were unmarried, and one had entered a convent). The fractional genealogies that follow show class-specific patterns of family participation in the military. As elite families splintered or died out, their main branches withdrew from the military shortly after independence, while their poorer cousins were more likely to remain in the army. Military families of modest means persisted in the service until mid-century, while poor families, most likely to constitute military clans, experienced great difficulty in maintaining their position.

A partial genealogy of the Vilasboas family (Figure 6.2) illustrates both the strategies for concentrating wealth and an elite family's gradual withdrawal from the army. The Baron of Maragogipe, an army officer and militia

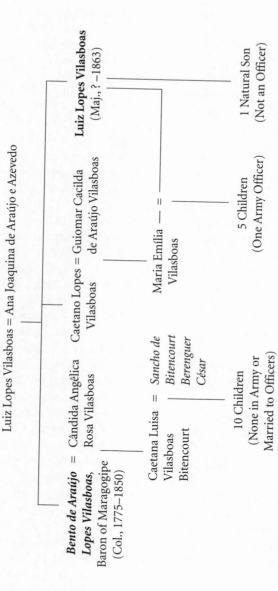

FIGURE 6.2 The *Vilasboas* family. Bold denotes regular army officers; italics denote militia or ordenanças officers.

SOURCES: Invs. in APEB/SJ/IT: Baron of Maragogipe, 01/95/136/01; Luiz Lopes Vilasboas, 08/3354/09.

colonel, left three complete sugar plantations in 1850. His brother, Major Luiz Lopes Vilasboas, who remained in the regular army, left an estate worth slightly more than one-fourth that of his ennobled brother, a substantial part of which consisted of a share in a sugar mill of which he had not yet taken possession. Even his marriage to his niece, which would have permitted him to inherit from a third brother, not an army officer, did not bring his fortune up to the level of the baron. By mid-century, none of the colonel's grandchildren had entered the army or married an officer, while only one of the major's sons was an officer in 1863. The main branches of the Vilasboas family left the military while those who would not inherit their principal assets persisted longer in the service, a pattern discerned among the Bahian planter elite generally by James Wetherell, who lamented their dispersal through the empire as sons relied "on their father's friends to procure for themselves civil or military employment."[141]

In contrast, the Baltazar da Silveira family lingered in the army through mid-century, despite (or because of) declining fortunes. Their nominal hereditary nobility—all the male members of the family bore the honorific "Dom"—protected neither their wealth nor their army rank. Most members of this family have already been discussed: Dom Carlos, married to a merchant's daughter and the artillery lieutenant colonel whose technical knowledge was found wanting in 1788; the elder Dom Luiz, the reputed "wimp" in 1822; and Dom Brás, the Cachoeira militia colonel who placed his sons, Dom José and the younger Dom Luiz, in the army during the independence war. None of Brigadier Dom Carlos's sons and grandsons attained his grade and wealth (Figure 6.3 and Table 6.1); by 1870, none of Dom José's nephews (to whom he left his property) and Dom Carlos's great-grandsons had chosen a military career, although all could easily have claimed cadet status. Several factors explain the professional and economic decline of the Baltazar da Silveira's third generation. The younger Dom Carlos's commitment to a career in Bahia (at a time when careers required officers to serve throughout Brazil), clear in an 1847 petition against transfer out of Bahia, where he would "better reconcile the interests of the service with his own," and his eventual ill health hindered his advance.[142] His older brother, Dom José, whose earlier enlistment permitted him to rise rapidly in the 1820s, spent ten years away from Bahia in the late 1830s and early 1840s before returning as a major to command the recruitment depot in 1847. A "good officer," according to none other than Emperor Pedro II himself, Dom José retained this post until 1865, when he led an infantry battalion from Salvador into the Paraguayan War. He enjoyed sufficient status to marry a daughter of the

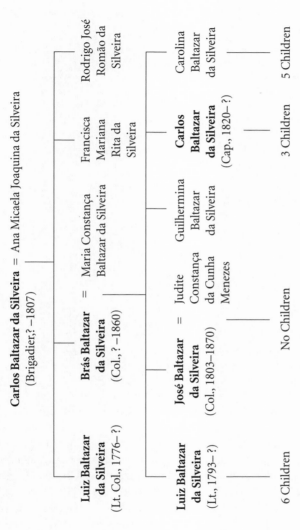

Carlos Baltazar da Silveira = Ana Micaela Joaquina da Silveira
(Brigadier, ? –1807)

Luiz Baltazar da Silveira (Lt. Col., 1776–?)

Brás Baltazar da Silveira (Col., ? –1860) = Maria Constança Baltazar da Silveira

Rodrigo José Romão da Silveira

Luiz Baltazar da Silveira (Lt., 1793–?)

José Baltazar da Silveira (Col., 1803–1870) = Judite Constança da Cunha Menezes

Guilhermina Baltazar da Silveira

Francisca Mariana Rita da Silveira

Carlos Baltazar da Silveira (Cap., 1820–?)

Carolina Baltazar da Silveira

6 Children   No Children   3 Children   5 Children

FIGURE 6.3 The Baltazar da Silveira Family. Bold denotes army officers.

SOURCES: Invs. in APEB/SJ/IT: Carlos Baltazar da Silveira, 01/99/144/01; Brás Baltazar da Silveira, 07/2823/02; José Baltazar da Silveira, 07/3029/07; will, J. B. Silveira, 20 Jan. 1865, APEB/SJ/IT, 05/2189/2658/08; FOs in AHE/FO: Luiz Baltazar da Silveira (uncle and nephew), II-21-176; J. B. Silveira, IV-22-104; C. B. Silveira, II-11-84; FOs in AHE/RQ: C. B. Silveira, C-29-850; B. B. Silveira, AHE/RQ, B-46-1281.

TABLE 6.1

Declining Fortunes: The Baltazar da Silveira Family's Wealth
at Death, 1807–1870

| Name and Year of Death | Value of Estate | Number of | | | Cash and Bonds |
		Slaves	Urban Houses	Suburban Farms	
Carlos Baltazar da Silveira, Brigadier, 1807	24:813$301	35	4	2	0
Brás Baltazar da Silveira, Colonel, 1860	21:851$848	18	3	1	0
José Baltazar da Silveira, Colonel, 1870	13:351$104	0	2	0	4:670$671

NOTES: Constant 1822 mil-réis deflated by sterling exchange rate; includes slaves freed by testamentary provisions.

SOURCES: Invs. in APEB/SJ/IT: C. B. Silveira, 01/99/144/01; B. B. Silveira, 07/2823/02; J. B. Silveira, 07/3029/07.

Baron of Rio Vermelho, but apparently did not benefit materially from this alliance.[143]

As elite families withdrew from the officer corps, poorer families remained, although they faced many of the same problems that dogged the Baltazar da Silveiras. All six of Surgeon Major Manoel Coelho dos Santos's sons entered the army at the rank of cadet (Figure 6.4). Their two sisters apparently had not married by 1860. Neither wealthy nor particularly successful in their careers, the Coelho dos Santos brothers are perhaps typical of the empire's military families, descended from men who left their sons only the status of cadet. As a result, the brothers had to work for their living. Antônio, Custódio, and Francisco spent years on campaign in the South,

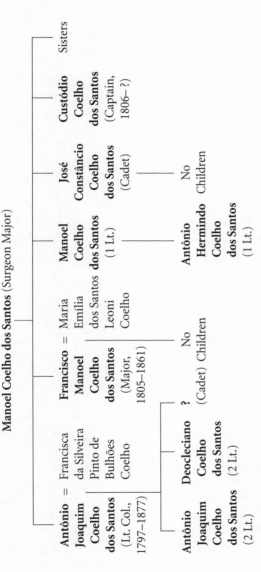

Manoel Coelho dos Santos (Surgeon Major)

António Joaquim Coelho dos Santos (Lt. Col., 1797–1877) = Francisca da Silveira Pinto de Bulhões Coelho	**Francisco Manoel Coelho dos Santos** (Major, 1805–1861) = Maria Emília dos Santos Leoni Coelho	**Manoel Coelho dos Santos** (1 Lt.)	**José Constâncio Coelho dos Santos** (Cadet)	**Custódio Coelho dos Santos** (Captain, 1806–?)	Sisters

António Joaquim Coelho dos Santos (2 Lt.) — **Deocleciano Coelho dos Santos** (2 Lt.)

? (Cadet) — No Children

António Hermindo Coelho dos Santos (1 Lt.) — No Children

FIGURE 6.4 The Coelho dos Santos family. Bold denotes army officers or cadets.

SOURCES: FOs in AHE/FO: Custódio Coelho dos Santos, II-12-13; Manoel Coelho dos Santos, VI-1-95; reqs. in AHE/RQ: C. C. Santos, C-63-1805; Francisco Manoel Coelho dos Santos, F-105-2901; Antônio Joaquim Coelho dos Santos (father), A-107-3156; Francisca da Silveira Pinto de Bulhões, F-7-297; cadet recognition file, A. J. C. Santos (father), AHE/RC, caixa 83, S-174; inv., F. M. C. Santos, APEB/SJ/IT, 03/1088/1557/02.

longing to return to Bahia. Francisco wrote his wife from Santa Catarina in 1839: "If I survive, I do not intend to tarry long, for I no longer have the patience to tolerate so many hardships."[144] On leave in Salvador in 1857, Custódio implored the war minister for a transfer to the local garrison, noting that "it is impossible for me to live in a cold country."[145] Ill health— in Francisco's case, insanity[146]—plagued the family, as did incompetence. Imprisoned for three years after the Periquitos' Revolt, Antônio returned to active service and in 1837 fought against the Sabinada. Nevertheless, "his bad, criminal, and negligent conduct" prompted the commission of the late 1830s to put him on the retired list. Although he returned to active service in the 1840s, one superior later judged him "so ignorant in all that pertains to military life that I do not consider him capable of anything." Eventually he outlived his detractors, earned promotions by seniority and ended his career in a sinecure, the command of Salvador's gunpowder depot. Despite the assistance of his son, retired Second Lieutenant Deocleciano, who did the depot's paperwork, the president recommended that Lieutenant Colonel Antônio be relieved of the post in 1877.[147] Two more of his sons joined the army, as can be inferred from his widow's request that one of them (a cadet) be transferred to Salvador to care for her in 1883.[148]

Only one inventory from the family, Francisco's, has survived. In 1861, he left a one-story house, two slaves, and furniture, all worth 3:304$729. The bitter fight between his widow and Francisco's surviving brothers over this modest estate, which turned on the status of the property that she had inherited from her parents and her gift of a young slave (now a valuable adolescent) to her niece in 1851, is a clear indicator of the brothers' poverty. The root of the problem lay in Francisco's long absences from Salvador and his failure to give formal authorization to his wife to manage his goods. The brothers argued that she had sold and given away property against Francisco's will, but the courts ruled that he had given informal consent.[149]

The Coelho dos Santos brothers, members of an ordinary military family, illustrate the transformation of the officer corps. Neither rich, well born, nor especially talented, the brothers entered the army for lack of alternatives, claiming their status as cadets. Like their richer counterparts, their material wealth suffered as their careers dragged them away from Salvador. And for lack of options, Antônio's sons followed their father into the army, at a time when more well-off families had long since left the corporation. For them, entry into the officer corps staved off downward social mobility as they struggled to maintain a middle-class existence.

Durable upward social mobility in the officer corps is difficult to document. Personal ability, assiduous attendance at the artillery regiment's school, and the favorable career prospects of the 1810s and 1820s probably facilitated the orphaned Cipriano Xavier de Jesus's rise from private to major by 1831, which he proudly recounted in his will, even as he emphasized his continuing poverty. He could not, however, pass on his career success to his sons—one entered the provincial civil service; a second was a thirty-year-old cadet with little prospect of advancement in 1831 (he still held the rank in 1847); and the third was the second lieutenant who left his family only a shack.[150]

The social mobility visible in the Bahian officer corps raises serious doubts about characterizations of it as a caste. When all officers are considered—and not just generals—the corps resembles the English aristocracy, which Lawrence Stone describes as "a bus or hotel, always full, but always filled with different people." The great military families of army hagiography may, in fact, be unusual when set in the context of the entire officer corps.[151] Its growth in the 1810s and 1820s and the promotion of sergeants to lieutenant throughout the nineteenth century brought in new families to replace those who dropped out. Through cadetship, these men's sons had privileged, though neither exclusive nor guaranteed, access to the officer corps. The disappearance of the planter-generals from the Bahian officer corps and the incorporation of the Bahian army into the Brazilian army impoverished the Bahian officer corps, which came to constitute a component of the middle class, its members dependent on the state for their often precarious livelihood.

Officers recognized the changes taking place in their world, struggling to comprehend them within the ideology of service and reward left to them by the colonial regime. A second lieutenant requested retirement in 1845 "to escape obligations that appear . . . incompatible, namely those of a married man and proprietor . . . and an active-duty army officer."[152] While colonial officership had rested on a patriarchal partnership between officers and the monarchy, the empire's national army displayed limited tolerance for such nonmilitary interests. Tension between these "incompatible obligations" permeates postindependence army-officer discourse, reflecting the material changes in their professional lives. The nationalization of their careers and their impoverishment rendered difficult, even impossible, the fulfillment of social roles other than that of army officer.

Emphatic declarations in officers' petitions equating military service with familial obligations underscore the degree to which it was becoming impossible to reconcile these aspects of their lives. A Bahian lieutenant serving in Rio Grande do Sul in 1839 requested a transfer back to Salvador because "the petitioner's family has great need of his presence," arguing that "any paterfamilias [*pai de família*] performs no lesser service in educating his children, turning them into good citizens."[153] Such petitions offer glimpses of a discussion among officers about the appropriate balance between personal interests and royal service. The transformation of the officer career lent urgency to this debate. As long as officers could expect to spend their entire careers in Salvador, they could readily reconcile personal and professional obligations; by the 1840s, this was no longer possible for those who wished to (or had to) pursue their careers. Officers with means could resolve the problem of competing interests by abandoning the army; many wealthy men did so. Those who remained faced a corporation increasingly intolerant of their extraprofessional concerns. When Francisco Manoel Coelho dos Santos requested transfer to Bahia in 1849, citing his fifteen-year absence which "brought disadvantages to his family and interests," his request was curtly dismissed: "he has the option of resigning his commission if he is fed up with military service."[154]

Military service quickly lost its lustre for Lieutenant Francisco de Paula Bahia, the only known mulatto militia officer to obtain a regular commission in reward for independence-war services. Serving in Rio Grande do Sul in 1829 when he learned of the death of his father, Bahia sought a transfer back to Salvador in order to take charge of "a numerous family"; unable to obtain it, he requested and received a discharge.[155] In contrast, the Coelho dos Santos brothers felt unable to take this step. Although they might complain, they had therefore to adapt to the new terms of service. Scattered evidence suggests that other officers did so as well, calling on colleagues to help mitigate the hardships of distant service by acting as agents for them, collecting dependents' pay and allowances, or submitting petitions on their behalf.[156]

The Bahian officers who remained in the army at mid-century demonstrated a greater loyalty to the corporation and to Brazil than had their predecessors. Fewer had social and economic ties to Bahia. Some, like Ladislau dos Santos Titara, cut them altogether. His use of "pátria" (homeland) and his literary production closely reflect the evolution of his career. In 1839, this second lieutenant presented the Instituto Histórico e Geográfico Brasileiro (Brazilian Historical and Geographical Institute) with the second volume of his epic poem, *Paraguaçu*, on the independence struggle in his native province, referring to Bahia as his pátria. Fifteen years later, a captain settled and married in Rio Grande do Sul, he offered his recently written history of the 1851–1852 campaign against Buenos Aires to the Institute, claiming to have been "solely guided by the love of [his] *pátria*," whose "honor and glory" and military exploits he had recorded for posterity.[157] Brazil was now his pátria. Titara's professional and intellectual trajectory—he died a major in Rio de Janeiro in 1861—embodies the evolution of the nineteenth-century army. The nationalization of the officer corps turned this Bahian literary patriot into a Brazilian nationalist writer. How many other officers shared his intellectual experience is not clear but the disappearance of petitions calling for a reconciliation of different types of service after mid-century is indicative of the new type of officer—poorer, more dependent on his salary, and more exclusively committed to the corporation.

From the exploits of Daniel Gomes de Freitas to the travails of the hapless Coelho dos Santos family, this chapter has ranged widely over the terrain of early-imperial army history. National Brazilian politics increasingly affected Bahia in the 1820s and 1830s, as the struggles among Exaltados, Moderados, and Caramurus led to transformations in the state apparatus. Emperor Pedro I's efforts to build a national army in the 1820s proved ephemeral, as the Moderado-dominated Regency dramatically cut the army size, returned army units to their home provinces, and chose to rely for security on civilian institutions such as the new police and the National Guard. Deeply embroiled in the radical politics of the early 1830s, a significant group of Bahia's officers advocated radical liberal reform; some took up arms to institute it. In the Sabinada, this radical project converged with a more mainstream army-officer position, one that rejected the Regency's military reforms as an attack on the army's corporate interests.

The Sabinada's defeat finally put an end to military rebelliousness in Bahia. Soon thereafter, the Regresso, with its emphasis on reestablishing order and centralizing power, built a national army, one whose officers lost ties to their provinces of origin. In their peripatetic careers, officers came to serve throughout the empire, and army battalions began rotating among provinces. These career changes impoverished the officer corps, as well-off families withdrew from the corporation, leaving fewer officers with significant material interests outside of the corporation.

Caught up in a process that they rarely controlled or influenced directly, Bahian officers experienced firsthand the painful and disorienting construction of a national Brazilian state apparatus. By mid-century, the national army matched the judiciary as a key institution of the imperial regime. To be sure, the mature empire was a civilian regime, and for the most part, Brazilian officers demonstrated an exemplary professional subordination to civilian authorities until the 1880s, even as the corporation was generally ignored.[158] It was, however, precisely this subordination that best suited the Bahian and Brazilian planter class. An army at the center of politics, such as Bahia's garrison in 1831–1833 or in 1837–1838, could only threaten their long-term interests. With the collapse of planter control over the Bahian army during the independence war, the only alternative was to cede control of the corporation to the central state. If that meant abandoning local autonomy and federalism for the sake of collective class interests, then it was a small price to pay. These larger considerations shaped officers' lives and also affected enlisted men's experience, the subject of the next chapter.

CHAPTER 7

Reforming the Rank and File

In February 1840, Santo Amaro's justice of the peace impressed José Inácio, a creole locally known as "Deputy." The man had earned his nickname for a remarkable political act in 1831. During the anti-Portuguese riots of that year, José, then a slave, had gone to the town council chambers, where he took a seat along with other patriots demanding the expulsion of Portuguese nationals. When challenged, he responded "that he was a citizen," beating on the table with an illegal dagger (*faca de ponta*), or according to the justice of the peace, driving the blade into the table.[1] Whether Deputy actually served in the army is not known, for it is virtually impossible to link recruitment notices to army data on individual soldiers. Nevertheless, the anecdote constitutes a fruitful starting point for an examination of recruitment, discipline, and the experience of enlisted men after independence, when liberal reform and the construction of a national army began to affect their lives.

Deputy's story is full of perverse ironies. At the time that he claimed citizenship, he could not have been impressed, for he was a slave. Moreover, before 1837, he might also have been spared enlistment on the grounds that he was a creole; racial preferences in recruitment were not abolished until that year. The 1824 constitution had obligated all Brazilians to defend the empire—making military service an attribute of citizenship—yet most enlisted men were impressed, often as punishment for vagrancy and other nonpolitical crimes. While Deputy claimed citizenship in the form of participation in deliberations over the future of his community, he received it in the form of impressment, which then led to six years of badly paid military service and subjection to corporal punishment, likely on one of Brazil's remote southern frontiers.

Unraveling some of these knotty contradictions is the aim of this chapter. The first section examines the failure to institute meaningful recruitment reform. While many liberal reformers found impressment offensive, they undertook few measures to modify it during their legislative ascendancy from the late 1820s to the mid-1830s. Nevertheless, the extensive debates about recruitment reform reveal much about deputies' understandings of citizenship and the role of patronage in Brazilian society. Liberals' only significant achievement was the reduction of the army's strength by more than two-thirds from the late 1820s to the early 1830s, a measure that effectively obviated the need for recruitment during most of these years. The Regresso's expansion of the army in the late 1830s and 1840s caused recruitment levels to increase significantly. The impact of these developments on recruitment practice in Bahia is the subject of the next section. Besides responding to the central state's demand for manpower, recruitment was also affected by the willingness and capacity of local authorities to impress vigorously. Indeed, the triangular relationship among state, local elites, and the free poor that had characterized colonial recruitment continued unchanged, save that critics of impressment gained a greater hearing.

A third section examines the rank and file's social composition. Amid the background noise generated by impressment, which so resembled that of the colonial period, it is easy to miss the changes in the army's social composition caused by the 1837 lifting of the color bar in recruitment, the shortening of service terms, and the Bahian garrison's incorporation into the emerging Brazilian army. Scattered quantitative evidence permits a systematic examination of these developments and their implications.

The failure to reform military discipline by abolishing corporal punishment or modernizing the army's discipline code strikingly parallels the failure of recruitment reform. It is of course not surprising that Brazilians should have retained corporal punishment in the armed forces, for European countries still practiced it, but real changes took place, particularly in the larger Brazilian societal context, in which corporal punishment became less and less acceptable, even as continued disdain for soldiers impeded its abolition. Unable to reform discipline at the highest level, the army undertook a number of lesser but still significant measures in Salvador's garrison to undermine soldiers' autonomy and shift the terms of negotiation over military discipline in the corporation's favor. Soldiers' rejection of corporal punishment and other aspects of military discipline is clearly visible in the

1831 mutiny and in the continuing high desertion rates. Finally, this chapter concludes with an examination of soldiers' relationship to urban society in the context of changing recruitment and discipline patterns. Frontline representatives of the state, soldiers faced the difficult task of policing the city while respecting the race and class hierarchies that their very existence threatened, one last irony that the case of Deputy casts into sharp relief.

Recruitment Reform: The Interminable Debate

As Pedro I was gradually moving toward a break with Portugal, he issued a new set of instructions for recruitment in July 1822. Initially applicable only to Rio de Janeiro, but extended to the rest of the empire in 1826, the instructions codified colonial practice and remained in force until 1875. In 18 articles, the document identified the classes of men subject to recruitment and expressed the government's goal of protecting those who performed what it perceived to be economically and socially necessary functions, thereby safeguarding the well-being of the larger society. Reprising the ambiguous colonial wording about race, the instructions subjected to forced recruitment all "single white, and also freed mulatto men [*pardos libertos*]" ages eighteen to thirty-five. Men in this age group who engaged in useful economic activities, however, were to be exempt: slave drivers, cowboys, artisans, coachmen, sailors, fishermen, one son of each farmer (*lavrador*), a certain number of clerks in each commercial establishment, and students. In addition to married men, the instructions also protected the older brother responsible for minor orphans and one son to support each widow. Properly enlisted and uniformed militiamen were also exempt, but the instructions qualified all of the exemptions with the clause, "only as long as they actually practice their trades and demonstrate good behavior."[2]

The July 1822 instructions are a quintessentially colonial document: Nothing in the text hints at the liberal principles that by virtue of João VI's recognition of the Cortes earlier that year nominally governed Brazil. Rather, the document unabashedly reiterated colonial recruitment prescriptions that sought to perpetuate and reinforce social hierarchies and patronage networks by leaving authorities broad leeway to interpret the law. Not only did this legislation direct recruiters away from the economically active, it also sought to encourage the "idle" and "vagrant" to seek the service of an employer or a militia commander and offered police and judicial authorities a convenient summary punishment that effectively removed "criminals" from their jurisdiction. Furthermore, some of the exemptions were less significant than they might seem: In a country in which only a small proportion of the population married in church, for example, the exemption of one widow's son protected only the few who had attained that level of social respectability.[3]

By the terms of the 1824 constitution, setting the army's strength and authorizing recruitment were parliament's prerogative.[4] In the 1826 parliamentary session, deputies passed several measures that, at the time, were intended to be temporary but ended up becoming permanent features of imperial Brazilian recruitment legislation. Furthermore, the debate reveals much about how liberal legislators reconciled themselves to forced recruitment. An especially brutal Cisplatine-War recruitment drive in Ceará (during which authorities took advantage of drought-induced dislocation to impress thousands of refugees in that province) lent urgency to deputies' work; one was even moved to tears at the suffering of recruits on troop transports arriving at the capital. Such "scenes of horror," he declared, were "unbelievable . . . in the nineteenth century, when we say that we have a constitutional system to govern us."[5]

Frustrated at the war ministry's inability or unwillingness to supply information about the army's condition, deputies quickly gave up hope of introducing significant reforms in recruitment during this session. Instead, they sought to assert legislative control over recruitment in a bill that extended the 1822 instructions to all of Brazil. Its sponsor, Brigadier Raimundo José da Cunha Matos, then Brazil's leading military expert, presented it as a temporary measure which would at least prevent the worst of the "arbitrary, despotic, and violent acts" perpetrated by recruiters by applying what he later called the "wise and wholesome instructions" to the entire country.[6] As far as Cunha Matos and his supporters were concerned, anything was better than the lack of legal sanction for recruitment, and late in the session, the instructions were incorporated into the law that set the army's strength for 1827–1828. Moreover, in this bill, deputies also mandated that recruitment be the responsibility of civilian presidents, not military governors of arms. No citizen, as a deputy explained, ought to be subject to military jurisdiction unless he were properly enlisted.[7]

In the second reading of the bill that sought to extend the 1822 instruction to all of Brazil, the liberal deputy Bernardo Pereira de Vasconcelos proposed to replace the clause "free whites, and also freed mulattoes" with "men." No debate about this amendment was recorded, but just before it was put to a vote, another deputy proposed that "men" be replaced with "Brazilian citizens." This wording passed, but then the Bahian deputy, José

Lino Coutinho, remembered that the constitution obliged all "Brazilians" to take up arms in defense of the empire, which terms the bill was now modifying. The observation set off a quick exchange about the meaning of the two terms. Some held that they were synonymous but Vasconcelos reminded legislators of the differences between active and passive citizens—those Brazilians who could vote and hold office and those excluded from the franchise by virtue of the constitution's income requirements for suffrage—and underscored that African freedmen were not citizens. Here Vasconcelos was apparently responding to an earlier suggestion that the article be re-worded so as to subject African freedmen to impressment. By this point, the debate was clearly out of order, and the Speaker advised deputies to fix the wording in the third reading. This clause was never again debated, however, and the bill died when the instructions were incorporated, without amendments, into the law that set the army's strength for 1827–1828.[8]

After 1826, to my knowledge, deputies never again discussed colonial racial preferences in recruitment, although they clearly remained on the books and were reiterated as late as 1836.[9] Cunha Matos presented a bill in 1827 that subjected to recruitment all "Brazilian-born free" men, but it apparently never reached the floor, and the debate over the clause in an 1831 bill that would have done the same includes no references to the racial preferences of the 1822 instructions that would have been modified by it.[10] In August 1837, when the continuing rebellions in Rio Grande do Sul and Pará demanded supplementary recruitment in excess of that authorized for the fiscal year, deputies passed a brief bill that subjected "Brazilian citizens" ages eighteen to thirty-five to recruitment, unless they enjoyed the 1822 ex-emptions, and permitted the impressed to present substitutes or buy their exemption for 400$000. Although race was never mentioned in this debate, the change of wording from the 1822 instructions was taken by the Regresso government to mean that "*pretos crioulos*" should not be exempt from re-cruitment and later commentators presented this executive decision as the measure that ended racial discrimination in recruitment.[11]

The brief debate over who should be subject to recruitment in 1826, however, reveals several important points about legislators' understandings of citizenship. As noncitizens, Africans could be easily excluded from the army.[12] Military service ought not fall solely on active citizens and legislation needed to declare explicitly that passive citizens were subject to military ser-vice as well. The status of Brazilian-born freed and free-born blacks was more ambiguous and their exclusion from recruitment marked them as less than even passive citizens under the law (just as in the colonial period, however, this exclusion was, paradoxically, a privilege that many an impressed man would have welcomed).

Forced recruitment, although widely condemned for its arbitrariness, was nevertheless broadly accepted. As Antônio Francisco de Paula e Holanda Cavalcanti de Albuquerque explained, it was actually constitutional, for those impressed had already "committed an act of omission" by failing to volunteer to defend the nation! With such attitudes prevailing even among even liberal deputies like Holanda Cavalcanti—who in later sessions emerged as one of the most eloquent and vocal critics of impressment even as he evolved from liberal to restorationist to supporter of the Regresso, finally emerging as a leading member of the Liberal Party in the 1840s[13]—it is not surprising that they failed to reform recruitment during their legislative ascendancy from the late 1820s to the mid-1830s. None of the major reform bills (those of 1827, 1831–1833, and 1834–1835) passed, although deputies indicted impressment on myriad grounds. Europe—the ever-present reference—offered three models for Brazilian reformers to consider, as deputies frequently explained: the British system of voluntary enlistments for relatively long ten-year terms; Prussian conscription of all eligible males for short service terms, followed by their enrollment in an army reserve and then the militia, the Landwehr (the only version of the French Revolution's *levée en masse* in existence in the mid-nineteenth century); and the French practice of selecting by lot only a portion of the eligible class for seven-year terms.[14] What Brazilians called simply "conscription"—the call-up of entire classes, whether in its French Revolutionary or Prussian conservative guises—was beyond the pale; advocates of reform invariably distanced themselves from anything that smacked of the militarization of Brazilian society. Conscription, declared a legislator in 1847, was "only suitable for democratic or absolutist governments," not constitutional regimes.[15]

Reformers thus grouped themselves around two poles. A draft lottery was first presented to the legislature in 1827 by Cunha Matos and repeatedly debated in subsequent years. While the details of the lottery bills varied considerably, they all shared a basic feature—the random selection of an annual contingent of recruits from a registry of eligible men. Who should be registered, of course, was a key issue; most bills included extensive exemptions from registration (when they did not, deputies were quick to propose amendments) and permitted cash commutation of military duties. At the second pole stood the advocates of voluntary enlistment [known to Brazilians as engagement (*engajamento*), for it usually entailed some form of extra compensation to the volunteer]. Any form of obligatory military service, held one deputy in 1831, was "an act of despotism," to which others retorted that neither Brazil had the means to pay sufficiently large enlistment bonuses to attract volunteers, nor Brazilians the inclination to serve voluntarily.[16] On occasion, a minority expressed support for the continuation of impressment. After all, they argued, why spend large sums of money to attract volunteers or coerce unwilling citizens through a draft lottery when the impressment of but a few of Brazil's numerous vagrants would resolve all of the army's manpower problems?[17]

Nothing demonstrates better the inability of legislators to agree on how to reform recruitment than the fate of the 1834 bill. When first presented by the army and navy committee, the bill proposed to replace impressment with a draft lottery; it metamorphosed under amendment into an engagement bill and finally passed in a form that ensured the continuation of impressment under the terms of the 1822 instructions. This legislative boondoggle began innocuously enough. In first reading, the bill survived a challenge from a competing one that sought to establish a national system of voluntary enlistments financed by municipal councils. Second reading offered little new; legislators simply amended the original version to increase the number of men exempt from the lottery. When the bill returned for the continuation of its third reading in 1835, however, an amendment requiring that recruitment be limited to engagement passed. This forced the bill back into committee for rewriting; when it returned for a fourth reading, the manifest impracticality of an all-volunteer army at a time when rebellions were breaking out in two provinces produced a compromise that, in effect, vitiated two years of legislative work. Volunteers would have to content themselves with higher salaries and shorter service terms than impressed men; if these incentives failed to convince enough men to sign up—a certainty—then forced recruitment would be undertaken.[18]

Thus, by default, the 1822 instructions remained in force until 1874, when a draft lottery bill finally passed. In all likelihood, liberals' suspicion of armies contributed to the failure of recruitment reform. Many shared Lino Coutinho's views: "I would really like it if there were not a single regular soldier in the empire, but rather that each citizen knew how to handle [arms], so that when necessary, he can take them up and become a soldier."[19] This rejection of regular armies in principle joined with suspicions of Emperor Pedro's motives in raising battalions of foreign mercenaries and in the Cisplatine War army buildup to lead liberals into reducing the corporation's size. Their preference for placing defense in the hands of citizens through a civilian militia (the National Guard) is the subject of the next chapter; for the army, it meant dramatic cutbacks, which conveniently obviated the need for objectionable recruitment. From well over 25,000 men during the Cisplatine War, the army shrank rapidly: In 1830, legislators set the strength for 1831–1832 at 12,000, reducing it over the next years to 6,320 for 1836–1837.[20] Returning battalions to their provinces of origin was often a prelude to disbanding them; the remaining soldiers who preferred to serve elsewhere were granted transfers. Service terms were cut to four and six years, respectively, for volunteers and impressed men, while all those who had already completed their service terms were ordered discharged forthwith.[21]

After the outbreak of rebellions in Rio Grande do Sul and Pará in 1835, policy toward the army shifted slightly. The legislators who had reiterated their support for impressment by gutting the 1834–1835 recruitment reform bill authorized the government to raise the army to its full strength of 6,320 in 1836. The following year, prior to the September Regresso, the minister of war sought legislative sanction for raising the army's size by 50 percent, but managed to get only a curious (and short-lived) provision that allowed the impressment of National Guardsmen.[22] A few days after the Regresso ministry came to power on 19 September, parliament voted an increase in the army's size to 8,200 men (12,000 in extraordinary times), figures raised the following year to 12,000 and 15,000; by the middle of the 1840s, they stood at 15,000 and 20,000.[23] This military buildup required a resumption of recruitment, which continued under the terms of the 1822 instructions, modified only so as not to exclude blacks. In 1841, service terms were lengthened to six and eight years for volunteers and impressed men respectively.[24] Moreover, the Regresso initiated army deployment policies very different from those of the liberals in the early 1830s.

Throughout these years, Brazilians stood in the uncomfortable position of having a constitutional regime that retained forced recruitment, a common paradox in Latin America at the time.[25] Under the circumstances, few defended impressment outright, although as late as 1840, the war minister praised recruitment's "healthy influence," claiming that the threat of impressment aided policing, increased "dedication to work," and improved "morality" by encouraging marriages.[26] Impressment's critics, by contrast, never ceased to condemn its flaws. In 1843, a new minister expressed a widespread sentiment when he remarked that forced recruitment was "not only improper for civilized nations" but also "highly impolitic," for the men so enlisted had "no interest" in maintaining the country's "internal and external security." Moreover, he continued, illiteracy among recruits reduced the pool of men qualified to serve as noncommissioned officers. Doctors argued that the violence of impressment ruined the health of many a recruit, while demographers argued that soldiers' bachelorhood impeded population growth. Others argued that the system's arbitrariness hurt economic production, for all able-bodied men (and not just vagrants) fled when press gangs approached. In 1830, Bahia's Conselho Geral (an advisory body to the president) expressed its concern about the "unconstitutionality of recruitment," for it left citizens unsafe even in their homes, the "inviolate asylum" protected by the charter.[27]

Time and again, condemnations of the "hunting of men" (*caçada humana*), a favorite contemporary cliché, rang through the halls of parliament as opposition deputies denounced abuses to demonstrate both the administration's perfidy and the damage done to society by violent impressment. In 1843, to cite a single example, a deputy took up the case of a man dismissed from his job in the Treasury and subsequently impressed, allegedly on the request of his mother, a baroness, who thus sought to prevent him from contracting an unsuitable marriage. Government responses to such charges took two directions: Invariably ministers pledged to root out violations of the law, often assuring deputies that they had already dealt with the authorities responsible. If the matter involved a specific recruit, they called on the man in question to present proof of the legal exemption from service that he or his advocates alleged. The recruit's failure to do so, of course, implied that he had been properly impressed in the first place.[28] Hiding behind the law which, by virtue of the 1822 instructions, authorized impressment on highly subjective grounds, forced debate back onto more congenial terrain.

The efforts to vest an ultimately arbitrary form of recruitment with the trappings of legality underscore the changes that had taken place since independence. As deputies understood in 1826, impressment could not continue without legal sanction. The constitutional jurist, José Antônio Pimenta Bueno, admitted that recruitment "affected individual liberties significantly"; thus, it was "indispensible that the law, and not arbitrary actions [*arbítrio*] . . . determine the terms of forced levies." As a result, there was no shortage of law regulating recruitment—the amendments to and commentary on the 1822 instructions run to more than fifty pages in an 1870 legal manual. Nevertheless, law and constitutional principles could not be easily reconciled with forced recruitment and Pimenta Bueno quickly dropped the subject in his treatise on constitutional law.[29] The contradiction between the constitution's guarantee of no arrest without charges (*culpa*

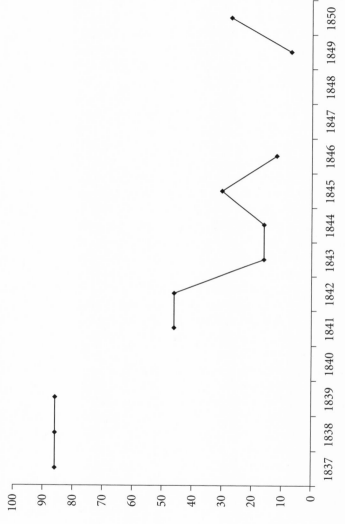

FIGURE 7.1 Recruitment Levels in Bahia, 1837–1850: Annual average number of men enlisted per month.
SOURCES: Reports on recruitment in APEB, BN/SM, AN/SPE, IGi; MG, *Relatório* (1839–1850).

formada) was quietly ignored when it came to impressment: Recruits could not appeal for habeas corpus because their arrests were presumed legal.[30]

Rather than prescribing rights that all Brazilians enjoyed or imposing burdens equally on the population, recruitment legislation served an essential hegemonic function by expressing an ideal of imperial and constitutional justice that could be selectively applied to ensure the smooth operation of patronage structures. These dynamics clearly appeared in the practice of recruitment in Bahia and the advocates of recruitment reform could not break these well-established and time-honored practices.

Recruitment Practice in Bahia

While deputies debated and tinkered with recruitment law, impressment continued in the provinces, providing grist for the mill of recruitment's critics. In Bahia, recruitment levels fluctuated dramatically in accordance with the army's size. Recognizing these fluctuations in recruitment modifies the image of a powerful state, dominating society and recruiting at will, that some have seen as characteristic of colonial and nineteenth-century Brazil. Moreover, given the challenges—to be sure, mostly rhetorical—to impressment, the practice lost some of its legitimacy, making for a complex dynamic relationship among the state, local elites, and the free poor.

After the flood of documentation during the Cisplatine War, recruitment notices virtually dry up in Bahian archives until the second half of the 1830s, when the Sabinada Rebellion's defeat prompted a surge in recruitment levels as former rebels and sympathizers were summarily removed from the province and even distant authorities such as the district judge of remote Vila Nova da Rainha ran out of handcuffs for his prisoners.[31] Between July 1837 and March 1839, the province supplied 1809 recruits (Figure 7.1) and it is clear that many more were impressed but later released.[32] This recruitment drive, exceptional in its political motives and in the broad consensus among the victors that it was essential, conveniently coincided with a period of rapid growth in the army, which readily absorbed the men.

Between the Cisplatine War and the Sabinada, however, military and civilian authorities in Bahia often seemed more concerned with implementing orders to discharge soldiers, which threatened to reduce the garrison to dangerously low levels, than with recruitment.[33] Only two brief recruitment drives were authorized during these years, one for 195 men in 1832 and another for 520 men in 1835. At least 19 volunteers responded to the proclamation that opened the former recruitment drive, but the quota proved difficult to fill. In 1833, the president received orders to reduce the garrison to 800 in the enlisted ranks, although he was permitted to recruit just enough men to maintain Salvador's two battalions at 400 men each, a responsibility that he turned over to the police, for justices of the peace were unwilling to prosecute it vigorously.[34] Indeed, these authorities sometimes even prevented volunteers from enlisting by refusing to issue the men certificates of good conduct.[35] To implement the first large recruitment drive in Bahia since the Cisplatine War, ordered in November 1835, the president commissioned special agents. While the *Diário da Bahia* angrily condemned this drive for its brutality and arbitrariness, the colonel in charge stressed that he had scrupulously adhered to the 1822 instructions, blaming his inability to impress more than 38 men in Nazaré on inclement winter weather and the flight of eligible men into the forests.[36]

In the early 1840s, recruitment took place on a more continuous basis, although authorities still spoke of the opening and closing of recruitment drives.[37] A thirteen-month drive in 1841–1842 saw 988 arrests, which produced 595 new enlistments (and caught 10 navy deserters).[38] Later in the 1840s, recruitment slowed, as might be expected by the defeat of rebellions in Rio Grande do Sul and Pará (Figure 7.1). In 1848, Bahia's president reported "much delay" in recruitment, while the war minister complained that the bans on recruitment 60 days before and 30 days after elections established in 1846 effectively prohibited impressment because of the frequency with which Brazilians went to the polls.[39] Given both these restrictions and the resistance of so many segments of society to recruitment, army authorities accepted that their battalions would rarely reach full strength, often satisfying themselves with two-thirds of their full complement, figures still difficult to maintain.[40]

Postindependence recruitment notices reflect the concerns about maintaining order expressed in the 1822 instructions, as local authorities repeatedly rid themselves of "troublemakers" by recommending that they suffer a stint in the army: "Vagrants" figure prominently among the men impressed, as do livestock rustlers and men accused of attempting to steal slaves, both of whom threatened the economic structure. Freedmen who failed to respect the masters who had liberated them (and thereby broke with the moral order of slavery) occasionally surface in recruitment notices. A final category of detainees includes violators of sexual standards, such as men who did not live with their wives or failed to keep promises of marriage after deflowering young women[41] and sometimes colorful bohemians such as the illiterate mulatto fisherman from Jaguaripe, Teodoro Ferreira Raigôzo, whom the justice of the peace described as follows: "[a] drunk, [a] rowdy, [and a] frequenter of Afro-Brazilian celebrations [*batuqueiro*] by profession. [He] is a fellow so dissolute that . . . that he has the habit of wandering naked at night [through] the streets of this town playing guitar and armed with a bottle of rum. [This is] his only occupation, even in daytime; when arrested, he was in this state".[42] The regional distribution of arrests for recruitment in the second half of 1841 also underscores the desire to keep order: more than 70 percent of the 197 men arrested were seized in Salvador and the Recôncavo, the heart of the plantation economy and its strategic urban center.[43] Here, where the police apparatus was strongest, recruitment served as an important coercive measure of last resort.

But it was only a measure of last resort. Recruitment's role in policing should not be exaggerated. Data from Rio de Janeiro, in fact, suggest that arrests for recruitment were but a tiny proportion of all arrests. In 1850, the capital's police jail received 1,676 new inmates, only 66 of whom were destined for the armed forces. Of these men, 31 were released.[44] Recruitment's limited impact derived from a simple consideration: The army could absorb only a small number of recruits each year and recruitment levels usually fluctuated in accordance with the corporation's need for soldiers. The arrest of men like Deputy and Raigôzo was merely an incidental, albeit highly beneficial, side effect of recruitment.

By maintaining a flexible and selective system of impressment, authorities assumed responsibility for maintaining the larger structures of patronage and clientage on which Brazilian society rested. Exhortations that recruiters scrupulously follow the letter of the law in impressment underscore the need to maintain an image of impartiality. Ostentatious displays of legalism and the continual release of impressed men by the provincial president, an imperial representative responsible for recruitment, but not directly involved in it, played a central role in moderating its excesses, as the hundreds of petitions received annually by his office demonstrate. Although he turned down most requests for the release of impressed men, the president corrected a sufficient number of abuses to maintain his image as an impartial authority, and more importantly, a source of patronage, just as, to cite a familiar example, eighteenth-century English gentlemen mitigated the effects of that country's law—replete with death-penalty offenses—to preserve their authority by interventions on behalf of the condemned.[45] Indeed, for this reason, the impressment of some men clearly and demonstrably exempt was probably essential to the continued viability of forced recruitment, for their later release reinforced presidential and monarchical authority.

The variable efforts of locally rooted recruiters reflected their attempt to balance dual roles as local potentates (and patrons) and agents of the central state. Although such local elites might thus hold the power to designate who would be drafted, the need to fulfill their obligations as patrons limited their ability to recruit arbitrarily. Local bosses could readily agree on the need to impress "vagrants" or to remove Sabinada rebels and sympathizers from the province. This agreement on fundamentals, however, left plenty of room for conjunctural issues such as elections and land disputes to divide local elites and separate them (or at least one faction) from the state, especially when wartime recruitment strained their reciprocal relations. In 1827, a militia cavalry captain charged with impressment accused an ordenanças captain of personally warning all eligible men to flee, "for he considered it improper that the cavalry recruit in his district." Issues other than decorum probably separated the two captains well before pressure to produce more recruits for the Cisplatine War prompted the cavalry captain to protect his own clients from the state's demands by recruiting the other's dependents. More commonly during this war, local authorities simply reported their inability to supply recruits despite their best efforts, obeying but not complying; an angry governor of arms attributed the small number of recruits to precisely such willful opposition from rural militia commanders.[46]

When steering recruiters away from their clients failed, local bosses sought the release of their dependents from the hands of recruiters. Faced with the frequent impressment of his subordinates, Salvador's National Guard commander stressed that it was his "obligation to offer protection to those who are worthy" of serving in this militia, even as he promised to turn the unworthy over to the army.[47] Recruiting agents, who claimed—and legally enjoyed—the right to impress whomever they could catch, regularly confronted National Guard officers or police subdelegates seeking to prevent such arrests.[48] In the remote and isolated interior, recruiters faced the threat of having their prisoners violently released.[49] Just as in the colonial period, behind many a complaint about impressment lay a patron's concern that one of his clients had been forcibly recruited; indeed one historian has attributed Moderados' anti-impressment rhetoric to the concerns of rural opposition groups in the capital's hinterland during the 1820s.[50] One president of Bahia, recognizing his reliance on local patrons who preferred to deflect recruitment away from their clients and recruiting agents either beholden to local elites or in constant conflict with them, attributed his inability to supply manpower to "the damned spirit of patronage that today permeates and disfigures everything."[51]

"Disfigurement" lies, of course, in the eye of the beholder and presidential fulmination against patronage leads naturally into a consideration of its beneficiaries, the free poor who constituted a third party in the tug-of-war over recruitment and who viewed patronage as a natural, necessary, and even "good" way of organizing society. Within this group, Joan Meznar has stressed the importance of the "honorable" poor, small farmers who performed their National Guard duties, fulfilled their familial obligations, and viewed army service with disdain. Stalwart clients of their planter patrons, these men reaped the rewards of their loyalty in the form of protection from recruitment. Often petty property owners in their own right but too weak to protect their farms, slaves, or cattle from the depredations of others, they were happy to see the press fall on men defined as vagrants. Indeed, they used recruitment to differentiate themselves from those whom they viewed as quite properly subject to impressment.[52] Thus, Manoel João, who claimed to have been "arbitrarily recruited" in 1848, described himself as "not one of those men [who are] the scourge of society," referring to his dutiful National Guard service and honest labor as a stonemason to justify his request for release.[53]

If protection from recruitment was thus a marker of honorable status and one of the perquisites of faithful clientage, the threat of recruitment hung over wayward clients. Coercion and force, as so many have noted, is the essential obverse of paternalism and protection in inherently unequal patron–client relations.[54] Just as local elites could protect their faithful followers, so they could also define the unfaithful as vagrants or criminals. When the "protector" of one Manoel Antônio Pereira could no longer tolerate his client's predilection for stealing from local farms and ranches, he requested that Santo Amaro's justice of the peace have him recruited in 1845. Petitions for the release of impressed men in turn contest local authorities' characterizations of the men, asserting that such assessments were the result of local political conflicts. Abuse of authority on the part of patrons, however, could result in their repudiation by clients. The latter always had the drastic option of leaving and thereby withholding their labor and services; others called upon patrons to live up to their ideals, ridiculing those who failed to do so. When Maragogipe's justice of the peace stepped down on the last day of 1838, the men whom he had been pursuing rang in the new year "playing guitars, singing, and insulting [him] in the streets where they wander with impunity."[55] In short, patrons and clients were bound together in reciprocal relations in which neither could easily violate norms.

Besides mocking unworthy and unreliable patrons, the free poor turned back to the first corner of the triangular relationship. In appealing to the presidency, these clients made good use of the competing institutions of the state apparatus, the conflicts of interest that separated men of property, and the state's need to legitimate and smooth over the rough edges of recruitment, seeking a restoration of the "justice" that all claimed to represent. To demonstrate their worthiness of this justice, petitions from the impressed stressed their respectability based on property ownership, legitimate marriage, sexual morality, and respect for authority, the lack of which were all associated with soldiers, carefully constructing, as Manoel João did, the image of an ideal member of the honorable poor.

Recruitment remained a complex tangle of social relationships. A welter of competing interests and patron–client ties that can be loosely grouped into a triangular pattern, oriented toward the state, the free poor, and local elites, produced a recruitment system that enjoyed strikingly broad support, except of course from the unfortunates actually enlisted after impressment. While liberals could readily identify the myriad ways in which impressment violated constitutional principles, advocates of recruitment reform could not cut through the patronage web without profoundly upsetting well-established social relationships.

Recruits and Soldiers: Profiling the Enlisted Ranks

While recruitment reform preoccupied legislators to an extraordinary degree considering how little they accomplished and presidents devoted much time to managing impressment, little can be learned about the enlisted men themselves from an analysis of recruitment alone. Rather, scattered quantitative evidence makes it possible to profile postindependence soldiers and trace their changing experience. In many ways, the rank and file's social composition was that which one might expect—poor, unskilled young men—but several important transformations can be documented during the first decades after independence. Both the expulsion of blacks from Salvador's battalions in the 1824–1825 purges (implicitly sanctioned by deputies when they retained the 1822 instructions) and the 1837 lifting of the color bar had important effects on Bahia's garrison, as did the shortening of service terms and the construction of a national Brazilian army after the late 1830s.

By the 1840s, contemporaries recognized notable changes in the racial composition of the rank and file. Colonel Henrique Marques de Oliveira

TABLE 7.1
Racial Patterns in Recruitment, Bahia, 1825–1849

	1825–1837		1838–1849	
	Number	*Percentage*	*Number*	*Percentage*
Preto	1	2.5	6	4.8
Crioulo	1	2.5	30	23.8
Cabra	2	5.0	28	22.2
Pardo	30	75.0	54	42.8
Mestiço	2	5.0	0	0
Branco	3	7.5	7	5.5
Indio	1	2.5	1	0.8
Total with race	40	100.0	126	99.9
No information	31		80	
Total	71		206	

SOURCES: Recruitment notices in APEB; BN/SM; AN/SPE, IG1.

Lisboa remarked: "Until 1831, we had our regular army units composed mostly of men of white or brown color [*cor branca ou parda*] and of the best-behaved sort, but since then . . . since [the creation of] the National Guard . . . almost all of our soldiers are of black color [*cor preta*]. . . [and] full of vices."[56] While Lisboa's lamentation resembles the jeremiad of an old soldier who had seen far too many changes in his lifetime, his observations can be largely confirmed in Bahian recruitment notices, in which authorities often, but not always, indicated the race of the impressed man (Table 7.1). After 1824, Bahian recruitment carefully followed the racial prescriptions of the 1822 instructions, and civilian authorities almost never presented the army with black recruits; the sole preto recruit identified between 1825 and 1837 was, incidentally, the man declined in 1825 because of his color. Special levies undertaken for the black Montevideo battalions later that year and again in 1828 further underscore the racial preference in normal recruitment.[57] There is also evidence of a nonblack garrison: The seventeen enlisted men who testified in an 1833 inquiry included six whites and eleven pardos, but no black men.[58] The 1837 ruling marked a major change, as pretos and crioulos came to constitute more than a quarter of recruits between 1838 and 1850. Mid-century visitors frequently also noted the presence of blacks in the rank and file: Alexander Marjoribanks described "nearly one-fifth" of the soldiers parading in Salvador on 2 July 1850 as "jet-black negroes," while the British minister described the bulk of the army in 1850 as "composed of free Negroes."[59]

This racial transformation—whose implications for army–society relations in Salvador will be examined below—was not the only change in the enlisted ranks after independence. Even after the Regresso lengthened service terms to six and eight years, they still stood at substantially less than the late colonial period's eight and sixteen years (for volunteers and recruits, respectively).[60] At the societal level, shorter service terms meant heavier recruitment (all other things being equal); for individuals, it meant that military service became a brief stage in their lives rather than effectively a lifetime occupation. An 1854 uniform requisition that recorded the enlistment date of one battalion's soldiers reveals this pattern. Not one of the men had completed sixteen years of service; the median soldier had served for slightly less than four years and 83 percent of them had served for less than six years.[61] While complaints that the army failed to grant timely discharges abounded and enlisted men could legally be held beyond their contracted term if service requirements demanded it, this evidence suggests that, by mid-century, few soldiers served much longer than one enlistment term.

As a result, ex-soldiers were far more common in imperial Brazilian society than they had been before independence. They are, unfortunately, difficult to trace. After collecting the pay that the army still owed them and soliciting transport to their home provinces, veterans disappear into the class of the free poor from which they had been recruited.[62] In 1836, Inácio Acioli de Cerqueira e Silva lamented that an independence war hero had been seen begging on Salvador's streets, and the justice of the peace of Santana Parish arrested a drunken and disorderly veteran. The impressment of some veterans likewise suggests that they returned to the class of "vagrants" or the idle poor (their prior service, however, usually but not always exempted such men from the obligation to enlist).[63] An ex-sergeant, by contrast, found work in the city's police, and in 1837, sought promotion to lieutenant in that corporation.[64]

Veterans' horizons might have been broadened by military service. The incorporation of Bahia's garrison into the emerging Brazilian army after the late 1830s, whose implications have already been traced for officers, meant that a good number of recruits from Bahia (and the rest of the Northeast) would end up serving outside the province, often in the South, the remote and cold frontiers that were the scene of imperial Brazil's foreign wars and

TABLE 7.2

Birthplace of Soldiers Serving in Bahia, 1825–1854

	Number	Percentage
Bahia	453	62.5
North	3	0.4
Northeast	103	14.2
Southeast	116	16.0
Center-west	1	0.1
South	9	1.2
Total other Brazil	232	31.9
Portugal	36	5.0
Other	4	0.6
Total foreign	40	5.6
Total known	725	100.0

SOURCES: "Relação dos desertores...Janeiro de 1825 a Março de 1827," BN/SM, II-33, 23, 28; 314 desertion notices, 1829–1850, APEB; SRs of 37 enlisted men discharged in 1835, AN/SPE, IG1, m. 116, fols. 395–404; FO of 137 enlisted men discharged on health grounds, 1847–1854, AN/SPE, IG1, m. 119–21.

the location of the longest rebellion against the regime. "Horror" at the prospect of being forced to leave home provinces, according to one deputy, contributed to the army's difficulty in finding manpower and a Salvador newspaper likened recruitment to "perpetual exile" in 1845. A young Bahian volunteer underscored this concern by seeking assurances that he would not be sent south in 1840.[65]

Even as Bahia became a province that exported recruits, Salvador's garrison remained primarily Bahian-born (Table 7.2). Most of the Portuguese-born deserters date from the 1820s; they were thus the natives of the former mother country who had cast their lot with the empire, automatically receiving Brazilian citizenship. Not one of these deserters was an African, evidence of their exclusion from the regular army. Indeed, the sole African-born recruit that I have identified during this period was quickly returned to Rio de Janeiro, for the army did not wish to pay the poll tax that Bahia levied on its freed African residents after the 1835 slave revolt.[66] This pattern of a primarily local-born garrison in a province that exported recruits suggests that volunteers—who enjoyed the right to select their unit—chose to stay in Salvador and perhaps also that officers in the provincial capital selected the best of the locally impressed men to keep in their battalions before sending the remainder to Rio de Janeiro.[67]

As might be expected from the class of men targeted by recruiters, few enlisted men had skills—only 32.3 percent of 504 soldiers reported knowing a trade.[68] The dishonorable poor, the vagrants, and the criminals targeted by the authorities charged with impressment were unlikely to have skills; on the other hand, unskilled men might have viewed the army as an opportunity. Edward M. Coffman has noted that, in the nineteenth-century United States, joining the army was a way by which men down on their luck could drop out of the labor market during hard times.[69] In Brazil's slave society, whose imperfect labor market offered far fewer opportunities to the free poor than did that of the United States, the prospect of bed and board at the state's expense must have been even more attractive to some. No doubt the threat of impressment weighed on the minds of others who hoped to evade the press gang by volunteering, a strategy that gained them shorter service terms and often also salary bonuses. A native of Maranhão requested enlistment in 1838 because "he finds himself far from his home [and] without relatives in this city [Salvador] who can aid him."[70] Tellingly, he did not refer to a lack of employment opportunities but emphasized his lack of family and (implicitly) patronage ties which might have permitted him to establish himself as part of the honorable poor.

The proportion of volunteers in the rank and file is difficult to establish, ranging from 10 to 40 percent in the available sources, assuming that engagements and substitutions were voluntary (Table 7.3). The war minister's data is skewed by the 1,809 men impressed after the Sabinada, who constitute almost half of the enlistments from Bahia between 1837 and 1850. After 1839, the proportion of volunteers approached 1 in 5, a more likely "normal" figure given the qualitative evidence of voluntary enlistments: Newspapers carried advertisements for substitutions, and according to the commander of arms, a temporary suspension of bonuses in 1843 caused the supply of volunteers to dry up and prompted the desertion of soldiers upset at this breach of contract.[71]

To recapitulate this section, the typical soldier in Salvador's garrison after independence was a young, Bahian-born, unskilled man; he had probably been impressed but certainly had volunteer comrades. He would probably serve only one enlistment term, hoping to avoid being sent out of the province. If he served for a longer period of time, he might have noticed a

TABLE 7.3
Enlistment Status of Soldiers, 1829–1854

	Enlistments 1837–1850		Deserters 1829–1850		Discharges 1847–1854	
	Number	Percentage	Number	Percentage	Number	Percentage
Voluntary	320	8.0	21	12.5	36	31.0
Impressed	3,582	89.5	139	82.7	68	58.7
Engaged/ substitutes	102	2.5	8	4.8	12	10.3
Total known	4,003	100.0	168	100.0	116	100.0
Unknown	0		146		21	
Total	4,003		314		137	

SOURCES: MG, *Relatórios* (1839–1850); 314 desertion notices in APEB; FO of 137 enlisted men discharged on health grounds, 1847–1854, AN/SPE, IG1, m. 119–21.

gradual transformation among his comrades. He was probably a mulatto man but he would have served alongside more and more black (and fewer white) men. If he talked to his battalion's veterans, he might have heard about significant changes in the disciplinary regimes under which he and his comrades lived.

Discipline Reform

Like recruitment, military discipline constituted a conundrum for statesmen and officers. Not only had the independence war changed the composition of the army's rank and file and politicized enlisted men, but Emperor Pedro I's hasty institution of flogging as an authorized punishment for desertion in 1823 had belied his earlier promise of a new military code, appropriate to "an army of disciplined citizens" that embodied "valor" and "civic virtue."[72] That this promise came less than a month after the promulgation of the 1822 recruitment instructions highlights the difficulty of implementing liberal ideals in Brazilian society. In the 1820s and early 1830s, Brazilians engaged in an extended debate over the nature of military discipline, discussions that ranged from the halls of parliament to soldiers' quarters. For all the noisy debate, however, remarkably little changed, and by mid-century, discipline in the army formally resembled that of the colonial period. What had changed, however, was the social context of military discipline, with both enlisted men and influential sectors of civilian society taking more vigorous stances against corporal punishment. Equally important, a series of administrative measures quietly chipped away at the connections with civilian society that so many colonial soldiers had enjoyed, thereby changing the terms of the soldier–officer "negotiation" over the nature of military service in Salvador.

Brigadier Raimundo José da Cunha Matos, the advocate of draft lotteries, struggled to produce a new army discipline code during the 1820s. Although he completed a voluminous draft, the project died when he was not reelected in 1830, notwithstanding the fact that the 1824 constitution promised the promulgation of such an ordinance.[73] His frequent speeches in parliament reveal some of his ideas and suggest that he envisaged doing away with corporal punishment, replacing it with "houses of correction and discipline," in which frequent drill and scant diets would correct soldiers' faults.[74] Cunha Matos's ideas pointed to the "modern" forms of discipline that Michel Foucault and others have analyzed and interpreted. Most officers, however, could only envisage enlisted men as quasi-slaves, particularly given the darkening of the ranks that took place during these years. While Cunha Matos might lament the lack of respect that officers had for enlisted men, negative views of soldiers were widely shared. One Salvador newspaper proclaimed that soldiers' "submissive, dependent, and semi-slave condition" rendered them dangerous.[75]

In 1828, parliament briefly debated the practice of flogging soldiers guilty of first and second desertion. Deputies condemned Pedro's suspension of a colonial law by simple decree and called for a return to the 1805 ordinance that had established hard labor as the principal punishment for deserters.[76] Cunha Matos claimed that flogging had entered the Luso-Brazilian military when it came under British influence in the eighteenth century. He called on his colleagues to recognize enlistees as "free citizens," noting that "lashes [*chibatadas*] are only appropriate for vile slaves."[77] Here, of course, Cunha Matos was pointing to the close association of whipping and slavery, and through his opposition to flogging, sought to restore the distinction between slaves and soldiers blurred since 1823 by both the introduction of whipping and the enlistment of freedmen.

No deputies spoke in favor of flogging soldiers, but one worried that the proposed measure might undermine discipline.[78] They rather dwelled on procedural matters and the fine differences between chibatadas, *açoites* (both floggings), and *espadeiradas* (blows with the *espada de prancha*, the flexible, edgeless sword authorized for beating soldiers by the Articles of War). The constitution only mentioned açoites among the "cruel punishments" explicitly abolished for citizens and a deputy wondered whether that included chibatadas and espadeiradas. Ever the legalist, Cunha Matos explained that açoites were applied to the buttocks, while chibatadas and blows with the espada de prancha fell on the back; hence both of the latter needed to be mentioned if the motion were to ban them.[79] Notwithstanding Cunha Matos's eloquence and the legislature's sanction of the antiflogging resolution, no action was taken until 1831, when the Moderado government restored the 1805 ordinance, following it with a general ban on flogging.[80] A worried commander of arms wrote from Bahia that he could not keep order among the "robbers, criminals, and perverse men" whom he commanded, requesting that the ban on flogging not be interpreted to mean all forms of corporal punishment. The war minister concurred and the espada de prancha remained officers' disciplinary weapon of choice.[81] Thus, the peculiar significance of the whip in a slave society brought about the abolition of flogging, while the retention of the espada de prancha underscored how little had changed.

Anticorporal punishment rhetoric, repeated in the liberal press, resonated among soldiers.[82] In 1827, a corporal sentenced to be flogged for desertion publicly refused to undergo his punishment, "invoking in loud voice the August Name of His Imperial Majesty," who according to the soldier, did not approve of the sentence. The governor of arms dismissed the corporal's views by blaming the incident on the machinations of a captain and immediately ordered the sentence carried out for fear that the spectacle would undermine the battalion commander's moral authority.[83] In 1835, a prisoner in Fort São Pedro "incit[ed] soldiers to disobedience" during public punishments by reminding them "of the age in which we live and the barbarity with which we punish." Many soldiers, according to their commanding officer, were convinced that, "although he [the prisoner] is crazy, he speaks truths."[84] An insubordinate soldier retorted to a sergeant that he would not suffer the "lash [*chibata*]" in 1837, a remark that either reveals the continued practice of flogging in the garrison, or more likely, the soldier's perception that other forms of corporal punishment were little different from whippings, a position that medical doctors began to take in the 1840s and 1850s.[85]

Notwithstanding such opposition to corporal punishment from inside and outside the army, the corporation officially retained the practice until the 1870s. Corporal punishment was the logical counterpart of impressment and the darkening of the enlisted ranks only reinforced this connection. Indeed, without meaningful recruitment reform, few could view soldiers as citizens and full members of society. As in impressment, much of the discussion about corporal punishment focused on ensuring that it was conducted in a legal, rather than arbitrary, manner so as to protect the moral authority of both officers and the corporation whom they represented. In 1830, the provincial president exhorted the commander of arms to prevent the arbitrary punishments of which, from time to time, the press accused the army.[86] A few years earlier, the *Constitucional Bahiense* denounced the administration of eighty lashes to a corporal absent for eighteen hours while many "desertions" of two or three days went unpunished (according to the 1805 ordinance, seven days had to pass before an absence became a desertion).[87] Here, of course, the goal was the preservation of officers' moral authority vis-à-vis their men by ensuring that the former followed the army's rules in their dealings with the latter.

Military discipline was, in the late colonial period, a complex interaction among soldiers, officers, and civilian society, a pattern also visible in the debate over corporal punishment. Quietly, without fanfare, army authorities shifted the terms of this interaction in their favor after independence by imposing greater control over soldiers' lives, as evidence from Salvador's garrison reveals. The colonial practice of granting lengthy furloughs disappeared altogether, while fewer and fewer soldiers resided off-base.[88] When the patriot army demobilized in 1823, the garrison resumed paying rations in cash, much to the annoyance of the commander of the artillery brigade from Santa Catarina that arrived in 1825. He complained that his men lacked the means of obtaining food that natives of Bahia enjoyed.[89] Although the soldiers could purchase food from petty food-sellers, the implication of the artillery commander's remark is clear: Without ties of family and friendship to women who would prepare food for his men, they would suffer privations as strangers to Salvador. In 1828, the army reestablished messes throughout the empire, a measure that in Salvador coincided with the arrival of non-Bahian units to garrison the city, setting off a scramble to find suppliers and outfit kitchens.[90] Ending furloughs, restricting off-base residence, and establishing messes constituted efforts to gain control over enlisted men's lives.

Furthermore, there are signs of greater army interest in drill and training, suggested both by the proliferation of drill manuals and Salvador's Depósito de Recrutas (Recruitment Depot), created in 1842, which served as a boot camp for new recruits.[91] In 1824, the war ministry distributed standard drill manuals to Brazil's garrisons, and during the Cisplatine War, the Bahian government underlined the importance of training by printing 60 copies of the official infantry regulations.[92] Less is known about the practice of drilling troops, for commanders rarely reported on these matters to civilian authorities.[93] Given the small size of the garrison and the frequent complaints of insufficient troops to perform regular duties, drill likely fell by the wayside.

The removal of Bahian battalions from Salvador in the 1820s and again in the 1840s and its converse—the stationing of non-Bahian units in the city—further separated soldiers from urban society. As the war minister explained in 1845, keeping soldiers in one place for long periods of time was "harmful to discipline."[94] Soldiers' long-term relationships with family, friends, lovers, and dependents—the society that surrounded the barracks—suffered as a consequence. This community only rarely can be seen, and it may be worthwhile to pause for a moment to describe one soldier's lover and the artifice that they used to win precious time together. Private Bernardo de Sena claimed in 1836 that Josefa Senhorinha was his minor sister and that he and an uncle paid for her to attend school. As such, she had free entry to Fort São Pedro; dressed in colorful African garb (*pano da costa*) and carrying a basket on her head, she regularly brought him food. She also "repeatedly" sought Bernardo's discharge. Her attire, however, raised suspicions in the commanding officer's mind. Admitting that "the habit does not make the monk," he nevertheless doubted that a woman dressed as Josefa was "honest and discreet" (*recatada*), especially after he caught the two in each other's arms "doing things that are not appropriate for a sister [and brother]."[95]

Josefa was well advised to seek her lover's discharge. A small force from Salvador had sailed for Maranhão in early 1836, and the following year, a larger contingent embarked for Rio Grande do Sul, while battalions' systematic rotation among Brazilian garrisons began in the 1840s. Already in 1825, the departure of the city's battalions to fight in the Cisplatine War prompted "great sorrow" in Salvador, at least somewhat mitigated by the payment of small stipends to destitute dependents.[96] When the Minas Gerais Battalion (a mobilized militia unit from that province which had been stationed in Salvador since 1823) returned home in 1829, some of its men joined the battalions stationed in Bahia, presumably because they had married or otherwise established themselves in Salvador.[97] With the increasing frequency of embarkations, more and more soldiers faced this problem; in 1838, two sergeants attempted to resolve it in different ways: one sought a dispensation on the grounds that he was "married and poor" while the other requested permission to take his wife and children with him, as a third sergeant, Manoel Luciano da Câmara Guaraná, had done in 1836.[98] Requests for leave to attend to family matters or collect inheritances reveal soldiers' continued connections to civilian society; the army's refusal of some of these requests points to the increasing difficulty that soldiers faced in maintaining these ties.[99]

Ultimately, none of the piecemeal discipline reforms changed the substance of the army's internal regime, to which officers could not envisage an alternative. Indeed, rather than reforming the soldiers whom they commanded, officers readily took advantage of provisions that allowed them to send troublesome enlisted men out of the garrison or to the navy. A soldier who had injured two civilians in 1835 received 50 blows with the espada de prancha and a recommendation that he be sent to the navy which, according to the commander of arms, would "remove arms from the hands of a dangerous individual"; sending him to the navy would make him "one less vagrant," his likely occupation were he dishonorably discharged.[100] With attitudes such as these prevailing among officers, discipline reform was bound to fail.

As in the colonial period, most soldiers likely preferred to resist military discipline in subtle ways that eluded officers and are difficult for historians to assess. Desertion remained the most significant and best documented military crime. Fully 20 (15 percent) of 137 soldiers whose careers are known because they were later discharged on grounds of ill health had deserted once during their career; in 1829, the army posted a national desertion rate of 7.4 percent among all enlisted ranks, the only such figure available before 1857, when the rate stood at 9.2 percent.[101] Officers sometimes suspected political motives in desertions, particularly when eighteen privates disappeared from Salvador's garrison over two days in 1829. Despite recapturing seven of them, the governor of arms could find no evidence for his suspicions.[102] Desertions were apolitical individual acts that nevertheless cumulatively made a mockery of the army's disciplinary regime.

Statements from a handful of deserters have survived. Some claimed to have deserted to avoid punishment for lesser faults, in one case, sleeping while on guard. Easy riches beckoned Private Antônio Martins in 1830 when he followed a corporal in the search for the latter's "former life" among counterfeiters where they "would work little and earn much" producing false copper coins. Desertion at the time of embarkations from Salvador suggests a desire to remain with family and friends, as do reports that deserters could be found in the homes of their relatives. The 1829 desertion of a soldier in the company of a young slave woman has all the marks of an elopement.[103]

Officers offered few solutions to the problem of desertion. Stymied by Salvador's military geography and the support that deserters received in civilian society, the governor of arms was once reduced to fulminating against local authorities "so negligent that they do not attempt to arrest strangers" and calling for the establishment of checkpoints on the main roads leading out of Salvador, reiterating the 1816 call for a rural constabulary. In 1844, the cavalry commander railed against the "scandalous protection" afforded deserters by the masters of boats that plied the Bay of All Saints.[104] The proliferation of police and militia corporations offered deserters another opportunity to escape the army, at least for a time confounding authorities. Ten days after deserting in 1843, a cavalry soldier turned up in the National Guard, the civilian militia; in the same decade, the police had to deal with at least two army deserters in their ranks (for its part, the army discovered a navy deserter who had volunteered in 1833).[105]

As a substitute for the separation of Bahian soldiers from society within Salvador—impossible given the military geography of the city—the army sought to man the province's units with recruits from other regions of Brazil. By exchanging Bahian draftees for men impressed in northern provinces, authorities hoped to prevent desertion, but even soldiers from as far away as Ceará deserted "in their majority" in 1851.[106] In any case, the volunteers who accounted for a good proportion of the rank and file retained the right to choose their unit and usually opted to remain in Bahia. Unable to forestall or repress desertion directly, the Brazilian government periodically pardoned the offenders. Brazil's emperors issued at least a dozen general desertion pardons for first and second simple desertion between 1822 and 1850, at an average interval of slightly more than two years. As in the colonial period, deserters well understood this. One disingenuously claimed that he "supposed that in going to his birthplace [Sergipe] to serve as a soldier, he was not committing a crime." He implicitly contradicted himself when he admitted that he knew of the 23 February 1843 pardon. He did not, however, claim its benefits when he enlisted in Sergipe, for it had already expired.[107] Those deserters who turned themselves in voluntarily when no amnesties were in force perhaps sought to suffer the lighter punishments imposed on those who gave themselves up, hoping to enjoy a later pardon. One of the army deserters serving in the police identified himself as soon as he heard of a pardon, seeking to be formally discharged and remain in the police.[108]

As a result of the changes in the army's discipline regime, a repeat of the 1798 Tailors' Conspiracy became increasingly unlikely. By the 1830s and 1840s, enlisted men lacked the freedoms enjoyed by the soldiers of the 1790s. They rarely lived off-base, nor did they have the time to work in civilian occupations. Enlisted men were not unaffected by the political turmoil of the 1830s; unlike in 1798, they rarely played a leading role in it. Military discipline, not larger political questions, lay at the core of the mutiny of artillery soldiers in Fort São Pedro on 1 September 1831. At the time, officers' control over enlisted men in the recently returned Bahian battalions was precarious at best. On 24 August, the British consul reported the Fourteenth Battalion's refusal to parade until its commander "pledged his honour that their arrears of pay should be forthwith discharged" and similar mutinous sentiments pervaded the Thirteenth and Fifteenth Battalions.[109] A week later, the artillery mutinied. The soldiers' demands were simple: According to the commander of arms, they no longer wished to sleep in the barracks, eat in the mess, or wear leather collars.[110] The first two demands struck directly at the efforts to gain more effective control over enlisted men. Many of the old soldiers likely remembered the days of frequent furloughs and cash rations. Confinement to barracks was no doubt especially galling to men who had been absent from Salvador for four or five years. The uncomfortable stiff neckstocks that so many nineteenth-century soldiers sported were a common cause of complaint in the British army.[111] Of course, the soldiers' final demand—for their discharges—effectively rendered the first three redundant. At the time, the army was rapidly disbanding battalions and discharging enlisted men; the mutineers perhaps simply sought to hurry the process along. Apparently authorities did exactly that, for less than two weeks later, the United States consul reported that many discharged mutineers were "lurking about the city."[112]

Opinion in Salvador ran strongly against the soldiers. The commander of arms publicly called his rebellious subordinates "the scourge of society, the terror of families, and a band of robbers and assassins," while the radical liberal *Nova Sentinela da Liberdade* also condemned them even as it continued to count on military participation in its federalist campaign, warning a cavalry officer in mid-September not to arrest those of his subordinates who "said that Federation [was] a good [form of] Government," for such a regime was inevitable.[113] Other newspapers denounced all forms of soldiers' politics: *O Investigador Brasileiro* carried an article extracted from a Rio de Janeiro newspaper that lambasted the "*sans culotte*" officers who inspired loose and dangerous talk among "ignorant soldiers."[114] During the wave of discharges in 1831 and 1832, the army made a point of ridding the corporation of politicized enlisted men, including a sergeant who demonstrated "abysmal military conduct," and more important, was a "declared anarchist and enemy of order."[115]

Other than these hints that enlisted men shared radical liberal ideals, there are few indications of how soldiers viewed the political unrest of these years. None of the surviving inquests into rebellions included them in the way that the trial of the Tailors' Conspiracy focused on enlisted men. For military and civilian authorities (and the city's elite) it was easier to dismiss soldiers, both in the sense of removing them from the corporation (or from the province) and in the sense of denying that they could hold political views. Blaming the machinations of radical liberal officers (of whom there were many) was a far more acceptable explanation for soldiers' unrest. As a result, there is remarkably little evidence of enlisted men's role in the greatest of the military rebellions, the Sabinada. It was not simply, as F. W. O. Morton has argued, the occasion for soldiers to desert; had soldiers done so in significant numbers, the rebellion would have collapsed at once.[116] In February 1838, the rebels' First Battalion (formerly the Third Infantry) reported only 4 desertions among its 608 enlisted men, an annual rate of 7.1 percent, typical of that time.[117] How the rebel officers managed to convince soldiers to follow them remains unclear. The rebel government raised their salaries substantially, finally making good on an offer often made by Exaltados when they sought soldiers' support.[118] Sabinada rhetoric ran strongly against corporal punishment. The rebel press pointed to the contradictions between it and the constitution's abolition of cruel and unusual punishment. After describing the flogging of a black man on board a navy ship blockading Salvador and recounting the threats that he had heard from officers who desired to whip all the city's blacks and mulattoes into submission, the author of a letter to the editor concluded: "I am convinced either that the Constitution was not made for creoles or mulattoes or that these men are traitors for they always speak of the Constitution and the Law, while doing things that I have not seen since the days of [Salvador's occupation by] the Portuguese [troops]."[119] These two elements do not constitute a convincing explanation, however, and the answer may lie in the relationships cultivated between officers and soldiers that do not appear in the documentation. Perhaps the junior officers in the two rebel battalions had succeeded in building a following among their enlisted men. Sergeants likely played a key role as well: At least one had recruited soldiers for the rising.[120] The quick, unambiguous initial success of the rising probably also encouraged enlisted men to remain loyal to their officers.

From the 1820s to the 1840s, the interaction between soldiers, officers, and society that lay at the core of military discipline changed significantly. Corporal punishment became increasingly illegitimate on ideological grounds and soldiers sensed this shift; they also perceived, as the 1831 artillery mutiny suggests, that the army had begun to curtail their freedoms and sap their ties to urban society. For many soldiers, as many as one in ten each year, desertion constituted a legitimate and reasonable response to the conditions of service; that the government and the army could only envisage pardons as the solution to desertion reveals how little had changed since the colonial period.

Comrades: Community and Identity

Soldiers' place in urban society was profoundly shaped by their role as an integral part of the city's police apparatus. The Guarda Militar de Polícia (Military Police Guard) created shortly after the Periquitos' revolt was in effect an army battalion designated a police force. The early 1830s saw the creation of two new police corporations, the Guarda Municipal Permanente (Permanent Municipal Guard) and the National Guard, a civilian militia. The latter is the subject of the next chapter, while the former was a civilian but militarized police force, paid by the provincial government. The army did not, however, lose its role in policing during this period, and the guards that soldiers mounted at strategic points throughout the city constituted an integral part of Salvador's police apparatus.

Although the garrison was considerably smaller in the 1830s and 1840s than it had been in the 1810s, rarely approaching half of its former size (see the Appendix, Figure A.1), soldiers nevertheless remained a significant and visible part of urban society. Despite the establishment of central messes, they constituted an important market for the food-sellers, who crowded around the barracks on payday and were allowed to set up shop inside the Forte do Mar for the convenience of its garrison and the prisoners housed there. In 1839, a soldier slipped out of the palace guard to buy some sweets at a nearby food stand, unfortunately failing to return before the duty officer inspected the detachment.[121] Soldiers were also highly visible on Salvador's streets as they marched to their guard posts and conducted the prisoners sentenced to hard labor who carried water to Salvador's barracks and government buildings. Parades and inspections took place in Salvador's squares, as can be inferred from an 1830 incident in which a civil servant was arrested for passing through the ranks of soldiers on Piedade Square.[122]

Soldiers often acted violently in the course of their ordinary duties, in some cases literally riding roughshod over civilians. Maria Dundas Graham described the modus operandi of patrols in 1821: "In cases of riot and quarrels in the street, the colonel generally orders the soldiers to fall on with canes and beat people into their senses."[123] For the most part, such violence did not bother the Bahian upper class, so long as it did not touch them. Thus, the inquest into the death of "an old woman, whose name is not known," trampled by a mounted Lieutenant José Baltazar da Silveira in 1828, absolved the rider, concluding "that the death resulted more from frailty and old age than from the light blow and bruise" suffered by the victim.[124]

From the wealthy to the honorable poor, Brazilians shared an ideology that distinguished clearly between house and street; the former represented patriarchal order, stability, and protection, while the latter signified disorder and the rough application of laws that failed to recognize status differences.[125] Respectable householders, however, regularly had to leave the protective walls of their houses to transact business in the public world of the street. There, where rich and poor mingled daily, social distinctions required constant reinforcement, all the more so because the disorderly world of the street put soldiers into positions of authority over honorable citizens, patriarchal householders and their dependents, and even members of the mostly white upper class. In apparently petty but profoundly important conflicts, soldiers and civilians struggled over status in the streets. When soldiers roughed up slaves, either in the course of their duties or to confirm for themselves their superiority as free men, they challenged the authority and patriarchal protection of those masters whose slaves they victimized. Thus owners "acrimoniously denounced" such abuses, calling for the punishment of the soldiers in question as a means of reestablishing their patronage.[126] Similarly, denunciations of random violence or other crimes perpetrated by soldiers were frequent. In 1837, for example, a man complained that soldiers from the guard at the medical school had stolen two chickens; an angry justice of the peace demanded that the officer in charge hand over the suspects at once.[127] Although commanders could not always identify the guilty soldiers (who may have been victims of their own bad reputation), the oft-repeated calls for the control of such abuses reflect a recognition that they belied the paternalist authority of the upper class.

Soldiers also threatened racial hierarchies, for enlisted men were ever more likely to be black or mulatto than the middle and upper class members of society whom they protected. In 1830, the celebrations of the heir apparent's birthday were marred when a sergeant ordered a woman to go home, striking her with a cavalry crop. The woman loudly complained to the Viscount of Pirajá, organizer of the festival and a man who cultivated something of a populist image. Pirajá promptly arrested the soldier, later explaining that using a whip on a "white person" was inappropriate for soldiers charged with maintaining public order.[128] Another incident merits close examination because of its unusually rich detail. In 1843, the police subdelegate of Sé Parish took offense when the sentinel at the presidential palace tried to enforce a ban on canes in the building. According to the sub-delegate, the soldier told him, "Oh young sir [*senhor moço*], leave the cane for one cannot enter with it." An indignant subdelegate, noting that the sol-dier was a "crioulo," reminded him that "those were not appropriate words to direct at people going into [the palace]," to which the soldier responded that he "did not know with whom he was talking, for he did not recognize frock coats and jackets."[129] When the subdelegate continued to lecture the soldier on matters of civility, the private cut him off: "Shut up. I don't want to talk to you nor am I here to listen to you."

After the subdelegate reported the soldier to the commander of the palace guard, the private claimed that the subdelegate had threatened him: "I'll make you and other blacks like you acknowledge authorities, [you] uppity [*atrevido*] [black]." The officer, who claimed to know the subdelegate to be a prudent man, initially doubted the soldier's version of the incident; his conversation with the subdelegate, however, confirmed it:

> "Doctor, how did this occur?"
> "Your soldier . . . attacked me."
> "How, Doctor?"
> "As soon as I tried to go in . . . , he addressed me:
> 'Young sir, one can't go in with a cane.'"
> "But where is the insult in this . . . ?"
> "It's clear . . . don't you consider it a crime when a black calls a white man 'Young sir'?"

The officer tried to placate the "increasingly enraged" subdelegate, who kept repeating his question. Finally, he appealed to the subdelegate's patriotism:

> "But Doctor . . . if he is a black, why are you so upset at his words, when he has no others more polite with which to address people like you? Besides, don't you see that the Nation relies on these, and other blacks, in times of danger. . . . They risk their lives and obtain the peace for you and others to live the good life [*lançarem a mão no bolo da fortuna*], while they get their [paltry wage of] 90 réis, and the Count of Lipes's [sic] [punishments] on their back."

The subdelegate's version of this conversation describes a mutual exchange of insults culminating in each dismissing the other's credentials, the subdelegate's law degree and the officer's stripes. Both agreed that a large crowd, including both the other soldiers of the guard and civilians, witnessed the verbal conflict.[130]

What was at stake? Both the subdelegate and the officer had good reason to color their reports, given the highly public nature of the incident. Little more than five years had passed since the massacre of Sabinada supporters, mostly men of color, in March 1838, and the subdelegate may have been especially sensitive to receiving orders from a black man and what he perceived to be indiscipline among soldiers. Moreover, the lifting of the color bar in recruitment was, by then, darkening the rank and file to a noticeable degree. The private's lack of respect for him, he argued, would lead to the "dire consequence" of insubordination among soldiers and the undermining of his moral authority. The subdelegate's rudeness and his presumption in demanding satisfaction facilitated the officer's support for the soldier. Still, corporate loyalty failed to bridge the class and race divide within the army. As far as the patronizing officer was concerned, "innocent words from an ignorant soldier" hardly merited such a reaction. His remarks about the subdelegate's making his fortune while others fought to protect it probably contained a personal element as well, for the officer, Lieutenant Luiz Baltazar da Silveira, belonged to a family that was then suffering a marked material decline.

Police work thus brought the army into close contact with Salvador's population. On city streets, soldiers—often lower class men of color—faced the difficult task of employing violence in defence of order without antagonizing the city's elites and their respectable dependents. Honor, status, and class hierarchies required continual reinforcement in the world of the street; soldiers and civilians constantly fought over the appropriate definitions of their respective places. And soldiers also fought with the members of other military and paramilitary corporations, the police and the National Guard. Different disciplinary regimes, notably the lack of corporal punishments in the police and the Guard, combined with salary differentials (police soldiers earned more than those in the army) and class distinctions (explicit in the income requirements for Guard membership) set these corporations apart. Service, however, threw them together, for their duties overlapped significantly, with all three corporations policing the city and the Guard substituting or supplementing the army in garrison duties.

Two related incidents in May 1839 reveal the patterns in these conflicts. A police soldier, Tomás de Aquino, and the Second Artillery's staff sergeant apparently had both been involved with the same woman. Aquino, drunk, armed, and spoiling for a fight, entered the sergeant's quarters and began breaking dishes, loudly insulting the noncommissioned officer. The barracks guard promptly arrested Aquino, dragging him to the stockade as he shouted insults against the artillerymen. The next day, a police patrol arrested an artillery soldier for disorderly conduct at Gravatá Fountain, where he had allegedly been preventing slaves from filling their water barrels. Many artillery soldiers, armed with swords, set off in hot pursuit to free their comrade; after considerable difficulty, an officer prevailed upon them to desist. That the incidents were discussed together highlights their connection: The arrest of the police soldier likely encouraged the police patrol to deal severely with the army soldier at the fountain. As far as the army soldiers were concerned, however, both Aquino's invasion of their quarters and the arrest of their comrade were intolerable affronts.[131]

Similar corporate loyalties appeared in an 1845 incident that took place while the Invalids' Company and a National Guard battalion shared Palma Barracks. When guardsmen tried to imprison a drunken invalid, Luiz Gomes Luvais, who had allegedly stolen an orange, an invalid corporal took his comrade's side. He incited the private to resist imprisonment—"Do not obey, Luvais, for civilians do not command us"—and, arming himself with a stick, joined the fray. Other reports add details to the incident. Luvais claimed that "the barracks were his and did not belong to civilians, whom he would never obey, nor officers of the National Guard, and that he would only obey his Captain Silva." Another witness noted that Luvais called the guardsmen a "mob of bailiffs" (*cambada de meirinhos*),[132] a disparaging reference to the petty civil servants who often served in the Guard. In this case, loyalty to comrades, resentment at the interlopers who occupied the invalids' quarters, and an element of class hostility expressed themselves in the invalids' corporate loyalty.

Rather than a loyalty to the army as an institution, these brawls reflect the loyalty to companions in arms that sociologists have identified as soldiers' primary motivation in combat.[133] Although soldiers did not usually identify wholeheartedly with the army hierarchy, many identified sufficiently with their comrades that they willingly risked life and limb, as well as the wrath of their superiors, to defend them against perceived aggressions from other corporations. Tense relations with some members of urban society reinforced soldiers' corporate loyalty.

This chapter began with the impressment of José Inácio, nicknamed "Deputy" for his political statement in 1831. No doubt Santo Amaro's justice of the peace considered impressment the simplest way to get rid of a dangerous individual whose presence continued to remind slaves and the free lower classes of the limits to their citizenship. Yet men like José Inácio would end up defending the nation against external enemies and policing the country's major cities. For soldiers, "citizenship" meant corporal punishment, tedious duties, low pay, and subjection to officers. Little wonder that the author of Brazil's first novel, Manuel Antônio de Almeida, could write in *Memórias de um sargento de milícias* (*Memoirs of a Militia Sergeant*, 1852–1853) that "to be a soldier was at that time [the 1810s], and perhaps still is today, the worst thing that could befall a man."[134]

The continuities that Almeida saw, however, must be set against important changes in soldiers' experience. As service terms shrank, soldiering no longer was a lifetime occupation. The lifting of the color bar in 1837 notably darkened the enlisted ranks by the 1840s. And the army quietly closed off some of the avenues that linked soldiers to civilian society by curtailing their freedoms and moving enlisted men around their country. Soldiers resisted these changes taking place in their lives, and through desertion, maintained an open channel to society, yet it is clear that such connections were increasingly difficult to maintain. The effective exclusion of soldiers from the "high politics" of the 1830s, so different from their centrality in 1798, reveals much about disdainful attitudes toward the enlisted ranks and their declining status. The uncomfortable position of nonwhite soldiers charged with maintaining law and order in Salvador, in which they sometimes exercised authority over the white upper class (and the resulting conflicts) also demonstrates these attitudes. Soldiers no doubt wisely learned how best to avoid incidents such as the conflict over the cane.

The extensive debates about discipline and recruitment reform in the 1820s and 1830s reveal the limits of liberalism in nineteenth-century Brazil. The campaign against corporal punishment focused on the use of the whip, whose significance in a slave society made it inappropriate for use on soldiers, but the army retained the espada de prancha. Draft lotteries with their implications of equality among all men were ultimately unpalatable to parliamentarians, but so were the inevitable excesses of forced recruitment, which authorities struggled to mitigate and they balanced the diverse interests at stake in impressment. Liberals' failure to undertake significant recruitment and discipline reform stemmed not just from their inability or unwillingness to break with the patronage structures of Brazilian society; it also reflects their ambivalence toward the army. The corporation figured in their plans as a marginal and peripheral institution, one that would be supplemented, if not replaced altogether, by a civilian militia, the National Guard.

CHAPTER 8

From Militia to National Guard

In late May 1831, as news that the imperial legislature was debating a National Guard bill reached Salvador, the commander of arms solicited orders to begin recruiting for the militia and to appoint officers to its vacant posts, expecting that the proposed Guard would be based on the existing corporation.[1] He was, of course, wrong in this regard: The new corporation would be a civilian institution over which he would have no authority at all, while the militias were simply disbanded. This officer's mistaken expectations underscore the extent to which the National Guard represented a break with the past but also suggest that the militia influenced Brazilians' interpretions of their experience with the Guard.

The debate over the militia and the establishment of the National Guard in 1831 raised many of the questions about race, citizenship, and class relations that Brazilians had debated as they struggled to reform the recruitment and discipline of enlisted men. The Guard is an institution familiar to historians of Brazil as the embodiment of the alliance between planters and monarchy that lay at the core of the imperial regime, but the early Guard differed significantly from the post-1850 institution. Most studies of the Guard recognize its initial democratic features, notably elected officership, a novelty that did not last past the end of the 1830s in most provinces.[2] What is less well understood, however, is the extent to which the Guard was influenced by the militias and ordenanças that it replaced. Officers, "simple guards," and the civilian authorities who struggled to manage the new corporation did not begin with a *tabula rasa*; their understanding of the militia and its faults shaped the Guard. Furthermore, the Guard in major cities such as Salvador functioned very differently from its rural counterpart; it was effectively organized almost at once and some of its members were usually on active duty throughout the 1830s and 1840s.

In this regard, the Guard differed little from Salvador's militia, which saw extensive service in the 1820s. Black and mulatto officers and soldiers numerically dominated the militia at this time. During the 1820s, the militia was the frequent object of reform proposals that drew on a well-established antimilitia rhetoric. For liberals, the militia's subjection to the regular army was the antithesis of the liberal citizenship that they envisaged; following French examples, they sought to create a Brazilian version of the *Garde Nationale* that would incorporate the virtuous citizenry and embody the nation. Strikingly absent from the debates over the militia were references to its racial segregation. One of the few militia reform measures to pass before 1831 concerned the paid militia officers promoted according to the 1802 ruling; legislators discussed it without acknowledging the disparate impact that the bill would have on black and mulatto officers, whom they deprived of the salary increases that their white counterparts received.

In Salvador, the creation of the National Guard in late 1831 and early 1832 was a difficult process, raising fundamental questions about the extent and nature of citizenship. By the mid-1830s, the Guard and its ideals were widely rejected, sometimes on the same mundane grounds that men had long opposed militia service—it was simply too burdensome. Those elected to officer posts in 1832 also often repudiated the Guard, either because its ersatz officership dependent on reelection could not measure up to the real and permanent officership of the militia or because they lacked effective authority over their men. And those excluded from the Guard, notably black militia officers, rejected it as well, drawing on their experience in the militia to condemn the Guard's exclusionary practice, and indeed, Brazilian liberalism more broadly. The Sabinada Rebellion marked an important stage in the Guard's rejection; the rebels abolished the new corporation and restored the black and mulatto militia battalions, receiving especially strong support from black officers.

In the aftermath of the Sabinada, the Bahian government reorganized the Guard, restoring some of what the victors then perceived as the militia's desirable features. All of the elected officers were cashiered and only those deemed reliable were reappointed; officers in the new Guard held their commissions for life, as had officers in the old militias. Equally important, the new Guard gave commanders the authority to enroll guardsmen and to call them up for paid service in detachments, much as had been the case in the militia. In the 1840s, Salvador's Guard was a far more militarized corporation than it had been in the 1830s, reflecting the social philosophy of the Regresso and its rejection of the liberal experiments of the 1830s.

From the 1820s to the 1840s, state–society relations as reflected in Salvador's militia and National Guard underwent important modifications. While the colonial militia had tied racially segregated merchant and artisan elites to the state, only the black and mulatto militia elites survived the independence war unscathed, and indeed, with much enhanced standing. The National Guard effectively sidelined these men in 1831 as it sought to incorporate property-owners into a liberal and color-blind institution. This experiment's perceived failure prompted the creation of the more militarized Guard of the 1840s, which was commanded by a core of civil-servant officers, often rather modest property-owners, but men closely tied to the state. While nominally color-blind, this corporation clearly reflected the urban racial hierarchy and afforded no separate spaces for nonwhites. Equally important, its dominance by civil servants demonstrates an assumption of responsibility for policing and maintaining order by the state, as the Brazilian planter class adopted forms of indirect control over military institutions.

Between Militia and National Guard, 1825–1831

By 1825, Salvador's militia had been reorganized along colonial lines, with black, mulatto, and white infantry battalions and a white artillery corps (see the Appendix, Figure A.3). Its officers were patriots to a man, for those who had failed to leave Salvador during the independence war had been summarily set aside in 1823. The corporation's weight had shifted toward the black and mulatto battalions as the Portuguese merchant-officers who had dominated the white regiments left Brazil or found themselves labeled enemies of the new nation and excluded from the militia. After passing its great test in 1824 by remaining loyal to the provincial government during the Periquitos' Rebellion, the militia settled into the routine of assisting in garrison duties and aiding in the city's policing. With the departure of most regulars in 1825 and 1826, militia service became especially burdensome, and until the end of the decade, some militiamen were almost always on active service, for which they were paid at the regular army salary rates; detachments from the suburban and Recôncavo militia were also called in to aid in policing Salvador.[3]

Sources on these years of intense militia work are few and scattered; like those of the colonial period, they frequently indicate that officers had difficulty maintaining discipline. After an 1828 inspection to ensure that the militia had been properly reorganized according to the 1827 decree that imposed a national numeration on the battalions, the governor of arms complained of much diminished numbers. Commanders repeatedly found themselves packing off "incorrigible" or "insubordinate" militiamen to the navy.[4] Militiamen did not always receive respect from the city's population. While responding to a fire alarm in 1827, some artillery soldiers suffered insults from civilians; a few weeks later, a black sergeant was prevented from arresting a refractory soldier by a doctor in whose house the man resided.[5] With the election of the first justices of the peace in the late 1820s, militia officers faced a new threat, for the new judges enjoyed the right to name block inspectors, posts that exempted men from militia service. Before long, the militia began losing men to the proliferating inspectorships, much to the annoyance of officers whose authority was thus undermined by civilians.[6] Despite these obstacles, militia officers produced a reasonably satisfactory number of soldiers for unpaid garrison and police duties and supplied regular levies to serve as paid soldiers alongside the regulars or the police.

Given the militia's social composition, reliance on it for policing meant that blacks and mulattoes had responsibility for Salvador's security in the 1820s. In 1829, the Treasury's refusal over a technicality to pay some mobilized black officers prompted an observation from the governor of arms that it "would be imprudent . . . to offend for so little [money]" men who were so important to public security. The British consul also recognized this, pointing out in 1827 that "the number of black and mulatto troops in this city exceeds greatly at present that of any other description . . . which makes the position of the white population one of great danger." The departure of regulars for the Cisplatine War had left Salvador in the hands of the non-white militia, but as the consul admitted, this was "not an object of much immediate apprehension" among Bahians.[7]

In 1829, when the arrival of the first regulars from southern Brazil permitted the government to begin releasing militiamen from service, the governor of arms thanked the "brave citizens" who had so willingly abandoned their personal interests in response "to the call of Authorities and the homeland." This proclamation hints at some of the changes in the militia's role in the 1820s: Its soldiers were now citizens, not merely subjects. Furthermore, such citizens held a special place in society. In early 1830, when

100 militia soldiers were back in the barracks serving with the regulars, the president described the militia as "the principal force of a free nation."[8] This rhetoric, it must be emphasized, referred to a segregated corporation, in which blacks and mulattoes significantly outnumbered whites. While there is little indication of how these men viewed their militia service, they likely saw it as a way to associate themselves with the state and to gain power, much as their independence war service had given them a new sense of assertiveness.

The militia was the object of considerable criticism during Pedro I's reign: Many held that militia (and ordenanças) service drew men away from agriculture and other useful occupations, and officers were condemned as imperious potentates whose impositions aggravated the condition of a long-suffering population.[9] In early 1824, when Salvador's town council examined the draft of Pedro's constitution, councilors proposed a clause that would exempt militiamen from being called to serve outside their home districts, except in case of foreign invasion. The militia battalion from Minas Gerais, which had arrived in Salvador in 1823 and would remain there until the end of the decade, was a graphic example of what could happen to militiamen converted by fiat into regular soldiers. Not only would such militiamen be obliged to spend long periods of time away from home, they also became subject to regular army discipline, including corporal punishment.[10]

Two major militia reform bills were debated in the legislature before 1831, revealing deputies' additional concerns, notably the militia's subordination to the regular army, a liberal theme familiar to students of Mexican history. Diogo Antônio Feijó, who would oversee the National Guard's creation as minister of justice in 1831, asked in 1828: "Can a people enjoy liberty when it is governed militarily? Brazil," he continued, "is divided . . . into companies; there is no man who does not have his captain." Both of the reform bills sought to demilitarize the militias, separating them from the army and eliminating militiamen's obligation to perform police duties.[11] The institution of elected justices of the peace in 1828 offered a civilian alternative to the ordenanças for local administration, but bills to abolish this colonial corporation failed to pass, as did all the measures to reform the militia. In these debates, however, there were hints of more substantial changes to come. In 1828, one deputy called for a national guard or a national militia to be composed of the "middle class" to defend liberty, the constitutional monarchy, and the "established order."[12]

As they debated the militia and the ordenanças, deputies were addressing the very nature of the Brazilian state and wrestling with their colonial heritage. Most concurred that a liberal and constitutional regime could not be a militarized one, as colonial government had been. Constitutional liberties had to be defended by the citizens who enjoyed them. Who should be admitted to the status of citizen was, of course, the key issue. Before examining the National Guard law—Moderados' answer to this question—one additional aspect of Brazil's colonial heritage that deputies only debated implicitly must be noted: racial segregation in the militia and the special status that colonial legislation afforded black and mulatto officers.

The only significant militia bill passed in Brazil's first legislature concerned the status of the corporation's paid officers. In the white militia, these were the army sergeants and captains promoted to lieutenant and major after their transfer from the regulars; in the black and mulatto battalions, they were the men promoted from within the militia according to the terms of the 1802 ruling that established a separate career path for paid officers in the nonwhite militia. By 1826, a mass of contradictory provisions left these militia adjutants and majors earning salaries in accordance with the pay scales in force at the time of their appointment, rather than the higher 1821 and 1825 army salary tables.[13] To rectify this obvious inequity, Deputy and Brigadier Raimundo José da Cunha Matos drafted a brief bill to grant all actively serving paid militia officers salaries at the regular army rate. Equal pay for equal work proved a compelling argument and the measure seemed destined to pass in its entirety. Late in the afternoon of a rather tedious second reading in 1827, the prominent liberal deputy, Bernardo Pereira de Vasconcelos, proposed an "editorial amendment" that restricted the salary provisions to militia officers who had transferred from the regulars, perhaps responding to concerns that the bill would reward the holders of irregular patronage appointments in the militia. Vasconcelos then launched into a vigorous defense of equal pay for equal work, observing that the current regime of unequal salaries depending on time of appointment was "opposed to all the principles of our legislation and that of all civilized Europe." The amendment passed with no significant discussion, as did the bill, which the emperor signed into law in 1829.[14]

The 1829 law illustrates the problem that liberal legislation posed for black and mulatto officers. Strictly speaking, it rested on the old principle that only regular army officers could serve as militia adjutants and majors. While it recognized militia adjutants and majors as fully equal to their regular counterparts, it did not—rhetoric about equal pay for equal work notwithstanding—accord this recognition to the adjutants and majors promoted from within the militia under the terms of the 1802 ruling. As a result, the Henriques' last commander, Francisco Xavier Bigode, who had returned to his old post on Manoel Gonçalves da Silva's death in 1828, continued to draw only 26$000 monthly, instead of the 50$000 that white majors transferred from the regulars earned under the 1825 pay scale. While these men had played a leading role in the fight for independence and had supported the imperial regime in its crisis of 1824, the new Empire often did not satisfy their aspirations.

The striking absence of any reference to black officers in the salary debate reveals Brazilian liberals' reluctance to deal directly with racial questions. While liberal military jurists like Cunha Matos readily condemned the colonial legacy of overtly discriminatory legislation (and Vasconcelos had sought to end racial discrimination in recruitment for the regulars),[15] they demonstrated greater ambivalence when faced with the social and legal spaces that the colonial regime had provided for black and mulatto Brazilians. Indeed, by refusing to discuss them, legislators were implicitly defining the Brazilian officer corps as an exclusively white institution, one in which there was no room for black men. Similar ambivalence characterized the army's policy on appointments to adjutancies in the black and mulatto battalions of Salvador. Although the militia had been reorganized in Bahia along colonial lines and the 1802 legislation remained on the books, no adjutant competitions were held in the 1820s; no regular officers requested assignment to the vacant majorships in Bahia's black and mulatto battalions. When the adjutants, Captains Joaquim José de Santana Gomes and José Maria Cirilo da Silva, requested the posts in 1827, arguing that the 1802 promotion provisions should apply and citing their special training in Rio de Janeiro, the Conselho Supremo Militar (the army's highest court) judged that such promotions "would necessarily result in the unpleasant situation [*desgosto*] of having regular army captains serving under the orders of officers whose different color is repugnant to and offends the sensibilities of white men."[16] Having thus clearly identified the problem as racism in the armed forces, the court washed its hands of the issue by referring it to the emperor. He apparently failed to rule on the petition and the abolition of the militia in 1831 rendered it irrelevant.

In 1831, amid the social and political unrest that wracked Rio de Janeiro in the aftermath of Pedro's abdication, the Moderado-controlled legislature hastily passed several measures to ensure security in the capital, extending them to the entire country. Preferring not to rely on the army and the military police, deputies first mandated the creation of civilian municipal guards, shortly thereafter replaced by the National Guard. Unfortunately, the legislature kept a poor record of its debates in that turbulent year, but it is clear that these were attempts to place responsibility for public security directly in the hands of those property-holding citizens who would most benefit from it.[17] Copied closely from the French law of 22 March 1831, the Brazilian Guard law also shares affinities with the measures that established civic militias in Mexico and Chile during the 1820s and 1830s.[18]

The Brazilian law's preamble proclaimed the new Guard's purposes to be "defending the Constitution, the liberty and integrity of the empire," "maintaining obedience to the law," and "conserving or reestablishing order and public tranquility." The law abolished the militia and the ordenanças, replacing them with a civilian corporation, organized by parish and subject to the ministry of justice, not the ministry of war. Its members in the country's four largest cities were to be electors ages twenty-one to sixty, in other words, free-born men who earned at least 200$000 per year. Elsewhere, the Guard was to consist of voters, free and freed men who earned at least 100$000. These men would, in turn, elect captains, lieutenants, and noncommissioned officers from among their number; captains, lieutenants, and sergeants would elect their battalion's standard-bearers, adjutants, majors, and lieutenant colonels. The latter held the post, not of commander, but of battalion head (*chefe*), a change of terminology that underscored the non-military nature of the new corporation. The provincial president would appoint the heads of the legions into which battalions were organized and the superior commanders who led the Guard in each judicial district. Civil servants, including artisans employed in government arsenals and workshops; students; and professionals such as lawyers, doctors, surgeons, and pharmacists could request enlistment in the reserve, which exempted them from Guard duties.[19]

The issue of membership in the Guard was controversial at the time and remains so. As many historians have noted, the income requirements for Guard membership (and voting) were quite low, including most salaried employees and independent artisans; even army enlisted men arguably earned just enough in salary and rations to make them eligible to vote. In short, nineteenth-century Brazil had an unusually broad electorate.[20] Nevertheless, the Guard clearly excluded slaves and urban plebeians, certainly the majority of the male population. The Guard furthermore abolished the segregation characteristic of the colonial militia. As Cunha Matos tersely put it, the Guard law "mixed up the colors and there are no separate white, mulatto, and black [*preto*] units: Rights are equal." If the Guard was, on paper, liberal in this regard, as Jeanne Berrance de Castro has argued, the 1831 law clearly excluded freedmen altogether from Guard membership in cities like Salvador. A cabinet-maker and former sergeant in the black militia, freed at his baptism, knew the law and flatly refused to have anything to do with the Guard (or any other civilian patrols) in July 1832 for precisely this reason.[21] The prospect that a former slave might be elected to command his former master, which figured prominently in contemporary criticism of the Guard, was thus limited to smaller cities and rural areas.[22] In October 1832, a revision of the Guard law eliminated the theoretical possibility that this might occur by restricting officership to those men eligible to be provincial electors, thereby excluding freedmen, and raising the income requirement for officers to double that of enlisted men to 400$000 in major urban centers and to 200$000 in the rest of the country, bringing the Guard in line with the constitution, which also required higher income for office-holders.[23] The efforts to disqualify freedmen drew a vigorous protest from Bahian deputy Antônio Pereira Rebouças, who reminded his colleagues of the services performed by black militia officers such as Colonel Neves in 1824, who would now no longer be eligible for a command in the country's militia (at the same time, however, Rebouças repeatedly advocated raising substantially the income requirements for service in the Guard).[24] Thus, while the original law had entirely excluded freedmen from the Guard in large cities, the 1832 revisions included them but barred them from election to officership.

As did its French counterpart, the National Guard placed responsibility for the nation's defense in the hands of property-holding males. Membership in the Guard was to constitute a form of active and self-conscious citizenship. The capital's *Aurora Fluminense* hailed the new corporation as "the Nation . . . in arms" and emphasized its difference from the old militias, militarized and subordinate to the regulars.[25] Elected officership heralded an important democratization of Brazilian society, while the end of segregation offered a liberal model of social relations; both broke in important ways with the country's colonial heritage in military affairs. Like the 1824 constitution, however, Guard legislation drew clear, if relatively inclusive, barriers around that citizenship and democratization.[26]

The National Guard in Salvador, 1831–1837

Along with the return of Bahian regular battalions to Salvador and their rapid disbanding in the second half of 1831, the National Guard was an institutional reform that came to Bahia from Rio de Janeiro, and one that did not necessarily respond to Bahian concerns. While the Guard was quickly established in Salvador, many of the men enrolled soon rejected the new corporation and its central premise that property-holding citizens would voluntarily collaborate in a democratic organization to maintain order. So did key individuals excluded from the Guard, notably black and mulatto militia officers. This rejection of the Guard culminated in the Sabinada Rebellion of 1837–1838, which abolished the liberal corporation and restored the segregated militias. Paradoxically, it took the liberal reforms of the 1830s to push black officers, supporters of the imperial regime throughout the 1820s, into the radical liberal camp.

In 1831, politics and institutional reform in Salvador followed Rio de Janeiro's lead: Amid political turmoil and military unrest, civilian municipal guards were created in the middle of the year, followed by the National Guard.[27] In November, newspapers were carrying advertisements for copies of the Guard law, which officers and men would need to carry out their duties. The president set an example by wearing his Guard uniform to public functions.[28] In late 1831 and early 1832, enlistment boards identified eligible guardsmen, although it is not clear how they determined the income levels required for membership; one board reportedly examined citizens' qualifications "with all caution" before enlisting them. Two conflicts over eligibility for officership later in the decade suggest that, especially in marginal cases, it was easy to question a man's eligibility on the grounds of inadequate income.[29]

After eligible guardsmen were indentified in 1831–1832, the new companies assembled for elections in February and March 1832. Held in the parish church, the votes followed many of the procedures familiar from Richard Graham's study of imperial elections.[30] The formal election acts submitted by justices of the peace unfortunately reveal little about the social dynamics or personal ambitions that were at stake in the 1832 (and 1836) contests. Sometimes few men showed up: Only 32 of the 117 members of one company in Penha Parish gathered to elect their officers, but other companies produced more respectable turnouts. Supplementary elections were frequent as captains were subsequently elected majors and lieutenant colonels.[31] Men who missed votes occasionally complained, and in 1836, one justice of the peace had to suspend an election because the guardsmen insisted upon voting for a man who had moved out of the parish.[32] None of these complaints, however, amounted to much and it appears that most elections ran smoothly.

After the company elections, battalions were formed and instructors were appointed to begin training them; the army cutbacks meant that numerous underemployed officers and sergeants eagerly sought the new jobs. Arms requisitions reveal a corporation ready for duty in the second quarter of 1832, although it sometimes proved difficult to obtain the weapons that had been entrusted to militiamen. Tailors must have done a brisk business in the uniforms that guardsmen acquired at their own expense; by mid-April 1832, 190 men in the Third Battalion alone had outfitted themselves.[33]

In the middle of 1832, the Guard began regular police patrols, which commanders coordinated with the local justices of the peace. Both the militia and the municipal guards were then disbanded. Some observers viewed the new corporation favorably: the United States consul reported in early 1833 that Salvador had been "very quiet for a long time . . . owing to the government discharging nearly all the regular soldiers and depending on the militia [sic] for protection."[34] All was not, however, well with the Guard, and its officers were already reporting problems familiar from the militia. Guardsmen exploited all of the provisions that permitted them to be transferred to the reserve and therefore escape duties; as early as June 1832, the head of Sé Parish's battalion worried that the ease with which men acquired certificates of attendance at schools would alone reduce his unit to but "a few zealous citizens." The president responded quickly to this concern and ordered that patrols be organized from among citizens not enlisted in the Guard. Justices of the peace from Santo Antônio além do Carmo and Rua do Paço hailed the measure as long overdue, while their counterpart in Pilar worried that most of the non-Guards in his parish were men of "irregular conduct."[35] Regardless of these differing assessments of the men not enlisted, the proposal demonstrates a quick abandonment of the Guard's central premise that respectable citizens should look after their own security.

Manpower problems are a constant refrain in Guard correspondence. In 1837, an angry battalion head sarcastically remarked on the "amphibious" nature of a recently qualified guard who confessed to earning his living in commerce, even as he presented a certificate declaring him to be a music student.[36] Justices of the peace named block inspectors from among the Guard's ranks, thereby sparing favored individuals the burden of patrols.[37] Guard service interfered with the regular operation of government offices. While the minister of justice might insist that civil servants share in the burdens of upholding public security, the army paymaster demanded that his doorman be dispensed from nighttime rounds so that he could open the office on time.[38] Those born in Portugal sought to be excused on the grounds of foreign nationality, even though all Portuguese residents in Brazil before independence had automatically received citizenship. Such "adoptive" citizens, some alleged, went so far as to declare that they had fought against independence, the only reasons for denying them citizenship, prompting calls for their deportation.[39]

Under these circumstances, it should come as no surprise that the archives are full of complaints about inadequate performance of duties, as guardsmen missed patrols and failed to show up for duty.[40] In this regard, the Guard differed little from its militia predecessor. What was different, however, was that officers now lacked effective means to compel guardsmen to serve. Few took the Guard's cumbersome discipline councils seriously; guardsmen facing charges in these tribunals of their peers were barred from service, which was exactly what many wanted in the first place. As the minister of justice explained, guardsmen accustomed to the "severe disciplinary regime of the militia completely flout the Guard law's penalties." When a sergeant attempted to arrest some of the forty men sentenced to brief prison terms of less than five days for assorted faults in October 1832, he faced a remarkable list of excuses: three claimed to be too ill to go to prison; another argued that he had several sick family members to care for; still another agreed to go, but only after receiving a written notification stating the reasons for his arrest, which would satisfy him that the sentence was legal. The arrested often spent little time in prison; in 1836, they regularly left their cells in Barbalho Fort to sleep at home.[41]

As in Rio de Janeiro, Salvador's National Guard simply did not function effectively except in times of crisis. During the April 1833 revolt of prisoners in the Forte do Mar, guardsmen, regular soldiers, and police cooperated willingly; the Fifth Battalion's drill instructor, Army Lieutenant João Francisco Cabuçu, rushed to the justice of the peace's house, where he helped organize the battalion into patrols.[42] If it was easy to demonstrate patriotism during such crises, the daily grind of Guard service was much less attractive. Some guardsmen quickly made explicit their rejection of the corporation: in April 1832, the head of the Fourth Battalion reported that his men were "saying . . . that they did not want to be citizens." In 1837, a guardsman and former black militia soldier went further, skipping drills and cutting his uniform in half, turning the pieces over to his officer. Others found service degrading, particularly when they were detailed to conduct the chain gangs that carried water to public buildings. If this was citizenship, few wanted it. Frustrated officers recognized their problem: "Men are not always impelled by motives of mere patriotism," wrote the battalion heads of the First Legion in 1833, adding that their experience demonstrated "that only punishment" could induce "many to serve."[43] The Guard had offered Salvador's middle classes and established artisans the opportunity to share in a collective defense of class interests. The 1831 law had made Guard service an essential attribute of citizenship, but the new corporation had failed to attract a durable commitment from its members. This was, of course, not surprising given that these men had other interests. It was, moreover, inefficient for the larger society to rely for security on men employed in regular occupations.[44]

Officership in the National Guard was as problematic as service as simple guardsmen. Those who struggled to make the Guard work in the 1830s no doubt wished for some of the authority that their militia predecessors had enjoyed. Not only did they lack the power to sentence guardsmen to the regulars (who, in any case, were not usually recruiting in the early 1830s) but the transitory nature of Guard officership, subject to reelection, upset many who refused to relinquish their ranks when required to do so. These men could or would only see officership as a permanent condition, as it had been in the militia. Indeed, even after Guard commissions had been made lifetime appointments, a police guard could taunt a Guard lieutenant by telling him that, even though he were "today an officer . . . tomorrow [he] could be a soldier [sic]." In 1836, with a second round of Guard elections looming, the minister of justice doubted that the corporation would survive the efforts of officers to be reelected or the discontent of those who failed to win posts. Ultimately, he concluded, "it is not prudent to confide the security of the Nation entirely to the ballot box."[45]

Committed National Guard officers were relatively rare once the crises of the early 1830s had passed; many simply gave up serving once they discovered the burdens that they had assumed. Their reasons varied: Inability to get along with subordinates prompted a captain to seek a transfer to the cavalry as a simple guard; failing that, he claimed to have moved to Itaparica even though his dry goods store was in Salvador. Another alleged that, although he met the income requirements for the post of second lieutenant to which he had been elected in 1836, he could not afford to buy a uniform. In 1834, no less than four captains of the Second Battalion had abandoned their posts; while one was sick and another had arranged to be removed from the Guard roll, the other two included one absent without leave for a year and another who "almost never shows up."[46] The frequency with which Guard correspondence was signed by men acting far above their rank is a telling indication of the lack of commitment to the corporation on the part of many officers. Guardsmen, however, minded little. In a special 1834 election to replace the Fifth Battalion's head, absent from Salvador for more than ten months, the officers and sergeants blithely reelected the incumbent who would likely vex them little.[47]

By 1837, the National Guard and its model of liberal citizenship had been widely rejected in Salvador. Citizenship was not worth the trouble to many guardsmen; elections tended to produce lax officers unsatisfactory to the provincial government. More important, as the president explained shortly after the Sabinada, "the greatest proprietors and the wealthiest citizens refuse to serve in a military corporation in which they enjoy no ascendancy."[48] Thus, the Guard could not effectively bind elites to the state as the colonial militias had. Those officers who struggled to make the Guard work wished for the military authority that their militia predecessors had enjoyed; in 1835, the war minister had expressed his preference for "the old militas" over the National Guard.[49] Proposed revisions to the Guard law sought to end elected officership for all ranks higher than captain and subject elected officers to confirmation by provincial presidents. They were apparently not debated, and in the 1834 devolution of powers to the provinces, the Additional Act, responsibility for the Guard was transferred to the new provincial legislatures, almost all of which eliminated or severely curtailed elected officership by 1838, the year in which Bahia did so.[50] Before then, however, the Sabinada intervened in Salvador, revealing a different, racially based rejection of the National Guard.

Racial Politics and the Sabinada, 1831–1838

Jeanne Berrance de Castro has argued that the ending of elected officership in the National Guard was a racially motivated measure designed to prevent the election of blacks and mulattoes.[51] This raises the larger question of Guard officers' social origins. Unfortunately the lack of a professional cadre to administer the corporation in the 1830s meant that records were kept in unsystematic fashion, while the impermanence of officership meant that those elected could not use their rank after they stepped down, making them difficult to identify in inventories. Scattered data on the 164 officers identified for the period of 1831 to 1837 suggest that they were a diverse lot. A young Francisco Gonçalves Martins, the future Baron and Viscount of São Lourenço, scion of a sugar planter family destined for a career in the magistracy and imperial politics, was elected head of Sé Parish's battalion in 1832. He did not long serve in that capacity, becoming district judge of Salvador in 1833 and chief of police just in time to repress the 1835 slave revolt and later the Sabinada, the start of a career that would see him serve as provincial president for two long terms.[52] A large number of civil servants and men employed in commerce won election: The foreman of Salvador's public granary was elected captain in Conceição da Praia in 1832 and adjutant in 1836. Several men who later described themselves as registered merchants can also be identified.[53] Men of more modest means are, except in rare cases, more difficult to identify.

Given the silence about race in Guard documentation, it is impossible to test Castro's assertion directly, save in one instance, the 1836 elections in Santo Antônio além do Carmo Parish. According to *O Defensor do Povo*, a radical liberal newspaper that in its few suriving issues often discussed racial questions, all but one of the elected posts in the Second Company were filled by "citizens of brown color" (*cor parda*). A tailor, Captain Joaquim de Souza Vinhático—owner of a small house, one slave, and a small suburban farm—headed the pardo slate by winning an absolute majority of the votes. The election was bitterly contested, and the defeated incumbents—all white men—took to calling the company "Ninety-Third Battalion" (the old mulatto militia unit's designation) and its officers "darkies" (*fuscos*). One was even overheard saying that he would now raise his slaves' children to become Guard officers, while white guardsmen sought transfers out of the company.[54] Elected officership could, as in this case, lead to highly undesirable outcomes, at least from the perspective of the white local notables who suddenly lost their privileged position to a pardo man of relatively modest means. While this case suggests that there is an element of truth in Castro's argument, Thomas Flory has argued that the real issue in the National Guard was broader: Elected officership in general was threatening because of its potential to upset the social order, of which race was only a part.[55]

Moreover, racial questions in the Guard were considerably more complicated than the election of nonwhite officers, as the experience of black and mulatto militia officers demonstrates. The Guard law specified that the militia would be abolished as soon as the Guard was created. Paid militia officers were to revert to the regulars, with the exception of those who had never served in the army, in other words, those promoted from within the black and mulatto militia. Unpaid militia officers with more than twenty-five years of service were excused from the Guard, while the rest had to be enrolled, provided of course that they met the requisite income and status qualifications. They could be elected officers, again, provided that they were free-born and enjoyed sufficient income, but they could refuse election to posts below their militia ranks. Few militia officers appreciated their reduction to "simple guards," and the minister of justice blamed delays in organizing the Guard on these men's opposition in 1832.[56]

More important, militia officers fared poorly in the two rounds of Guard elections held in Salvador (1832 and 1836) and I can identify with certainty only five who won posts in the new corporation, two from the white militia and three from the mulatto battalion.[57] While the militia and the Guard were functionally similar, 1832 thus marked an important turning point as a new group of men took charge of the city's part-time military. Several factors probably contributed to this turnover. In all likelihood, many guardsmen wanted a fresh start and were unwilling to elect the men who had ordered them around during the 1820s. If, as so much evidence from the late colonial period and early 1820s suggests, black officers were significant and respected community leaders, then their failure to win election may also be attributed to the parish-level organization of the Guard, which would have split the black vote. Unfortunately, these remain hypotheses, for there is no indication of who the losers in Guard elections were; thus, I cannot be certain that militia officers ran in significant numbers for office in the Guard.

It is, however, clear that black, and to a significantly lesser extent, mulatto militia officers came to reject the Guard, and more fundamentally, the liberalism that underlay it. The abolition of their corporation must have come as a shock to Salvador's militia officers. April 1831 had marked a high point in the militia's involvement in urban politics, but scarcely four months later, it was slated for abolition. The mulatto colonel, Antônio Lopes Tabira Bahiense, formally commanded the April 1831 protests against the Portuguese-born commander of arms, João Crisóstomo Calado, and Lieutenant Colonel Francisco Xavier Bigode led the black battalion to Barbalho Fort, where the protestors gathered before their triumphant march into the city. Militia officers had also demonstrated their moderation and loyalty to the new regime during the social and military unrest that rocked the city during the winter of 1831.[58] Despite this prominence, many of the militia's functions were taken over by the civilian Municipal Guard hastily created in mid-1831, and within a year, the Guard sidelined black and mulatto officers altogether. Bigode; his adjutant, Joaquim José de Santana Gomes; and the mulatto adjutant, José Maria Cirilo da Silva, had no right to return to the regular army (for they had not served in it), and they were retired on their major and adjutants' salaries.[59]

Enforced retirement did not, however, eliminate these three men from Bahian politics. Through their protests against the 1829 salary law, the evolution of their thinking about the Brazilian state can be traced. Although narrowly focused on the issues of professional recognition and salary increases, these petitions hint at larger political discussions among black and mulatto officers that eventually led many to reject the Brazilian state altogether. Immediately after the 1829 salary law, they began a long and ultimately unsuccessful campaign to have themselves recognized as officers (as they had been under the colonial regime) and to receive the salary increases denied them since the early 1820s.[60] After 1831, their petitions took on a more assertive tone (they were free from direct military obligations) and addressed larger questions as they analyzed Brazilian liberalism and compared colonial and imperial racial policies. In 1832, Bigode described his monthly pay as "inadequate for his necessary sustenance and decency" and stressed that his salary was not in accordance with constitutional provisions that "the Law be equal for all, whether it protects, punishes, or rewards." He then identified himself as being "of black color" (*cor preta*), an unusual explicit assertion of racial identity in petitions, and recounted his career, emphasizing that his promotion to the post of major had come under the terms of the 1802 ruling, which, although issued "in times of darkness," contained clauses "that appear full of light and [the] impartiality that a free Constitution today affirms, for it was determined that [to the posts of] senior officers and adjutants of that unit, and that of the mulattoes, be always promoted . . . individuals of the same colors when they demonstrated the necessary qualifications." He continued paraphrasing the 1802 ruling, recalling that the then "Head of the Nation" had instituted this policy "to exile from society odious concerns over incidents of color" and to demonstrate that he considered "all black and mulatto men . . . worthy of all military honors and posts."

Having thus demonstrated that the "spirit of partiality" had been "banished" more than 30 years ago, Bigode turned to the 1829 law which excluded "only black and mulatto officers" from its benefits. The interpretation of salary laws against the interests of himself "and others of his class and color" was an "error" for it perpetuated "in constitutional times of equality . . . the same odious prejudices that in absolutist and despotic times had been banned." He only briefly referred to his services at independence—this was no petition for special favor—and concluded by calling on the young emperor to restore black and mulatto officers to a place of equality with all other militia officers, by which "Your Imperial Majesty would extirpate a pernicious abuse and an odious vice, demonstrate the Name of Constitutional, and prove that it is your will that the law be equal for all."[61]

The mixture of liberal ideals (including quotations from the constitution) with a defense of segregated institutions in this petition reflects not just

Bigode's personal interest in receiving a salary increase (and quite possibly back pay). He spoke for all the men of "his class and color," who no doubt had time to analyze their condition during their unwanted retirement. Equality before the law was, for Bigode and his colleagues, meaningless unless it recognized the racial distinctions that colonial legislation had embodied. Furthermore, Bigode's praise of what he considered the enlightened and liberal racial policy of the absolutist monarchy demonstrates his understanding that, given the racial hierarchies of Brazilian society, a color-blind liberalism would simply give free reign to the "odious prejudices" that had been held at bay by his and his colleagues' special status in the military.[62]

Bigode's petition had the same fate as those of Gomes and Cirilo; Bahian military and civilian authorities commented favorably, both on his civil and military conduct and on the argument that he and his colleagues had been considered equal to regular officers. Authorities in Rio de Janeiro rejected the request. No doubt familiar with Bigode and Gomes's travails, the contemporary historian of Bahia, Inácio Acioli de Cerqueira e Silva, observed that, notwithstanding all of their services, "disdain and humiliation" were the Henriques's only recompense. In 1835 and 1837, Bigode submitted virtually identical petitions; both went to the Conselho Supremo Militar, which twice ruled against him, legalistically applying the 1829 salary law. The last petition was formally turned down in Rio de Janeiro on 5 September 1837, and the news must have reached Bigode only a few weeks before the outbreak of the Sabinada Rebellion on 7 November 1837.[63]

As it did in so many other aspects of Bahian life, the Sabinada marked a major turning point for both the remnants of Salvador's militia and the city's National Guard. What role militiamen played in organizing the rebellion is not known, but it marked an important shift in alliances for Salvador's black officers who, until 1837, had stood firmly against radical liberal opposition politics. Lieutenant Cabuçu, who blamed "the blacks [*negros*] and their battalions" for "terrifying all" at the end of the revolt, pointed to a key aspect of the Sabinada: the support that it elicited from black officers. Moreover, he clearly identified the source of the terror as negros, not pardos.[64] For mulatto officers, the Sabinada once again demonstrated their ambiguous place in Bahian society, as they exhibited but lukewarm support for the rebellion. Only one white militia officer, an artillery second lieutenant, joined the Sabinada.[65] While the rebels abolished the National Guard and restored the black and mulatto militias, fourteen Guard officers joined the revolt (three of them, however, had been officers in the mulatto militia).

What did the Sabinada offer these men? For black militia officers the answer is clearest and best documented. The rebellion offered them a restoration of the position in the state apparatus from which they had been evicted in 1831. Bigode personally invited his old companions at arms to join in the republic's defense, as did an Henriques captain, José de Santa Eufrásia.[66] Fully fourteen officers who signed the 1824 oath of allegiance to the constitution appear among the thirty-one officers in the restored Henriques of 1837; several more of them had been sergeants before 1831. Dubbed the "Homeland's Loyal Volunteers," the black militia battalion once again took pride of place as the First Battalion of the Second Line. They saw action against the planter-led forces that besieged Salvador, and according to sympathetic chroniclers, acquitted themselves well.[67]

More important, the Sabinada placed race on the political agenda. One letter to the editor of a rebel newspaper articulated the frustration that many free black Brazilians felt at the increasingly elitist nature of Brazilian liberalism. *O Novo Diario da Bahia's* declaration that "they are warring against us, because they are whites, and in Bahia there must be no blacks [*negros*] and mulattoes [*pardos*], especially in office" must have had special appeal for Bigode, who had experienced firsthand this sort of exclusion. The article went on to observe that only blacks and mulattoes who "are very rich and change their liberal opinions" could hold office in Brazil, pointedly citing Antônio Pereira Rebouças as an example.[68] Bigode was neither rich nor did he change his "liberal opinions"; instead, he implemented in the Sabinada the ideals that he had been advocating since the early 1830s—a liberalism that acknowledged race and rested on black institutions. Late in the rebellion, some black militia officers adopted an even more radical position: Santa Eufrásia was heard to demand that it was time "for blacks [*negros*] to govern the republic," rather than whites.[69] With demands that blacks assume the reins of government, he had moved far beyond simply the defense of institutional space for blacks in the state apparatus.

As the rebels' language makes clear, they were speaking about Brazilians, not Africans, who carefully excluded from the rebellion. The extent to which this explicit racial politics threatened Bahian and Brazilian social hierarchies can best be gauged from the repression that followed the revolt. As the Sabinada defenses crumbled during three terrible days in mid-March 1838, Bigode surrendered, only to be murdered after his incarceration in Palma Barracks, allegedly on the orders of the commander of loyalist forces, none other than General Calado, whom he had helped expel from Bahia in 1831. A wounded Santa Eufrásia eluded capture for a month, but committed suicide rather than fall into the hands of the authorities; another captain was shot at "point-blank range" when he tried to surrender. The adjutant, Captain Gomes, survived by going underground and only turned himself in long after the pogrom had subsided.[70] Further indirect evidence for the massacre of the Henriques's leadership can be found in the desultory prosecution against these men. Of the thirty-one commissioned officers in the rebel unit, only nine were in custody. How many of the other twenty-two suffered Bigode's fate or enjoyed Gomes's luck is unknowable but their absence from the trial record gives pause. The crushing of the Sabinada marked the elimination of the Henriques's leadership, men who had developed a racially based critique of the Brazilian state, drawing on their experience in the colonial militia. In this sense, the Sabinada was the Bahian equivalent of Cuba's Escalera of 1843–1844, the repression of which largely destroyed the Afro–Cuban militia and cabildo leadership.[71]

Mulatto militia officers were less amenable to the racial politics of the Sabinada's black officers. Eleven joined the rebellion; three of them, Lieutenants Alexandre Ferreira do Carmo Sicupira, João Lício Rodrigues Banha, and Manoel Inácio da Conceição Bahia, had long histories of participation in radical liberal politics.[72] The reconstituted mulatto battalion contained only five officers and three sergeants from the mulatto militia and it was far less active in the Sabinada's defense than the black battalion; it was apparently kept inside Salvador to police the city.[73] Tomás Alves de Otan e Silva, the highest ranking rebel mulatto militia officer and commander of the rebel battalion, read the handwriting on the wall in early March 1838; for his refusal to follow orders, he was arrested by the rebel authorities on 2 March. Captain José Maria Cirilo da Silva, the mulatto adjutant who had joined Bigode and Gomes in their campaign to revise the 1829 salary law, carried on half-heartedly to the end as battalion major.[74] Some pardo officers were conspicuous by their absence from the Sabinada, notably Tabira Bahiense, the mulatto militia's last commander, and retired Lieutenant Colonel Pedro Inácio de Porciuncula, Cirilo's father, who appeared as a key prosecution witness in the trials.[75]

The ambivalence of pardo officers toward the Sabinada's racial politics and its restoration of the militia is not surprising. More than a few of them, like the wealthy Joaquim da Silva Braga, the building contractor who died in 1844, stopped using their militia ranks after 1831, thus distancing themselves from their past as pardo officers. Needless to say, Braga was not involved in the Sabinada. By contrast, black officers clung to their militia ranks and uniforms, the symbols of their former status; as late as 1848, one requested to be buried in full uniform. With the elimination of segregated corporations, mulatto officers, especially those with means, could bid to become white men, while black officers could not; constructions of whiteness were, after all, more credible the less the African ancestry. To be sure, no firm conclusions about these men's sense of self can be drawn on the basis of this limited evidence but it is significant that, in 1860, the sixty-nine-year-old widowed Cirilo was a white man.[76]

It is still more difficult to analyze the motives of the fourteen National Guard officers involved in the rebellion; three of them had been officers in the mulatto militia. They constituted 12.5 percent of the 112 Guard officers identified in a June 1838 report.[77] None served in the First or Third Guard Infantry Battalions (Sé and Conceição da Praia Parishes, respectively the centers of government and commerce). The perception of the Third Battalion as a den of iniquitous Portuguese led the lusophobic rebel government to abolish it before the rest of the Guard.[78] The rebel Guard officers were thus from poorer parishes; they also held low ranks: Only one was captain (Vinhático) and the rest were lieutenants. The entire command of Salvador's Guard left the city, playing a major part in the siege and defeat of the rebellion, as Chief of Police Martins later emphasized.[79] According to trial testimony, the most active rebel Guard officer was the pardo tailor, Captain Vinhático, whose controversial election has already been analyzed (that he had been killed during the recapture of Salvador may have made him a convenient scapegoat). The surviving fourteen included a tinsmith who owned a hardware store, a scribe, the administrator of a commercial house, a farmer, and two who vaguely described themselves as being in business.[80] The rebel Guard officers were thus a marginal minority in the corporation; the three who had been officers in the mulatto militia reinforce this impression. That such men had managed to win election in the mid-1830s, however, suggests that the Guard was, to some degree, a popular institution.

These patterns of participation in the Sabinada suggest several conclusions about racial politics. In the atmosphere of increasingly binary racial politics—*brancos* versus *classes de cor*—the pardo militia officers had difficult choices to make. Relatively few of them joined the rebellion and it is clear that the Sabinada's racial politics was most fully embraced by black officers, who looked back to their experience in the militia to reject the liberalism of the Guard. This, in turn, marked an important change from the 1790s, when mulattoes were perceived to be the most radical advocates of change and blacks more subordinate. Then, of course, it had been pardo enlisted men who faced the clearest discrimination while, in the 1830s, it was black officers who suffered most. The former left their stamp on the Tailors' Conspiracy while the latter indelibly marked the Sabinada. And the post-Sabinada repression took this into account: Bigode was murdered, Otan survived; Gomes felt that he needed to hide while Cirilo faced trial. Within the National Guard, officer support for the Sabinada came from men like Vinhático, a pardo artisan who had tried to use the National Guard as an institution through which to claim a higher status in society. Rebuffed in these efforts, he likely found the Sabinada's racial discourse appealing.

The New National Guard, 1838–1850

With the Sabinada defeated, the provincial assembly moved quickly to reform the National Guard. A law of July 1838 authorized the president to appoint officers to all posts in the corporation, subject to their meeting the income requirements established in 1832, to residing in the municipality, and to "having rendered services in defense and support of the monarchical-constitutional system," which meant having opposed the Sabinada Rebellion. Officership in the new Guard was a permanent condition and the law established retirement provisions for those who had completed twenty-five years of service or became incapacitated. For guardsmen, the greatest innovation was the abolition of qualification boards; enlistments henceforth would be done by Guard commanders.[81]

The Viscount of Pirajá eagerly anticipated that the new law would "give the government considerable power," a hope shared by the *Correio Mercantil*,[82] and they would not be disappointed as the second half of 1838 saw a complete overhaul of Salvador's Guard. All of the officers elected in 1836 were stripped of their posts and only 41 of 112 were reappointed, judging by an incomplete June 1838 list of officers and the 1845 city almanac.[83] Promotion criteria in the new Guard resembled those of the old militias, as commanders constructed their model of the ideal officer by stressing economic success, good conduct (especially anti-Sabinada service), and seniority. In justifying his recommendation for adjutant, the commander of the Fourth Battalion explained that the man "had means, belonged to a distinguished family, and has [performed] relevant services."[84] With the establishment of clear criteria for promotions, protests against preteritions soon piled up on the president's desk, and the Guard came to resemble the army in this respect.[85] The use of "head" to refer to battalion commanders gradually gave way to "commander," further underscoring what had changed.

The new Guard, however, differed in a key way from both the army and the militia in that a somewhat vaguely worded clause in the 1838 law appeared to permit officers to request dismissals or decline appointments. Facing fairly frequent refusals to assume officer posts in 1838 and 1839, the superior commander condemned these men's lack of "honor" and "nobility." Other officers more sensibly argued that it was better to release officers "fed up with public service."[86] By the early 1840s, this issue had lost its salience, suggesting that the Guard officer corps became a somewhat self-selected corporation.

Three partially overlapping sets of data on the social origins of the new Guard's officers reveal a predominance of civil servants and merchants. The 1845 almanac listed all of the Guard's officers for the municipality and judicial district of Salvador, including its outlying suburbs. Almost half of the officers identified elsewhere in the almanac were civil servants, while just over one-fourth were merchants, and most of the rest professionals or white-collar employees such as warehouse administrators. Artisans are strikingly absent from Guard, in sharp contrast to their prominent place among militia officers (Table 8.1 compared with Table 4.2). The almanac did not record suburban sugar planters and landowners such as the new superior commander, the Viscount of Rio Vermelho, but his distillery in Agua de Meninos was listed.[87] Nor did it record clerks and employees of mercantile houses who can be readily identified in other documentation. The eighteen legion and battalion heads and acting heads in November 1845 largely conform to this pattern (Table 8.2). The superior commander characterized most as "proprietors," a vague term that disguised wide differences in wealth. The sugar planters and most of the generic "proprietors" commanded the suburban battalions, leaving the two urban legions under civil servants, professionals, and a few merchants. National Guard officers' wealth and slave holding at death on average exceeded that of militia officers by threefold (32:794$171 to 9:996$586 and 33.1 to 9.1; Table 8.3 compared with Table 4.3), but the average value of Guard officer estates masks wide differences in wealth between the professionals and civil servants, who lagged far behind merchants and sugar planters.

A closer examination of Salvador's Guard officers in 1845 reveals distinct differences between the suburban battalions commanded by sugar planters and landowners and the urban battalions proper, headed by merchants and civil servants, and through the latter, closely tied to the state apparatus. The suburban Third Legion exemplifies the textbook interpretation of the

TABLE 8.1
National Guard Officer Occupations, 1845

	Serving	Retired	Total
Civil servant	42	4	46
Merchant/shopkeeper	22	5	27
Professionals			
Administrator	3	1	4
Lawyer	3	0	3
Teacher	3	0	3
Broker	4	1	5
Banker	0	2	2
Doctor	7	0	7
Total professionals	20	4	24
Artisans			
Typographer	2	0	2
Silkworker	1	0	1
Portrait painter	1	0	1
Total artisans	4	0	4
Distillery owner	1	0	1
Total known	89	13	102
Unknown	170	8	178
Total officers	259	21	280

SOURCE: *Almanach . . . 1845.*

Guard as a corporation that reinforced the power of the rural landed class and mirrored social hierarchies in the countryside. The Baron (future Count) of Passé, owner of five sugar mills and 496 slaves in 1877, commanded this legion from his plantation at Pindoba, while the legion's major owned a single sugar plantation nearby. A considerably more modest planter and honorary army colonel, Alexandre de Lacerda Seabra, led the Fourth Battalion, while three of his captains, the brothers Fabrício, Silvestre, and Domingos Cardoso de Vasconcelos, exemplify the lesser notables on whom fell so much of local administration. Resident in Paripe parish, they owned a few slaves, small ranches, and a lime works. A fourth captain, Domingos Pereira Soares, also owned a lime factory and described himself as a sugar cane farmer.[88]

TABLE 8.2

National Guard Commander Occupations, 1845

Merchant/proprietário	2
Broker/proprietário	1
Civil servant/proprietário	2
Civil servant	5
Lawyer/proprietário	2
Sugar planter/proprietário	2
Proprietário	4
Total	18

SOURCES: "Relação dos Chefes de Legião e Com.des ... ," 10 Nov. 1845, APEB, m. 6455; *Almanach ... 1845*; wills and invs. of National Guard officers, APEB/SJ/IT and APEB/SJ/LRT.

Not surprisingly, merchant officers were far more common inside Salvador. Most had managed to wind up their business affairs before their deaths, investing profits from commerce in real estate, stocks, and bonds or transferring the ownership of commercial houses to heirs, or as Francisco José Godinho had done, his son-in-law. This Portuguese-born Guard officer—a retired major in 1845—owned forty-nine houses in Salvador and Santo Amaro and had converted more than half of his estate of over 483:000$000 into financial instruments. He transferred his commercial house in Santo Amaro to his clerk and protegé, provided that the man marry his daughter. Only Godinho's wealth was exceptional—most other merchants followed his strategies as they approached retirement.[89] Merchant officers were typically involved in a variety of activities. Two who died in midcareer had sugar, coffee, tobacco, and timber on hand for export and stores full of imported dry goods and foodstuffs. Captain Félix Ribeiro Navarro and his partner owned a haberdashery and traded in slaves on the coast of Africa. Two others were less lucky in that business, leaving their heirs claims against the British government for the seizure of slavers.[90] As the example of retired Major Godinho suggests, successful merchants tended to avoid taking on Guard responsibilities; few led battalions or legions. Those who did during these years, notably João Alves Pitombo and Justino Nunes de Sento Sé, left estates worth considerably less than the average for merchant officers.[91] In the long run, National Guard work was not compatible with mercantile success.

This, in turn, left command of the urban National Guard in the hands of civil servants. A visitor to the Customs House in November 1845 might have mistaken it for the Guard's headquarters. No less than four of the commanders in Table 8.2 worked there, and a fifth, a customs broker, likely spent much time there; ten more officers were on its staff. While the imperial and provincial civil services may have offered their employees a secure and generally comfortable living, and contributions to the pension fund (*montepio*) ensured their widows and children some sustenance, bureaucratic careers were not paths to great wealth. More than a few left only pensions to their successors.[92] The civil servant commanders in 1845 were men of but modest means. Lieutenant Colonel José Maria Servulo Sampaio, employed in the presidential secretariat in 1845, died bankrupt in 1864 after having sunk his and his wife's savings into a small sugar mill (*engenhoca*), which burned to the ground in 1863. Colonel Joaquim Antônio da Silva Carvalhal underscored his close links to the state in his will, describing his many services: army cadet during the independence war, election as Guard adjutant in 1834 and major in 1836, senior clerk of the customs house in 1838, a post that he held until his retirement in 1861. He was not wealthy. In 1878, his house carried a hefty mortgage and he had borrowed money to keep up his contributions to the pension fund.[93] The customs broker, Lieutenant

TABLE 8.3

National Guard Officers' Average Wealth and
Slaveownership at Death, 1845–1885

	Average Wealth	Number	Number Holding Slaves	Average Size of Holding
Civil servants	8:289$239	9	4	3.3
Professionals	5:568$932	4	4	6.5
Merchants	78:388$461	11	10	11.7
Sugar planters	92:267$085	3	3	268.0
Other land owners	7:281$293	6	6	19.7
Unknown	4:017$980	7	6	2.3
All officers	32:794$171	40	33	33.1

NOTES: Constant 1822 mil-réis deflated by sterling exchange rate; includes slaves freed by testamentary provisions.

SOURCES: *Almanach . . . 1845*; forty invs., APEB/SJ/IT.

Colonel Joaquim Proto Dourado, owned 15 slaves, but little else on his death in 1851; his widow borrowed to pay for the funeral.[94] Colonel Inácio Acioli de Cerqueira e Silva, the historian of independence in Bahia, also fits this pattern. Described as a "proprietor" in 1845 and listed as a lawyer in the 1845 almanac, he had been employed as manager of the São João Theater in the 1830s. He twice won election as alderman, and in 1850, the Brazilian legislature debated whether to grant him the right to practice law throughout the empire, notwithstanding his not having completed his education in Portugal. According to his biographer, however, he died poor in Rio de Janeiro, living on a pension conceded to him to write a history of Brazil, a literary trajectory strikingly similar to that of the army officer–poet, Ladislau dos Santos Titara.[95] Acioli and Carvalhal were also honorary majors in the army, half-pay commissions liberally granted in reward for service against the Sabinada.

The close connection of these Guard commanders to the state is significant: Instead of tying merchant and artisan elites to the state as had the old militia, the Guard of the 1840s expanded the bureaucracy's influence into urban society. One simple reason helps explain the dominance of the Guard by civil servant officers. Unlike merchants or artisans, bureaucrats continued to draw salaries while serving in the Guard; their personal interests did not suffer when they were called away from work, for they received whichever was higher—their government pay or their officers' salary.[96] Thus, the Customs House, which employed almost one-fourth of the urban Guard's commanders in 1845, ten other officers, and likely many more guardsmen, in effect granted the Guard an important subsidy in the larger state interest of maintaining control over the corporation and ensuring that it was available to maintain order. To be sure, this control over the Guard came at a price: Paperwork fell behind in many government departments, including the army arsenal. At other times, the Guard suffered. Lieutenant Colonel Evaristo Ladislau e Silva, a battalion commander and lawyer who often did government legal work, apologized in 1841 for failing to attend promptly to Guard correspondence beceause he was "overloaded" with work at the Treasury.[97]

On the surface, the post-1838 urban Guard thus more resembles a corporation of the autonomous powerholders whom Raimundo Faoro has seen as central to Luso-Brazilian history than the mechanism of planter–monarchy alliance analyzed by Fernando Uricoechea.[98] This contrast should not, however, be exaggerated. The core of the imperial alliance lay in the countryside and urban society was heavily dependent on the Recôncavo; moreover, the Sabinada's defeat had demonstrated the Recôncavo's predominance over Salvador. In this light, the new Guard might better be seen as an institution indirectly controlled by the planter class through the state apparatus, much as the national army officer corps that took shape in the 1840s did not require direct participation by the planter class.

Not only did the 1838 law end the practice of electing Guard officers in the interest of giving the government control over the officer corps, it also gave these officers the power to enlist their guardsmen, dispensing with the cumbersome qualification boards. While this measure sought to give officers more control over the rank and file, guardsmen still enjoyed the right to request transfer to the reserve on the grounds outlined in 1831, and several categories of men, notably foreigners, remained exempt. More than a few natives of Portugal rediscovered their citizenship when Guard service became onerous or when they fell afoul of their officers.[99] Innundated with medical excuses and certificates of attendance at schools in 1839, Superior Commander Rio Vermelho declared that he no longer trusted Salvador's doctors to make accurate diagnoses and expected that enrollment in the Lyceum would soon exceed that of the Guard.[100] Requests for exemptions not founded in law frequently arrived on officers' desks. In February 1839, two merchants requested release from Guard service for some of their clerks; one explained that all of his employees were essential, for his firm was then handling the cargoes of five ships in port. To the other request, Lieutenant Colonel Pitombo responded that no law authorized excuses on these grounds; were there one, added this merchant-officer, he would long since have taken advantage of it to relieve his chief clerk.[101] A sergeant seeking to be excused from all Guard service explained in great detail that as manager of a distillery he was the essential employee at an establishment that directly or indirectly produced more than 2:140$000 annually in imperial and provincial tax revenue, worth far more to the state than the services that he might provide as a Guardsman.[102]

This inelegant scramble to evade Guard duties by stretching the terms of legal exemptions differed little from what had taken place before 1838. In 1839, Rio Vermelho blamed "those who transplanted to Brazil a law which might have been appropriate for France because of its large population," without making clear who should serve in Brazil; what he did not want but seemingly could not prevent was a Guard rank and file composed solely of "artisans and day laborers." Ten years later, he went so far as to propose turning the Guard into a paid corporation. Rio Vermelho's allusions to France, however, were strikingly misplaced: Paris's National Guard suffered from the same problems with which he struggled.[103] When no obvious crisis loomed, few willingly spent the night on patrol or their Sundays on guard at the presidential palace—it was simply too tempting to become a free rider.

To deal with this problem, the framers of the 1838 law granted commanders the authority to imprison their subordinates for up to fifteen days, but this power proved difficult to exercise. Some refractory guardsmen could not be found: In early 1839, one reportedly lived as a recluse in the warehouse where he worked to elude his captain.[104] Sometimes justices of the peace cooperated with officers seeking to arrest insubordinates; other times they did not. The justice of the peace of Santo Antônio além do Carmo prevented Guard officers from exercising authority over their men in 1841, "because he believes that nobody should be arrested except on his orders, and that the Guard is subject to him."[105] In 1845, a block inspector let several arrested guardsmen escape, to which the acting superior commander responded that it was "an offense against discipline and the impartial administration of justice to tolerate the conduct of National Guardsmen who, enjoying some fortune or protection, do not spare the means, however repugnant, of avoiding service, egotistically leaving it to only the poor and the less protected." Of course, presidents were themselves major contributors to this problem. Even the transfer of the power to name block inspectors from the elected judges of the peace to appointed police delegates and subdelegates in 1842—one of the Regresso's major reforms—did not eliminate the conflicts over the appointment of inspectors. One officer hoped in 1843 that the "battalion of inspectors" would be returned to the Guard, but the new subdelegate of Pilar argued that there were not enough qualified nonguardsmen for the posts in his parish. In early 1845, three of Salvador's battalions still reported seventy-two block inspectors withdrawn from their rolls.[106] Presidents furthermore continued to dispense guardsmen from service: In 1841, 151 men from the Second Battalion were formally excused by the president, a figure equal to 45 percent of the 355 men showing up for duty (210 more were unaccounted for and 60 were sick).[107] Enmeshed in the webs of patronage that structured society, Guard officers could only exercise their authority to the extent that it did not threaten that of other, more powerful patrons.

Frequent call-ups for regular army service made the post-1838 Guard less attractive for the rank and file. In the 1830s, Guard service had consisted principally of unpaid police work and occasional Sunday garrison duties. The 1831 law made provisions for forming detachments of guardsmen to serve as regular troops in cases of emergency, but the complex and cumbersome procedures established for designating guardsmen for these detachments proved most unsatisfactory when the rebellions in Rio Grande do Sul and Pará broke out in 1835. In 1836, the government attempted to rectify this problem by authorizing Guard commanders to select recruits for these detachments. The bill aroused a storm of opposition from liberal deputies who accused the government of seeking to restore the militias and desiring to use the Guard for electoral purposes; the threat of being so drafted would no doubt have impeded the free exercise of the franchise.[108] With Brazil's military and political situation worsening in 1837, the government obtained the curious authorization to recruit for the regulars within the Guard noted in the last chapter, despite vigorous opposition from the Guard's defenders.[109] The first government of the Regresso abruptly changed course, suspending the Guard impressment provisions four days after it came to power and introducing a bill to call up 4,000 guardsmen to serve for one year. Officers were to select the men, beginning with the unmarried, while those who failed to report for duty could be sentenced to the regulars for two years.[110] The Sabinada intervened in Bahia, preventing this call-up, which would have been the first in the province, for earlier shortfalls in regular troops had been made up with rotating unpaid Guard drafts; Bahian authorities had apparently refused to create detachments during the 1830s.[111]

After 1838, call-ups of National Guardsmen were frequent, and for most of the 1840s, Salvador had at least a company or two of guardsmen "quartered" (*aquartelado*) as regular soldiers. In 1842, the provincial government was authorized to raise a provisional corps of 400 guardsmen.[112] These levies, reminiscent of the militias in the 1820s, were the least popular of the Guard's duties. As early as 1838 and 1839, Guard commanders had attempted to mitigate their burdens, first by offering to do garrison duties for shorter ten-day shifts and then in rotating daily unpaid shifts, which they judged "less onerous" for their men.[113] Each order to "quarter" guardsmen elicited a flood of petitions from the designates, in which they typically alleged that family obligations and business interests prevented them from undertaking the task.[114] Enough of these requests were ignored to keep more than 350 guardsmen in the barracks in 1843 and about 200 in 1844, the only years for which I located this data.[115] Not only was this service onerous, but Guardsmen assigned for six-month terms to these units often found themselves serving much longer, as their battalions failed to supply replacements. To petitions for release, presidents usually responded that the men would be discharged as soon as new levies arrived.[116]

Moreover, quartered guardsmen and those in the provisional corps came under regular military discipline and were subject to corporal punishment and the full panoply of desertion penalties. President and Commander of Arms Francisco José de Souza Soares de Andréia doubted the wisdom of these provisions and argued that ten guardsmen who were technically ineligible for the 1845 desertion pardon because they had aggravated the offense by taking uniform pieces or equipment ought to be pardoned anyway, for guardsmen could not be held to the same standards as regular soldiers.[117] Service as regular soldiers blurred the distinction between the army and the Guard that had been so important to the framers of the 1831 law. If the citizens of the Guard could be reduced by fiat to the status of regular soldiers, then little distinguished the Guard of the 1840s from the militias of the 1820s. The vision of a self-conscious, respectable property-holding citizenry responsible for their own security embodied in the original Guard was thoroughly buried by the call-ups of the 1840s.

There were, nevertheless, reasons to join the Guard, including of course the protection from the army recruitment that obedient guardsmen enjoyed and the opportunity to associate oneself with potential patrons. Guard officers repeatedly emphasized that it was their obligation both to protect worthy and dutiful guardsmen, even as they despatched the unworthy to the regulars or the navy.[118] Furthermore, as Antônio Edmilson Rodrigues and his colleagues have noted, the very existence of the Guard served an important function in maintaining order, if only by subtly regulating society and specifying individuals' places in it.[119] In 1845, the president reported that the city's Guard battalions counted 4,467 men of all ranks, a figure slightly larger than the militia at its peak of 4,043 in 1812 (Table 4.1), although the 1845 figure was likely a smaller proportion of the city's population than the 1812 enlistment.[120] Over time, service became routine; loyalties (and antipathies) developed among officers and men. In 1847, the acting superior commander, Sento Sé, heartily disliked Carvalhal, then commanding the First Legion.[121] Two years earlier, when President Andréia ordered portions of two battalions into the barracks in response to a rumored slave conspiracy, the men of the First Battalion refused to go unless the entire detachment were commanded by their lieutenant colonel. Andréia smelled sedition and promptly exercised his prerogative to suspend the First Battalion for one year, landing regular soldiers to ensure compliance; he and progovernment newspapers blamed the Second Legion's head, Colonel Inácio Acioli, then publishing a newspaper critical of the provincial administration.[122] While the real reasons for this "rebellion" remain unclear, it suggests an element of corporate identity in the Guard that extended beyond officers to at least

TABLE 8.4
Occupations of National Guardsmen, 1838 and 1847

| | 1838 | | 1847 | |
	First Infantry	Third Infantry	Third Caçadores	Fourth Caçadores
Artisans	34	4	32	59
Commerce	34	127	0	0
Civil service	6	0	0	0
Farmer (*roceiro/ lavrador*)	0	0	22	1
Other	1	1	2	0
Total	75	132	56	60

SOURCES: "Lista dos Guardas Nacionaes Alistados . . ." and "Lista dos Guardas Nacionaes Soltr.os alistados . . . ," ca. Aug. 1838, APEB, m. 3534; "Relação das Praças da 1.a Comp.a da G.N. . . ."; "Relação das Praças da 2.a Cia . . . ," 21 Dec. 1847, APEB, m. 3377.

some guardsmen. So too does the willingness of guardsmen to squabble with regular soldiers that was a notable feature of the Guard–army conflicts analyzed in the previous chapter.

A smattering of sources makes it possible to profile the new Guard's rank and file (Table 8.4). The Third Infantry Battalion, based in the city's commercial center, Conceição da Praia Parish, was dominated by men employed in commerce, clerks and shopkeepers; the First Infantry Battalion (Sé Parish, the center of government) included a few low-level civil servants, with the rest of its contingent divided equally between artisans and commercial employees. Salvador was, of course, a major port and center of international trade and constituted an important market for urban trades; the 1838 contingents nicely reflect this urban pofile. The 1847 contingents drawn from suburban parishes reveal the importance of agriculture, likely market gardening, on the city's outskirts. To some extent, this data may exaggerate the Guard's modest social origins, for designated Guardsmen could hire substitutes, provided that the men met Guard qualifications. It is not, unfortunately, known how many of these men were substitutes, but given detachments' prominence, these quartered guardsmen were the corporation's most visible members. The 1847 contingents also mirror Salvador's racial

TABLE 8.5

Race of Two National Guard Companies, 1847

	Officers		*Sergeants and Corporals*		*Guardsmen*	
	Number	*Percentage*	*Number*	*Percentage*	*Number*	*Percentage*
Branco	7	100	6	28.5	9	7.8
Pardo			5	23.8	43	37.1
Cabra			5	23.8	20	17.2
Crioulo			5	23.8	44	37.9
Total	7	100	21	99.9	116	100.0

SOURCES: "Relação das Praças da 2.a C.ia . . ." and "Relação das Praças da 1.a Comp.a . . .," 21 Dec. 1847, APEB, m. 3377.

hierarchy: All of the officers and one-fourth of the sergeants and corporals were white, while only 9 of 116 guardsmen were white (Table 8.5).

The contrast between these companies and the Santo Antônio além do Carmo company headed by Captain Vinhático in 1836 is striking. In the new National Guard, social hierarchies were secure, and white men did not have to worry about receiving orders from pardo officers; officers were not likely artisans either. The 1838 Guard reform produced a corporation closely tied to the state through its civil-servant officers, respectful of social hierarchies and capable of functioning effectively by supplying contingents to serve alongside the regulars.

Brazilians' unwillingness to pursue the democratization promised in the 1831 law killed the liberal Guard of the 1830s. In the debates about reforming the Guard in the 1840s, deputies frankly admitted as much. It would simply not do to have "notable men" elected corporals or to have sugar planters serving under their slave-drivers; the central issue in the 1830s was not the election of nonwhites or even ex-slaves as officers, but simply the election of officers.[123] Given that the provincial legislatures had, like Bahia, each done away with elected officership in slightly different fashion, the corporation of the 1840s was a peculiar compromise between liberal Guard and colonial militia, belonging to none of the known categories of military institutions, as one deputy declared in 1841.[124] Its diverse provincial organization belied its name and left ministers of justice unable to report effectively about its state.[125] Reform bills of the 1840s sought to impose some national order onto the Guard but deputies failed to agree on how best to revise the 1831 and 1832 laws. Some called for the restoration of the militias, while others defended the liberal institution of the 1830s and railed against efforts to militarize the Guard, particularly an 1843 bill that proposed to staff the Guard with large numbers of regular officers. Deputies' fears of placing power to appoint Guard officers in partisan hands proved an important stumbling block in 1846.[126]

Examining the Guard together with the militias reveals the important transformations in state–society relations that took place after independence. The story is one of racially based exclusion, as the black and mulatto militia pillars of the colonial regime were sapped by the reform bills of the 1820s and then roughly kicked out from under the state in 1831. Liberal reformers could not leave room for black and mulatto officers, and the massacre of black officers in March 1838 was the only solution that could be envisaged to their rejection of Brazilian liberalism. The liberal and democratic Guard edifice constructed in 1831 and 1832 proved a shaky foundation on which to build a new order in a racially divided slave society. Liberal idealism quickly gave way to cynical realism among Guard officers, while guardsmen rejected a citizenship that merely masked expectations of continued subordination to social superiors. The only possible solution was the militarization, or better, "militia-zation" of the Guard in 1838 coupled with a strong dose of state control over the institution's officer corps in the form of civil-servant officers.

Conclusion

The middle decade of the nineteenth century is conventionally presented as the Brazilian empire's apogee. After the final defeat of Rio Grande do Sul's Farroupilha Rebellion in 1845, the empire faced only one more regional revolt, the Praieira in Pernambuco, quickly smashed in early 1849. By the early 1850s, the differences between the political parties that had coalesced during the 1840s faded almost to insignificance (from 1853 to 1856, Liberals and Conservatives sat together in the same cabinet). The much stronger imperial government, generally under Conservative control after September 1848, implemented several signficant reforms. It put an end to the slave trade by the mid-1850s, thereby resolving one of the country's pressing foreign-policy problems (British naval forces were seizing slavers in Brazilian waters) and demonstrating a significant degree of autonomy from planter interests. In 1851–1852, Brazil intervened decisively in Argentine affairs, contributing troops to the alliance of Montevideo and Entre Rios that overthrew Juan Manuel de Rosas in Buenos Aires. Important army reforms and an overhaul of the National Guard also came in the early 1850s.[1]

In Bahia, the late 1840s were tense years. In February 1848, rumors of another radical liberal and federalist rebellion ran rife in Salvador. Proclamations calling for separation from Rio de Janeiro appeared on city streets; like so many of their predecessors, they railed against excessive taxation that only served to keep the court in luxury, condemned palace camarillas, and called for military support. One ended with "vivas" to a republic. The *Correio Mercantil*'s editors could not determine the rumors' origins, but another newspaper attributed them to an unlikely alliance of Conservatives (Saquaremas) and the radical liberals associated with *O Guaicuru*. The British consul took the rumors seriously, judging that "the majority of the inhabitants appears to be in favor of a disunion."[2] This crisis subsided almost as suddenly as it had erupted, however, and the commander of arms advised the president not to call up extra guardsmen, for such an action might lend credence to the rumors. A routine transfer of an artillery battalion out of the province in April 1848 was greeted with equaminity, except that the commander of arms grumbled (as his predecessors so often did) that he would not have enough soldiers on hand to carry out garrison duties.[3]

The fall of the Liberal ministry in September 1848 (which provoked radical liberals in Pernambuco, the Praieira faction, to rebel) brought Francisco Gonçalves Martins to the Bahian presidency. He oversaw a hasty embarkation of the First Infantry to join the imperial forces in Pernambuco, while 200 Guardsmen entered Salvador's barracks to replace them. The new president welcomed the authorization to increase the cavalry to 100 men, for he considered slave revolt an imminent danger; he also requested weaponry to arm the Guard more effectively, receiving 500 rifles from Rio de Janeiro.[4] Opposition newspapers expressed sympathy for the Praieira rebels; one lamented the sending of troops to the "fratricidal struggle." Rumors of conspiracies and handbills accusing Martins of seeking to hand Brazil over to Portuguese and Africans appeared in early 1849, but chief of police João Maurício Wanderley did not take them too seriously, according to his biographer, recognizing that the plotters lacked the means to carry out their plans.[5]

The failure of the 1848 and 1849 crises to produce serious consequences in Bahia requires explanation. At least part of the answer lies in the significantly different nature of the province's garrison, especially when compared to the mid-1830s. Unlike in 1837, the battalions in Salvador lacked Bahian roots. Provincial authorities reported no signs of disloyalty among the regulars, and the National Guard effectively relieved them when necessary. The policy of rotating battalions among provinces and officers among battalions appears to have had the desired effect of securing army loyalty to the imperial regime. Furthermore, the by-then customary practice of keeping some Guardsmen in the barracks had made this corporation a more effective military institution. Had a rebellion broken out, at least some Guardsmen would have been ready, in contrast to the ineffectual loyalist mobilization on the night of 6 November 1837.

To be sure, not all were happy with the institutional changes that had taken place in the armed forces in the 1840s, the editors of *O Guaicuru* among them. In 1845, they had extolled the former practice of returning troops to their home provinces at the end of campaigns, worrying with good reason that the Bahians who had fought against the Farroupilha Rebellion, finally defeated, would never return home. *O Guaicuru* was not alone in its advocacy of federalism in military affairs, but those who called for a return to pre-Regresso army deployment policies made no headway.[6]

Rather, in the early 1850s, the Brazilian government further institution-alized the policies and practices sketched out during the 1840s, notably an 1850 promotion law that made formal education a requirement for officer advancement. This measure was followed by an expansion and overhaul of army education establishments, which became ever more central to offi-cer culture. Administrative reforms, including the creation of an adjutant general's department in the capital, improved management of army per-sonnel matters, as evidenced by the uninterrupted annual publication of an almanac after 1851. Still, these measures only accelerated tendencies already visible in the 1840s, and those who have analyzed the army reforms of the 1850s overlook their essential prerequisite—the creation of a national army in the 1840s.[7]

The institutional evolution of the army to about 1850 analyzed in this book from the perspective of Bahia's officers had important consequences for state–society relations. While the Bahian planter class lost direct, per-sonal control over the officer corps in Salvador, through alliance with the imperial regime, it gained a centrally administered, loyal, and obedient force, exemplary in its subordination to civilian authorities until the 1880s. Dur-ing these years, however, officers gradually nurtured a national corporate identity in opposition to civilian politicians who allegedly despised the army and failed to attend to its material and professional needs. First surfacing explicitly in the 1850s in *O Militar*, an army newspaper published in Rio de Janeiro, and growing stronger after the failure of post-Paraguayan War modernization programs, this corporate identity proved to be an effective rallying cry for those in the army who overthrew the empire in 1889. Instead of fomenting regional rebellions as the Bahian garrison had done in the 1830s, the Brazilian army acted on the national stage after 1889, with the victors in the often-bitter internal army politics always claiming to speak for the corporation as a whole and indeed for the entire nation as well.[8] Salvador's garrison became increasingly marginal in the larger corporation, its officers' politics reflecting national issues.[9]

In 1850, parliament finally passed a new National Guard law, finding a middle ground between those who sought to militarize the corporation and those who called for a return to the liberal and democratic institution of the early 1830s. The 1850 Guard law strikingly resembled the 1838 Bahian Guard reform, as it included permanent appointive officers, the enlistment of guardsmen by officers, the obligation to do police and garrison duties, and the responsibility to act as an army reserve. While retaining the notion of Guard membership as an attribute of citizenship (and the 1832 income requirements for membership), legislators thus excised the principal liberal features from the corporation. By standardizing Guard procedures throughout the country, the 1850 law also restored the Guard's national character (in the sense of institutional uniformity across the country), further reinforcing central power by giving the minister of justice the power to name its most senior officers.[10]

In Bahia, the Guard was completely overhauled in the early 1850s, and for the first time, systematic enlistments were done throughout the province (and not just in Salvador); in 1854, the minister of justice reported 71,405 men enrolled in the province, a figure that would rise to 111,813 in 1863.[11] In this, its third incarnation, the Guard functioned much as it had from 1838 to 1850, but the Paraguayan War (1865–1870) proved to be both its apogee and undoing. Recruitment on a scale never before seen in Brazil, much of it conducted within the Guard, blurred the distinction between regulars and guardsmen even more effectively than the short-term detachments and provisional corps of the 1840s had done. More than one-third of the 15,267 men contributed by Bahia to the war effort were guardsmen designated for regular service, and by the end of the conflict, Guard battalions in Salvador had effectively collapsed, proving unable to muster more than a handful of men for holiday parades in the early 1870s.[12] In recognition of this fact, the Guard was reformed once again; in 1873, it was reduced to a ceremonial institution whose members were freed from the obligation to perform police duties and gathered only once per year for inspections. In this form, the Guard lingered on until 1918.[13]

In contrast to the National Guard's four incarnations in scarcely more than four decades, forced recruitment changed remarkably little. A draft lottery bill finally passed in 1874, and legislators coupled it with measures to make military service more palatable to the men of higher social classes who would now run the risk of having their names drawn. They abolished corporal punishment, the privileges of cadets, and the use of soldiers as officers' personal servants. On paper at least, parliament finally accomplished what Raimundo Jose da Cunha Matos had attempted in the 1820s. Faced with popular resistance and considerable foot-dragging on the part of local authorities charged with implementing this cumbersome law, however, the imperial government soon abandoned efforts at enforcing it.[14] As late as 1888, Salvador saw razzias little different from those witnessed by Luiz dos Santos Vilhena or Thomas Lindley almost a century earlier. Only in the 1910s was a system of selective service finally established in Brazil.[15]

Salvador's experience of Brazilian independence was quite similar to that of the other principal port cities of the North and Northeast, Recife, São Luiz, and Belém. To be sure, the political trajectories of these provinces differed, but each saw significant periods of social unrest that raised many of the issues analyzed here for Bahia: doubts about the relationship with Rio de Janeiro, radical liberal demands for change, factional conflicts among elites, slave revolts, lower-class mobilizations that sought to broaden the meaning of liberalism and extend citizenship, and complex racial politics. Major rebellions, in fact, took place in (or in the hinterlands of) each of these cities.[16] Some of them, in fact, strikingly resembled the military rebellions of Salvador. The Setembrizada, an enlisted men's mutiny in Recife (14 September 1831), for example, differed little from the artillery mutiny two weeks earlier in Salvador, save that it was not contained in the barracks. Rather, enlisted men controlled the capital of Pernambuco for a few days, until rural militia forces, supplemented by the Municipal Guard and armed law students, violently repressed it.[17] More generally, outside the region that came to dominate Brazil—the Rio de Janeiro/São Paulo/Minas Gerais axis— independence and incorporation into the Brazilian empire were deeply conflictual processes that followed distinct courses in each province. In short, there is no single, linear narrative of Brazilian independence.

Some aspects of the Bahian story recounted here can be more easily generalized to the rest of Brazil than others. In all likelihood, the dynamic of patronage and clientage and the struggles among state, local elites, and free poor over impressment differed little in other provinces, as evidence from Minas Gerais and Paraíba suggests.[18] Just as the Sabinada prompted an unprecedented wave of impressment in Bahia, so the defeat of the Praieira in 1849 provided the occasion for the victors to impress thousands of the vanquished in Pernambuco, giving Bahia a respite from forced recruitment altogether between November 1848 and October 1849.[19] In Maranhão, impressment became a political issue during the Balaiada Rebellion (1838– 1841) in ways that it never did in Bahia. That the leaders of this movement were members of the rural free poor caught up in a breakdown of patron– client ties amid the factional disputes in that province's political elite at a time when the Brazilian state was actively recruiting contributed to this outcome; the Balaios likely opposed impressment less on principle than because it touched them "unfairly."[20] Elsewhere, impressment appears to have been less controversial, at least in a popular political sense: Even after the massive impressment of the Paraguayan War years, the free poor of the rural Northeast were still willing to take up arms to frustrate the implementation of the draft lottery in the mid-1870s, apparently because it threatened the familiar, time-honored, and acceptable mechanisms of patronage.[21]

The colonial and early-imperial racial preferences in recruitment, while noted by some historians, have yet to be analyzed elsewhere in Brazil.[22] The discovery of systematic series of data on soldiers in the form of troop registries may make possible more research on this point, but given that the standard service record form contained no information on race, I suspect that these documents will actually be of limited use. How racial preferences were played out in, for example, a province such as Pará, whose population had a mostly indigenous ancestry, remains a question for further research. There, in the early 1830s, some authorities complained about a largely Indian garrison, but after the outbreak of the Cabanagem Rebellion in 1835 shifted to a discourse that emphasized binary categories of whites and nonwhites.[23] Nevertheless, if the changing racial composition of the rank and file in Bahia can be generalized to at least the main plantation regions of Brazil, then it certainly helps to makes sense of several developments. The low status from which the army suffered in the nineteenth century had much to do with the darkening of the rank and file: Certainly a pamphleteer who blamed the former slaves and "sons of old Ethiopia" in the army for the reluctance of "good citizens" to serve in the 1870s could not have credibly made his argument half a century earlier.[24] The failure of recruitment and discipline reform derived in important ways from the rank and file's social and racial composition. And, as I have argued, these racial preferences had important implications for soldiers' politics. Enlisted men's sensitivity to the racial epithets cast by the Portuguese troops stationed in Bahia after 1817—a phenomenon noted throughout Brazil—makes more sense when it is recognized that they were whites and pardos, men who distinguished themselves from blacks and slaves.[25] The inability of the pardo and white enlisted men involved in the Tailors' Conspiracy to make common cause with pretos reflects real social networks fostered and reinforced by discriminatory recruitment. The nagging problem of runaway slaves in the ranks that the army faced before 1888 was likely a direct consequence of the broadening of recruitment that began around the time of independence.[26]

The almost complete lack of research on black and mulatto militias elsewhere in Brazil makes it difficult to assess the experience of Bahia's black and mulatto officers. Until the mid-1810s, the black officers of Pernambuco closely resembled their Bahian colleagues; Henry Koster described them as significant community leaders and noted their worries about being replaced by white officers (the Englishman doubted that João VI would take such an impolitic step).[27] In 1817, however, at least one of Recife's black regiments joined the republican rebellion under its major, Joaquim Ramos de Almeida, and numerous black and mulatto militiamen participated in the revolt.[28] Apparently these battalions survived the defeat, and they resurfaced in the Confederação do Equador of 1824. At one point during the Pernambucan resistance to Rio de Janeiro, the black commander, Major Agostinho Bezerra Cavalcante, dissuaded the pardo major, Emiliano Felipe Benício Mundurucu, from leading his battalion in sacking the commercial district. This service was not enough to spare Cavalcante the firing squad in 1825; Mundurucu escaped into exile and was reportedly still collecting army pay in 1839. For Pernambuco's black and mulatto officers, the Confederação do Equador was their Sabinada.[29]

Only scattered material is available on the black and mulatto officers elsewhere in Brazil. The 1802 ruling and the 1829 salary law applied throughout Portuguese America, and officers of the numerous companies and battalions of pardos and Henriques in Minas Gerais must have faced problems similar to those of their Bahian counterparts after independence, but they remain unstudied.[30] Nonwhite militiamen in Rio de Janeiro reportedly wore portraits of Jean-Jacques Dessalines, the recently crowned emperor of Haiti, in 1805. Maria Graham saw Rio de Janeiro's black officers pledge loyalty to Pedro I in 1823, but there are indications that their battalions were quietly disbanded in the 1820s.[31] Only future research on how these militia officers responded to the difficult choices of the independence era will tell whether Bahian black officers' ambivalence toward liberal reform and radical politics was typical.

The transition from militia to National Guard in Salvador, followed by the corporation's reorganization in 1838, marked a key change in state–society relations that remains unstudied elsewhere. The impressive personnel turnovers in 1831 and 1838 and the elimination of black and mulatto officers from Salvador's part-time military reveal something of the turmoil of these years, while the civil-servant National Guard officers of the 1840s demonstrate the provincial state's assumption of responsibility for managing policing and discipline of the urban population, a dramatic departure both from the liberal assumption that property-holding citizens would collaborate in maintaining their collective security and from the colonial practice of tying racially segregated urban merchant and artisan elites to the monarchy through militia commissions. Again, only systematic research in other centers will reveal whether Salvador's Guard was typical or unusual in this regard.

The patterns discerned among Bahia's army officers are likely typical of northern and northeastern military centers. Most Brazilian army historiography focuses on the development of national army in the struggles against the Spanish empire in the eighteenth century and its nineteenth-century successor states.[32] Until the Cisplatine War, however, these "Brazilian" forces consisted of soldiers and officers recruited from Rio de Janeiro, its hinterland, and points south. By contrast, the other major northeastern centers had, like Bahia, army garrisons with few connections outside of the respective captaincy. Their officers and men were gradually drawn into the "Brazilian" army from the 1820s, a process that became effective only in the 1840s.

This study has, through the armed forces in Bahia, examined the construction of the Brazilian state from below and from the periphery to the center. My emphasis on the close connections between state and society and the evolving bargain between the Bahian planter class and the two imperial centers with which it contended supports the views of those who have questioned the Brazilian state's autonomy.[33] Of course, state autonomy is a relative quality, and more than a few decisions emanating from Lisbon and Rio de Janeiro during these years hardly served the Bahian planter class's interests, such as the stationing of Portuguese troops in Salvador in 1817, the military "reforms" of the early 1830s that ultimately led to the Sabinada Rebellion, or the preoccupation with external defense as opposed to policing the slave population. No doubt, too, the Bahian planter class would have been better served by the retention of the Portuguese imperial monarchy in Rio de Janeiro, which might have avoided the political and social turmoil of independence. The creation of the Brazilian imperial state necessitated a realignment of planter-class control over the armed forces, which came through the Regresso and its creation of a national army, as well as the locally managed National Guard reform in Salvador. Both processes were strikingly parallel in that the state apparatus figured prominently in the new mechanisms of control over armed forces, whether through the civil-servant officers of Salvador's Guard or the loyalty to Brazil fostered among army officers by the Regresso's creation of a national army. The outcomes of both, too, it bears repeating, more effectively served the interests of the Bahian planter class than the chaotic military structures of the immediate postindependence period.

These were, of course, abstract, long-term processes that few contemporaries recognized, much less the men and women whose lives were most affected by them. For officers, their symptoms figured more prominently, as they complained about the inability to reconcile personal and professional interests or about the hardships of serving in the cold and unpleasant South. Enlisted men's ties to family and community in Salvador suffered as more and more of them were sent out of Bahia and as the army gradually imposed more control over their lives. Nevertheless, through desertion and their continual resistance to military discipline, they retained a degree of control over their own lives. In this sense, military institutions must ultimately be seen as the product of an interaction among soldiers, officers, and society.

Few of those touched by the armed forces would disagree that independence brought far-reaching changes to their lives. They often disliked them, but would not likely have spoken about the continuities from colonial regime to independent empire. To be sure, the Bahian planter class managed to preside over an ultimately conservative revolution of independence, as F. W. O. Morton has effectively put it, but their rule would never be the same. Bahia (and Brazil) went through its version of the liberal-democratic revolutions that swept the Atlantic World during these years, leaving a substrate of liberal ideals and challenges to colonial society. While slavery lasted until 1888, the institution was far less legitimate after the 1820s. Impressment may have continued with little outward change—the unfortunates roughed up and dragged to the barracks would have thought so—but the larger institution and practice of forced recruitment lost legitimacy and became an object for reformers' efforts. Here, the ethic of patronage existed uncomfortably with the ethic of liberalism and its emphasis on equality, a tension identified by Emília Viotti da Costa.[34] Similarly, the restrictions hedged up around corporal punishment point to the ambivalence with which legislators viewed the practice. Militiamen became citizens, all the more explicitly in the National Guard. While such citizenship was relatively broad by contemporary standards, it was nevertheless clearly circumscribed by property requirements. It entered Brazilian political discourse as an ideal that unmasked the realities of hierarchy and inequality, making them more difficult to maintain. To be sure, the Regresso did away with the most liberal and democratic features of the Guard, but it did not eliminate them entirely. The point here is, of course, not to condemn Brazilian liberalism for its failure to go far enough; rather, it is to understand the interaction between liberal reformers and their ideals and Brazilian society and its colonial heritage. Nowhere was this interaction more fraught with ambivalence than in the politics of race.

Throughout these years, race was never far from the surface of Bahian politics. Its manifestations in the armed forces closely paralleled the shifting racial categories used by the state. While the state upheld a three-category system of brancos, pardos, and pretos, both in the militia and in recruitment for the regulars, these three categories mattered, as is clear from the inability to forge an effective preto–pardo alliance in the Tailors' Conspiracy and in the different trajectories of black and mulatto militia officers. As the liberal state gradually abandoned institutionalized racial discrimination along these lines, racial politics assumed increasingly binary forms, the clearest expression of which came in the Sabinada. That not all "pardos" joined the classes of color furthermore underscores the socially constructed nature of racial difference.

Bahia's black officers incorporated all of the complexities of Brazilian racial politics. Some may find troubling Joaquim José de Santana's betrayal of the Tailors' Conspiracy, these men's slave holding, or their inability to tranform personal ties with Africans into a politically meaningful alliance, but these are ahistorical judgments. A recognition that "race" alone did not define political lines renders these men's actions comprehensible; class, status, national origin, and their corporate vision of Brazilian society profoundly shaped their political actions. In many respects, they resembled the *gens de couleur* of Saint Domingue, as they sought a greater role in society, taking advantage of the opportunities that the Age of Revolution offered, without necessarily wishing to overthrow larger structures such as slavery or the exclusion of Africans from the nation.[35]

Race, furthermore, was not an a priori category; its meaning and political significance evolved in tandem with the state's use of racial categories. Pardo identity, already weaker in the Fourth Militia Regiment than preto identity in the Henriques, could not survive the abolition of the militia and elite discourse about dangerous classes of color. The prominent place of pardo soldiers in the Tailors' Conspiracy and its formulation of an anti-discrimination ideology reflected their particular place in a white corporation. How postindependence enlisted men viewed their place in society is unfortunately impossible to analyze given the silencing of soldiers in the historical record. Race was certainly a key subtext in soldier-civilian conflicts, and the victors in the Sabinada characterized their enemies as blacks and

Africans, a strategy that built unity among all those who defined themselves as not members of the dangerous "classes of color."

That no racial discourse emerged from the officer corps is not surprising, but such an assertion perhaps misrepresents the issue. Whiteness was, as I have argued, an attribute of officership, and this gave all officers a strong incentive to uphold their whiteness. The difficulty of finding regular officers willing to transfer to the black and mulatto militias underscores the importance of whiteness to men who willingly forwent the significant career advance that such a transfer entailed. One of the few who accepted transfer into the pardo militia, Antônio Manoel de Melo e Castro, the well-connected but illegitimate pardo son of a high official and a man married to the daughter of an African slave, is the exception that proves the rule. After independence, "pardo" officers like those about whom Felisberto Caldeira Brant Pontes complained in 1824, had no incentive whatsoever to call attention to their African ancestry. Whether this constitutes their acceptance of hegemonic Brazilian racial structures or simply reflects a rational calculation of their personal and professional interests is of course unknowable.[36]

For Brazilian military men, the structures of racial discrimination thus shaped the publicly articulated patterns of racial politics. Elsewhere, this is a common enough phenomenon, although not always sufficiently recognized. Ben Vinson III has shown for colonial Mexico that, with the elimination of corporate privileges for nonwhite militiamen, free-coloreds ceased to identify themselves as such when making claims on the state.[37] More than a few modern imperial powers have identified "martial" races among their colonized populations, relying on them to staff colonial armies, and in consequence, shaping postcolonial ethnic politics.[38]

The racial politics of the Bahian military raises a final comparative point. It has become by now a truism that clearly defined and institutionalized racial discrimination against all people of African descent is far more likely to foster organized resistance (and a broader African-American identity) than diffuse and informal practices of racism such as those that increasingly prevailed in Brazil after independence. In the Americas, Cuba and the United States have seen far more vocal and active African-American political movements than Brazil and the other societies whose racial structures more closely approximate those of Brazil.[39] The experience of Bahia's armed forces in the independence era confirms this tendency, as racial politics closely conformed to the patterns of discrimination. The abolition of formal racial discrimination in the armed forces, a process completed in the 1830s with the establishment of the National Guard and the lifting of the color bar in recruitment for the regulars ultimately made racially based politics less likely. The remaining diffuse and informal practices of racism, replete with individual exceptions, furthermore, permitted Brazilians to cultivate the ideology of their society as a racial democracy.[40] When faced with real challenges from below, as in the Tailors' Conspiracy, the Periquitos' Rebellion, or the Sabinada, however, Brazilian elites have not hesitated to resort to force to maintain social and racial hierarchies. Distinctions among pardos and pretos may have been useful for maintaining social order, but when faced with real challenges, the only difference that mattered to those in power was the one between themselves and the dangerous classes of color.

APPENDIX

THE SIZE AND ORGANIZATION
OF SALVADOR'S GARRISON

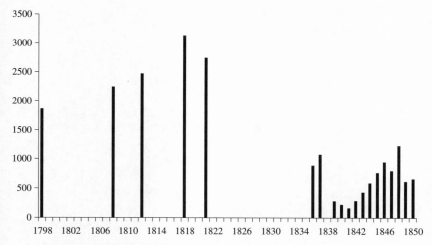

FIGURE A.1 Salvador's Army Garrison Size, 1798–1850. All ranks.

SOURCES: Reports on the garrison's size, AN/SPE, IG1; APEB; BN/SM; MG, *Relatório* (1839–1850); *Idade de Ouro do Brazil*, 20 Feb. 1821, p. 4.

	1790s	1809	1817	1819	1820	1822	1823	1824	1825	1826	1827	1828	1829	1831	1832

Unit: —1 Reg. ——————————— d | 1 BC—13 BC ——— t (to South) ——— t—**2 BC**—t (from Rio) | t—13 BC–9 BC (from South) ———

Unit: —2 Reg.—Legião de Caçadores ——— d | 2 BC—14 BC ——— t (to South) ——— t—**5 BC**—t (from São Paulo) | t—14 BC–10 BC–d (from South) ———

Unit: —Art. Reg. ——— d | 3 BC—d | Guarda Militar de Policia ——— d

Unit: t—**12 Reg.**—t (from Lisbon, to Santa Catarina) | t—**12 Reg.**—t (from Santa Catarina, to Lisbon) | 4 BC—15 BC ——— t (to South) ——— t—**20 BC**—t (from Piauí) | t—15 BC—d (from South) ———

Unit: t—**2**—t **Reg.** (from Lisbon, to Recife) | Art.—7 Art. Corps Corps —t (to South) ——— **5 Art.**—t **Corps** (from Montevideo) | t—7 Art.— 3 Art. Corps Corps (from South)

Unit: Cavalry Squadron —t (to South) ——— t——— Cavalry Squadron (from South) ——— d

Unit: t (from Minas Gerais) ——— **Minas Gerais Battalion** ——— t (to Minas Gerais)

Unit: t—**Art.**—t **Brigade** (from Santa Catarina, to South)

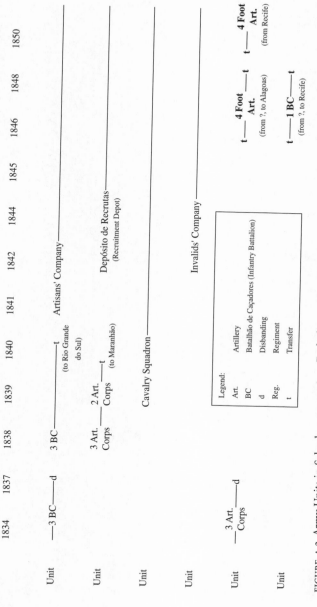

FIGURE A.2 Army Units in Salvador, 1790s–1850. Excluding wartime periods (1822–1823, 1837–1838). Bold denotes non-Bahian units.

SOURCES: Vilhena, *Recopilação*, 1:250; army organization legislation in *CLB*, "Chronica dos acontecimentos"; Silva, *Memorias; Idade de Ouro do Brazil*, 1817; correspondence about army deployment in APEB, AN/SPE, IG1; MG, *Relatório* (1839–1850); BN/SM; Paula, "Organização."

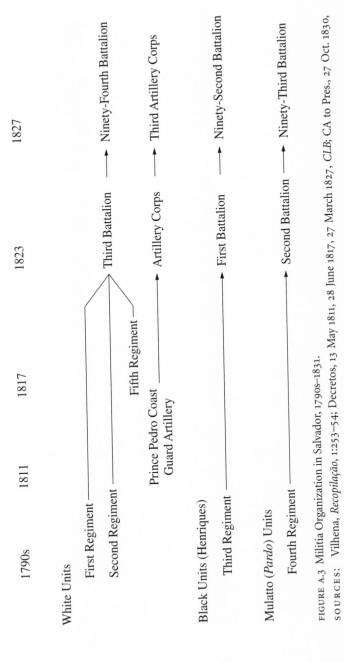

| 1790s | 1811 | 1817 | 1823 | 1827 |

White Units

First Regiment ─────────────────────────────────┐
Second Regiment ────────────────────────────────┤→ Third Battalion ───→ Ninety-Fourth Battalion
                           Fifth Regiment ───────┘

Prince Pedro Coast
Guard Artillery ──────→ Artillery Corps ───────→ Third Artillery Corps

Black Units (Henriques)

Third Regiment ──────────────────────→ First Battalion ───→ Ninety-Second Battalion

Mulatto (*Pardo*) Units

Fourth Regiment ──────────────────→ Second Battalion ───→ Ninety-Third Battalion

FIGURE A.3 Militia Organization in Salvador, 1790s–1831.
SOURCES: Vilhena, *Recopilação*, 1:253–54; Decretos, 13 May 1811, 28 June 1817, 27 March 1827, *CLB*; CA to Pres., 27 Oct. 1830, AN/SPE, IG1, m. 115, fols. 57v–61r.

NOTES

The following abbreviations have been used throughout these notes and in the bibliography:

AAPEB *Anais do Arquivo Público do Estado da Bahia*
ABN *Anais da Biblioteca Nacional*
ACD *Anais da Câmara dos Deputados*
ADI *Archivo Diplomático da Independência*
Adj. Adjutant
AHE Arquivo Histórico do Exérctio
    FO Fés de Ofício
    RQ Requerimentos
    RC Reconhecimentos de Cadetes
AIGHB Arquivo do Instituto Geográfico e Histórico da Bahia
AIHGB Arquivo do Instituto Histórico e Geográfico Brasileiro
AM Arquivo Municipal (Salvador)
AN Arquivo Nacional (Rio de Janeiro)
    SAP Seção de Arquivos Particulares
    SPE Seção do Poder Executivo
      GIFI Grupo de Identificação de Fundos Internos
APEB Arquivo Público do Estado da Bahia (Seção de Arquivo Colonial e Provincial, unless otherwise indicated)
    SJ Seção Judiciária
    LRT Livros de Registro de Testamentos
    IT Inventários e Testamentos

Art. Artillery
AS *Anais do Senado*
BN Biblioteca Nacional (Rio de Janeiro)
    SM   Seção de Manuscritos
        DB   Documentos Biográficos
Brig. Brigadier
CA Comandante das Armas (Commander of Arms of Bahia, unless
    otherwise indicated)
Cap. Captain
Cap.-mor Capitão-mor (Captain-Major)
Cav. Cavalry
CI Conselho Interino (Interim Council)
CLB *Collecção das Leis do Império do Brazil*
CLRB *Coleção das Leis e Resoluções da Bahia*
Col. Colonel
Com. Commander/Commanding
Comp. Company
CR Carta Régia
CS Comandante Superior (National Guard)
CU Conselho Ultramarino
FO *Fé de ofício* (Service record)
GA Governador das Armas (Governor of Arms of Bahia)
Gov. Governor (of Bahia)
GN Guarda Nacional (National Guard)
HAHR *Hispanic American Historical Review*
IG Inspetor General (Inspector General of Bahia)
Inf. Infantry
Interr. *Interrogatório* (Interrogation)
Inv. *Inventário* (Inventory)
JLAS *Journal of Latin American Studies*
JP Juiz de Paz (Justice of the Peace)
LBR *Luso-Brazilian Review*
Lt. Lieutenant
m. *maço*
Maj. Major
MG Ministro da Guerra (Minister of War)
MGE Ministro da Guerra e Estrangeiros (Minister of War and
    Foreign Affairs)
MI Ministro do Império [Minister of Empire (Interior)]
Min. Minister
MJ Ministro da Justiça (Minister of Justice)

MNE	Ministro dos Negócios Estrangeiros (Minister of Foreign Affairs)
MMU	Ministro da Marinha e Ultramar (Minister of Navy and Overseas Dominions)
NARS	National Archives and Records Service (United States)
OD	*Ordem do Dia* (Order of the Day)
PAEB	*Publicações do Arquivo do Estado da Bahia*
PC	*Processo Crime* (Criminal Trial)
Req.	*Requerimento* (Petition)
PRE	Presidente do Real Erário (President of the Royal Exchequer)
Pres.	President (of Bahia, unless otherwise indicated)
PRO, For. Off.	Public Record Office, Foreign Office (Great Britain)
RIGHB	*Revista do Instituto Geográfico e Histórico da Bahia*
RIHGB	*Revista do Instituto Histórico e Geográfico Brasileiro*
Rio	Rio de Janeiro (City)
Squad.	Squadron
TAm	*The Americas*
Test.	Testimony
VP	Vice-President (of Bahia)

Unless otherwise indicated, all correspondence was issued in Salvador.

Introduction

1. Downing, *Military Revolution;* Tilly, "Reflections," 73–76; idem, "War Making"; idem, *Coercion,* chap. 3. A recent exception is López Alves, *State.*

2. Major works on the late-colonial Latin American militaries include Archer, *Army;* Campbell, *Military;* Kuethe, *Military Reform* and *Cuba;* Marchena Fernández, *Institución, Oficiales,* and *Ejército.* For a few exceptions to the lack of studies of postindependence militaries, see DePalo, Jr., *Mexican National Army;* Meisel, "War." On Brazil, see the little-known work of McBeth, "Politicians," "Brazilian Army," and "Brazilian Recruit."

3. Faoro, *Donos;* Pang, *Pursuit,* chap. 8; Pang and Seckinger, "Mandarins."

4. Freyre, *Masters.*

5. Goffman, *Asylums,* 1–124; Foucault, *Discipline,* 218.

6. On these two approaches to states, see Skocpol, "Bringing," 27–28; Corrigan and Sayer, *Great Arch,* 1–10.

7. See Joseph and Nugent, eds., *Everyday Forms;* Mallon, *Peasant;* Taylor, "Global Process," 140–66.

8. Schwartz, *Sovereignty;* Alden, *Royal Government;* Maxwell, *Conflicts.* See also Schwartz, "Colonial Past," 180–82.

9. J. M. Carvalho, *Construção* and *Teatro.* See also R. Graham, *Patronage;* I. R. Mattos, *Tempo;* Uricoechea, *Patrimonial Foundations.*

10. A classic statement of this view is Stein and Stein, *Colonial Heritage*. For Brazil, see Russell-Wood, "Preconditions," 39; E. V. Costa, *Brazilian Empire*, 23; and J. H. Rodrigues, who sees independence as a failed revolution, *Independência*, 1:170, 5:229–34, 249.

11. Fernandes, *Revolução*, 31.

12. The most influential recent work in this vein has been Mallon, *Peasant;* but see, from a very different perspective, Rodríguez O., *Independence*. See also the monographs cited below in notes 30 and 32.

13. Hobsbawm, *Age;* Palmer, *Age*.

14. Langley, *Americas;* Liss, *Atlantic Empires*.

15. Novais, *Portugal;* Novais and Mota, *Independência*.

16. See Fragoso, *Homens;* Neves, "Imperio." On Bahia, see Lugar, "Merchant Community," chaps. 1–2.

17. J. H. Rodrigues, *Independência*, 1:95–97, 183–85, 301, 321; 2:86; 3:17, 35–40, 191; 5:250; Tavares, *Independência;* M. J. M. Carvalho, "Cavalcantis"; Assunção, "Elite Politics." Surveys of the period that recognize these dynamics include Barman, *Brazil;* C. H. S. Oliveira, *Independência*.

18. Vilhena, *Recopilação*, 2:931.

19. Turner, *Citizenship*, 26. For analyses of citizenship from different perspectives, see Marshall and Bottomore, *Citizenship;* Turner, ed., *Citizenship;* Waldinger, Dawson, and Woloch, eds., *French Revolution;* Brubaker, *Citizenship*.

20. Forrest, "Citizenship," 153.

21. DaMatta, *Casa*, 61.

22. E. V. Costa, *Brazilian Empire*, chap. 2. See also Dias, "Ideologia"; Schwarz, *Misplaced Ideas*, 19–31; J. H. Rodrigues, *Independência*, 1:32.

23. Malerba, *Brancos;* Flory, *Judge*, chaps. 1–2.

24. Schwartz, "Colonial Identities," 186; Wagley, "Concept," 531–32; Harris, *Patterns*, 56.

25. Winant, *Racial Conditions*, 14–17; Fields, "Slavery," 100, 109–10.

26. Lovell and Wood, "Skin Color," 94–106.

27. Marx, *Making*.

28. Thompson, *Making;* Parker, *Idea;* I. R. Mattos, *Tempo*.

29. On Brazil, see Fernandes, *Negro;* Andrews, *Blacks*, 71–81. For other societies, see Chance and Taylor, "Estate"; Omi and Winant, *Racial Formation*, 24–35; Roediger, *Wages*, 7–11.

30. Van Young, ed., *Mexico's Regions;* Anna, *Forging;* Guardino, *Peasants;* Mörner, *Region;* Walker, *Smoldering Ashes;* Thurner, *Two Republics;* Chambers, *Subjects*.

31. The relative lack of regional political histories of the Brazilian empire is all the more surprising given the importance of this genre to Old Republic historiography, Levine, *Pernambuco;* Love, *São Paulo* and *Rio Grande do Sul;* Wirth, *Minas Gerais;* Pang, *Bahia*. A few exceptions include M. J. M. Carvalho, "Hegemony"; Assunção, "Elite Politics"; Bieber, *Power;* Mosher, "Pernambuco."

32. For one recent example, see Hamnett, "Process," 282. Recent works that take this approach include Walker, *Smoldering Ashes;* Chambers, *Subjects;* Uribe-Uran, *Honorable Lives.*

Chapter 1

1. Kindersley, *Letters,* 24; Keith, *Voyage,* 17; Fitz-Roy, *Narrative,* 2:62–63.

2. Kindersley, *Letters,* 32.

3. Taunay and Dénis, *Brésil,* 4:134–35; Maximiliano, *Viagem,* 470; Beyer, "Ligeiras notas," 275–76; Spix and Martius, *Viagem,* 2:146, 153.

4. Mattoso, *Bahia, século XIX,* 43–44, 88.

5. Spix and Martius, *Viagem,* 2:152.

6. Schwartz, *Sugar Plantations;* Eltis, *Economic Growth,* 243–44; Russell-Wood, "Ports," 207. On Bahia's slave trades, see Verger, *Fluxo;* J. C. Miller, *Way,* 452–57, 482–89, 510.

7. Barickman, *Bahian Counterpoint,* 9–16, 28–33, 44–65, 100–102, 147–53; Schwartz, *Sugar Plantations,* chap. 15; Wimmer, "African Producers," chaps. 5–6; Lugar, "Portuguese Tobacco Trade," 41–69.

8. Barickman, *Bahian Counterpoint,* 33–41; Schwartz, *Sugar Plantations,* 415–34; Morton, "Growth," 43–49.

9. On sertão population growth, see Mattoso, *Bahia, século XIX,* 62–65, 73–75, 88–90, 92–94, 466–67. On its society, see Levine, *Vale,* chap. 2; E. F. Neves, *Comunidade,* chaps. 3–6.

10. For one such project, see Navarro, "Itinerario." On the South Coast, see Barickman, " 'Tame Indians,' " 331–37, 355; Mattoso, *Bahia, século XIX,* 65–66, 90–92.

11. Azevedo, *Povoamento,* 331, n. 239.

12. On merchants, see Lugar, "Merchant Community," chaps. 1–2; Kennedy, "Bahian Elites," 420–24; Mattoso, *Bahia, século XIX,* 490–94. On Portuguese shopkeepers, see Viana, *Antigamente era assim,* 186–89. On African foodsellers, see Brelin, *De passagem,* 104; Wetherell, *Brazil,* 29–30; Câmara Municipal, Sessão Ordinária, 1 April 1841, *Atas* (1841–1843), fol. 37, AM.

13. Reis, *Slave Rebellion,* 164–65; idem, " 'Revolution.' "

14. Flexor, *Oficiais,* 39–40, 44, 47, 53–55; Russell-Wood, "Ports," 225–26, 232–33; Mattoso, *Bahia, século XIX,* 533–35; M. J. S. Andrade, *Mão de obra,* 129–30.

15. M. J. S. Andrade, *Mão de obra,* 129–30; Mattoso, *Bahia, século XIX,* 542. Domestic servants in Salvador have yet to find their historian, but see for Rio, S. L. Graham, *House.*

16. Fraga Filho, *Mendigos,* chaps. 1–3.

17. Reis, *Morte;* Harding, *Refuge;* Reis, *Slave Rebellion,* chap. 6.

18. Mattoso, *Bahia, século XIX,* 440, 447; Reis, *Slave Rebellion,* 177.

19. Req., Abbess to Queen, ca. 1770s (copy), BN/SM, II-33, 29, 47; "Parecer," 6 Jan. 1827, BN/SM, II-34, 6, 19; "Planta do Quartel de S.to Antonio da Mouraria . . . ,"

ca. 1848, AN/SPE/IG1, m. 119, fol. 225. Salvador's growth has been traced by Simas Filho, "Cidade"; on its forts, see Campos, *Fortificações;* Falcão, *Fortes.* On Caribbean garrison towns, see Marchena Fernández and Gómez Pérez, *Vida.*

20. Reis, *Slave Rebellion,* chap. 3; idem, "Recôncavo"; Schwartz, *Sugar Plantations,* chap. 17.

21. The following discussion is based on Azevedo, *Povoamento,* 181–200, 218–28; Mattoso, *Bahia: a cidade,* 127–49, and *Bahia, século XIX,* 100–14; Nascimento, *Dez freguesias,* 61–108.

22. M. C. Cunha, *Negros,* 22.

23. Tannenbaum, *Slave,* 42–57; M. C. Cunha, "Silences," 427–41; idem, *Negros,* chap. 2; Degler, *Neither Black nor White,* 40–41.

24. Algranti, *Feitor,* 202–5; Brown, " 'On the Vanguard,' " 224–36; Kraay, " 'Shelter,' " 645–48, 651.

25. Mattoso, *Bahia, século XIX,* 161.

26. M. I. C. Oliveira, *Liberto,* 21–31; M. C. Cunha, *Negros,* chaps. 1–2. On manumission and freedpeople, see also Nishida, "Manumission"; Mattoso, *To Be a Slave,* chaps. 7–9.

27. Calculated from M. J. S. Andrade, *Mão de obra,* 188, 195, 197.

28. Reis, *Slave Rebellion,* 6; Nascimento, *Dez freguesias,* 95.

29. M. C. Cunha, *Negros,* 74–86; Reis, *Slave Rebellion,* chap. 12.

30. Kennedy, "Bahian Elites," 415–16, 435–36; Morton, "Conservative Revolution," 47–49, 54; Borges, *Family,* 243–44.

31. Vilhena, *Recopilação,* 1:140.

32. Reis, *Slave Rebellion,* 23–28. See also Mosher, "Pernambuco," chap. 4.

33. Brading, *First America,* 293–421, 561–602.

34. Schwartz, "Formation," 36–40; Barman, *Brazil,* 25–30; Maxwell, *Conflicts,* 84–98.

35. Russell-Wood, "Preconditions," 23, 32; Barman, *Brazil,* 137–38.

36. See, for example, Cardozo, "Azeredo Coutinho," 98; Maxwell, "Generation," 125–44.

37. Skidmore, *Black into White;* Schwarcz, *Espetáculo* and *Retrato;* C. M. Azevedo, *Onda;* Andrews, *Blacks;* Peard, *Race,* chap. 3.

38. Mattoso, *Bahia, século XIX,* 582. This point has recently been developed for colonial Spanish America, Jackson, "Race," 152–53, 173; Cahill, "Colour," 325–27.

39. Russell-Wood, "Ports," 223. See also Mattoso, *Bahia, século XIX,* 106. For more sophisticated analysis, see Nazzari, "Vanishing Indians," 503–9, 515–24; Barickman, "Cores," 11–14; S. C. Faria, *Colônia,* 138.

40. For one exception, see Lewin, "Grande Romano," 152–70.

41. Taunay and Dénis, *Brésil,* 4:98. See also Koster, *Travels,* 2:175.

42. Degler, *Neither Black nor White,* xix, 107, 203–4.

43. Nascimento, *Dez freguesias,* 95. On the association of *preto* with African and slave, see Reis and Silva, *Negociação,* 45; H. M. M. Castro, *Cores,* 34–35.

44. H. M. M. Castro, *Cores,* 34, 107; S. C. Faria, *Colônia,* 137, 138–39, 307; Barickman, "Cores," 40–42.

45. Advertência, ca. 1781, BN/SM, II-34, 4, 38.

46. Harris et al., "Who Are the Whites?" See also the rejoinder by Edward Telles, "Who Are the Morenos?" and Harris et al.'s "A Reply to Telles." On phrenology, see Schwarcz, *Espetáculo,* 48–54.

47. "Compromisso da Irmandade de Nossa Senhora do Terço . . . 1817," AN, códice 815.

48. Much scholarship on race in modern Brazil demonstrates the lack of meaningful differences in the life experiences of pardos and pretos on the basis of census data, Andrews, *Blacks,* 249–58; Lovell and Wood, "Skin Color," 91–94, 104–6.

49. "Slaves Rebel in the Captaincy of Bahia (1814)," in Conrad, ed., *Children,* 405–6; Maxwell, "Generation," 129–30; Felisberto Caldeira Brant Pontes to Luiz José Carvalho e Mello, London, 1 Oct. 1824, *ADI,* 2:128. See also J. H. Rodrigues, *Independência,* 2:46–49.

50. Skidmore, *Black into White,* 63–69.

51. J. J. do C. M., *Carta.* The *Carta* has been analyzed by J. H. Rodrigues, *Independência,* 2:122; E. Silva, *Prince,* 143–44, 196–97, n. 31; and Bieber, who suggests that its author was José Inácio do Couto Moreno, a Portuguese resident of Minas Gerais, "Postmodern Ethnographer," 62–64. For a Bahian statement of J. J. do C. M.'s views, see *Echo da Patria,* 19 Aug. 1823, *AAPEB* 10 (1923), 88.

52. P. Garcia, *Cipriano Barata,* 75, 130–31.

53. Vilhena, *Recopilação,* 1:49.

54. Mattoso, *Bahia, século XIX,* chap. 31; Reis, *Slave Rebellion,* 10–13.

55. Morton, "Conservative Revolution," 47–49; Mattoso, *Bahia: a cidade,* 161; Mattoso, *Bahia, século XIX,* 596–97.

56. Vilhena, *Recopilação,* 1:43.

57. Mattoso, *Bahia, século XIX,* 178–92; Borges, *Family,* 48, 115–18, 237–43, 262. On family law, see Mattoso, "Família"; M. B. N. Silva, "Family."

58. Morton, "Conservative Revolution," 49–50, 55–56; Mattoso, *Bahia: a cidade,* 159–69; *Bahia, século XIX,* 579–601. On students, see also Pinho, "Bahia," 300.

59. Reis *Slave Rebellion,* 12–13; Schwartz, *Sugar Plantations,* chap. 16.

60. Miguel Antonio de Mello to MMU, 30 March 1797 (draft), AIHGB, lata 358, doc. 28.

61. Vilhena, *Recopilação,* 1:135; Gov. to MMU, 4 April 1799, *ABN* 36 (1914), 131.

62. S. L. Graham, *House,* 10–12; Mattoso, *Bahia, século XIX,* 422. For a blessing, see will, José Mendes da Costa Coelho, 12 Dec. 1857, APEB/SJ/IT, 04/1465/1934/21, fol. 3r.

63. M. C. Cunha, *Negros,* 48–52.

64. Test., Alexandre Theotonio de Souza, 28 Aug. 1798; Antonio Ignacio Ramos, 19 Sep. 1798, *ABN* 43–44 (1920–1921), 104, 130.

65. R. Graham, *Patronage,* chaps. 3, 8, and 9; Needell, *Tropical* Belle Epoque, 129–31; E. V. Costa, *Brazilian Empire,* xx–xxiv and passim.

66. Mattoso, *Bahia, século XIX,* 497; req., Manoel dos Santos to Gov., ca. 1810, APEB, m. 247-6.

67. Nascimento, *Dez freguesias,* 114; Mattoso, *Bahia, século XIX,* 156–57.

68. Schwartz, *Sugar Plantations,* 406–12; Mattoso, *Bahia, século XIX,* 175; Borges, *Family,* 113, 164–65; 222–24; Prado Júnior, *Colonial Background,* 336–37; S. C. Faria, *Colônia,* 212–17.

69. Borges, *Family,* 36, 70, 234–36; Prado Júnior, *Colonial Background,* 334–39; Lewin, *Politics,* chap. 3.

70. Test., Antonio Joaquim Imbú, 9 May 1833, "Autuação de trez sumarias ... 1833," fol. 47r, APEB, m. 2853.

71. Wimberly, "Expansion," 79; M. I. C. Oliveira, *Liberto,* 58–73; idem, "Viver," 177–87.

72. Mattoso, *Bahia, século XIX,* chap. 30 (quote 582). See also Borges, *Family,* 281–82.

73. E. V. Costa, *Brazilian Empire,* 239–43; R. Graham, "Free African Brazilians," 41–45; Russell-Wood, *Black Man,* 201–2.

74. On the colonial state's structures, see Mattoso, *Bahia, século XIX,* 223–30; Morton, "Conservative Revolution," 60–92; Alden, *Royal Government,* 29–44; Barman, *Brazil,* 18–25; Prado Júnior, *Colonial Background,* 351–98.

75. Taunay and Dénis, *Brésil,* 4:115.

76. Schwartz, *Sovereignty,* 3–21.

77. Faoro, *Donos.* For English-language statements of this view, see Pang, *Pursuit;* Pang and Seckinger, "Mandarins." The most elegant of Faoro's critics have, like Pang, written on the Brazilian Empire, R. Graham, *Patronage;* I. R. Mattos, *Tempo;* J. M. Carvalho, *Construção* and *Teatro;* Schwartz, *Sovereignty.*

78. Maxwell, *Pombal,* 88–90, 124.

79. Maxwell, *Conflicts,* 98–114.

80. Barman, *Brazil,* 9–11; Novais, *Portugal,* 287–98; P. O. C. Cunha, "Fundação," 136–41; Lyra, *Utopia,* 66–83, 107–8.

81. Higgs, "Unbelief," 20.

Chapter 2

1. Baud, "Herinneringen," 1:197.

2. I. A. C. Silva, *Memorias,* 3:148.

3. CR, 24 Feb. 1808, in I. A. C. Silva, *Memorias,* 3:51, n. 100; CR, 31 Aug. 1809, *CLB.*

4. Schaumburg-Lippe, *Schriften,* 2:111.

5. Delson, "Beginnings," 555–57; Kennedy, "Bahian Elites," 427–28; Schulz, *Exército,* 25–33; Dudley, "Professionalization," 122–23.

6. Geyer, "Past," 183–85, 190–91, 198–200, 204; Hatch, "Introduction," 1–2. This discussion also draws on Skelton, *American Profession,* xi–xvi, chaps. 5, 13; Huntington, *Soldier,* chaps. 1–3; Janowitz, *Professional Soldier,* chap. 1.

7. Soares, *Santo Antonio,* 9–22; Caldas, *Notícia,* 342–43.

8. Cidade, *Cadetes,* 19; R. V. Cunha, *Estudo,* 1:15–18.

9. Corvisier, *Armies,* 106–7; Cidade, *Cadetes,* 19.

10. Vilhena, *Recopilação,* 1:257–58.

11. McBeth, "Brazilian Generals," 136–37. For contemporary references to underage cadets, see IG to Gov., 12 Aug. 1813, APEB, m. 247-8. For underage cadets not permitted to accrue service time, see MGE to Gov., Rio, 5 Feb. 1817, BN/SM, II-33, 17, 36, doc. 40; and MGE to Gov., Rio, 6 June 1818, BN/SM, II-34, 2, 42, doc. 19.

12. Morton, "Military," 254–55; FOs of 149 officers, 1770–1850, AHE/FO and RQ.

13. IG to Gov., 10 Dec. 1814, APEB, m. 247-8; will, Manoel José de Carvalho, 6 July 1815, APEB/SJ/LRT, vol. 5, fol. 93r–94v. The cadet was promoted in September, FO, Pedro Ribeiro Sanches, AHE/FO, VI-9-162.

14. Barretto, *Indice,* 115–16. The artillery class is described by its first teacher in req., José Antonio Caldas to King, ca. 1766 (copy), BN/SM, II-33, 27, 30.

15. Lindley, *Narrative,* 52.

16. Test., Hermógenes Francisco de Aguilar, 9 Jan. 1799, *AAPEB* 36 (1959), 324; IG to Gov., 13 Nov. 1810, APEB, m. 247-5. On Guibert (Jacques Antoine Hippolyte) and his influence, see Corvisier, ed., *Dictionary,* 340. No manuscript or published work by Guibert appears among the volumes seized from Hermógenes's library, Mattoso, *Presença,* 28–33.

17. Theodoro José Guilherme de Sá, *Memória sobre os conhecimentos necessarios a hum official militar . . .* (Salvador, 1816), cited in R. B. Castro, *Primeira imprensa,* 129–30; *Manual do engenheiro . . . acompanhados de algumas noções sobre outros objectos militares,* advertised in *Idade de Ouro do Brazil,* 11 Feb. 1814, 7.

18. Regulamento, 18 Feb. 1763, in R. J. C. Mattos, *Repertório,* 1:4.

19. IG to Gov., 9 April 1813, APEB, m. 247-8; 10 April 1817, APEB, m. 247-12.

20. Reqs., Antonio de Bitencourt Berenguer Cezar to Queen, ca. 1799 (copy), BN/SM, II-33, 22, 28; Jozé Eloi Pessoa to Gov., ca. 1812, APEB, m. 247-7.

21. Gov. to MGE, ca. Dec. 1819, AHE/RQ, H-14-396.

22. Req., Pedro José dos Santos to King, ca. 1820, AHE/RQ, P-31-919; Felisberto Caldeira Brant Pontes to José da Silva Lisboa, 22 Nov. 1819, in Barbacena, *Economia,* 24.

23. Gov. to MMU, 22 July 1788, *ABN* 34 (1912), 89.

24. Req., José Pedro de Menezes to Gov., ca. 1817, APEB, m. 247-12.

25. Gov. to King, 24 May 1796, APEB, m. 137; Col. Com., First Reg., "Proposta . . . ," 1 Sep. 1806, BN/SM, II-33, 17, 22; Com., Presidio de São Paulo, to Gov., 20 Nov. 1802, *ABN* 36 (1914), 497.

26. Marquis of Lavradio to Count of Valadares, 21 June 1768; José de Meneses, 1 Feb. 1769; Marquis of Louriçal, 29 May 1769, in Lavradio, *Cartas,* 22, 97, 192.

27. FO, Francisco de Paula Miranda Chaves, AHE/FO, III-21-54; req., Vicente de Souza Velho to Prince Regent, AHE/RQ, V-24-602.

28. Vilhena, *Recopilação*, 1:44–45. Of course, since the 1760s, officers with commissions signed by the king were considered noble, R. J. C. Mattos, *Repertório*, 2:191.

29. One such ceremony is described in test., Firmiano Joaquim de Souza Velho, 29 Oct. 1798, *ABN* 43–44 (1920–1921), 148–49. The practice is criticized in CS to Pres., 3 May 1834, APEB, m. 3528.

30. "Plano do Fundo de Piedade . . . ," ca. 1800, AIHGB, lata 28, doc. 5; Lindley, *Narrative*, 148; MGE to Gov., Rio, 22 Dec. 1810, BN/SM, II-33, 24, 41.

31. Inv., Joaquim de Mello Leite Cogominho de Lacerda, APEB/SJ/IT, 01/04/04/07, fol. 53r; will, Manoel Luiz de Menezes, 5 June 1830, APEB/SJ/IT, 03/747/1272/02.

32. The extent of the colonial *foro militar* is described in Sampaio, *Instrucçoes*, 7–10.

33. Vilhena, *Recopilação*, 1:269.

34. Vilhena, *Recopilação*, 1:45, 267, 261.

35. N. Z. Davis, *Fiction*.

36. Req., Alexandre Theotonio de Sousa to Queen, ca. 1801, BN/SM, II-33, 17, 4.

37. Req., Thomas Franco to King, ca. 1810 (copy), AN/IG1, m. 112, fol. 137.

38. M. J. N. Silva, *Synopsis*, 2:403; FO, Manoel Fernandes da Silveira, 24 Jan. 1817, APEB, m. 247-12; notarized gift, 23 Jan. 1798 (copy), AN/SPE/IG1, m. 112, fol. 84r.

39. Wills, José Ignacio Acciavoli de [Vasconcellos] Brandão, ca. 1826, APEB/SJ/IT, 04/1663/2132/03, fol. 10r; Luiz Correa de Moraes, 6 Aug. 1833, APEB/SJ/IT, 05/2004/2475/07, fol. 6r; Joze Correia de Aguiar, 19 Sep. 1843, APEB/SJ/LRT, vol. 30, fol. 166r; Luis Lopes Villasboas, 22 Oct. 1850, APEB/SJ/IT, 08/3354/09, fol. 16v; speeches, José Paulino de Almeida e Albuquerque and Raimundo José da Cunha Mattos, 27 May, *ACD* (1830), 1:250.

40. See, for instance, Prince-Regent to Gov., Lisbon, 10 Jan. 1805, BN/SM, II-33, 29, 92; req., José Maria de Gouvea Portugal to Queen, ca. 1809, AN/SPE/IG1, m. 112, fol. 73r–v.

41. MMU to Gov., Queluz, 18 Feb. 1803, BN/SM, I-31, 30, 112; MGE to Gov., Rio, 22 Jan. 1817, BN/SM, II-33, 17, 36, doc. 14.

42. IG to Gov., 25 Aug. 1820, APEB, m. 247-12.

43. Req., Herculano Antonio Pereira da Cunha to King, ca. 1819, AHE/RQ, H-14-396.

44. Kennedy, "Bahian Elites," 428; Morton, "Military," 256; McBeth, "Brazilian Generals," 141.

45. Lago, *Brigadeiros*; Silva, *Generais*; Lago, *Generais*. For a recent example of prosopography, see Hughes, *King's Finest*.

46. Test., João Gomes de Carvalho, 23 April 1799, justificação, José Gomes de Oliveira, *ABN* 45 (1922–1923), 311.

47. Test., João de Deus do Nascimento, 9 Oct. 1798, *ABN* 45 (1922–1923), 135.

48. PRE to Gov., Rio, 20 Nov. 1817, BN/SM, II-33, 31, 16, doc. 242; MGE to Gov.,

Rio, 30 Jan. 1818, BN/SM, II-33, 35, 11, doc. 304; Schwartz, *Sugar Plantations,* 272, 277; M. B. N. Silva, *História,* 62–63.

49. Morton, "Military," 254.

50. On these conflicts, see Alden, *Royal Government,* 59–275.

51. Published biographical information on these men includes Aguiar, *Vida;* Calogeras, *Marques;* Lago, *Brigadeiros,* 27–29, 111–12; Silva, *Generais,* 1:58–69; Dória and Fonseca, "Marechal José Inácio Acciaiuoli."

52. MMU to Gov., Queluz, 8 Jan. 1801, BN/SM, I-31, 27, 11.

53. Inv., Acciavoli, APEB/SJ/IT, 04/1663/2132/03.

54. Barbacena, *Economia;* Pinho, "Pesquizas"; Mattoso, *Bahia, século XIX,* 256.

55. M. B. N. Silva, *História,* 115–16; Alvará, 18 Oct. 1820, BN/SM, II-34, 5, 109, doc. 2; Lago, *Brigadeiros,* 53–54, 104.

56. Burkholder and Chandler, *From Impotence,* 15–80; Socolow, *Bureaucrats,* chap. 7; Archer, *Army,* 198–200; Marchena Fernández, *Ejército,* 162–76; idem, *Oficiales,* 112–24; G. M. Miller, "Status," 667.

57. Inv., Cogominho, APEB/SJ/IT, 01/04/04/07; Barbacena, *Economia,* 5, 25, 26, 55, 162, 170.

58. Inv., Acciavoli, APEB/SJ/IT, 04/1663/2132/03, fols. 36r–38r.

59. Brant to Matheus Pereira d'Almeida, 4 Dec. 1819, Barbacena, *Economia,* 37; Maria Bárbara Garcês Pinto de Madureira to Luís Paulino d'Oliveira Pinto da França, 15 and 21 April 1822, in França, ed., *Cartas,* 38, 43.

60. Luís Paulino to Henrique Garcez Pinto de Madureira, Rio, 15 March 1818, in França, ed., *Cartas,* 147. On the importance of personal management, see Bittencourt, *Longos serões,* 1:135.

61. Maria Bárbara to Luís Paulino, 2 March 1822, in França, ed., *Cartas,* 18–19; Luís da França Pinto Garcez to Maria Bárbara, Aramaré, 19 Feb. 1822, *ibid.,* 14.

62. "Auto para sequestro nos bens de José Gomes de Oliveira Borges . . . ," 24 Sep. 1798, *ABN* 43–44 (1920–1921), 190.

63. Vilhena, *Recopilação,* 1:110; Florencio José Correa de Melo to Gov., 14 May 1800, BN/SM, I-31, 30, 91; Lindley, *Narrative,* 106–7; Lavradio to João Gomes de Araujo, 27 July 1768, in Lavradio, *Cartas,* 45.

64. Req., Maria Thereza Xavier to King, ca. 1817, APEB, m. 247-11; statement of debts, inv., Cogominho, APEB/SJ/IT, 01/04/04/07, fol. 48r.

65. Lindley, *Narrative,* 99–102,

66. Luís da França to Maria Bárbara, Aramaré, 19 Feb. 1822, in França, ed., *Cartas,* 16; test., João de Deos, 12 Sep. 1798, *ABN* 45 (1922–1923), 126; "Dividas activas . . . ," inv., Manoel Pinto de Assunção, APEB/SJ/IT, 03/972/1441/12, fols. 16v–18v; Rebouças, "Recordações," 464, n. 14; test., Manoel Pereira de Santa Thereza, 24 Sep. 1798, *AAPEB* 35 (1959), 100; test., João de Deos, 9 Oct. 1798, *ABN* 45 (1922–1923), 140; Lindley, *Narrative,* 53, 95; Huell, "Mijne Eerste Zeereis," 226.

67. For estimates of Spanish-American regulars' strength, see Marchena Fernández, *Ejército,* 128.

68. In early 1821, this battalion counted 407 men in its enlisted ranks; it was likely somewhat larger in 1818, *Idade de Ouro do Brazil,* 20 Feb. 1821, 4.

69. Decreto, 31 Aug. 1809, *CLB.* On the qualifications of the cavalry captains, see Governing Junta to MGE, 28 July 1809, AN/SPE/IG1, m. 112, fol. 39r. For the captain's offer, see Luiz Barbalho Munis Fiuza Barretto to Brig. Com., 1 July 1810, APEB, m. 247-5; IG to Gov., 1 Dec. 1812, APEB, m. 247-7.

70. "Rellação das Pessoas que . . . contribuirão . . . ," ca. March 1810, AN/SPE/IG1, m. 112, fols. 107r–9v. For his hopes, see IG to Prince Regent, 27 June 1809, AN/SPE/IG1, m. 112, fols. 97v–100r. On economic difficulties, see Governing Junta to MGE, 22 March 1810, AN/SPE/IG1, m. 112, fol. 106r–v.

71. Gov. to MI, 27 June 1811, AN/SPE/IG1, m. 112, fol. 181r.

72. Mott, *Escravidão,* 11–18; Reis, *Slave Rebellion,* 42–44.

73. IG to MGE, 8 May 1810, AN/SPE/IG1, m. 112, fols. 116r–19r.

74. Some documents pertaining to this meeting have been published by Britto, "Levantes," 85–94, who notes the nonconfidence motion. Arcos's slave policy is analyzed by Reis, *Slave Rebellion,* 44–53. The proposed slave code can be found in BN/SM, DB, C9.5, doc. 6. For the rebukes, see MI to Gov., Rio, 27 July 1816, BN/SM, II-33, 24, 35; MI to IG, Rio, 14 Sep. 1816, AN/SAP, códice 607, vol. 1, fol. 20.

75. For warnings of the threats, see MMU to Gov., Ajuda, 10 March 1793, AIHGB, lata 109, doc. 9; Queluz, 2 Nov. 1798, BN/SM, II-33, 21, 48; I. A. C. Silva, *Memorias,* 3:16.

76. Test., Joze de Freitas Sacoto, 18 Oct. 1798, *AAPEB* 35 (1959), 129; Gov. to MMU, 17 June 1798, *ABN* 36 (1914), 35.

77. Mattoso, *Presença,* 148–59.

78. Mattoso, *Presença;* Ruy, *Primeira revolução;* Ramos, "Social Revolution"; Jancsó, *Bahia;* Tavares, *História da sedição;* Mattos, *Comunicação;* Morton, "Conservative Revolution," chap. 4; Garcia, *Cipriano Barata,* chap. 3.

79. Russell-Wood, "Colonial Brazil," 126, n. 108.

80. Test., Joze Raimundo Barata de Almeida, 2 Nov. 1798; and Cipriano Joze Barata de Almeida, 18 Oct. 1798, *AAPEB* 35 (1959), 121, 180. See also Jancsó, "Sedução," 429–35.

81. Mattoso, *Presença,* 148; test., José Felix, 5 Sep. 1798, *ABN,* 43–44 (1920–1921), 111; 10 Sep. 1798, *AAPEB* 35 (1959), 56.

82. Despite having been identified as attending seditious gatherings, Lieutenants Vicente Ferreira Lopes and Francisco de Santa Anna were not arrested, test., Domingos de Abreu Godinho, 15 Oct. 1798, *AAPEB* 35 (1959), 3; Ricardo Bernardino Guedes, 25 Sep. 1798, *ABN* 43–44 (1920–1921), 146.

83. Test., Joze Gomes de Oliveira Borges, 6 Sep. and 26 Oct. 1798, *AAPEB* 35 (1959), 85, 88.

84. Test., Hermógenes, 11 Jan. 1799, *AAPEB* 36 (1959), 328–29.

85. Test., J. F. Sacoto, 18 Oct. 1798, *AAPEB* 35 (1959), 132; Manoel de Santa Anna, 11 Feb. 1796, *AAPEB* 36 (1959), 295.

86. Test., M. Santa Anna, 11 Feb. 1799, *AAPEB* 36 (1959), 295.

87. *Alamanch . . . 1812*, 126.

88. Gov. to Paulo Fernandes, 8 Nov. 1811, AIHGB, lata 581, pasta 16; PRE to Gov., Rio, 21 Jan. 1813, BN/SM, II-34, 5, 107; *Idade de Ouro do Brazil*, 20 May 1812, 1.

89. Quintas, *Revolução;* Mota, *Nordeste;* Leite, *Pernambuco 1817;* Lyra, *Utopia*, 163–67; Barman, *Brazil*, 57–60.

90. Aguiar, *Vida*, 18.

91. "Chronica dos acontecimentos," 64.

92. Carvalho, "Revisitando," 187; Mota, *Nordeste*, 51–52; Quintas, *Revolução*, chap. 5; Leite, *Pernambuco 1817*, 177–89.

93. PRE to Gov., Rio, 11 Sep. 1817, BN/SM, II-33, 13, 31; I. A. C. Silva, *Memorias*, 3:70–71; Instructions, ca. 1818 (draft), BN/SM, II-34, 2, 29; MI to Conde da Villaflor, Rio, 3 Jan. 1821, BN/SM, II-34, 2, 41, doc. 62; Barman, *Brazil*, 61–62.

94. Tavares, *História da Bahia*, 168; Val, "Formação," 634; Mattoso, *Bahia, século XIX*, 617, 622–25. See also Araujo, "Politique," 117–18.

95. FOs, Francisco da Costa Branco, AHE/FO, III-20-8 (maj., 1819); F. P. M. Chaves, AHE/FO, III-21-54 (brevet maj., 1817; maj., 1818). Brant was promoted to marshal in 1819, as noted above.

96. Decreto, 16 Sep. 1799, in M. J. N. Silva, *Synopsis*, 2:144–45. F. J. C. Mello to Gov., 14 May 1800, BN/SM, I-31, 30, 91.

97. Morton, "Military," 254, 257; req., Pedro Alexandrino de Souza Portugal to Prince Regent, ca. 1805 (copy), BN/SM, II-33, 29, 89; Lago, *Brigadeiros*, 136.

98. Req., José Gonçalves Galeão to Prince Regent, 15 Oct. 1805, BN/SM, II-33, 19, 54.

99. Morton, "Military", 264–65; Kennedy, "Bahian Elites," 430–31.

100. Req., P. J. Santos to King, ca. 1820, AHE/RQ, P-31-919. See also reqs., M. F. Silveira to Queen, ca. 1795, BN/SM, II-33, 26, 40; Luiz de Betencourt Berenguer Cezar to Prince Regent, ca. 1810, APEB, m. 247-6; João José dos Reis to Prince Regent, ca. 1809, AHE/RQ, JJ-107-2863.

101. Barman notes this pattern for Portuguese immigration more generally, *Brazil*, 17–18.

102. Morton, "Conservative Revolution," 234.

103. MGE to Gov., Rio, 28 March 1817, BN/SM, II-33, 17, 36, doc. 78; 22 Oct. 1817, BN/SM, II-33, 35, 16, doc. 212.

104. *Idade de Ouro do Brazil*, 23 Dec. 1817, 1; "Chronica dos acontecimentos," 74.

105. PRE to Gov., Rio, 18 May 1820, BN/SM, II-34, 2, 43, doc. 52.

106. Test., Lucas Dantas de Amorim Torres, 25 Sep. 1798, *AAPEB* 36 (1959), 608; Mattoso, *Presença*, 156, 157.

107. FOs of 149 officers, 1770–1850, AHE/FO and RQ; McBeth, "Brazilian Generals," 130.

108. Morton, "Military," 255; see also Mattoso, *Bahia, século XIX*, 226.

109. Com. of Troops to Gov., 25 Feb. 1803, *ABN* 37 (1915), 85; Koster, *Travels,* 2:176; Spix and Martius, *Viagem,* 2:149.

110. Hoetink, *Two Variants,* chap. 4.

111. Luiz Gonzaga das Virgens e Veiga's notebooks, *AAPEB* 36 (1959), 461–76, 492–99, 523–67. This material has been analyzed by Jancsó, "Sedução," 394–98.

112. Test., Joaquim Antonio da Silva, 5 Sep. and 2 Nov. 1798, *AAPEB* 35 (1959), 106–9, 111–15; atestado, Joze Francisco de Souza e Almeida, 20 March 1803; FO, J. A. Silva, AHE/RQ, JJ-119-3113.

113. Decreto, 4 Feb. 1820; Provisão, 26 Oct. 1820, in Cidade, *Cadetes,* 26–28; R. V. Cunha, *Estudo,* 1:23–25.

Chapter 3

1. Florencio José Correa de Melo to Gov., 14 May 1800, BN/SM, I-31, 30, 91, fol. 79r; L. A. O. Mendes, "Discurso," 287.

2. Morton, "Military," 257–59; McBeth, "Brazilian Recruit," 72; Cidade, "Soldado," 3, 45–47; Kennedy, "Bahian Elites," 429; Mattoso, *Bahia: século XIX,* 226; Beattie, "Transforming," chap. 1; Aufderheide, "Order," 113–17.

3. Vilhena, *Recopilação,* 1:45.

4. Morton, "Military," 258; R. Graham, "Free African Brazilians," 35.

5. Peregalli, *Recrutamento,* chap. 3. McBeth, "Brazilian Recruit," 74–75; Prado Júnior, *Colonial Background,* 362–63; Beattie, "Transforming," 45–56, 53, 65–66. See, by contrast, F. F. Mendes's argument that coercive recruitment reflects state weakness, "Economia moral"; idem, "Tributo," 153–66.

6. Vilhena, *Recopilação,* 1:266. For official concerns about recruitment's impact on commerce and agriculture, see CR, 24 Feb. 1808, BN/SM, I-9, 2, 5.

7. Vilhena, *Recopilação,* 1:141, 256, 287–90, 292.

8. Req., Manoel Antonio da Silva Serva to King, ca. 1810s, BN/SM, II-33, 21, 26.

9. This view is well established in the historiography of Argentina, Slatta, *Gauchos,* chap. 8; Rodriguez Molas, *Historia,* 278–81. In contrast, however, see Salvatore, "Autocratic State," 259–62, 264; idem, "Reclutamiento," 33–35, 37, 46; Meisel, "War," 49–50, 55–56.

10. Vilhena, *Recopilação,* 1:257. See also Kraay, "Reconsidering," 23–24, 30–32.

11. This triangular pattern in recruitment has also been identified by F. F. Mendes, "Tributo," 93, 142, 320.

12. "Instrucções . . . para o recrutamento . . . ," 16 Aug. 1816, *CLB;* Gov. to Cap.-mor of Cachoeira, 16 Aug. 1814, APEB, m. 169.

13. Vilhena, *Recopilação,* 2:481; A. J. Costa, "População," 242.

14. MMU to Gov., Ajuda, 12 May 1775, BN/SM, II-33, 29, 34.

15. Aufderheide, "Order," 101; "Rellação . . . dos presos . . . ," Maragogipe, 8 Nov. 1810, BN/SM, I-31, 29, 61; Cap.-mor to Gov., Maragogipe, 7 March 1797, BN/SM, II-33, 23, 28; Vilhena, *Recopilação,* 1:257, 266.

16. Câmara to Gov., Maragogipe, 14 Aug. 1775, BN/SM, II-33, 21, 93; Câmara to Gov., Jaguaripe, 26 Oct. 1776, 12 July 1797, BN/SM, I-31, 30, 13; II-34, 5, 51; Vilhena, *Recopilação*, 1:257, 2:942.

17. Cap.-mor to Gov., Jaguaripe, 12 Dec. 1774, BN/SM, I-31, 28, 9; Cap.-mor to Gov., Maragogipe, 13 Feb. 1799, 10 Jan. and 30 July 1808, BN/SM, II-33, 23, 23; II-31, 28, 44; I-31, 28, 42; Cap.-mor to Gov., Agoa Fria, 9 April 1810, APEB, m. 247-5.

18. Jeronimo da Costa e Almeida to Gov., Maragogipe, 15 May 1775, BN/SM, II-33, 21, 84; Antonio José Calmon de Sousa e Eça to Gov., Jacoruna, 27 Aug. 1802, BN/SM, II-33, 18, 45.

19. Cap.-mor to Gov., Maragogipe, 30 July 1808, BN/SM, I-31, 28, 42; "Lista de Officiais, Inferiores e Soldados . . . que se achão incapazes . . . ," 1 Dec. 1812, APEB, m. 247-7.

20. Castro, *Ao sul;* Metcalf, *Family,* 120–52; Dias, "Sociabilidades"; S. C. Faria, *Colônia,* 396–98. For the application of these insights to recruitment, see Meznar, "Ranks," 340–47; Kraay, "Reconsidering," 16–18.

21. Reqs., Thomê Machado de Barcellos to King, n.d., BN/SM, II-34, 5, 23; Gonçalo Pereira de Brito to Queen, Cachoeira, ca. 1792 (copy), BN/SM, II-33, 21, 113; Cap.-mor to Gov., Maragogipe, 30 July 1808, BN/SM., I-31, 28, 42; req., Manoel Luiz Gonsalves Braga to Gov., ca. 1814, APEB, m. 247-8.

22. Lindley, *Narrative,* 195–96.

23. Brig. Com., First Reg., to IG, 6 July 1816, APEB, m. 247-10; req., Anna Rita de Araujo to King, ca. 1817, APEB, m. 247-12.

24. Titara, *Complemento,* 206–7, n. 264; reqs., Antonio da Cunha Pereira to Pres., ca. 1830, APEB, m. 3756; Felix Jose de Medina to Pres., ca. 1836, APEB, m. 3777; Tesoureiro Geral das Tropas to Pres., 20 May 1829, APEB, m. 3221.

25. Decreto, 13 May 1808, *CLB;* FOs in AN/SPE/IG1, m. 116, fols. 395–404.

26. Sodré, *História militar,* 132–33; McBeth, "Brazilian Recruit," 80–81.

27. Lippe, *Regulamento . . . infantaria,* 228–37.

28. Beresford, *Regulamento,* 2.

29. Bebiano, "Mecanismos," 1041, 1050–55; Foucault, *Discipline,* 135–94.

30. McNeill, *Keeping,* 3, 131–32.

31. This section owes much to the following studies of military discipline: Loriga, *Soldats,* chaps. 2, 4–6; Smith, *Between Mutiny and Obedience,* chaps. 1, 3–8.

32. "Chronica dos acontecimentos," 71; test., José Felix, 5 Sep. 1798, *ABN* 43–44 (1920–1921), 112.

33. Here, of course, I am distinguishing between what Scott has called subalterns' public and hidden transcripts, their stated compliance with rules coupled with their rejection of them in practice, *Domination,* 2–5.

34. Reis and Silva, *Negociação,* chap. 1; for the United States, see Genovese, *Roll, Jordan, Roll.*

35. Foucault, *Discipline,* 141–69; Goffman, *Asylums,* 1–124.

36. D. J. A. Rebello, "Corographia," 161; Victor Lourenço La Beaumelle to Pres., 27 June 1825, APEB, m. 3729.

37. Vilhena, *Recopilação,* 1:267.

38. Ibid., 1:267–68.

39. On historians' neglect of women's roles in militaries, see Hacker, "Women," 671. For one exception, see Salas, *Soldaderas.*

40. IG to Gov., 23 Nov. 1810, APEB, m. 247-4. Two privates mentioned the gardens in 1822, test., Francisco Ribeiro and Luiz da França, March 1822, *AAPEB* 27 (1941), 72, 74.

41. Mattoso, "Conjoncture," 41–43.

42. Mattoso, *Presença,* 149, 150, 151, 153, 156, 157; test., Ignacio da Silva Pimentel, 3 Sep. 1798, *AAPEB* 35 (1959), 45; Manoel Felix de Jesus, 29 Oct. 1798, *ABN* 43–44 (1920–1921), 150.

43. Luiz Gonzaga das Virgens e Veiga's notebooks, *AAPEB* 36 (1959), 467. On the the *quarta,* see Barickman, *Bahian Counterpoint,* 46.

44. Test., Miguel dos Anjos, José Joaquim de Almeida, Francisco Simoens o Novo, Ignacio Correa de Vasconcellos, Antonio Manoel de Araujo, March 1822, *AAPEB* 27 (1941), 69, 56, 119–20, 140, 153.

45. Myerly, *British Military Spectacle,* 10–11, 77–78; Joseph, *Uniforms,* 65–83.

46. On the sale of uniforms, see Brig. Com., Art. Reg., to IG, 7 July 1810, APEB, m. 247-5; IG to Gov., 1 Dec. 1812, APEB, m. 247-7.

47. Lindley, *Narrative,* 87; IG to Gov., 1 Dec. 1812, APEB, m. 247-7.

48. Prince Regent to Gov., Quelus, 10 May 1799, BN/SM, II-33, 29, 18; CR, ca. March 1800, *ABN* 36 (1914), 236; Decreto, 31 Aug. 1809; Alvará, 12 March 1810, *CLB.*

49. Cap.-mor to Gov., Maragogipe, 20 June 1798, BN/SM, II-33, 23, 31; Conselhos de Investigação, March 1822, *AAPEB* 27 (1941), 73, 74, 101, 103, 170; Bernardino Alves de Araújo, "Artigos da minha justificação," AHE/RQ, B-27-788; test., José Antonio dos Santos, 29 Oct. 1798, *ABN* 43–44 (1920–1921), 149; Lindley, *Narrative,* 247; IG to Gov., 21 Jan. 1817, APEB, m. 247-12.

50. Marquis of Lavradio to Conde de Prado, 21 July 1768; to Joaquim Inácio da Cruz, 1 May 1769, in Lavradio, *Cartas,* 30–31, 174.

51. Vilhena, *Recopilação* 1:35, 108.

52. Lippe, *Regulamento . . . cavallaria,* 55; atestado, Carlos Balthazar da Silveira, 3 April 1803, AHE/RQ, JJ-119-3113; Brig. Com., Legion, to IG, 28 March 1814, APEB, m. 247-9.

53. Gonzaga's notebooks, *AAPEB* 36 (1959), 472; test., Romão Pinheiro, 2 Nov. 1798, *AAPEB* 36 (1959), 632.

54. Gov. to MGE, 30 June 1808, APEB, m. 145, fols. 235v–37r; "Epochas da Bahia . . . ," 21 June and 2 July 1808, BN/SM, II-33, 32, 53; "Chronica dos acontecimentos," 50; Huell, "Mijne Eerste Zeereis," 275–80. Unfortunately, none of these accounts records the names of the accused and his victim.

55. Huell, "Mijne Eerste Zeereis," 277.

56. Vilhena, *Recopilação*, 1:268.

57. Lippe, *Regulamento* . . . *cavallaria*, 177.

58. Lindley, *Narrative*, 70. For British officers' views of discipline, see Steppler, "British Military Law," 859; Dinwiddy, "Early Nineteenth-Century Campaign," 329; Burroughs, "Crime," 560–61.

59. McBeth, "Brazilian Recruit," 71, 81.

60. "Traslado das tres denuncias . . . ," in I. A. C. Silva, *Memorias*, 3:120; test., Caetano Vellozo Barreto, 4 Sep. 1798, *AAPEB* 35 (1959), 105; "Chronica dos acontecimentos," 53; Jozé Ferreira de Castro, Parte, 16 March 1815; req., idem to [Gov.], ca. 1815; IG to Gov., 31 March 1815, APEB, m. 247-10.

61. Decisão 12, 3 March 1812, *CLB;* GA to Pres., 16 Nov. 1829, APEB, m. 3399; M. J. N. Silva, *Synopsis*, 2:294–95, 347.

62. Gov. to MMU, 20 Jan. 1799, in Vilhena, *Recopilação*, 2:379; req., Pedro Ramos and Francisco Pereira de Castro to Gov., ca. 1815; IG to Gov., 10 April 1815, APEB, m. 247-10. For another case investigated, see IG to Gov., 1 Dec. 1812, APEB., m. 247-7.

63. Wirtschafter, *From Serf*, 149–51.

64. Vilhena, *Recopilação*, 1:258–60; Morton, "Conservative Revolution," 73.

65. Wirtschafter, *From Serf*, 110; Coffman, *Old Army*, 193.

66. The distinction between management and repression is Smith's, "Disciplinary Dilemma," 48.

67. M. J. N. Silva, *Synopsis*, 1:346–62; Sampaio, *Instrucções*, 70–80; Titara, *Auditor*, 191–99.

68. Gilbert, "Why Men Deserted," 561–62; Corvisier, *Armée*, 2:703–13; Burroughs, "Tackling Army Desertion," 32–37; Hartnagel, "Absent without Leave," 216–18; Forrest, *Conscripts*, chap. 8.

69. Cap.-mor to Col. [Com. Forces in Sergipe], Lagarto, 3 July 1816, APEB, m. 232; test., Manoel de Santana, 11 Feb. 1799, *AAPEB* 36 (1959), 294.

70. Bando, 16 April 1793, BN/SM, II-33, 21, 56, fol. 2r; req., Custodio Gonçalves do Couto to Prince Regent, ca. 1812, BN/SM, II-33, 20, 67.

71. Vilhena, *Recopilação*, 1:266; Lindley, *Narrative*, 155; GA to Pres., 8 Aug. 1824; req., Germano Pereira to GA, ca. 1824, APEB, m. 3364.

72. Lavradio to Conde de Azambuja, 13 March 1769, in Lavradio, *Cartas*, 137; proposed slave code (copy), São Francisco, 24 Feb. 1816, BN/SM, DB C9.5, doc. 6.

73. Cap.-mor to Col. [Com. Forces in Sergipe], Lagarto, 3 July 1816, APEB, m. 232 (Sergipe was then a district of Bahia); Cap.-mor to Gov., Maragogipe, 20 March 1797, BN/SM, II-33, 23, 29.

74. FO, Gonzaga, *AAPEB* 36 (1959), 425; list of court-martial cases, APEB, m. 143. For a reference to an individual petition for clemency, see IG to Gov., 6 Nov. 1812, BN/SM, II-33, 22, 71.

75. "Lista de Officiaes, Inferiores, e Soldados . . . ," 1 Dec. 1812, APEB, m. 247-7; "Relação dos Individuos . . . ," 1 April 1817, BN/SM, II-33, 17, 36, docs. 83, 84.

76. Will, Manoel José de Carvalho, 6 July 1815, APEB/SJ/LRT, vol. 5, fols. 93r–94v.

77. See the entries for 29 Nov. 1794, and 12 and 14 Sep. 1795, in Gonzaga's notebooks, *AAPEB* 36 (1959), 464, 468; test., R. Pinheiro, 15 Sep. 1798, *AAPEB* 35 (1959), 53; test., Hermogenes Francisco de Aguillar, 9 Jan. 1799, *AAPEB* 36 (1959), 322.

78. IG to Gov., 10 July 1817, APEB, m. 247-11; Luís da França Pinto Garcez to Maria Bárbara Garcês Pinto de Madureira, Aramaré, 19 Feb. 1822, in *França*, ed. *Cartas*, 16; req., Luciano de Brito to [Pres.], ca. 1825, BN/SM, II-33, 31, 4, no. 1, doc. 18.

79. IG to Gov., 11 July 1816, 4 Nov. 1815, APEB, m. 247-10; req., Antonio Ramos to Gov., ca. 1810, APEB, m. 247-6; req., Joaquim Francisco de Lucena Maxado to Gov., ca. 1815, APEB, m. 3781; Morton, "Conservative Revolution," 77.

80. Reqs., Jozé Ricardo to Gov., ca. 1815, APEB, m. 247-10; Felipe Neri Leite to IG, ca. 1815, APEB, m. 247-9.

81. Req., José Bernardo de Miranda to [King], ca. 1763 (copy), BN/SM, II-34, 6, 43; FOs, Manoel José Vieira, AHE/FO, XIX-3-32, VI-2-113; req., J. Ricardo to Gov., ca. 1815, APEB, m. 247-10; req., José Pedro de Alcantara to Emperor, 18 Aug. 1860, with enclosed FO, 16 Aug. 1860, AHE/RQ, JZ-136-3937.

82. Reqs., Jozé Joaquim dos Santos to King, ca. 1818, AHE/RQ, JJ-272-6530; Roberto da Costa e Souza to [Queen], ca. 1791 (copy), BN/SM, II-33, 29, 13; Jozé Gôes Souza e Oliveira to King, ca. 1811, BN/SM, II-33, 22, 71; Lucas de Queiroz Ponte to King, ca. 1816, BN/SM, II-33, 17, 36, doc. 22.

83. IG to Gov., 20 July 1820, AHE/RQ, B-27-783.

84. "Chronica dos acontecimentos," 51; Luís Paulino d'Oliveira Pinto da França to Henrique Garcez Pinto de Madureira, Rio, 15 March 1818, in *França*, ed., *Cartas*, 147.

85. Test., Lucas Dantas de Amorim Torres, 6 Nov. 1798, *AAPEB* 35 (1959), 274; Francisco Marinho, 14 Sep. 1798; João Francisco de Magalhães, *AAPEB* 36 (1959), 399, 412.

86. Test., R. Pinheiro, 15 Sep. 1798, *AAPEB* 35 (1959), 53; Pedro Nolasco de Sá Marinho e Azevedo, 28 Aug. 1798, *AAPEB* 36 (1959), 389.

87. Redlich, *German Military Enterpriser*, 2:208.

88. M. J. N. Silva, *Synopsis*, 1:155; "Auto para sequestro nos bens de Caetano Veloso Barreto . . . ," 11 Oct. 1798, *ABN* 43–44 (1920–1921), 197; Vilhena, *Recopilação*, 1:66, 130.

89. Req., Barnabé Vellozo to King, ca. 1819; atestado, Joaquim de Mello Leite Cogominho de Lacerda, 23 Feb. 1818 (copy); Col. Com., First Reg., to IG, Salvador, 22 July 1820, AHE/RQ, B-27-783. For another reference to soldiers paying each other to do guard duties, see test., Joze Gomes de Oliveira Borges, 26 Oct. 1798, *AAPEB* 35 (1959), 89.

90. Test., João da Costa Ferreira, 15 Sep. 1798; Salvador Pereira Sudré, 15 Oct. 1798, *ABN* 43–44 (1920–1921), 122, 142; Joze Joaquim de Siqueira, 1 Sep. 1798, *AAPEB* 35 (1959), 81.

91. "Auto de sequestro nos bens de Lucas Dantas de Amorim Torres," 20 Sep. 1798, *ABN* 43–44 (1920–1921), 182; "Traslado das tres denuncias . . . ," in I. A. C. Silva, *Memorias,* 3:113, 117; "Auto para sequestro nos bens de Ignacio da Silva Pimentel . . . ," 24 Sep. 1798; "Auto para sequestro nos bens de José Joaquim de Siqueira . . . ," 28 Sep. 1798, *ABN* 43–44 (1920–1921), 191, 194.

92. Test., João de Deos do Nascimento, 9 Oct. 1798; Dantas, 17 Oct. 1798, *ABN* 45 (1922–1923), 140, 96.

93. McBeth, "Brazilian Recruit," 71.

94. On these aspects of slavery, see Reis, *Slave Rebellion,* chap. 9; Barickman, " 'Bit of Land,' " 657–62; Karasch, *Slave Life,* 302–16, esp. 315.

95. Vilhena, *Recopilação,* 1:111.

96. "Instruções," 16 Aug. 1816, *CLB;* Gov. to Prince Regent, 15 Nov. 1804, APEB, m. 142; Gov. to MMU, 8 Aug. 1793, 24 May 1797, 21 Oct. 1799, *ABN* 34 (1912), 290, 448; 36 (1914), 158.

97. Koster, *Travels,* 2:184, see also 2:68, 2:176; Rugendas, *Viagem,* 277, 146.

98. Vilhena, *Recopilação,* 1:267; Lindley, *Narrative,* 87; IG to Gov., 21 Oct. 1816, APEB, m. 247-10.

99. *ABN* 43–44 (1920–1921), 45 (1922–1923); *AAPEB* 35–36 (1959).

100. Hoetink, *Two Variants,* chap. 4; Cope, *Limits,* chaps. 3–4.

101. Test., J. J. Siqueira, 1 Sep. 1798, *AAPEB* 35 (1959), 80–81.

102. Test., J. Felix, 5 Sep. 1798, *ABN* 43–44 (1920–1921), 111–12; 10 Sep. 1798, *AAPEB* 35 (1959), 56; M. Santana, 11 Feb. 1799, *AAPEB* 36 (1959), 297; Dantas, 20 Sep. 1798, *AAPEB* 36 (1959), 602.

103. Reqs., Gonzaga, *AAPEB* 36 (1959), 522, 523, 582. The *alvará* of 16 Jan. 1773 is noted in R. J. C. Mattos, *Repertório,* 2:112.

104. Gov. to MMU, 20 Oct. 1798, in I. A. C. Silva, *Memorias,* 3:122, 124; test., João de Deus, 11 Nov. 1798, *ABN* 45 (1922–1923), 119.

105. Test., I. S. Pimentel, 3 Sep. 1798, *AAPEB* 35 (1959), 42.

Chapter 4

1. Vilhena, *Recopilação,* 1:253–54. On Henrique Dias, see Mello, *Henrique Dias.*

2. McAlister, *"Fuero,"* v; Kuethe, *Cuba,* 174–76. On Brazil, see Morton, "Military," 263–68; Leonzo, "Defesa," 373–75.

3. Decreto, 13 May 1811, *CLB;* "Chronica dos acontecimentos," 54.

4. Turnbull, *Voyage,* 23.

5. Vilhena, *Recopilação,* 1:254. On the ordenanças, see Leonzo, "Companhias"; Kuznesof, "Clans"; Prado Júnior, *Colonial Background,* 364–65, 378–84.

6. Reqs., Marcellino da Silva Torres to Gov., ca. 1796 and 1819; idem to Pres., ca. 1829, APEB, m. 3756.

7. L. A. O. Mendes, "Discurso," 287. For assessments of militia uniforms, see invs. in APEB/SJ/IT: Manoel Ferreira Dias, 04/1771/2241/10, fols. 6v–7r; Silverio Leonardo da Conceição Passos, 04/1654/2123/08, fols. 4v–5r; José Antonio Guimarães, 03/1350/1819/03, fol. 23v.

8. Req., Manoel de Gouvea to Queen, ca. 1801 (copy), APEB, m. 100, doc. 53.

9. IG to Gov., 23 Oct. 1816, APEB, m. 247-10.

10. Maj. Com., Fourth Reg., to Prince Regent, 6 Feb. 1808, BN/SM, II-34, 2, 33; "Proposta . . . 3 Regimento de Mil.cas," 17 Jan. 1821, APEB, m. 247-12.

11. "Provincia da Bahya. Proposta do 1.o Regim.to de Milicias," 14 Dec. 1814; IG to Gov., 16 Dec. 1814, APEB, m. 247-8.

12. IG to Gov., 16 Dec. 1814, APEB, m. 247-8.

13. Req., Felipe Benício to Gov., ca. 1812; Lt. Col. Com., Third Reg., to IG, ca. 1819, APEB, m. 247-8.

14. Kennedy, "Bahian Elites," 431.

15. IG to Gov., 25 Nov. 1815, APEB, m. 247-9; 3 Nov. 1815; 30 March 1816; 28 Aug. 1816, APEB, m. 247-10; Lugar, "Merchant Community," 220.

16. Req., Francisco Teixeira da Mata Bacelar to Gov., ca. 1811, APEB, m. 247-8.

17. Will, Bonifacio Duarte Benfica, 18 Jan. 1816, APEB/SJ/LRT, vol. 6, fol. 88v; "Rellação das cinco Praças do Batalhão de Cassadores da 2.a Linha do Exército N. 92 . . . ," BN/SM, I-31, 15, 19; "Lista dos homens pardos q' não tem praça em corpo algum das Tropas de Milicia . . . ," n.d., *AAPEB* 36 (1959), 444–45.

18. IG to Gov., 27 July 1812, APEB, m. 247-8; Decreto, 9 Oct. 1812, *CLB.*

19. IG to Gov., 15 July 1820, APEB, m. 247-12; 8 May 1814, APEB, m. 247-8.

20. Req., Manoel Joze Guedes to Gov., ca. 1819, APEB, m. 247-12; IG to Gov., 27 May 1814, APEB, m. 247-8; 23 June 1812, APEB, m. 247-7; GA to Pres., 5 Jan. 1827, APEB, m. 3367; IG to Gov., 6 May 1815, APEB, m. 247-10.

21. IG to Gov., 25 Jan. 1814, APEB, m. 247-9

22. Vilhena, *Recopilação,* 1:253.

23. Lists of Militia Officers, 4 Oct. 1803, BN/SM, II-34, 5, 80; Decisões 150 and 181, 18 Aug. and 26 Oct. 1830, *CLB.*

24. Parecer, 27 Aug. 1807, APEB, m. 103, doc. 82A.

25. See, especially, Fernández, "Social World," 62; Leonzo, "Defesa," 352; Lugar, "Merchant Community," 217–19.

26. Spix and Martius, *Viagem,* 2:153.

27. Koster, *Travels,* 2:185; M. D. Graham, *Journal,* 141; Taunay and Dénis, *Brésil,* 4:97.

28. See, for example, Hanger, "Privilege," 85; Booker, "Needed," 273–76; Klein, "Colored Militia," 25–26; Voelz, *Slave,* 415–24.

29. Gov. to MMU, 19 Dec. 1799; Com. of Troops to Gov., 6 June 1800, *ABN* 36 (1914), 172, 257.

30. Vilhena, *Recopilação*, 1:270.
31. Huell, "Mijne Eerst Zeereis," 241.
32. "Chronica dos acontecimentos," 53.
33. Andrews, *Blacks*, 249–58; Lovell and Wood, "Skin Color," 91–94, 104–106.
34. F. J. Davis, *Who Is Black?* That this was not always the case, however, is stressed by Williamson, *New People.*
35. Nazzari, "Vanishing Indians," 520–23.
36. Titara, *Paraguassú*, 493, n. 2; Ruy, *Primeira revolução*, 79. See also the concerns about mulattoes in São Paulo's white militia regiments, Leonzo, "Defesa," 318.
37. Vinson III, "Free Colored Voices," 171–72; idem, "Bearing Arms," 188, 434. See also Howard, *Changing*, 30, 34.
38. Vinson III, "Bearing Arms," 170–93.
39. Vilhena, *Recopilação*, 1:140; Mattoso, *Bahia, século XIX*, 535.
40. I have used the same classification of artisan trades as Chance, *Race*, 160.
41. Seed, "Social Dimensions," 600–2.
42. For an indebted merchant, see inv., Caetano Maurício Machado, APEB/SJ/IT, 03/1145/1614/06. On the decline of Salvador's merchants after independence, see Lugar, "Merchant Community," 178–79, 184, 192–93.
43. Inv., Joaquim da Silva Braga, APEB/SJ/IT, 03/1100/1569/04.
44. See, for instance, Thompson, *Making*, 9–11; Parker, *Idea*, 7–14.
45. For classification of brotherhoods, I have relied on Salles, *Associações*, 47; Mulvey, "Slave Confraternities," 64–68; Mulvey, "Black Brothers," 275–79; Russell-Wood, "Prestige," 64–66; Nishida, "From Ethnicity," 331–35; 343, n. 4.
46. Wills in APEB/SJ/IT: Innocencio José da Costa, 4 Aug. 1804, 08/3465/02; Manoel de Oliveira Barroso, 17 Nov. 1807, 04/1513/1982/04, fols. 59r–70r; wills in APEB/SJ/LRT: Constantino Vieira de Lima, 10 Feb. 1816, vol. 6, fol. 115r–v; Francisco Alvares Guimarães, 28 July 1839, vol. 27, fol. 17r; João Dias Coelho, 31 May 1854, vol. 37, fols. 196r, 198v; João Antunes Guimarães, 5 Nov. 1845, vol. 32, fol. 5v.
47. Wills in APEB/SJ/LRT: B. D. Benfica, 18 Jan. 1816, vol. 6, fol. 88r; Francisco José da Cunha, 12 Feb. 1821, vol. 22, fols. 180v–81r; Manoel Alvares da Costa, 6 Oct. 1826, vol. 17, fol. 78r; will, J. Antonio Guimarães, 21 Nov. 1814, APEB/SJ/IT, 03/1350/1819/03, fols. 10r–v.
48. Wills in APEB/SJ/LRT: Custódio Gomes de Almeida, 6 Nov. 1820, 04/1748/2218/01, fols. 3r–4v; Manoel Pinto da Assunção, 27 April 1832, 03/972/1441/12, fol. 5r.
49. Wills in APEB/SJ/IT: José da Costa Faria, 19 July 1803, 05/2023/2494/11, fol. 4v; Joaquim de Santana Neves, 7 July 1831, 01/2014/2485/03, fols. 5v–6v; Marcos Berlink, 11 Feb. 1848, 04/1858/2329/03, fol. 6r; will, Joaquim Félix de Santana, 25 Dec. 1814, APEB/SJ/LRT, vol. 7, fols. 32r–v;
50. Wills in APEB/SJ/IT: J. C. Faria, 19 July 1803, 05/2023/2494/11, fol. 4r; Neves, 7 July 1831, 01/2014/2485/03. In this regard, Bahia's black officers were very similar to

their counterparts in Havana and Buenos Aires, Deschamps Chapeaux, *Batallones,* 55–60; Howard, *Changing,* 30–36; Andrews, "Afro-Argentine Officers," 96–97.

51. FO, José Raimundo de Barros, APEB, m. 247-10; will, J. F. Santana, 25 Dec. 1814, APEB/SJ/LRT, vol. 7, fol. 31v. Neves's will is silent on his status at birth; his service record is also silent on his filiation, but Antonio Pereira Rebouças cited Neves to demonstrate the importance of freedmen in the Bahian military, speech, 25 Aug., *ACD* (1832) 2:200–1; FO, Neves, AHE/RQ, JZ-90-2705.

52. Wills in APEB/SJ/LRT: Manoel Pereira da Silva, 9 March 1814, vol. 5, fol. 52r; M. Berlink, 11 Feb. 1848, 04/1858/2329/03, fol. 6r; FO, Francisco Xavier Bigode, AHE/RQ, F-148-3781.

53. Querino, *Costumes,* 33–34; Harding, *Refuge,* 93–96, 195–204.

54. Reis, *Slave Rebellion,* 225–26.

55. Oliveira, "Viver," 182; idem, *Liberto,* 55–58.

56. Wills in APEB/SJ/LRT: M. P. Silva, 9 March 1814, vol. 5, fol. 52r; J. F. Santana, 25 Dec. 1814, vol. 7, fols. 31v–33v, 38v; will, Neves, 7 July 1831, APEB/SJ/IT, 01/2014/2485/03, fols. 4r, 6r, 7r, 8v.

57. Wills, J. F. Santana, 25 Dec. 1814, APEB/SJ/LRT, vol. 7, fols. 30v–40v; Neves, 7 July 1831, APEB/SJ/IT, 01/2014/2485/03, fols. 4r–8v.

58. Will, M. O. Barroso, 17 Nov. 1807, APEB/SJ/IT, 04/1513/1982/04, fol. 61r–v.

59. Wills and invs. in APEB/SJ/IT: C. G. Almeida, 6 Nov. 1820, 04/1748/2218/01, fols. 3r–v; J. S. Braga, 03/1100/1569/04; S. L. C. Passos, 04/1654/2123/08; Marcellino Alvares da Costa, 03/1059/1528/24.

60. Inv., C. G. Almeida, APEB/SJ/IT, 04/1748/2218/01, fols. 3v, 18r–19v; "Informação dos Officiaes do 4.o Regim.to de Milicias . . . ," 31 Dec. 1809, APEB, m. 247-6.

61. Will, I. J. Costa, 4 Aug. 1804, APEB/SJ/IT, 08/3465/02; Gov. to MMU, 20 Jan. 1799, in Vilhena, *Recopilação,* 2:372.

62. Inv., Manoel Ferreira da Silva, APEB/SJ/IT, 04/1731/2201/02, fol. 17v; will, C. V. Lima, 10 Feb. 1816, APEB/SJ/LRT, vol. 6, fol. 116r.

63. Req., J. Antunes Guimarães to Emperor, ca. 1841, AHE/RQ, JJ-41-1136; req., Ignacio Antunes Guimarães (son) to King, ca. 1810s, BN/SM, DB, C.876.30.

64. Inv., I. A. Guimarães (son), APEB/SJ/IT, 04/1668/2138/06; *Almanach . . . 1812,* 132; Ruy, *História,* 357.

65. Will, J. Antunes Guimarães, 5 Nov. 1845, APEB/SJ/LRT, vol. 32, fol. 7r, 8r–v; Martins, Barrozo, Dourados, and Carvalho to Jozé Bruno Antunes Guimarães, Liverpool, 12 Aug. 1809, BN/SM, II-33, 32, 54, no. 2; "Censo dos Pays de família e seus filhos," Santana Parish, 1 July 1824, APEB, m. 3513; reqs., I. A. Guimarães (son) to Emperor, ca. 1825, BN/SM, DB, C.876.30; J. Antunes Guimarães to Emperor, ca. 1820s, BN/SM, DB, C.801.14.

66. FOs, J. Antunes Guimarães, AHE/RQ, JJ-41-1136; Bruno, BN/SM, DB, C.624.6; I. A. Guimarães (son), BN/SM, DB, C.876.30; Acting MGE to Gov., Rio, 27 Aug. 1817, BN/SM, II-33, 22, 22.

67. Inv., C. M. Machado, APEB/SJ/IT, 03/1145/1614/06, fol. 19r.

68. "Representação dos Mestres de Campo e Coronéis...," 12 Aug. 1796; atestado, Jozé Pires de Carvalho e Albuquerque, 15 Aug. 1796, BN/SM, II-33, 29, 48; Gov. to Luiz Pinto de Sousa, 15 July 1796, *ABN* 34 (1912), 395.

69. CR, 22 March 1766; Aviso, 30 May 1767, in R. J. C. Mattos, *Repertório,* 2:323–24.

70. Maxwell, *Pombal,* 130; Boxer, *Race Relations,* 73–74; Carneiro, *Preconceito,* chap. 3.

71. Vilhena, *Recopilaçao,* 1:254; Provedor-mor da Fazenda to Viceroy, 18 Aug. 1739, in Silva, *Memorias,* 4:57, n. 27; atestado, Justino Joze de Campos, Fort São Pedro, 26 Nov. 1799, AHE/RQ, JZ-90-2705; atestado, Manoel de Abreu Carvalho Contreiras, Bateria de São Paulo, 2 Jan. 1805, AHE/RQ, JZ-173-4911. The CU noted in 1800 that the governor had ordered that both black and mulatto regiments take their turns mounting the palace guard, implying that both had been barred from doing so earlier, Consulta, 13 Jan. 1800, APEB, m. 91, fol. 229v.

72. Vilhena, *Recopilação,* 1:253–54.

73. Portugal's successor makes this clear in Gov. to MMU, 10 July 1804, *ABN* 37 (1915), 155.

74. Test., Antônio Rodrigues Machado, 17 Aug. 1798; Domingos da Silva Lisboa, 27 Aug. 1798, *AAPEB* 36 (1959), 386, 430.

75. Test., Lucas Dantas de Amorim Torres, 20 Sep. 1798, *AAPEB* 36 (1959), 601; Mattoso, *Presença,* 148.

76. Test., Manoel Faustino dos Santos Lira, 25 Sep. 1798, *AAPEB* 35 (1959), 14.

77. Test., João de Deus do Nascimento, 11 Sep. 1798, *ABN* 45 (1922–1923), 119.

78. "Traslado das tres denuncias"; Gov. to MMU, ca. 1799, in Silva, *Memorias,* 3:115, 125; test., Francisco Vicente Vianna, 3 Sep. 1798, *ABN* 43–44 (1920–1921), 107; req., Joaquim José de Santana to Queen, ca. 1800 (copy), APEB, m. 91, doc. 78A.

79. Gov. to Queen, 14 June 1800, APEB, m. 140, fol. 61v.

80. Provedor da Real Fazenda to MMU, 10 Oct. 1798, *ABN* 36 (1914), 43. For contemporary views of mulatto pretensions, see Vilhena, *Recopilação,* 1:46; Spix and Martius, *Viagem,* 2:129.

81. MMU to Gov., Queluz, 20 April 1800, APEB, m. 91, doc. 75.

82. This policy has been analyzed for São Paulo by Leonzo, "Defesa," 307–12.

83. Decisão 1, 3 Jan. 1809; CR, 30 Oct. 1810; Decreto, 17 Dec. 1811; Decisão 12, 3 March 1812, *CLB;* IG to Gov., 10 Oct. 1812, APEB, m. 247-7; *Manobra.*

84. IG to Prince Regent, 27 June 1809, AN/SPE/IG1, m. 112, fol. 102v; PRE to Gov., Rio, 12 April 1817, BN/SM, II-33, 17, 36, doc. 101.

85. Gov. to MMU, 20 June 1806, *ABN* 37 (1915), 387; "Informação dos Officiaes do Distinto Regimento 1.o de Milicias," 3 March 1810, APEB, m. 247-6; reqs. and FO, F. A. Guimarães, AHE/RQ, F-45-1541. João Joaquim de Freitas Henriques, Guimarães's successor, appears as a regular major in *Almanach ... 1812,* 122.

86. "Relação dos Officiaes Promovidos . . . ," 28 June 1817, BN/SM, II-33, 17, 36, doc. 152.

87. Russell-Wood, *Black Man,* 92–93.

88. Alvará, 17 Dec. 1802 (copy), AN/SPE, GIFI, 12.4, 4H-50, fols. 916v–17r. The genesis of this ruling has been analyzed by Morton, "Conservative Revolution," 145–47.

89. Morton, "Conservative Revolution," 147–49.

90. IG to Gov., 7 Feb. 1808; Gov. to Prince Regent, 9 Feb. 1808, BN/SM, II-34, 2, 23.

91. Consulta, CU, Lisbon, 13 Jan. 1800 (copy), APEB, m. 91, fol. 232r.

92. Boxer has noted that the Angolan military was more integrated than that of Brazil, *Race Relations,* 31–33.

93. Jose Francisco da Silva to Adj.-General, Rio, ca. April 1824, AHE/RQ, JJ-237-5790; will, M. O. Barroso, 17 Nov. 1807, APEB/SJ/IT, 04/1513/1982/04, fol. 61r, 63v. For career information on these three men, see "Informação dos Officiaes do 4.o Regim.to de Milicias," 31 Dec. 1809, APEB, m. 247-6. F. W. O. Morton identifies Melo e Castro as a Portuguese-born officer, "Conservative Revolution," 149. While this may be true, Melo e Castro's marriage and transfer to the Fourth Regiment suggest that his slave's assessment of him as pardo was widely shared. After all, Portuguese birth did not necessarily imply whiteness, as Domingos da Silva Lisboa, mentioned above, demonstrates.

94. IG to Gov., ca. 1809, APEB, m. 247-4; "Informação dos Officiaes do 3.o Regimento de Milicias," 31 Dec. 1809, APEB, m. 247-6; IG to Gov., 24 May 1811, BN/SM, II-33, 22, 65, doc. 3.

95. Col. Com., Third Reg., to Gov., 15 Dec. 1814; IG to Gov., 16 Dec. 1814, APEB, m. 247-8.

96. FO, Bigode, AHE/RQ, F-148-3781; "Proposta dos Postos que se achão vagos do Terceiro Regimento," 15 Dec. 1814, APEB, m. 247-8; IG to Gov., 9 Oct. 1820, APEB, m. 247-12.

97. "Informação dos Officiaes do 4.o Regim.to de Milicias," 31 Dec. 1809, APEB, m. 247-6; FO, Jozé Maria Cirillo da Silva, AHE/FO, V-1-8.

98. Spix and Martius, *Viagem,* 2:153.

99. MGE to Gov., Rio, 14 May 1817, BN/SM, II-33, 17, 36, doc. 140.

Chapter 5

1. Felisberto Caldeira Brant Pontes to Joaquim Pereira d'Almeida, 31 Oct. 1820, in Barbacena, *Economia,* 174; and Count of Palmela, 21 Dec. 1820, BN/SM, II-33, 22, 74.

2. Morton, "Conservative Revolution," 376.

3. The following narrative is based on B. H. Amaral, *História;* Pinho, "Bahia," 244–67; Tavares, *Independência;* idem, *Levante;* Morton, "Conservative Revolution,"

chaps. 8–9; Araujo, "Politique"; Cavalcanti, "Processo." On the Luso-Brazilian political context, see Barman, *Brazil*, chaps. 3–4; Macaulay, *Dom Pedro*; J. H. Rodrigues, *Independência*, vols. 1, 3, and 4; Bethell, "Independence"; Russell-Wood, ed., *From Colony*; Novais and Mota, *Independência*; C. H. S. Oliveira, *Independência*; E. V. Costa, *Brazilian Empire*, chap. 1.

4. Barman, *Brazil*, 73, 81–82, 86–87.

5. Leite, *Pernambuco, 1824*; M. J. M. Carvalho, "Hegemony," chap. 1.

6. Inácio Luís Madeira de Melo to King, 7 March 1822, in B. H. Amaral, *História*, 124; Cap.-mor to Madeira, Cachoeira, 16 April 1822, *AAPEB* 27 (1941), 9.

7. On the meaning of "anarchist," see Ribeiro, " 'Pés-de-chumbo,' " 157.

8. "Felicitação do Conselho Interino a S. M. em Dezembro de 1822," *RIGHB* 13 (1897), 443; "Proclamação, Bahia em Camara," 23 Aug. 1823, *AAPEB* 10 (1923), 32–33.

9. Tavares, *Independência*, 63–65.

10. Proclamação, Manoel Pedro de Freitas Guimarães, 10 Feb. 1821, in B. H. Amaral, *História*, 16; Holanda, "Herança colonial," 9. See also Barman, *Brazil*, 65–67.

11. "Vereação extraordinaria," Santo Amaro, 29 June 1822, in B. H. Amaral, *História*, 202; Ata, Câmara, São Francisco, 29 June 1822, in I. A. C. Silva, *Memorias*, 3:350.

12. I. L. C. Souza, *Pátria*, 173–74, 178–80.

13. CI to MI, Cachoeira, 29 Oct. 1822, *RIGHB* 13 (1897), 439; Pedro Labatut to MI, n.p., 16 April 1823, in Brazil, Arquivo Nacional, *Junta*, 52–53; Mattoso, *Bahia, século XIX*, 274; P. C. Souza, *Sabinada*, 46; J. H. Rodrigues, *Independência*, 4:99–103.

14. Reis and Silva, *Negociação*, 80. See also Mattoso, *Bahia, século XIX*, 452.

15. U. S. Consul to Secretary of State, 15 Sep. 1822, NARS, T-432, roll 2; CI to Labatut, 21 and 23 Nov. 1822, *AAPEB* 41 (1973), 31, 33. Reis describes the revolts in *Slave Rebellion*, 53–54.

16. Maria Bárbara Garcês Pinto de Madureira to Luís Paulino d'Oliveira Pinto da França, 13 April 1822, in França, ed., *Cartas*, 36; French Consul to Min. of Navy, on board *Amazone*, 21 June 1822, *AAPEB*, 41 (1973), 121. For examples of rhetorical use of the metaphor of slavery, see Labatut to Madeira, ca. Oct. 1822; portaria of CI, 29 Jan. 1823, in B. H. Amaral, *História*, 282, 396.

17. "Copia do Recurso," 302–3, 305.

18. A. M. Souza, "Breve notícia," 121. *Diario Constitucional*, 3 April 1822, 3; "Apontamentos," BN/SM, II-31, 36, 1. This issue is analyzed by J. H. Rodrigues, *Independência*, 2:89–90, 121–22.

19. Resolução, CI, 23 Oct. 1822 (copy), BN/SM, II-34, 10, 11; Salvador Pereira da Costa to CI, Nazaré, 30 Jan. 1823, BN/SM, II-33, 36, 6.

20. Req., residents to Câmara, Jaguaripe, 12 Feb. 1823, *AAPEB* 10 (1923), 62.

21. I. A. C. Silva, *Memorias*, 3:267; Rebouças, "Recordações," 455–56; M. Garcia, *Historia*, 12–14; E. L. Silva, *Recordações-biographicas*, 13.

22. Morton, "Conservative Revolution," 236; I. A. C. Silva, *Memorias*, 3:267–70.

23. Proclamation, 10 Feb. 1821; Manifesto, 11 Feb. 1821, in I. A. C. Silva, *Memorias*, 3:268–69, n. 9; 279.

24. Morton, "Conservative Revolution," 238; P. Garcia, *Cipriano Barata*, 46–47.

25. *Idade d'Ouro do Brazil*, 15 Feb. 1821, 1–2; 17 Feb. 1821, 3; 19 Feb. 1821, 2–3; 26 Feb. 1821, 3–4, 1 March 1821, 4.

26. *Idade d'Ouro do Brazil*, 19 Feb. 1821, 1; Mota, *Nordeste*, 195.

27. M. Garcia, *Historia*, 19–24; E. L. Silva, *Recordações-biographicas*, 15; Rebouças, "Recordações," 457; Veterano, *Estatua*, 10–17; J. H. Rodrigues, *Independência*, 1:44–45; Barman, *Brazil*, 68–69.

28. Lago, *Brigadeiros*, 128. Critical assessments of Freitas Guimarães can be found in Com., Art., to Governo Geral, 20 May 1810, APEB, m. 247-5; MGE to Gov., 1 April 1817, BN/SM, II-33, 17, 36, doc. 81.

29. Ata, Câmara, 10 Feb. 1821, in B. H. Amaral, *História*, 28. His critics include a chartitable Maria Bárbara to Luís Paulino, 2 March 1822; and the blunt Bento da França Pinto de Oliveira to Luís Paulino, 6 March 1822, in França, ed., *Cartas*, 20, 21.

30. M. B. N. Silva, "Repercussões," 186.

31. M. D. Graham, *Journal*, 152, 153.

32. Junta Provisória to Felippe Ferreira de Araujo e Castro, 8 March 1822, in I. A. C. Silva, *Memorias*, 3:470. See also Câmara to King, 16 March 1822, in I. A. C. Silva, *Memorias*, 3:479.

33. M. Garcia, *Historia*, 52–55; I. A. C. Silva, *Memorias*, 3:289–92; Rebouças, "Recordações," 460–64; *Idade d'Ouro do Brazil*, 6 Nov. 1821, 1–4; 9 Nov. 1821, 1.

34. Morton, "Conservative Revolution," 241; I. L. C. Souza, *Pátria*, 181–83; B. H. Amaral, *História*, 57; M. Garcia, *Historia*, 55. On Caldeira, see Tavares, *Levante*, 21–22.

35. Test., Manoel Joze de Carvalho, Joze Ribeiro da Conceição, and Miguel dos Anjos, March 1822, *AAPEB* 27 (1941), 98, 43, 71, 96.

36. Bento da França to Luís Paulino, 30 June 1822, in França, ed., *Cartas*, 72.

37. Test., M. J. Carvalho, March 1822, *AAPEB* 27 (1941), 98.

38. These men are listed in *O Independente Constitucional*, 22 Dec. 1823, 4 (APEB, m. 3765).

39. França, ed., *Cartas*, 133.

40. Conselho de Investigação, Manoel de São Boaventura Ferraz, 7 Feb. 1824, AHE/RQ, M-160-4138.

41. Req., Joaquim de Oliveira Santos to Pres., ca. 1828, APEB, m. 3765.

42. Tesoureiro Geral das Tropas to Pres., 14 Feb. 1828, APEB, m. 3765; GA to Pres., 27 Oct. 1827, APEB, m. 3367.

43. In addition to the officers mentioned below, Acciavoli had retired; Godinho and Cogominho passed away in 1811 and 1818 respectively.

44. *Diario Constitucional,* 16 Feb. 1822, 1–2; 6 March 1822, 2.

45. Brant to MNE, 12 Feb. 1824, *ADI,* 2:8. On his subsequent career, see Aguiar, *Vida;* Calogeras, *Marquez.*

46. "Relação nominal dos oficiaes da Provincia da Bahia," ca. Nov. 1835, AN/SPE/ IG1, m. 116, fols. 430–36. About half of the folios are missing.

47. On Lima, see P. Silva, "Brigadeiro," xii–lviii; on Pirajá, see P. C. Souza, *Sabinada,* 53–55. On independence services, see Pirajá to Min. of Navy, AIGHB, pasta 77, doc. 28.

48. On Castro, see Tranajura, "José Antônio da Silva Castro," 123–37; Tavares, *Levante,* 9–10. Castro's inv. reveals his wide landowning, APEB/SJ/IT, 03/1021/ 1490/01.

49. Brant to MNE, 12 Feb. 1824; London, 5 Jan. 1825, *ADI,* 2:8, 186.

50. Madeira to King, 17 March 1822, in B. H. Amaral, *História,* 125.

51. Halperin Donghi, "Revolutionary Militarization," 84.

52. Handbill, João Primo, 23 July 1823, in R. B. Castro, *Tipografia,* 154; Rebouças, "Recordações," 462, n. 10; "Cópia do recurso," 22 Aug. 1822, *RIGHB* 58 (1932), 303; test., Ignacio Correa de Vasconcellos, *AAPEB* 27 (1941), 138.

53. I. A. C. Silva, *Memorias,* 3:282, n. 17; req., José Francisco Soares to Emperor, 14 Sep. 1831, AHE/RQ, JJ-242-5884.

54. Req., José and Luís Baltasar da Silveira to Emperor, ca. 1824; GA to MG, 19 May 1824, AHE/RQ, JJ-193-4683.

55. Rebouças, "Recordações," 494–98; I. A. C. Silva, *Memorias,* 3:370–72, 400–1; 4:59, n. 28.

56. Titara, *Paraguassú,* 157–63, n. b.

57. Brant to MNE, 12 Feb. 1824, *ADI,* 2:8.

58. Tavares, *Independência,* 115–19.

59. CI to MI, Cachoeira, 17 Dec. 1822, *RIGHB* 14 (1897), 549; Labatut to CI, Cangurungú, 9 March 1823, BN/SM, II-31, 36, 9, doc. 16. On Labatut's conflict with the CI, see Ruy, *Dossier.*

60. CI to MI, Cachoeira, 16 April 1823, *RIGHB,* 17 (1898), 353.

61. I. A. C. Silva, *Memorias,* 4:2–25.

62. U. S. Consul to Secretary of State, 21 Nov. 1824, NARS, T-432, roll 2; I. A. C. Silva, *Memorias,* 4:181; A. M. Souza, "Breve noticia," 128–29.

63. Morton, "Conservative Revolution," 290; M. Garcia, *Historia,* 137–41.

64. Lago, *Brigadeiros,* 128; GA to MG, 3 June 1824, AN/SPE, IG1, m. 249, fol. 427; "Noticia sôbre a morte . . . ," BN/SM, II-33, 35, 10.

65. "Relação de Officiaes que . . . se fazem indignos de continuar no Serviço," 16 Aug. 1824, AN/SPE/IG1, m. 249, fols. 423–24.

66. "Memoria," 250; Acting GA to GA, 12 April 1824, APEB, m. 3465; L. C. Andrade, "Cel. Felisberto Gomes Caldeira," 220, 221; "Tropa da Bahia," *Grito da Razão,* 6 May 1825, 2.

67. Acting GA to GA, 12 April 1824, APEB, m. 3465.

68. *O Independente Constitucional,* 22 Dec. 1823, 3 (APEB, m. 3765).

69. Req., Bernardino Alves de Araujo to Emperor, ca. 1832, AHE/RQ, B-27-788; Titara, *Paraguassú,* 117, n. 2; 294–95, n. 3; justification of officers, 30 Oct. 1824, in I. A. C. Silva, *Memorias,* 4:194–97.

70. "Memoria," 311; French Consul to Min. of Navy and Colonies, 27 Oct. 1824, *AAPEB* 39 (1970), 167; Brant to MNE, 12 Feb. 1824, *ADI,* 2:7; Pres. to Min. of Navy, 25 May 1824, *AAPEB* 13 (1925), 60.

71. Acting GA to MG, 25 Nov. 1824, AN/SPE/IG1, m. 249, fol. 410. On the repression, see Tavares, *Levante,* 34–35; Morton, "Conservative Revolution," 297–98.

72. GA to Pres., 24 Dec. 1824, BN/SM, II-31, 36, 15; "Plano da Organização de hum Corpo de Policia da Cidade da Bahia," Rio, 28 Feb. 1825, BN/SM, II-33, 31, 36.

73. GA to MG, 28 Jan. 1825, AN/SPE/IG1, m. 249, fol. 457r; 23 March 1825, in R. B. Castro, *Tipografia,* 131; L. C. Andrade, "Cel. Felisberto Gomes Caldeira," 225; "Chronica dos acontecimentos," 86.

74. Test., Joze Maria Barreto Falcão and Francisco Simões o Novo, March 1822, *AAPEB* 27 (1941), 32, 117; *Grito da Razão,* 23 March 1825, 3; Morton, "Conservative Revolution," 298.

75. Edital, 14 May 1825 (copy); "Relação dos Reos Militares," 6 June 1825, AN/SPE/IG1, m. 114, fols. 534, 537r–v; "Noticia sôbre a morte," BN/SM, II-33, 35, 10; Minutes, 20 June, *AS* (1836), 121–22.

76. The little that has been written on Bahian slave recruitment is deeply contradictory: B. H. Amaral, *História,* 7, 272, 285, 291–92; Ferraz, "Escravo"; Morton, "Conservative Revolution," 267–68; Reis and Silva, *Negociação,* 90, 97; Araujo, "Politique," 1:222–25; J. H. Rodrigues, *Independência,* 3:90, 213–14. On slave recruitment elsewhere in the Americas, see Sales de Bohigas, "Esclavos."

77. Test., J. M. B. Falcão, João Joze do Prado, J. R. Conceição, Joze Joaquim de Almeida, Frederico Antonio Pinto, March 1822, *AAPEB* 27 (1941), 32, 38–39, 42, 55–56, 66.

78. I. A. C. Silva, *Memorias,* 4:59, n. 28; B. H. Amaral, *História,* 450.

79. CI to Caps.-mores, Cachoeira, 13 April 1823; CI to MI, Cachoeira, 16 April 1823, in Brazil, Arquivo Nacional, *Junta,* 29, 21; req., João de Deos Lima to Governo, ca. June 1823, APEB, m. 3486.

80. Dores, "Diario," 32; "Lista da Guerrilha Voluntaria do Pedrão," *RIGHB* 48 (1923), 387–89.

81. CI to Labatut, Cachoeira, 22 Nov. 1822, *AAPEB* 41 (1973), 28.

82. CI to MI, Cachoeira, 23 Dec. 1822, *RIGHB* 14 (1897), 561, 563; I. A. C. Silva, *Memorias,* 3:401; Titara, *Paraguassú,* 452, n. j.

83. CI to Labatut, Cachoeira, 12 and 14 April 1823, *AAPEB* 41 (1973), 88, 89; Labatut to CI, Cangurungú, 16 April 1823, in I. A. C. Silva, *Memorias,* 4:2, n. 2.

84. "Termo de Veriação," Jaguaripe, 23 April 1823, *AAPEB* 10 (1923), 63–65.

85. *Idade d'Ouro do Brazil,* 28 Jan. 1823, 1.

86. Joaquim Pires de Carvalho e Albuquerque to Maj. Com., Fixed Art., Rio, 16 March 1825, AHE/RQ, JJ-237-5790; OD, 6 June 1822, BN/SM, II-33, 36, 35.

87. CI to MI, Cachoeira, 16 April 1823, *RIGHB* 17 (1898), 362–64.

88. Bando, 31 July 1823, *AAPEB* 10 (1923), 69.

89. José Joaquim de Lima e Silva to MI, 16 July 1823, BN/SM, II-31, 35, 4.

90. Decisão 113, 30 July 1823, *CLB*.

91. M. I. C. Oliveira, "Viver," 191.

92. MJ to Pres., Rio, 22 Sep. 1825, APEB, m. 755, fol. 450.

93. Antonio de Souza Lima to GA, Itaparica, 30 July 1825 (copy), APEB, m. 3365.

94. Lt. Col. Com., Art., to Pres., 9 May 1825, BN/SM, II-33, 31, 4, no. 5, doc. 19; Lt. Col. Com., Fourteenth Inf., to GA, 23 March 1827, APEB, m. 3367; R. J. C. Mattos, *Repertório,* 1:229.

95. A. M. Souza, "Breve noticia," 126; Bahia, Junta Provisória, *Relatório* (1823), 4–5; Rebouças, "Recordações," 497; I. A. C. Silva, *Memorias,* 3:372.

96. Antonio [Pires de Carvalho e Albuquerque] to Brother, n.p., 26 Sep. 1822, BN/SM, II-34, 2, 40, no. 4; CI to Caps.-mores, Cachoeira, 18 Oct. 1822 (circular), APEB, m. 1618, fol. 28r; and to Labatut, 29 March 1823, *AAPEB* 41 (1973), 82; I. A. C. Silva, *Memorias,* 4:28–29, n. 13.

97. U. S. Consul to Secretary of State, postscript of 9 Sep. to letter of 24 Aug. 1823, NARS, T-432, roll 2; French Consul to Min. of Navy and Colonies, 6 March 1824, *AAPEB* 39 (1970), 157.

98. Ata, Câmara, 17 Dec. 1823, in I. A. C. Silva, *Memorias,* 4:110; *Grito da Razão,* 13 Feb. 1824, 1–2; 2 March 1824, 6; 13 April 1824, 1.

99. OD, Rio, 6 June 1823; MG, Portaria Circular, 28 May 1824, BN/SM, II-31, 35, 12, no. 2; Decisão 251, 3 Nov. 1825, *CLB*.

100. Pres. to Emperor, 8 May 1824, AN/SPE, códice 603, vol. 1, fol. 66v; Brant to MNE, 12 Feb. 1824, *ADI,* 2:8; MNE to Brant, Rio, 10 March 1824, *ADI,* 1:59–60.

101. I. A. C. Silva, *Memorias,* 4:179; French Consul to Min. of Navy and Colonies, 24 Nov. 1824, *AAPEB* 39 (1970), 168.

102. Pres. to MG, 28 Oct. 1824, BN/SM, II-33, 22, 1, doc. 20; Acting GA to Pres., 24 Nov. 1824, BN/SM, II-34, 1, 3, doc. 210; "Memoria," 326.

103. "Noticia sôbre a morte," BN/SM, II-33, 35, 10; *Grito da Razão,* 6 May 1825, 4.

104. GA to Pres., 9 Feb. 1825, APEB, m. 3365; GA to Pres., 24 Nov. 1824, BN/SM, II-34, 1, 3, doc. 208; Lt. Col. Com., Guarda Militar de Polícia, to Pres., 20 May 1829, APEB, m. 6304.

105. "Instruções . . . ," 10 July 1822, *CLB;* GA to Pres., 6 July 1825, APEB, m. 3365.

106. "Relação dos desertores . . . de Janeiro de 1825 a Março de 1827," 28 July 1827, BN/SM, II-33, 32, 28.

107. "Memoria," 316, n. 55.

108. "Proclamação . . . ," 1 Sep. 1823, *AAPEB* 10 (1923), 71.

109. Andrews, *Afro-Argentines,* 96–101.

110. GA to Pres., 30 Dec. 1825, BN/SM, II-33, 31, 4, no. 12, doc. 8; "Copia do recurso," 314.

111. Req., João do Prado Franco to Pres., ca. 1826, APEB, m. 3366.

112. Test., Manoel Alves do Nascimento, Antonio Gomes da Cunha, F. A. Pinto, Antonio Joaquim, March 1822, *AAPEB* 27 (1941), 51, 61, 66, and 111. Slaves rarely wore shoes, which served as badges of freedom, Karasch, *Slave Life*, 130.

113. Titara, *Paraguassú*, 179; test., Luiz Manoel and Miguel Ferreira, March 1822, *AAPEB* 27 (1941), 169, 173.

114. Test., Antonio Jozé de Souza Almeida e Aragão, March 1822, *AAPEB* 27 (1941), 128.

115. Titara, *Paraguassú*, 193–94, n. 4; 483, n. 4; *O Independente Constitucional*, 22 Dec. 1823, 4 (APEB, m. 3765).

116. Titara, *Paraguassú*, 506, n. e.

117. GA to MG, 12 Aug. 1824, AHE/RQ, F-148-3781; *Echo da Pátria*, 19 Aug. 1823, *AAPEB* 10 (1923), 87; Titara, *Paraguassú*, 539; I. A. C. Silva, *Memorias*, 4:55; "Chronica dos acontecimentos," 80.

118. Lt. Col. Com., Militia Art., to Pres., 7 March 1825, BN/SM, II-33, 31, 4, no. 3, doc. 14; Lt. Col. Com, First Militia, to Governo Provincial, 4 Nov. 1823, *AAPEB* 10 (1923), 54.

119. Mappas diarios, 20 Nov. 1824, BN/SM, II-34, 1, 2, docs. 128, 129; II-34, 1, 3, doc. 207; lists of signatories in APEB, m. 2171.

120. See, for example, "Proposta dos Officiaes para o Batalhão Numero Primeiro de Segunda Linha . . . ," 6 March 1824 (copy), APEB, m. 3762.

121. Req., Francisco Xavier Bigode to Emperor, ca. 1824, AHE/RQ, F-148-3781.

122. "Informação dos Officiaes do 4.o Regim.to de Milicias . . . ," 31 Dec. 1809, APEB, m. 247-6; FO, Paulo Maria Nabuco de Araujo, BN/SM, DB, C.194.20; Titara, *Paraguassú*, 286, n. 4.

123. GA to José Bruno Antunes Guimarães, 14 Jan. 1814; FO, Bruno, BN/SM/DB, C.624.6.

124. Mott, *Sergipe*, 28.

125. Req., Dionizio Ferreira de Santa Anna to Emperor, ca. 1825, and supporting documents, AHE/RQ, D-14-396. For other heroic reqs., see in AHE/RQ, Jozé Fernandes do Ó to Emperor, ca. 1824, JJ-229-5575; Amaro Ferreira to Emperor, ca. 1825, A-54-1719; Joaquim de Santa Anna Neves to Emperor, ca. 1824, JZ-90-2075; Francisco de Paula Bahia to Emperor, ca. 1824, F-117-3156.

126. José Vicente de Santa Anna to Emperor, ca. 1824; war ministry summary, 21 July 1824, AHE/RQ, JZ-173-4911.

127. "Proclamação," Abrantes, 20 Nov., 1824, BN/SM, II-31, 36, 8, no. 6.

128. Marginal notes on Pres. to MI, 2 May 1824, BN/SM, II-31, 36, 9.

129. *Grito da Razão*, 14 Nov. 1824, 3; 29 Dec. 1824, 3; Manoel Gonçalves da Silva to Pres., 19 Nov. 1824, APEB, m. 3693; Officers to Pres., Abrantes, 27 Nov.

1824, BN/SM, I-31, 36, 8, doc. 60; Lt. Col. Brigade Com. to Col. Com., Divisão Constitucional e Pacificadora, Armações, 30 Nov. 1824, BN/SM, I-31, 23, 8.

130. *Grito da Razão*, 24 Dec. 1824, 5; 29 Dec. 1824, 3; "Memoria," 348–50. Querino incorrectly places Gonçalves at the head of his battalion in late November 1824, *Bahia*, 300.

131. On the composition of these tribunals, see I. A. C. Silva, *Memorias*, 4:206; marginal note to form letter from José Egídio Gordilho de Barbuda, 14 Dec. 1824 (copy), AN/SPE, IG1, m. 249, fol. 402; "Noticia sôbre a morte," BN/SM, II-33, 35, 10.

132. Req., J. F. Ó to Emperor, ca. 1824, AHE/RQ, JJ-229-5575; interr., J. F. Ó, 20 Nov. 1839, PC, 1.0 B.m da 2.a L.a, fol. 131r, APEB, m. 2838; req., A. Ferreira to Emperor, ca. 1825, AHE/RQ, A-54-1719.

133. GA to Pres., 7 Oct. 1824, AHE/RQ, JZ-62-1831.

134. FO and req., F. P. Bahia, 19 Aug. 1829, AHE/RQ, F-117-3156; req., Bruno to Emperor, ca. 1826, BN/SM/DB, C.624.6.

Chapter 6

1. *Aurora da Bahia*, 3 Oct. 1838, 6.

2. I. A. C. Silva, *Memorias*, 4:213–18; U.S. Consul to Secretary of State, 11 March 1826, NARS, T-432, roll 3; "Chronica dos acontecimentos," 88–90; "Proclamação," 9 March 1826, *AAPEB* 10 (1923), 160–61; Decreto, 30 Jan. 1826, *CLB*; Ruy, *História*, 280–84; I. L. C. Souza, *Pátria*, 254–55.

3. Seckinger, *Brazilian Monarchy*, 59–73; J. A. S. Souza, "Brasil e o Prata," 324–28; Barman, *Brazil*, 126–29.

4. Article 101, "Constituição Política do Império do Brasil," *CLB*; P. O. C. Cunha, "Fundação," 253.

5. Articles 91–95, "Constituição Política," *CLB*.

6. R. Graham, *Patronage*, 103–9; Barman, *Brazil*, 124; J. M. Carvalho, *Desenvolvimiento*, 25. In this respect, the Brazilian constitution was comparable to liberal constitutions in contemporary Spanish America, Rodriguez O., *Independence*, 91–92; Anna, *Forging*, 124–25; Guardino, *Peasants*, 174; Halperin Donghi, *Aftermath*, 115–18; Bushnell, *Reform*, 17, 22–23.

7. Article 179, "Constituição Política," *CLB*. Barman notes that these guarantees were fuller than those of the contemporary United States constitution, *Brazil*, 124, 279, n. 126; they did, however, appear in some liberal Spanish American constitutions, Chambers, *Subjects*, 184; Bushnell, *Reform*, 10, 101; Collier, *Ideas*, 157.

8. E. V. Costa, *Brazilian Empire*, 59–61.

9. Barman, *Brazil*, 139–51; Macaulay, *Dom Pedro*, chap. 6; P. O. C. Cunha, "Fundação," 398–400; Flory, *Judge*, chaps. 3–4.

10. Barman, *Brazil*, 153–59; Macaulay, *Dom Pedro*, 213–53; I. L. C. Souza, *Pátria*, 340–50.

11. Nabuco, *Estadista*, 60.

12. Barman, *Brazil*, 161–69; P. P. Castro, "Experiência," 9–19.

13. Barman, *Brazil*, 172–87; Flory, *Judge*, chap. 7; P. P. Castro, "Experiência," 27–54.

14. The following discussion is based on I. A. C. Silva, *Memorias*, vol. 4; Pinho, "Bahia," 273–84; Morton, "Conservative Revolution," chaps. 9–11; Reis, *Slave Rebellion*; idem, "Elite baiana"; Aras, "Santa federação"; Vianna Filho, *Sabinada*; P. C. Souza, *Sabinada*; Kraay, " 'As Terrifying.' "

15. See, for examples, Thurner, *From Two Republics*; Szuchman, *Order*; Mallon, *Peasant*; Guardino, *Peasants*; Anna, *Forging*.

16. "Catalogo dos jornaes," 411–16.

17. On lusophobia, see Reis, *Slave Rebellion*, 23–28; Chasteen, "Cabanos"; Mosher, "Pernambuco," chap. 4; P. O. C. Cunha, "Fundação," 382–91. For Mexico, see Sims, *Expulsion*.

18. P. O. C. Cunha, "Fundação," 382.

19. Dias, "Interiorização," 169. On Bahia's federalist movement, see Aras, "Santa federação," 93–210.

20. *O Censor*, Nov. 1837, 199; *O Democrata*, 8 March 1834, 129; *Nova Sentinella da Liberdade*, 4 Sep. 1831, 241. See also *Novo Diario da Bahia*, 9 and 11 Aug. 1837, *PAEB*, 4:396–403; *O Genio Federal*, 5 June 1834, 1.

21. "Proclamação de Sergio Velloso . . . ," 10 March 1838, *PAEB*, 2:87.

22. "Breve dissertação sobre a legitimidade," *Sentinella da Liberdade*, 31 Jan. 1831, 9–36; *A Luz Bahiana*, 27 Oct. 1837, 1–2; "A fidalguia ou nobreza não deve ser hereditária," *Sentinella da Liberdade*, 9 March 1831, 90; *Novo Diário da Bahia*, 26 Dec. 1837, 1.

23. E. V. Costa, *Brazilian Empire*, 59–61, 76–77.

24. Untitled proclamation, 16 Sep. 1826, APEB, m. 3366.

25. *Nova Sentinella da Liberdade*, 12 June 1831, 25; 7 July 1831, 105–6; *O Sete de Novembro*, 25 Nov. 1837, 2.

26. "Creação do Batalhão 'Libertos da Pátria,' " 3 Jan. 1838, *PAEB*, 2:83–84. See also Kraay, " 'As Terrifying,' " 517–18; P. C. Souza, *Sabinada*, 146–57.

27. Reis, *Slave Rebellion*, 203–4.

28. Carlos Joaquim de Magalhães Cerqueira to Viscount of Pirajá, Cachoeira, 18 April 1831, BN/SM, I-31, 15, 37; U. S. Consul to Secretary of State, 24 Feb. 1832, NARS, T-432, roll 3; [Pres.?] to José Lino Coutinho, 28 Feb. 1832, BN/SM, II-33, 32, 46; Pres. to MJ, Pirajá, 29 Nov. 1837, *PAEB*, 4:436.

29. José Xavier Pitanga to Lt. Com., Itapagipe, 24 Jan. 1838, PC, J. X. Pitanga, fol. 25r, APEB, m. 2838.

30. Reis, *Slave Rebellion*, 38; Freitas, "Narrativa," 268, 281.

31. Aras, "Santa federação," 169; CA to MG, 2 May 1831, AN/SPE, IG1, m. 251, fol. 139v; Letter from Bahia, *Jornal do Commercio*, 30 Jan. 1838, 2; Francisco Ramiro de Assis Coelho to Regent, 11 Dec. 1837, AIHGB, lata 213, doc. 11, fol. 1v.

32. Acting CA to MG, 2 May 1831, AN/SPE/IG1, m. 251, fol. 139r; *Nova Sentinella da Liberdade,* 29 May 1831, 4; 24 June 1831, 74. See also Tavares, "Cipriano José Barata de Almeida," 142–43.

33. Flory, "Race," 208–11.

34. *Nova Sentinella da Liberdade,* 12 June 1831, 25; *O Democrata,* 7 May 1836, 324–25; Flory, "Race," 207; Cipriano Barata de Almeida, "Dezengano ao publico...," quoted in Morel, "Entre paixão," 125.

35. "O que he a facção recolonisadora," *Nova Sentinella da Liberdade,* 16 June 1831, 36; Schwartz, "Formation," 15.

36. Nabuco, *Estadista,* 77; Flory, "Race," 213–15; Spitzer, *Lives,* 119–25; Kraay, "'As Terrifying,'" 517.

37. *O Defensor do Povo,* 13 Feb. 1836, 2–3; 16 Dec. 1836, 1–4.

38. For different interpretations of this phenomenon, see Degler, *Neither Black,* chap. 5; R. Graham, "Free African Brazilians," 42–43; E. V. Costa, *Brazilian Empire,* 239–43; Spitzer, *Lives,* 125–26.

39. *Supplemento à Gazeta da Bahia,* 2 Dec. 1831, 2.

40. Nabuco, *Estadista,* 58.

41. Decisão 249, 31 Oct. 1825, *CLB;* MG, *Relatório* (1828), 39; (1830), 5; speech, Raimundo José da Cunha Mattos, 10 Aug., *ACD* (1826), 4:111. For deputies' concerns, see the debates of 12 and 25 Aug., *ACD* (1828), 4:72–76, 136–41; 20 May, *ACD* (1829), 1:105–7.

42. Decreto, 1 Dec. 1824, *CLB;* Decisão 129, 14 June 1825, *CLB;* Decreto, 27 Nov. 1829, *CLB;* CA to Pres., 22 Dec. 1829, APEB, m. 3399; Lei, 4 Dec. 1822, *CLB.*

43. Session of 15 May, *ACD* (1830), 1:151–53.

44. Req., Jozé Vicente de Amorim Bezerra to Emperor, ca. 1828, AN/SPE/GIFI, 12.4, 4H-170, fols. 73r–91v. See also reqs. in AHE/RQ, Jozé Francisco Soares to Emperor, 14 Sep. 1831, JJ-242-5884; Polidoro Henriques de Lemos to Emperor, Rio, ca. 1831, P-49-1410; Bernardino Alves de Araujo to Emperor, ca. 1832, B-27-788.

45. J. A. A. Amaral, *Indicador,* vol. 1, part 1, 90.

46. Req., Manoel Garcez Pinto de Madureira to Emperor, ca. 1839, AHE/RQ, M-82-2345.

47. MG, *Relatório* (1829), in *ACD* (1829), 2:59.

48. Speech, J. L. Coutinho, 12 June, *ACD* (1829), 2:84; *O Bahiano,* 9 May 1829, 3; 1 Sep. 1829, 1–2.

49. Morton, "Conservative Revolution," 299.

50. Speeches, J. L. Coutinho, 3 Aug., *ACD* (1826), 4:20; Bernardo Pereira Vasconcelos, 4 Oct., *ACD* (1827), 5:104; McBeth, "Brazilian Army," 118; Coelho, *Busca,* chap. 2.

51. Provisão, 1 Feb. 1826, in *O Independente Constitucional,* 26 Aug. 1826, 1 (APEB, m. 3765). On the rebuke, see the debate of 11 Aug., *ACD* (1828), 4:63–64.

52. Lei, 24 Nov. 1830; Decreto, 20 Dec. 1830, *CLB;* on the budget cuts, see *ACD* (1830), 2:308–14, 3:409–10.

53. "Um brado da verdade e patriotismo," *Sentinella da Liberdade*, 15 Jan. 1831, 5–7; *Nova Sentinella da Liberdade*, 21 Aug. 1831, 197.

54. Decreto, 4 May 1831, *CLB*.

55. Holloway, *Policing*, 68–69, 88–89.

56. P. P. Castro, "Experiência," 14–25; McBeth, "Brazilian Army," 125–26.

57. *Nova Sentinella da Liberdade*, 18 Aug. 1831, 187; Kaxangá, *Oração*; Hum Bahiano [to Pres., ca. Aug. 1831], APEB, m. 2857.

58. I. A. C. Silva, *Memorias*, 4:283.

59. Aras, "Santa Federação," 108–22.

60. Arnizau, "Memoria"; *Grito da Razão*, 27 Feb. 1824, 2; sugar planters to Pres., [c. 1830]; CA to Pres., 22 Sep. 1832, APEB, m. 3449. See also Reis, *Slave Rebellion*, 58–59, 65.

61. Pres. to MG, 14 Oct. 1831, APEB, m. 680, fols. 19r–v.

62. Pres. to MG, 27 Oct. 1834, APEB, m. 681, fols. 135v–36r; 10 Feb. 1835, AN/SPE, IG1, m. 116, fol. 407r–v.

63. "Relação dos officiaes . . . que se achão em outras provincias . . . ," 3 Aug. 1833, AN/SPE, IG1, m. 252, fol. 353.

64. These provisions were established by the annual laws that set the army's strength, 30 Aug. 1831, 25 Aug. 1832, 3 Sep. 1833, 22 Aug. 1834, 26 Aug. 1835, 10 Oct. 1836, 28 Sep. 1837; Decreto 43, 15 Oct. 1836, *CLB*.

65. CA to Pres., 18 March, and 11 and 29 May 1833, AN/SPE, IG1, m. 115, fols. 292r, 312r, 303v. On the number of *avulsos*, see speech, José Inácio Borges, 20 June, *AS* (1835), 137.

66. Pres. to MG, 25 Oct. 1837, AHE/RQ, M-187-5018.

67. Speech, MG, 27 June, *ACD* (1837), 1:347.

68. Req., Francisco Manoel da Silva Cardoso to Emperor, ca. 1836, AHE/RQ, F-107-2939.

69. See the salary tables in Decreto, 25 March 1825, *CLB*.

70. João Carneiro da Silva Rego to Secretário do Governo, 10 Jan. 1834, AN/SPE, IJJ9, m. 337, fol. 4r; *Gazeta Commercial da Bahia*, 18 Jan. 1836, 1.

71. Calculated from 71 FOs, Bahian officers in AHE/FO.

72. For the professions of loyalty, see Pres. of Sociedade Militar to Pres., 15 Jan. 1833, APEB, m. 3807; CA to MG, 16 Jan. 1834, AN/SPE, IG1, m. 376r.

73. CA to Pres., 13 July 1833, APEB, m. 3372.

74. Pres. of Sociedade Militar to CA, 4 Feb. 1833, APEB, m. 3428. On enlisted men's voting rights, see R. J. C. Mattos, *Repertório*, 2:62–64. Lei, 19 Aug. 1846, *CLB*, disenfranchised them. JPs' reluctance to permit soldiers to vote is mentioned by Com., Third Infantry, to CA, 8 Sep. 1836, APEB, m. 3373.

75. *O Militar*, 9 May 1833, 77–78 (APEB, m. 2853); req., Bahian officers to Provincial Assembly, ca. May 1835 (copy), AN/SPE, IG1, m. 116, fols. 379–86.

76. *O Democrata*, 7 Feb. 1834, 113; P. P. Castro, "Experiência," 26; Decisão 772, 7

Dec. 1833, *CLB;* J. V. A. Bezerra to José Martiniano de Alencar, 22 May 1833, *ABN* 86 (1966), 425–26.

77. Titara, *Paraguassú,* 566–70. The lists of subscribers to I. A. C. Silva's *Memorias* only appear in the original edition (Salvador, 1835–1837), 1:341–49, 2:375–76, 3:257, 4:349–51.

78. Baptismal Certificate, Daniel Gomes de Freitas, Santana Parish, 15 Sep. 1806 (copy); FO, D. G. Freitas, 4 Oct. 1828, AHE/RQ, D-5-135.

79. Req., D. G. Freitas, 12 June 1829, AHE/RQ, D-5-135.

80. Decreto 56, 13 April 1831, *CLB;* "Resultado do exame a que procedeu a Commissão . . . ," 1 Sep. 1831, AHE/RQ, D-5-135; "3.o Corpo d'Artr.a de Posição . . . Relação Estatística Criminal . . . 1.o trimestre do anno de 1832," AN/SPE, IG1, m. 115, fol. 241r; CA to Pres., 5 May 1836, APEB, m. 3373; 23 Sep. 1835, APEB, m. 3454.

81. Inspector of Treasury to Pres. of São Paulo, [São Paulo?], 18 Dec. 1841; Pres. of São Paulo to MG, São Paulo, 29 Oct. 1844, AHE/RQ, D-5-135.

82. Freitas, "Narrativa"; P. C. Souza, *Sabinada,* 49.

83. M. J. N. Silva, *Synopsis,* 2:197; Bueno, *Direito,* 96. The proposal to buy out commissions was made by MG, 6 May, *ACD* (1833), 1:82; 28 June, *ACD* (1834), 1:197.

84. Aviso Circular, 27 Feb. 1833, J. A. A. Amaral, *Indicador,* vol. 1, part 1, 229.

85. Proclamation of Sérgio José Velloso, *Jornal do Commercio,* 27 Nov. 1837, 2.

86. Kraay, " 'As Terrifying,' " 510–15.

87. Proclamations of J. C. S. Rego, 7 and 30 Nov. 1837, *PAEB,* 2:59–60, 79.

88. MG to Pres., Rio, 23 March 1838, *PAEB,* 5:340; "Rellação Nominal dos Alferes de Commissão," 18 Oct. 1838, AN/SPE, IG1, m. 116, fol. 846; Decreto 244, 22 Aug. 1840, *CLB;* "Proposta da organização do 3.o Esquadrão de Cavallaria . . . ," 15 Oct. 1839, BN/SM, I-31, 14, 54.

89. Quoted in Nabuco, *Estadista,* 69. J. M. Carvalho notes that the first references to this speech date from 1897, and that it has not been located in the press or parliamentary debates of the 1830s, "Introdução," 9, n. 1.

90. On Regresso thought, see Flory, *Judge,* chap. 8; I. R. Mattos, *Tempo,* 138–55.

91. Barman, *Brazil,* chaps. 7–8; P. P. Castro, "Experiência," 55–67.

92. Pinho, *Cotegipe,* 167; idem, "Bahia," 284–85.

93. See, however, the pioneering work of A. B. Souza, *Exército,* 26–27, 84–88, 105–12, 181.

94. Speech, F. R. A. Coelho, 27 May, *ACD* (1835), 1:115.

95. Speeches, MG, 5 and 17 May, *ACD* (1838), 1:48–49, 129.

96. Speech, Francisco Alvares Machado de Vasconcelos, 18 June, *ACD* (1838), 1:367.

97. Speech, Antônio Paulino Limpo de Abreu, 18 July, *ACD* (1838), 2:151. See also his speeches, 15 and 28 June, *ACD* (1838), 1:345–46, 456. On the death of the

retirement measure in committee, see amendments proposed by the Navy and War Committee, 18 May, *ACD* (1838), 1:137; and the explanations offered by one of its members, 12 July, *ACD* (1838), 2:100.

98. Speech, José Joaquim de Lima e Silva, 15 June, *ACD* (1838), 1:341–42.

99. Speech, J. J. L. Silva, 13 July, *ACD* (1838), 2:109.

100. Lei 41, 20 Sep. 1838, *CLB*.

101. Regulamento 22, 9 Oct. 1838, *CLB*. The relatively brief debate on this bill can be followed in *ACD* (1838), 2:216–17, 243–48, 249–51, 276.

102. Pres. to MG, 6 June 1840, AN/SPE, IG1, m. 117, fol. 74r; speech, Manuel Inácio de Carvalho de Mendonça, 20 July, *ACD* (1840), 2:320. For protests and the reversal of retirements, see reqs., Manoel de São Boaventura Ferraz and José Cassiano da Costa to Emperor, 12 Aug. 1845 and ca. Oct. 1842, AHE/RQ, M-160-4138 and JJ-208-5084.

103. Decretos 72, 3 April 1841; 260, 1 Dec. 1841; 159, 25 April 1841; 251, 28 Nov. 1842 (which published the list of officers), *CLB*.

104. MG, *Relatório* (1841), 5–6; MG, *Almanak* (1844).

105. Reqs., Raimundo José dos Santos to Emperor, Belém, 29 Jan. 1848, AHE/FO, II-18-107; Jozé do Sacramento Mangueira to Emperor, 13 Oct. 1850, AHE/RQ, JZ-157-4468.

106. Speech, MG, 1 Aug., *ACD* (1838), 2:246.

107. Decreto 30, 22 Feb. 1839, *CLB*.

108. Lei, 6 Sep. 1850, *CLB*; Pondé, *Organização*, 213; Schulz, *Exército*, 26–30.

109. Speeches, Manuel Paranhos da Silva Veloso, 22 June, *ACD* (1837), 1:310; Francisco Gonçalves Martins, 5 July, *ACD* (1839), 2:87–88; MG, 6 July, *ACD* (1839), 2:97; Sebastião do Rego Barros, 9 July, *ACD* (1839), 2:138.

110. Of the 32 officers named to posts in the Third Infantry in August 1838, I can confirm the Bahian birth of 15; most of the rest had served in Bahia during the 1820s and 1830s, suggesting that they too were Bahians, "Relação dos Officiaes promovidos para o Terceiro Batalhão de Caçadores . . . ," Rio, 20 Aug. 1838, *PAEB*, 5:342–43.

111. Informações Semestrais, Fourth Art., 1 July 1847, APEB, m. 3778.

112. Marginal note on Pres. to MG, 30 April 1841, AN/SPE, IG1, m. 117, fol. 110v.

113. FOs, Martinho Baptista Ferreira Tamarindo, AHE/RQ, M-187-5018; Izidoro José Rocha do Brasil, AHE/FO, IV-16-79; Manoel Luciano da Câmara Guaraná, AHE/RQ, M-128-3277.

114. Reqs., Jozé Pinheiro de Lemos [Fontoura] to Emperor, Porto Alegre, ca. 1829, AHE/RQ, A-11-415; Antonio dos Santos Castro to Emperor, Rio, 4 May 1829, AHE/RQ, A-169-4370. For the importance of mathematics education in the 1830s, see Lt. Col. Com., Third Art., to CA, 31 Oct. 1837, APEB, m. 3428.

115. Paymaster to Pres., 26 Sep. 1832 and 5 Sep. 1833, APEB, m. 3718 and 3326. D. G. Freitas mentions his study in req. to Pres., 28 April 1836, APEB, m. 3373.

116. MG, *Relatório* (1839), table 3. On Brazilian military education, see Motta, *Formação.*

117. Informações Semestrais, Fourth Art., 1 July 1847, APEB, m. 3778.

118. J. M. Carvalho, *Construção,* 36, 55–60, 66–68, 79–91.

119. CA to Pres., 15 Oct. 1839, BN/SM, I-31, 14, 54.

120. Sodré, *História,* 111; C. Castro, *Militares,* 27.

121. CA to Pres., 20 June 1873 (secret), APEB, m. 3430; inventário, José Pedro d'Alcantara, APEB/SJ/IT, 03/1019/1988/06. The eight are Brigs. José Vicente de Amorim Bezerra, José Pedro de Alcantara, Manoel Joaquim Pinto Paca, Joaquim José Veloso, and Inocêncio Eustáquio Ferreira de Araujo; Lt. Gen. Luiz da França Pinto Garcez (the son of Marshal Luís Paulino d'Oliveira Pinto da França); and the father and son of the same name and rank, Marshals Alexandre Gomes de Argolo Ferrão, respectively the Baron of Cajaíba and the Viscount of Itaparica.

122. Inv., J. P. Alcantara, APEB/SJ/IT, 03/1019/1988/06; Acting Secretary of CA to Secretary of Pres., 19 Sep. 1866, APEB, m. 3413.

123. Inv., Baron of Cajaíba, APEB/SJ/IT, 01/96/139/02; will, Viscount of Itaparica, APEB/SJ/IT, 01/108/162/05; Lago, *Generais,* 11–18; A. Costa, "Genealogia," 116–17.

124. FO, Luiz da França Pinto Garcez, AHE/FO, II-22-38; A. P. M. Silva, *Generais,* 2:332–37; FO, Inocêncio Eustáquio Ferreira de Araujo, AHE/FO, IV-16-32.

125. FOs, José Joaquim Veloso, AHE/FO, IV-23-53; AHE/RQ, JJ-159-3972; Manoel Joaquim Pinto Paca, AHE/FO, IV-2-55, XIX-3-35; J. P. Alcantara, AHE/RQ, JZ-136-3937; J. V. A. Bezerra, AN/SPE/GIFI, 12.4, 4H-170, 76v; MG, *Almanak* (1860), 44–45.

126. For examples, see reqs., Manoel Ignacio de Barros Paim to Emperor, 31 May 1832, APEB, m. 3372; Pirajá to Pres., ca. 1833, APEB, m. 3363; José Antonio de Menezes Doria to Pres., ca. 1836, APEB, m. 3373.

127. Will, Cypriano Xavier de Jesus, 4 Aug. 1831, APEB/SJ/LRT, vol. 22, fols. 113v–14r. For another example, see will, Joze Correa de Aguiar, APEB/SJ/LRT, vol. 30, fol. 164v.

128. Req., Leopoldina Xavier de Jesus to Juiz dos Orphãos, 12 Dec. 1871; inv., Maria Leandra de Jesus and João Antonio Xavier, APEB/SJ/IT, 07/3029/02, fol. 2r.

129. For examples, see invs. in APEB/SJ/IT: Antonio Vicente Bellez, 04/1670/2140/12; Innocencio José da Silva, 05/2005/2476/05; Caetano Mauricio Machado, 04/1715/2185/06.

130. Reqs., J. A. Xavier to Emperor, ca. 1840; CA to Pres., 13 March 1840; 27 May 1858, AHE/RQ, JJ-41-1132.

131. Will, Antonio Marcelino da Costa Doria, 26 May 1851, APEB/SJ/IT, 05/2180/2649/26.

132. CA to Pres., 27 Sep. 1841, APEB, m. 3775; 17 Jan. 1854, APEB, m. 3386.

133. Partilha amigável, Francisco de Araujo Lima, APEB/SJ/IT, 03/1064/1533/02, fols. 3v, 7r.

134. João Francisco Cabussú to J. M. Alencar, 13 March, 30 April, 6 July 1833, and 11 April 1838, *ABN* 86 (1966), 324, 325, 326, 331–32. In 1845, he was listed as a bookbinder, *Almanach . . . 1845*, 216.

135. McBeth, "Brazilian Generals," 141. See also Schulz, *Exército*, 205–7; Hayes, *Armed Nation*, 51.

136. CA to Pres., 7 July 1841, APEB, m. 3775.

137. R. V. Cunha, *Estudo*, 1:56; will, Manoel da Silva Daltro, 19 Nov. 1839, APEB/SJ/LRT, vol. 27, fol. 147r.

138. CA to Pres., 30 April 1851, APEB, m. 3384; MG, *Almanak* (1857), part 2, 80; M. J. N. Silva, *Synopsis*, 2:272; Schulz, *Exército*, 206.

139. Req., Joaquim José Vellozo to Emperor, Rio, 29 Feb. 1848, AHE/RQ, JJ-159-3972; informações semestrais, Antonio José Maxado Belfort, 30 June 1847; Pedro José Vieira, 7 July 1847, APEB, m. 3778.

140. Req., José Coelho de Sampaio to Emperor, 6 Feb. 1854, AHE/RQ, JJ-211-5155; FO, Luiz Francisco Eufrazio, AHE/FO, II-22-71.

141. Wetherell, *Brazil*, 139–40.

142. Req., Carlos Balthazar da Silveira (grandson) to Emperor, 25 Oct. 1847, AHE/RQ, C-29-850.

143. Pedro, *Diário*, 64; FO, José Balthazar da Silveira, AHE/FO, IV-22-104; inv., J. B. Silveira, APEB/SJ/IT, 07/3029/07.

144. [Francisco Manoel] Coelho [dos Santos] to Maria [Emília dos Santos Leoni Coelho], Santa Catarina, 19 July 1839, inv., F. M. C. Santos, APEB/SJ/IT, 03/1088/1557/02, fol. 88r–v.

145. Custódio Coelho dos Santos to MG, 29 May 1857, AHE/RQ, C-63-1805.

146. After he was arrested for beating his wife in 1859, allegedly during a fit of insanity, Francisco was briefly interned in the old soldiers' hostel in Rio on his brothers' request, CA to Pres., 30 June 1859, APEB, m. 3398; req., C. C. Santos to Emperor, 16 Jan. 1860, AHE/RQ, C-63-1805.

147. Pres. of Rio Grande do Sul to MG, Porto Alegre, 4 Sep. 1840; CA to Pres., 19 Oct. 1853; Pres. to MG, 10 Jan. 1877, AHE/RQ, A-107-3156.

148. Req., Francisca da Silveira Pinto de Bulhões Coelho to MG, 9 Feb. 1883, AHE/RQ, F-7-297.

149. Inv., F. M. C. Santos, APEB/SJ/IT, 03/1088/1557/02.

150. Will, C. X. Jesus, 4 Aug. 1831, APEB/SJ/LRT, vol. 22, fol. 112r; informação semestral, Manoel Balthazar dos Reis, 30 June 1847, APEB, m. 3778.

151. Stone, *Crisis*, 23. On two military clans, see Fonseca, *Fonseca;* Barreto, *Menna Barreto*.

152. Req., José Nunes Bahiense to Emperor, ca. 1845, AHE/RQ, JZ-133-3815.

153. Req., Cypriano da Rocha Lima to Emperor, Porto Alegre, 5 April 1839, AHE/RQ, C-67-1900.

154. Req., F. M. C. Santos to Emperor, Alegrete, 17 Feb. 1849; informação, Pres. of Rio Grande do Sul, São Borja, 4 March 1849, AHE/RQ, F-105-2901.

155. Req., Francisco de Paula Bahia to Emperor, 19 Aug. 1829, AHE/RQ, F-117-3156.

156. CA to Pres., 30 Oct. 1837, APEB, m. 3410; Luís da França to [Pres.?], ca. 1840, APEB., m. 3814; req., Maria Joaquina Pimental Ferreira to Emperor, Rio, 16 Sep. 1845, AHE/RQ, M-187-5018; req., Vicente Inácio da Silva to Juiz dos Orfãos, ca. 1842, APEB/SJ/IT, 01/99/145/02, fol. 11r.

157. Ladislau dos Santos Titara to Instituto Histórico e Geográfico Brasileiro, 30 April 1839; idem to idem, Rio Grande, 24 Oct. 1854, *RIGHB* 86 (1975–1977), 166–67, 175. Both of Titara's historical works have been republished, *Paraguassú* and *Memórias*.

158. Schulz, *Exército*, chaps. 1–4.

Chapter 7

1. JP to Pres., Santo Amaro, 14 Feb. 1840, APEB, m. 2583; João Lourenço de Athaide Seixas, "Exposição dos acontecimentos da Villa de S.to Amaro da Purificação em Abril de 1831," APEB, m. 2852. See also Reis, *Slave Rebellion*, 39.

2. "Instruções . . . ," 10 July 1822, *CLB*.

3. On marriage rates, see Nascimento, *Dez freguesias*, 114–15; Mattoso, *Bahia, século XIX*, 151.

4. Article 15, "Constituição Política do Império do Brasil," *CLB*.

5. Speech, Lúcio Soares Teixeira de Gouveia, 10 Aug., *ACD* (1828), 4:103.

6. Indicação, Raimundo José da Cunha Mattos, 26 May; Projeto de Lei, 19 June; speeches, R. J. C. Mattos, 13 July; 10 Aug., *ACD* (1826), 1:137, 2:201, 3:161, 4:109.

7. Speech, Luís Francisco de Paula Cavalcanti de Albuquerque, 31 Aug., *ACD* (1826), 4:321–22.

8. See the debate of 4 Aug., *ACD* (1826), 4:35–37.

9. F. F. Mendes, "Tributo," 114.

10. Projeto de Lei, 8 Aug., *ACD* (1827), 4:75; debate of 16 Aug. *ACD* (1831), 2:43–44.

11. See the debate in *ACD* (1837), vols. 1–2; Lei 45, 29 Aug. 1837; Decisão 560, 3 Nov. 1837, *CLB;* R. J. C. Mattos, *Repertório*, 3:33; J. A. A. Amaral, *Indicador*, vol. 1, part 1, 37.

12. Malheiro, *Escravidão*, 1:2–3, 206, 209.

13. Speeches, Antônio Francisco de Paula e Holanda Cavalcanti de Albuquerque, 14 July, *ACD* (1826), 3:173; 25 Aug., *ACD* (1828), 4:138; 11 July, *ACD* (1837), 2:84. On his political trajectory, see Mosher, "Pernambuco," 99, 112–13; Barman, *Brazil*, 180–81, 198–99.

14. On these aspects of European recruitment, see Skelley, *Victorian Army*, 251; Howard, *Franco-Prussian War*, 11–14, 18–21, 29–35; Sales de Bohigas, "Some Opinions."

15. Speech, Dom Manoel de Assis Mascarenhas, 10 May, *ACD* (1847), 1:38–39. See also speech, R. J. C. Mattos, 8 Aug., *ACD* (1827), 4:75.

16. See the debate of 16 Aug., *ACD* (1831), 2:43; speech, Manoel Inácio de Carvalho Mendonça, 15 May, *ACD* (1847), 1:78.

17. Speech, Francisco de Souza Martins, 12 June, *ACD* (1834), 1:129. For other statements of this view, see H. J. Rebello, "Memoria," 27; *O Censor,* 6 Sep. 1837, 52–53.

18. *ACD* (1834), (1835); Lei 55, 6 Oct. 1835, *CLB.*

19. Speech, José Lino Coutinho, 3 Aug., *ACD* (1826), 4:20.

20. Leis, 24 Nov. 1830, 26 Aug. 1835, *CLB.*

21. Decretos, 1 Aug., 22 Aug., and 23 May 1831, *CLB.*

22. Speech, MG, 29 May, *ACD* (1837), 1:147; Lei 45, 29 Aug. 1837, *CLB.*

23. Leis 68, 28 Sep. 1837; 42, 20 Sep. 1838; 282, 24 May 1843, *CLB.*

24. Lei 190, 24 Aug. 1841, *CLB.*

25. Serrano Ortega, *Contingente,* 13–18; Thomson, "Indios," 208–12; Meisel, "War," chap. 3.

26. MG, *Relatório* (1840), 7.

27. MG, *Relatório* (1843), 20; Soisa, *Generalidades,* 19; H. J. Rebello, "Memoria," 26, 28; A. M. Souza, "Viagens," 37; Conselho Geral to Emperor, 30 Dec. 1830, AN/SPE, IG1, m. 251, fol. 50r; Article 179, "Constituição política," *CLB.*

28. On the baroness's son, see *ACD* (1843), 1:369, 372.

29. Bueno, *Direito,* 97–98; J. A. A. Amaral, *Indicador,* vol. 1, part 1, 34–90.

30. Decisão 83, 20 Oct. 1843, *CLB;* Titara, *Auditor,* 71.

31. Juiz de Direito to Pres., Vila Nova da Rainha, 7 and 29, Nov., 9 Dec. 1839, BN/SM, I-31, 15, 29.

32. MG, *Relatório* (1839), table 11; speech, MG, 21 June, *ACD* (1838), 1:400.

33. CA to Pres., 10 May 1832; Lt. Col. Acting Com., Ninth Inf., to CA, 16 June 1832; CA to Pres., 9 Aug. 1832, APEB, m. 3394.

34. Decretos, 9 and 24 July 1832, *CLB;* CA to Pres., 29 Oct. 1832, APEB, m. 3449; Decisão 457, 21 Aug. 1833, *CLB; Gazeta Commercial da Bahia,* 8 Nov. 1833, 2.

35. Lt. Col. Com., Third Art., to CA, 5 July 1832, APEB, m. 3389.

36. Decreto, 2 Nov. 1835, *CLB; Diario da Bahia,* 19 Jan. 1836; Col. Encarregado do Recrutamento to Pres., 17 Aug. 1836, APEB, m. 3485.

37. CA to Pres., 5 July 1841, APEB, m. 3775; Pres. to Chief of Police [and Delegados and Subdelegados], 21 Nov. 1848 (printed circular), APEB, m. 6456.

38. "Prov. da Bahia. Relação dos Recrutados . . . ," 12 July 1842, AN/SPE/IG1, m. 117, fol. 305v.

39. Pres., *Relatório* (4 April 1848), 12; MG, *Relatório* (1848), 30; Lei 387, 19 Aug. 1846, *CLB.* Eventually the ban was limited to general elections, Decisão 108, 6 Sep. 1848, *CLB.*

40. Marginal note on Pres. to MG, 24 Sep. 1829, AN/SPE, IG1, m. 114, fol. 21r; Col. Com., Fourth Art., to CA, 10 March 1848, APEB, m. 3422.

41. For one example of each, see João da Costa Ferreira to Pres., Feira de Santana, 11 Nov. 1838, APEB, m. 3814; Delegado to Pres., Santo Amaro, 25 May 1843, APEB, m. 6460; Manoel Diogo de Sá Barretto e Aragão to President, Limoeiro, 18 Jan. 1828, APEB, m. 3693; Lt. Col. Com., Second Battalion, GN, to Pres., 16 Aug. 1840, APEB, m. 3548.

42. JP to Pres., Jaguaripe, 17 Nov. 1844, APEB, m. 2442. In Salvador, Raigôzo made no attempt to have himself excused, and on 11 Feb. 1845, he enlisted in the Depósito de Recrutas, "Recrutamento da Provincia da Bahia de 1844 em diante," AN/SPE, IG1, m. 118, fol. 942.

43. "Rellações das praças recrutadas...," 26 July–20 Dec. 1841, APEB, m. 3775.

44. Holloway, Policing, 201.

45. Hay, "Property," 40–49.

46. Manoel Maciel de Sá Barretto to Lt. Col. Com., Forty-Third Cav., Bom Sítio, 16 July 1827 (copy), APEB, m. 3367; GA to VP, 19 June 1827, APEB, m. 3367.

47. CS to Pres., 5 Aug. 1839, APEB, m. 3539; 15 April 1840, APEB, m. 3548.

48. See for example, Cap. Encarregado do Recrutamento to Pres., 15 July 1841, APEB, m. 3687; 17 and 22 July 1841, APEB, m. 3485.

49. Lt. Col. Com., Forty-Third Cav., to GA, n.p., 20 July 1827 (copy), APEB, m. 3367; Innocencio Eustaquio Ferreira d'Araujo to Pres., n.p., 15 May 1829, BN/SM, II-33, 23, 41.

50. Lenharo, Tropas, 87–88.

51. Pres. to MG, 15 Jan. 1848, AN/SPE, IG1, m. 119, fol. 195r.

52. Meznar, "Ranks," 337–47.

53. Req., Manoel João to Pres., ca. 1848, APEB, m. 3486.

54. Hay, "Property," 61–63; Roniger, Hierarchy, 4–5.

55. JP to Pres., Santo Amaro, 9 Sep. 1845, APEB, m. 2593; req., Antonia Luiza dos Santos to President, ca. 1839, APEB, m. 3486; JP to Pres., Maragogipe, 4 Aug. 1839, APEB, m. 2471.

56. Speech, Henrique Marques de Oliveira Lisboa, 10 May, ACD (1847), 1:35.

57. Decisões 57, 244, 25, respectively of 5 March and 22 Oct. 1825, and 11 Feb. 1826, CLB, instituted and ended the first recruitment drive. On its implementation in Bahia, see GA to Pres., 19 Nov. 1825, APEB, m. 3365; 31 March 1826, APEB, m. 3366. The second was instituted by Decreto, 14 July 1828, CLB, and likely expired when peace came later that year.

58. "Devassa a ex-officio, Vila Nova da Rainha, Juizo Ordinario, Francisco de Souza Leitão," 1833, APEB, m. 2859.

59. Marjoribanks, Travels, 103; James Hudson to Lord Palmerston, Rio, 18 Feb. 1850, PRO, For. Off. 13, vol. 274, fol. 165.

60. Lei 190, 24 Aug. 1841, CLB.

61. "2.o Batalhão d'Artilharia á pé. Preciza-se para as praças ... ," 1 Jan. 1854, AN/SPE, IG1, m. 121, fols. 147–53.

62. For example, see req., Francisco José de Paula to Pres., ca. 1831, APEB, m. 3222.

63. I. A. C. Silva, *Memorias,* 3:399; JP, Santana Parish, to Pres., 26 Sep. 1836, APEB, m. 2686; req., Miguel da Roxa to CA, ca. 1833; CA to Pres, 30 Sep. 1833, APEB, m. 3372; CA to Pres., 29 March 1844, APEB, m. 3424.

64. Req., Henrique Nero da Silva to Pres., ca. 1837, APEB, m. 3777.

65. Speech, Joaquim Manuel Carneiro da Cunha, 11 Aug. *ACD* (1840), 2:572; "A Primeira Linha e a G. Nacional," *O Guaycuru,* 12 July 1845, 416; JP to Pres., Santo Amaro, 2 Jan. 1840, APEB, m. 2593.

66. CA to Pres., 15 Jan. 1844, APEB, m. 3424. On the poll tax, see Reis, *Slave Rebellion,* 6, 223–30; M. I. C. Oliveira, *Liberto,* 29–30.

67. Beattie analyzes this recruitment pattern for a later period in "Transforming," 303–31.

68. 314 scattered desertion notices, 1829–1850, APEB; FOs of 137 enlisted men discharged on health grounds, 1847–1854, in AN/SPE, IG1, m. 119-21; "Recrutamento da Provincia da Bahia desde 1844 em diante," AN/SPE, IG1, m. 118, fols. 858–73, 906–42; FOs of 37 enlisted men discharged in 1835, AN/SPE, IG1, m. 116, fols. 395–404.

69. Coffman, *Old Army,* 139–41, 334–35.

70. Req., Joaquim Ribeiro da Silva to Pres., ca. 1838, APEB, m. 3485.

71. *O Independente Constitucional,* 26 Aug. 1826, 4 (APEB, m. 3765); *Correio Mercantil,* 22 June 1840, 1; CA to Pres., 8 Feb. 1844, AN/SPE, IG1, m. 546. This Bahian data is consistent with midcentury national data in which the proportion of impressed men ranges from 55 to 70 percent, Beattie, "Transforming," 72; F. F. Mendes, "Tributo," 104.

72. "Manifesto . . . ," 1 Aug. 1822, *AAPEB* 10 (1923), 23.

73. Article 150, "Constituição Política," *CLB.*

74. Speeches, R. J. C. Mattos, 1 and 10 July, *ACD* (1828), 3:22, 84.

75. Speech, R. J. C. Mattos, 6 Aug., *ACD* (1827), 4:56; *O Censor,* Oct. 1837, 125. See also Cidade, "Soldado," 15; idem, *Cadetes,* 195.

76. Parecer, Commissão de Guerra, 17 June, *ACD* (1828), 2:143.

77. Speech, R. J. C. Mattos, 1 July, *ACD* (1828), 3:21–22. On the frequency of flogging in the eighteenth-century British army, see Gilbert, "Military and Civilian Justice," 51–55.

78. Speech, José Gervásio de Queiroz Carreira, 10 July, *ACD* (1828), 3:84.

79. Speech, R. J. C. Mattos, 10 July, *ACD* (1828), 3:83–84.

80. Decisões 120, 30 May 1831; 180, 16 July 1831, *CLB.*

81. CA to MG, 20 Aug. 1831, AN/SPE, IG1, m. 251, fol. 146r (with marginal comments).

82. *Nova Sentinella da Liberdade,* 4 Aug. 1831, 153.

83. GA to MG, 10 April 1828, AN/SPE, IG1, m. 250, fols. 833v, 838r.

84. Lt. Col. Com., Third Art., to CA, 5 March 1835, APEB, m. 3459.

85. Second Sergeant Com., Guarda da Ribeira, to Duty Major, 20 Jan. 1837, APEB, m. 3373; Soisa, *Generalidades,* 21–22; Bolivar, *Breves considerações,* 14, 24–25, 32.

86. Pres. to CA, 3 Aug. 1830; CA to Pres., 4 Aug. 1830, AN/SPE, IG1, m. 115, fols. 45r, 46r.

87. *Constitucional Bahiense,* 20 Dec. 1827, 3. See also ibid., 18 Jan. 1828, 1–4 (AN/SPE/IG1, m. 250); *O Bahiano,* 9 May 1829, 4.

88. I located only one case of off-base residence after independence, Com., Third Art., to Pres., 3 Sep. 1836, APEB, m. 3373.

89. Portaria, Governo Provisório, 10 Dec. 1823 (copy), APEB, m. 3368; Maj. Com., Santa Catarina Art., to GA, 3 Jan. 1825, APEB, m. 3365.

90. Lei, 24 Sep. 1828, *CLB;* GA to Pres., 10, 12, and 15 Dec. 1828, APEB, m. 3368; 5 May 1829, BN/SM, I-31, 13, 15.

91. Decreto A, 13 Oct. 1837, *CLB,* ordered the creation of the Depósito, which was not established until 1842, Joaquim Rodrigues Coelho Kelly, "Relatório," 27 July 1846, APEB, m. 3494-1.

92. Portaria Circular, 15 April 1824, *CLB;* R. B. Castro, *Tipografia,* 217.

93. See, however, one exception, CA to Pres., 21 May 1832, APEB, m. 3394.

94. Speech, MG, 4 April *ACD* (1845), 2:443.

95. Lt. Col. Com., Third Art., to CA, 2 Nov. 1836; CA to Pres., 10 Nov. 1836, APEB, m. 3373; req., Josefa Senhorinha to Pres., ca. Aug. 1836, APEB, m. 2686.

96. "Chronica dos acontecimentos," 87; req., Antonina Barretto Mello de Vasconcellos to Pres., ca. 1826, APEB, m. 3763.

97. Pres. to MG, 10 July 1829, AN/SPE, IG1, m. 114, fol. 15r–v.

98. Maj. Acting Com., Third Inf., to Pres., 4 Dec. 1838, APEB, m. 3777; req., Joze Telles de S. Anna to General das Armas [sic], ca. 1838, APEB, m. 3773; req., Manoel Luciano da Câmara Guaraná to CA, ca. 1836, APEB, m. 3400.

99. Reqs., João d'Amorim Bezerra to Pres., 29 April 1847; Francisco Tiberio Pereira Falcão to Pres., 13 Nov. 1850, APEB, m. 3773; CA to Pres., 9 Nov. 1847, APEB, m. 3444.

100. CA to Pres., 11 June 1835, APEB, m. 3387.

101. FOs of 137 discharged soldiers, 1847–1854, AN/SPE, IG1, m. 119–21; MG, *Relatório* (1830), 10; "Mappa demonstrativo das alterações," MG, *Relatório* (1858).

102. GA to Pres., 12 Sep. 1829, AN/SPE, IG1, m. 114, fol. 22r. See also MG, *Relatório* (1850), 21.

103. Maj. Com. to Pres., n.p., 26 Aug. 1845, APEB, m. 3696; "Ditto do Soldado ... Antonio Martins," 23 Nov. 1830, APEB, m. 3371. For desertion at the time of embarkation, see CA to Pres., 4 July 1836, APEB, m. 3458-1; for deserters found in the homes of their families, see Maj. Com. to Pres., Maragogipe, 21 May 1828, APEB, m. 3749. The elopement is noted in "Avisos," *O Bahiano,* 6 June 1829, 4.

104. GA to Pres., 8 Oct. 1829, BN/SM, II-33, 25, 66; 12 Sep. 1829, BN/SM, I-31, 14, 29; Lt. Com., Cav. Comp., to CA, 4 Dec. 1844, APEB, m. 3695.

105. CA to Pres., 14 Dec. 1843, APEB, m. 3449; req., Baldoino Ferreira Sant'Iago to Pres., ca. 1840s, APEB, m. 3496; CA to Pres., 3 Feb. 1847, APEB, m. 3445; 24 April 1833, APEB, m. 3372.

106. For discussion of this policy, see CA to Pres., 3 Aug. 1848, APEB, m. 3414; Pres. to MG, 30 Oct. 1849, AN/SPE, IG1, m. 119, fol. 303r; CA to Pres., 9 Oct. 1851, APEB., m. 3384.

107. Interr., 21 Oct. 1845, Conselho de Guerra, Antonio José Francisco dos Santos, APEB, m. 3682.

108. For the voluntary return of deserters, see GA to Pres., 11 April 1829, APEB, m. 3369; req., Maria do Rozario to Pres., ca. 1830, APEB, m. 3485; req., José Leão da Silveira Cohn to Pres., ca. 1848, APEB, m. 3422. For the deserter in the police, see req., B. F. Sant'Iago to Pres., ca. 1840s, APEB, m. 3496.

109. British Consul to Arthur Aston, 24 Aug. 1831 (copy), PRO, For. Off. 13, vol. 88, fol. 136.

110. CA to MG, 1 Sep. 1831, AN/SPE, IG1, m. 115, fol. 154.

111. Myerley, *British Military Spectacle*, 26, 78, 118.

112. U.S. Consul to Secretary of State, 13 Sep. 1831, NARS, T-432, roll 3.

113. OD, 2 Sep. 1831, *Supplemento a Gazeta da Bahia*, 3 Sep. 1831, 1; *Nova Sentinella da Liberdade*, 4 Sep. 1831, 233–34; 15 Sep. 1831, 268.

114. *O Investigador Brasileiro*, 15 Nov. 1831, 295.

115. CA to Pres., 4 June 1832, APEB, m. 3394.

116. Morton, "Military," 262.

117. PC, B.am N.o 1 da 1.a L.a, fols. 3–17, APEB, m. 2840-1.

118. "Memoria descriptiva," 262; CA to MG, 2 May 1831, AN/SPE, IG1, m. 251, vol. 139v; "Atas da Camara Municipal extraídas do Livro dos Anos de 1835 a 1838," *PAEB*, 5:113.

119. Letter from O Pescador, *O Sete de Novembro*, 14 Dec. 1837, 75–76. See also *Novo Diario da Bahia*, 7 Dec. 1837, 2; *O Novo Sete de Novembro*, 18 Dec. 1837, 2.

120. Test., Ignacio José Jambeiro, 15 May 1838, PC, Vereadores, fol. 45r, APEB, m. 2835; for earlier concern about sergeants' politics, see Pres. to MI, 19 Jan. 1833, BN/SM, II-34, 5, 79, no. 1.

121. Lt. Col. Acting Com., Ninth Inf., to CA, 9 Aug. 1832, APEB, m. 3394; test., Antonio Joaquim Imbú, 9 May 1833, "Autuação de trez sumarias . . . 1833," fol. 47v; APEB, m. 2853; Antonio Pedro Gurgalha to Pres., 28 Nov. 1826, BN/SM, II-34, 1, 6, doc. 6; "Guarda Principal," 3 Sep. 1839 (copy), APEB, m. 3814.

122. Francisco de Abreo Bahia Contreiras to Intendente de Marinha, 7 Jan. 1830, APEB, m. 3694.

123. M. D. Graham, *Journal*, 140.

124. FO, José Balthazar da Silveira, 26 Dec. 1848, AHE/FO, IV-22-104.

125. DaMatta, *Casa*, chaps. 1–2; S. L. Graham, *House*, 10–27. For this concept's application to recruitment in a later period, see Beattie, "House," 440–43.

126. "Parte geral da Guarda Policial," 20 July 1837, APEB, m. 3688; *O Tolerante na Bahia*, 25 April 1839, 1 (AHE/RQ, D-26-709); *O Mercantil*, 9 Dec. 1845, 3; Lt. Col. Com., First Art., to CA, 28 April 1846, APEB, m. 3690. See also Reis, *Slave Rebellion*, 190.

127. CA to Pres., 25 Jan. 1837; JP, Sé Parish, to Pres., 18 Jan. 1837, APEB, m. 3428. For other such denunciations, see *O Independente Constitucional*, 5 April 1824, 2 (AN/SPE/IG1, m. 249).

128. Viscount of Pirajá to Pres., 4 Dec. 1830, BN/SM, I-31, 15, 25, doc. 37. See also Lt. Col. Com., Guarda Militar de Polícia, to Pres., 5 Dec. 1830, BN/SM, I-31, 15, doc. 36.

129. The subdelegate had evidently used the question, still heard in Brazil, "Do you know whom you are talking to?" to assert his superiority, DaMatta, *Carnavais*, chap. 4.

130. Subdelegate, Sé Parish, to Pres., 28 April 1843; Luiz Balthazar da Silveira to Maj. Com., Depósito de Recrutas, 5 May 1843, APEB, m. 3376.

131. Second Cadet, Com. of Guard, to Oficial do Estado, 4 May 1839; Manoel José Vieira to Lt. Col. Com., Second Art., 7 May 1839; Lt. Col. Com., Second Art., to Pres., 7 May 1839; Theodozio Gomes to Com. Geral, 6 May 1839; José da Rocha Galvão to Com. Geral, 6 May 1839, APEB, m. 3688. For an analysis of such conflicts from the perspective of the police, see Brown, " 'Vanguard,' " 248–53.

132. Lt. Col. Com, Second Legion, to CS, 14 June 1845; Second Staff Lt. to Lt. Col. Com., Second Battalion, GN, 13 June 1845; test., Tertuliano da Silva Roza, 20 June 1845, Conselho de Investigação, Bento Pereira and Luiz Gomes Luvaes, APEB, m. 3376.

133. Holmes, *Firing Line*, 290–315; Henderson, *Cohesion*, 161–66.

134. M. A. Almeida, *Memórias*, 106.

Chapter 8

1. CA to MG, 24 May 1831, AN/SPE, IG1, m. 251, fol. 137. See also MG, *Relatório* (1831), 6.

2. Uricoechea, *Patrimonial Foundations;* M. A. Faria, "Guarda Nacional"; J. B. Castro, *Milícia;* Rodrigues, Falcon, and Neves, *Guarda Nacional.*

3. GA to Pres., 12 Nov. 1827, APEB, m. 3431; 8 Feb. 1828, APEB, m. 3368; 29 July 1829, APEB, m. 3370.

4. GA to Pres., 6 Feb. 1828, BN/SM, I-31, 13, 10; 30 Dec. 1828, APEB, m. 3368; GA to Pres., 31 July 1826, APEB, m. 3366; GA to VP, 1 Jan. 1827, APEB, m. 3367; GA to Pres., 17 June 1830, APEB, m. 3371.

5. Col. Com., Art., to GA, 7 Aug. 1827 (copy), BN/SM, II-33, 19, 6; GA to Pres., 15 Nov. 1827, APEB, m. 3431.

6. GA to VP, 1 Oct. 1828, BN/SM, I-31, 13, 10; GA to Pres., 17 Jan. 1829, APEB, m. 3370.

7. GA to Pres., 23 May 1829, BN/SM, I-31, 13, 15; British Consul to John Bidwell, 26 May 1827, PRO, For. Off. 13, vol. 41, fol. 92.

8. OD, 22 May 1829, *O Bahiano,* 26 May 1829, 1; GA to Pres., 22 May 1829, APEB, m. 3369; GA to Pres., 15 April 1830, BN/SM, I-31, 15, 19; Pres. to GA, 19 May 1830 (copy), AN/SPE, IG1, m. 115, fol. 37r.

9. "Apontamentos . . . por José Bonifácio de Andrade e Silva," AIHGB, lata 192, doc. 19; A. M. Souza, "Viagens," 41, 69; speeches, José Clemente Pereira, Bernardo Pereira de Vasconcelos, and José Bernardo Batista Pereira, 14 June, *ACD* (1826), 2:131, 132, 133; Antônio Francisco de Paula e Holanda Cavalcante de Albuquerque, 2 July, *ACD* (1828), 3:26; José Lino Coutinho, 17 June, *ACD* (1830), 1:426–27.

10. I. A. C. Silva, *Memorias,* 4:170; speeches, J. L. Coutinho, 14 June, *ACD* (1826), 2:133; 9 Aug., *ACD* (1827), 4:86.

11. Hale, *Mexican Liberalism,* 141–44; speech, Diogo Antônio Feijó, 1 July, *ACD* (1828), 3:16. See the texts of these bills in *ACD* (1827), 2:111–12; (1830), 1:172–73.

12. Speech, Francisco de Paula Souza e Melo, 2 July, *ACD* (1828), 3:28. For other examples, see speeches, Luís Francisco de Paula Cavalcante de Albuquerque and José da Cruz Ferreira, 14 June 1826, *ACD* (1826), 2:134, 135; *O Mensageiro da Bahia,* 20 March 1830, 126.

13. R. J. C. Mattos, *Repertório,* 3:167–69.

14. *ACD* (1826), 2:253; (1827), 3:222–23, 263–64, 267–75 (Quote, 273); Lei, 24 Sep. 1829, *CLB.* Concerns about patronage appointments appear in Pareceres, Commissão de Guerra, 1 June, *ACD* (1826), 2:9–10; 17 June, *ACD* (1828), 2:143–44.

15. R. J. C. Mattos, *Repertório,* 2:112, 322.

16. Consulta, Conselho Supremo Militar, 16 Feb. 1829, AHE/RQ, JJ-156-3932.

17. *ACD* (1831), 1:9, 18–19, 144, 159, 246, 264.

18. Girard, *Garde,* chap. 15; Sérgio Buarque de Holanda, preface to J. B. Castro, *Milícia,* xviii–xix; Santoni, "Fear," 270–73; idem, "Failure," 170–73; Anna, *Forging,* 156–57, 233; Hernández Ponce, "Guardia."

19. Lei, 18 Aug. 1831; chap. 6, "Constituição política do império do Brasil," *CLB.*

20. Holloway, *Policing,* 83–84; R. Graham, *Patronage,* 106–9; M. A. Faria, "Guarda," 169–74; J. B. Castro, *Milícia,* 108, 126–28, 155–57; Aufderheide, "Order," 110.

21. R. J. C. Mattos, *Repertório,* 2:324; J. B. Castro, *Milícia,* 135–45; Acting JP, Santo Antônio além do Carmo, to Pres., 19 July 1832, APEB, m. 2682.

22. J. B. Castro, *Milícia,* 137–38, 139–40. See also Flory, "Race," 220–21; Rodrigues, Falcon, and Neves, *Guarda,* 43–44.

23. Decreto, 25 Oct. 1832, *CLB;* Article 95, "Constituição Política," *CLB.* No debate on the Guard's reform was recorded by the chamber of deputies which only contracted for the publication of its proceedings until 3 Sep. 1832.

24. Speech, Antônio Pereira Rebouças, 25 Aug., *ACD* (1832), 2:200–1. The *Nova Sentinella da Liberdade* condemned Rebouças's position on income requirements, 26 Aug. 1831, 78, n. 2.

25. *Aurora Fluminense,* 15 Dec. 1831, 2396.
26. On this point, see especially Rodrigues, Falcon, and Neves, *Guarda,* 33–43.
27. I. A. C. Silva, *Memorias,* 4:282; *O Orgão da Lei,* 6 June 1832, 156.
28. *O Investigador Brasileiro,* 15 Nov. 1831, 298; *Gazeta da Bahia,* 16 Nov. 1831, 3; *O Orgão da Lei,* 6 June 1832, 155.
29. Acting JP, Conceição da Praia, to Pres., 25 Jan. 1832, APEB, m. 2682; Acting Head, Second Legion, to Acting CS, 31 July 1837, APEB, m. 3530; req., Bartholomeo Telles de Menezes to Acting CS, ca. 1836, APEB, m. 3532.
30. R. Graham, *Patronage,* chap. 4. Surprisingly little has been written on Guard elections, but see Rodrigues, Falcon, and Neves, *Guarda,* 200–5.
31. See the reports from JPs in APEB, m. 2682, 2686. On the Penha case, see Acta das Eleições, 26 Feb. 1832, APEB, m. 2682.
32. JP, São Pedro Velho, to Pres., 2 March 1832, APEB, m. 2682; JP, Santo Antônio além do Carmo, to Pres., 3 and 4 Feb. 1836, APEB, m. 2686.
33. Head, Fifth Battalion, to Pres., 21 March 1832, APEB, m. 3528; CA to Pres., 10 April 1832, 25 June 1832, APEB, m. 3394; Head, Third Battalion, to Pres., 16 April 1832, APEB, m. 3528.
34. Head, Fifth Battalion, to Pres., 19 June 1832, APEB, m. 3528; U.S. Consul to Secretary of State, 18 Feb. 1833, NARS, T-432, roll 3.
35. Head, First Battalion, to Pres., 13 June 1832, APEB, m. 3528; Acting JP, Santo Antônio além do Carmo, to Pres., 20 June 1832; JP, Rua do Paço, to Pres., 20 June 1832; JP, Pilar, to Pres., 19 June 1832, APEB, m. 2682.
36. Head, First Battalion, to Head, First Legion, 17 June 1837, APEB, m. 3530.
37. Acting CS to Pres., 3 Aug. 1833, APEB, m. 3528; 25 April 1836, APEB, m. 3532; Acting Head, Second Battalion, to Câmara Municipal, 15 April 1835, AM, Documentos Avulsos—Militares; Flory, *Judge,* 92–95.
38. Decisão 311, 12 June 1833, *CLB;* Paymaster to Pres., 27 Sep. 1834, APEB, m. 3718.
39. Acting Head, Third Battalion, to Acting Com., First Legion, 23 April 1834, APEB, m. 3528; *O Democrata,* Feb. 1834, 121–22.
40. For two examples, see Acting CS to Pres., 2 April 1836; CS to Pres., 25 April 1836, APEB, m. 3532.
41. MJ, *Relatório* (1833), 14; Govino Ribeiro do Nascimento, Parte, 9 Oct. 1832, APEB, m. 3528; Cap., First Comp., to Head, Third Battalion, 9 July 1836, APEB, m. 3532.
42. João Francisco Cabuçu to José Martiniano de Alencar, 30 April 1833, *ABN* 86 (1966), 325. For praise of all three corporations, see Pres. to MG, 29 May 1833, AN/SPE, IG1, m. 115, fol. 303r; *Diario da Bahia,* 30 April 1833, 284–85.
43. Head, Fourth Battalion, to Pres., 18 April 1832, APEB, m. 3528; Head, First Battalion, to Pres., 29 April 1837, APEB, m. 3530; Acting CS to Pres., 22 Jan. 1836; Acting Head, First Legion, to CS, 22 April 1836, APEB, m. 3532; Battalion Heads, First Legion, to CS, 6 Oct. 1833, APEB, m. 3528.

44. MJ, *Relatório* (1834), 12. See also Holloway, *Policing,* 154; Rodrigues, Falcon, and Neves, *Guarda,* 188–99.

45. Pres. to MJ, 23 Sep. 1833, AN/SPE, IG1, m. 707; Lt. Com., Guarda do Colégio, to CS, 27 July 1839, APEB, m. 3374; MJ, *Relatório* (1835), 35–36.

46. Acting Head, Third Battalion, to Acting Head, First Legion, ca. June 1834, Acting CS to Pres., 23 June 1834, APEB, m. 3528; Francisco de Borja Damazio to Head, Fourth Battalion, 26 Feb. 1836, APEB, m. 3532; Acting Com., Second Battalion, to Head, First Legion, 12 Oct. 1834, APEB, m. 3528.

47. Acting CS to Pres., 11 Nov. 1834; 9 Dec. 1834, APEB, m. 3528.

48. Pres. to MJ, 10 April 1838, *PAEB,* 3:393.

49. Speech, MG, 19 June, *AS* (1835), 134.

50. Bill proposed by the Acting MJ, 10 June, *ACD* (1833), 1:241; J. B. Castro, *Milícia,* 188–89.

51. J. B. Castro, *Milícia,* 141, 193.

52. Acting JP, Sé Parish, to Pres., 22 March 1832, APEB, m. 2682; Reis, *Slave Rebellion,* 192; Flory, *Judge,* 72–73, 74.

53. Req., Fellippe Duarte Vianna to Pres., ca. June 1837; atestado, Lt. Col. Head, Third Battalion, n.d., APEB, m. 3536; inv., Raimundo Francisco de Macedo Magarão, APEB/SJ/IT, 05/2906/2378/04; will, João Alves Pitombo, 29 Jan. 1850, APEB/SJ/IT, 05/1984/2456/05.

54. *O Defensor do Povo,* 13 Feb. 1836, 1–2; inv., Joaquim de Souza Vinhático, APEB/SJ/IT, 04/1601/2070/14.

55. Flory, "Race," 221.

56. Lei, 18 Aug. 1831; Decreto, 25 Oct. 1832, *CLB;* MJ, *Relatório* (1832), 4.

57. Comparison of 391 militia officers with 164 Guard officers mentioned in documentation for 1832–1837 or listed in "Rellação dos officiaes . . . ," 6 June 1838, APEB, m. 3534.

58. Proclamations of Coms., "Corpos, Tropa, e Povo," Barbalho Fort, 4 and 5 April 1831, in I. A. C. Silva, *Memorias,* 4:255–56, 262–63; "A queda dos tyran-nos da Bahia," *Escudo da Constituição Brasileira,* 11 April 1831, 300–1. The militia does not figure in the principal chronicles of the events of mid-1831, I. A. C. Silva, *Memorias,* 4:279–83; "Noticia sôbre a morte. . . ," BN/SM, II-33, 35, 10; Rebouças, *Recordações,* 92–98.

59. The mulatto colonel, Antônio Lopes Tabira Bahiense, who died in 1847, dis-appears from the record after 1831, inv., APEBa/SJ/IT, 08/3510/18. Unlike Bigode, Gomes, and Cirilo, he had not held a paid commission in the militia, Tesoureiro Geral das Tropas to Pres., 26 May 1831, APEB, m. 3222.

60. See their AHE/RQ files: José Maria Cirilo da Silva, JZ-116-3395; Joaquim José de Santana Gomes, JJ-156-3932; Francisco Xavier Bigode, F-148-3781.

61. Req., Bigode to Emperor, 5 April 1832, AHE/RQ, F-148-3781.

62. His position is strikingly consistent with calls for the restoration of segregated militias that appeared in the black press in Rio at about the same time, *O Homem de Cor,* 14 Sept. 1833, 1–2.

63. I. A. C. Silva, *Memorias,* 4:56, n. 27; CA to Pres., 25 April 1832; Pres. to MG, 28 April 1832; reqs., Bigode to Emperor, ca. 1835 and 29 June 1837; Consultas, Conselho Supremo Militar, 11 Jan. 1836 and 28 Aug. 1837, AHE/RQ, F-148-3781.

64. Cabuçu to J. M. Alencar, 11 April 1838, *ABN* 86 (1966), 332.

65. PC, Manoel Alves Fernandes Sucupira, APEB, m. 2836.

66. Interr., José de Carvalho, 28 Aug. 1838; Guilherme de Santana, 20 Nov. 1839, PC, 1.0 B.m da 2.a L.a, fols. 96v, 131r, APEB, m. 2838; Antonio de Souza Lima to Pres., Itaparica, 19 March 1838, APEB, m. 3698; OD 677, 24 Nov. 1837, *O Sete de Novembro,* 9 Dec. 1837, 56.

67. "Termo de Juram.to da Constituição . . . ," 4 May 1824, APEB, m. 2171; PC, 1.0 B.m da 2.a L.a, fol. 114r–v, APEB, m. 2838; "Noticia sôbre a morte," BN/SM, II-33, 35, 10; Freitas, "Narrativa," 266.

68. *O Novo Diário da Bahia,* 26 Dec. 1837, 2.

69. "Narrativa dos successos da Sabinada," 341.

70. "Noticia sôbre a morte," BN/SM, II-33, 35, 10; "Alleluia Bahianos," *Correio Mercantil,* 18 April 1838, 2; Alexandre Gomes de Argollo Ferrão to Joao Chrisostomo Callado, 20 March 1838, *PAEB,* 2:154; CA to Pres., 6 Aug. 1839, BN/SM, I-31, 14, 54.

71. PC, 1.0 B.m da 2.a L.a, APEB, m. 2838; Howard, *Changing,* 85–97; Klein, "Colored Militia," 24.

72. In the 1820s, they complained of being excluded from militia service because of their role in the Periquitos' Rebellion, req., Bernardino José Cardoso et al. to Pres., ca. 1825, APEB, m. 3766.

73. OD 8, 26 Dec. 1837, *O Novo Sete de Setembro,* 30 Dec. 1837, 4; Interr., Thomaz de Aquino Mangueira, 9 Oct. 1839, PC, Batalhão 4.0 de 2.a L.a, fol. 140v, APEB, m. 2840-1.

74. Interr., Thomas Alves d'Otan e Silva and Cirilo, 18 Nov. 1839, PC, Batalhão 4.0 de 2.a L.a, fol. 157r, APEB, m. 2840-1.

75. Test., Pedro Ignacio de Porciuncula, 4 Aug. 1838, PC, José Galdino Ribeiro Sanches et al., APEB, m. 2840; 7 Aug. 1838, PC, Ignacio J.e Aprigio da Fonseca Galvão, APEB, m. 2836.

76. Inv., Joaquim da Silva Braga, APEB/SJ/IT, 03/1100/1569/04; will, Marcos Berlink, 11 Feb. 1848, APEB/SJ/IT, 04/1858/2329/03, fol. 6r; test., Cirilo, 12 Oct. 1860, Justificação, Vicencia Maria dos Santos, APEB, m. 3769.

77. "Rellação dos officiaes . . . ," 6 June 1838, APEB, m. 3534.

78. *Diario da Bahia,* 9 Nov. 1837, 1.

79. Speech, Francisco Gonçalves Martins, 21 June, *ACD* (1838), 1:403.

80. See the interrs. in the following PCs: José Joaquim do Sacramento, fol. 14v; José Ferreira de Moraes e Silva, fol. 93v, APEB, m. 2841; B. T. Menezes, fol. 15r, APEB, m. 2836; Thomé da Costa Passos, fol. 17r, APEB, m. 2839; Hermenegildo Pereira d'Almeida; Erico Protestato da Fonseca, 52v–53r; Francisco de Paula Bahia, fol. 67r, APEB, m. 2843;

81. Lei 77, 14 July 1838; Resolução 107, 26 April 1839, *CLRBa*.

82. Viscount of Pirajá to Regent, 28 June 1838, *PAEB*, 5:372; *Correio Mercantil*, 17 July 1838, 1.

83. "Rellação dos officiaes . . . ," 6 June 1838, APEB, m. 3534; *Almanach . . . 1845*, 296–320.

84. Lt. Col. Com., Fourth Battalion, to Head, Second Legion, 31 Oct. 1840, APEB, m. 3539.

85. Reqs., Manoel Magalhães Requião to Pres., ca. 1840, APEB, m. 3762; Pedro Gonsalves de Castro to Pres., ca. 1840, APEB, m. 3541; CS to Pres., 30 Oct. and 20 Nov. 1840, APEB, m. 3548.

86. CS to Pres., 19 Nov. 1839, APEB, m. 3535; Col. Com., Second Legion, to Pres., 20 March 1839, APEB, m. 3538. For two letters declining appointments, see João Alvares de Araujo to Com., Fifth Battalion, 1 Nov. 1838; João Adrião Chaves to Acting Head, Second Legion, 31 Oct. 1838, APEB, m. 3534

87. On Rio Vermelho, see A. L. Souza, "Visconde," 221–27.

88. Invs. in APEB/SJ/IT: Conde do Passé, 01/93A/133/01; Manoel José de Teive e Argolo, 04/1903/2374/01; Alexandre Lacerda Seabra, 04/1676/2146/01; Fabrício Cardoso de Vasconcelos, 02/1890/1359/10; Silvestre Cardoso de Vasconcelos, 05/2170/2639/09, Domingos Cardoso de Vasconcelos, 04/1944/2416/08; will, Domingos Pereira Soares, 17 April 1862, APEB/SJ/IT, 07/2993/22.

89. Will and inv., Francisco José Godinho, APEB/SJ/IT, 03/1030/1499/10. For another example of these strategies, see will and inv., Vicente Ferreira de Freitas Guimarães, APEB/SJ/IT, 08/347/02.

90. See the following documents in APEB/SJ/IT: "Balanço da casa comercial . . . ," 30 April 1866, inv., Theodoro Teixeira Gomes, 01/83/115/04, fols. 23r, 25r; "Balanço Geral da Sociedade Bellens & Irmão," 9 Sep. 1862, 07/2959/02, fols. 23v–24r; will, Félix Ribeiro Navarro, 3 May 1850, 07/3189/01, fol. 7v; will, Manoel Rodrigues Valença, 1 Aug. 1876, fol. 1r; "Declarações de Justino Trajano de Sento Sé," 20 July 1892, inv., Justino Nunes de Sento Sé, 01/48/54/65, fol. 113r.

91. Invs. in APEB/SJ/IT: J. A. Pitombo, 05/1984/2456/05; J. N. Sento Sé, 01/48/54/65.

92. Will, Lourenço de Souza Marques, 6 Sep. 1888, APEB/SJ/LRT, vol. 62, fol. 33v; req., Francisco Antônio Filgueira Júnior to Juiz dos Orfãos, ca. June 1876, inv., Francisco Antonio Filgueira, APEB/SJ/IT, 04/1785/2255/04; req., Maxima Peixoto Botelho to Juiz dos Orfãos, ca. Nov. 1890, inv., José Sesinando Botelho, APEB/SJ/IT, 06/2666/05.

93. Inv., José Maria Servulo Sampaio, APEB/SJ/IT, 07/2921/05; will, Joaquim Antônio da Silva Carvalhal, 17 June 1878, APEB/SJ/LRT, vol. 55, fols. 10r–11v.

94. Inv., Joaquim Proto Dourado, APEB/SJ/IT, 04/1643/2112/09.

95. Miranda, "Noticicia," xvii–xxvii; *ACD* (1850, First Session), 1:142–44, 149–56; 2:332.

96. See, for example, "Relação das praças do 1.o B.am de C.es da G. N. aquartelado

q' São Empregados Publicos," 18 July 1849, APEB, m. 3572; Acting CS to Pres., 1 March 1841, APEB, m. 3545.

97. Director, Arsenal de Guerra, to Pres., 12 Nov. 1844, AN/SPE, IG1, m. 119, fol. 153; 27 Nov. 1845, APEB, m. 3349; Com., Fourth Battalion (Evaristo Ladislau e Silva), to CS, 3 May 1841, APEB, m. 3545.

98. Faoro, *Donos;* Uricoechea, *Patrimonial Foundations.*

99. Second Lt. Com., First Comp., to Maj. [Acting] Head, Fourth Battalion, 14 May 1839, APEB, m. 3538; Cap. João Francisco de Souza Paraiso to Maj. Acting Com., First Battalion, 21 Nov. 1838, APEB, m. 3534.

100. CS to Pres., 12 Nov. 1839, APEB, m. 3535.

101. Req., Joaquim José Rodrigues to Pres., ca. Feb. 1839, APEB, m. 3536; Lt. Col. Com., Second Battalion, to Pres., 22 Feb. 1839, APEB, m. 3538.

102. Req., Tomas Teixeira da Cunha to Pres., ca. 1847, APEB, m. 3566.

103. CS to Pres., 9 Aug. 1839, APEB, m. 3535; CS to Pres., 9 May 1849, APEB, m. 3572; Girard, *Garde,* chaps 16–19.

104. Cap., First Comp., to Lt. Col. Com., Second Battalion, 23 Feb. 1839, APEB, m. 3538.

105. Acting CS to Pres., 11 Jan. 1841, APEB, m. 3545. For a cooperative JP, see Lt. Col., Com., Second Battalion, to Pres., 21 Dec. 1838, APEB, m. 3534.

106. Lt. Col. Head to Com., Second Legion, 12 Sep. 1843, APEB, m. 3564; Subdelegado, Pilar, to Pres., 7 July 1845, APEB, m. 3555. See the lists of block inspectors submitted by Acting CS to Pres., 28 March 1845, APEB, m. 3555.

107. Acting CS to Pres., 9 April 1845, APEB, m. 3555; "Mappa do 2.0 B.m de G. N. Aquartelado no Q.el da Mouraria," ca. Feb. 1841, APEB, m. 3545.

108. Lei, 18 Aug. 1831; bill presented on 1 June, *ACD* (1836), 1:122–23; debates of 11 July and 28 Sep., *ACD* (1836), 2:63, 368–74.

109. Lei, 29 Aug. 1837, *CLB.* See speeches, B. P. Vasconcelos, 21 June, *ACD* (1837), 1:303; Saturnino de Souza e Oliveira, 10 July, *ACD* (1837), 2:80; A. P. Rebouças, 10 July, *ACD* (1837), 2:75–76; *O Censor,* 6 Sep. 1837, 54.

110. Decisão 482, 22 Sep. 1837, *CLB;* proposta, Min. of Finance, 22 Sep., *ACD* (1837), 2:271; Decretos, 9 and 15 Oct. 1837, *CLB.*

111. On the replacement of regulars by guardsmen, see Pres. to MG, 1 July 1836, AN/SPE, IG1, m. 116, fol. 466r; CA to Pres., 4 July 1836, APEB, m. 3458-1. For references to refusals to form detachments, see Decisão 115, 27 Feb. 1837, *CLB;* Acting CS to Pres., 26 April 1837, APEB, m. 3530.

112. For a typical report on the "quartering" of two companies, see Pres. to MG, 21 Dec. 1847, AN/SPE, IG1, m. 119, fol. 154r. On the provisional corps, see Decreto 188, 25 June 1842, *CLB.*

113. Acting Com., Second Legion, to CS, 28 Nov. 1838, APEB, m. 3530; Pres. to MJ, 14 Oct. 1839, AN/SPE, IJ1, m. 708, fol. 97r.

114. For examples of these petitions and comments on them, see Officers of Third Battalion to Acting Com., Aug. 1838, APEB, m. 3530; req., Francisco Rodrigues da

Costa to Pres., ca. 1839, APEB, m. 3546; Lt. Col. Com., Sixth Battalion, to Pres., 7 March 1839, APEB, m. 3535; req., Antonio Luiz Vieira to Pres., ca. 1844, APEB, m. 3539; Acting CS to Pres., 31 Dec. 1847, APEB, m. 3377.

115. "Mappa Diário da Força...," 25 Aug. and 16 Sep. 1843, APEB, m. 6460; MG, *Relatórios* (1844), tables 11, 13; (1845, First Session), table 10; "Mappa geral demonstrativo das Forças existentes...," MG, *Relatório* (1845, Second Session).

116. See the numerous petitions in APEB, m. 3551, 3553.

117. See the debate over this issue, 27 and 28 June *ACD* (1839), 1:562, 569; 3 July, *ACD* (1839), 2:55–56; Pres. and CA to MG, 14 May 1845, AN/SPE/IG1, m. 118, fols. 1050v–51r.

118. Head, Third Legion, to CS, 9 Aug. 1839, APEB, m. 3535; Manoel Vieira Machado to Pres., 13 Sep. 1841, APEB, m. 3781; Head, Third Legion, to CS, 21 July 1847, APEB, m. 3377; CS to Pres., 5 Aug. 1839, APEB, m. 3539; Lt. Col. Com., Sixth Battalion, to Pres., 20 May 1840; Maj. Acting Com., Fourth Battalion, to Pres., 20 Feb. 1840, APEB, m. 3548.

119. Rodrigues, Falcon, and Neves, *Guarda*, 124–28, 139–40; Holloway, *Policing*, 153.

120. Pres., *Relatório* (1845), table 7.

121. Manoel Gomes Tourinho da Silva to [Pres.?], 20 Dec. 1847, APEB, m. 3564.

122. Miranda, "Noticia," xiv–xv; Pres., *Relatório* (1846), 4–5; Chief of Police to Pres., 12 Dec. 1845, AN/SPE, IG1, m. 118, fol. 1017; Pres. to MJ, 20 Dec. 1845 (secret), AN/SPE, IJ1, m. 709; *O Guaycuru,* 17 Dec. 1845, 564–65. See also the legislative debate about this incident, speeches, José de Barros Pimentel, 18 July; João Maurício Wanderley, 24 July, *ACD* (1846), 2:227–28, 312. On the newspaper, see I. A. C Silva to Acting CS, 19 Dec. 1845, APEB, m. 3555.

123. Speeches, Paulino José Soares de Souza, 9 Oct.; Joaquim Manoel Carneiro da Cunha, 14 Oct., *ACD* (1843, Second Session), 3:337, 400.

124. Speech, Venâncio Henriques de Rezende, 6 Sep., *ACD* (1841), 3:88–89.

125. See the MJ's *Relatórios* for the 1840s.

126. See the texts of these bills in *ACD* (1843, Second Session), 3:309–13; (1845), 2:653–59. For an especially cogent argument in favor of restoring the militias, see Francisco José de Souza Soares de Andréia's report, Pres., *Relatório* (1845), 13–27. Key issues were raised in speeches, Manoel José de Albuquerque, 12 Oct.; Manuel Nunes Machado, 10 Oct. 1843, *ACD* (1843, Second Session), 3:343–52, 367; Herculano Ferreira Pena, 7 July; Joaquim Antão Fernandes Leão, 22 July; Antônio Manuel de Campos Melo, 6 July, *ACD* (1846), 2:72–73, 90–91, 287.

Conclusion

1. Barman, *Brazil,* 227–34; J. M. Carvalho, *Teatro,* 51–61; Iglésias, "Vida," 9–69; I. R. Mattos, *Tempo,* 171–91.

2. Proclamations, AN/SPE, IJ1, m. 710, fol. 10r, 59r, 60r–v; Pres. to MJ, 9 Feb. 1848 (secret), and 2 March 1848 (confidential), AN/SPE, IJ1, m. 710, fols. 50r–52v,

55r; *Correio Mercantil,* 16 Feb. 1848, 1; *O Bahiano,* reprinted in *Correio Mercantil,* 23 Feb. 1848, 3; British Consul to Viscount Palmerston, 24 Feb. 1848, PRO, For. Off. 13, vol. 261, fol. 17. See also Tavares, "Processo," 45–48.

3. *Correio Mercantil,* 4 March 1848, 1; CA to Pres., 15 March 1848, APEB, m. 3395; 25 April 1848, APEB, m. 3422; 2 May 1848 (confidential), APEB, m. 3378.

4. Pres. to MG, 19 Nov. 1848 (confidential), AN/SPE, IG1, m. 119, fols. 296r–98v; CA to MG, 19 Nov. 1848, AN/SPE, IG1, m. 252, fol. 396. On the Praieira Rebellion, see Mosher, "Pernambuco," chap. 5. Fear of slave revolt is analyzed by Graden, " 'This City,' " 138–40.

5. *O Fiscal,* 6 Dec. 1848, 84; Pinho, *Cotegipe,* 177–79.

6. "A primeira linha e a G. Nacional," *O Guaycuru,* 12 July 1845, 416. For other calls for military federalism, see speeches, Antônio Carlos Ribeiro de Andrada Machado, 6 and 9 July, *ACD* (1839), 2:103–4, 134; Antônio José Henriques, 29 May, *ACD* (1843, Second Session), 1:408–9; "Reflexões politicas," *Correio Mercantil,* 17 Oct. 1848, 2.

7. The standard interpretation is that of Schulz, *Exército,* chaps. 1–2; but see also Pondé, *Organização,* chaps. 4–5; Motta, *Formação,* 115–73; A. B. Souza, *Exército,* 123–48.

8. On *O Militar,* see Schulz, *Exército,* 38–51; A. B. Souza, *Exército,* 149–79. Schulz provides the standard interpretation of the army's role in the overthrow of the empire, *Exército,* chaps. 4–11. See also Dudley, "Institutional Sources"; idem, "Professionalization"; C. Castro, *Militares.* The army's corporate identity is presented uncritically in Hayes, *Armed Nation.* More sophisticated treatments of army ideology recognize the corporation's internal politics, C. Castro, *Militares;* McCann, "Formative Period; J. M. Carvalho, "Forças"; Smallman, "Military Terror."

9. Kraay, "Soldiers," 212–15.

10. Lei, 19 Sep. 1850, *CLB.* See also J. B. Castro, "Guarda," 281–82. Rodrigues, Falcon, and Neves argue that the 1850 law brought no real changes to Guard practice in Rio, *Guarda,* 294.

11. "Mappa da Guarda Nacional . . . ," 21 April 1854, MJ, *Relatório* (1854); Pres., *Relatório* (1 March 1863), 20.

12. "Mappa da força com que cada uma das Províncias do Imperio concorreu para a guerra do Paraguay . . . ," MG, *Relatório* (1872); Kraay, "Reconsidering," 10, 20–23; Pres., *Relatório* (17 Oct. 1871), 30.

13. J. B. Castro, "Guarda," 298.

14. Kraay, "Reconsidering," 26–30; Beattie, "Transforming," chaps. 3–5; idem, "House," 446–51; Meznar, "Ranks," 347–51; F. F. Mendes, "Tributo," 250–318; idem, "Lei," 267–91.

15. Kraay, "Reconsidering," 1–2; McCann, "Nation," 232–43; Beattie, "House," 460–69; idem, "Transforming," chaps. 5, 9.

16. The best recent works on these rebellions include M. J. M. Carvalho, "Hegemony"; Mosher, "Pernambuco"; Lindoso, *Utopia;* Janotti, *Balaiada;* M. J. V. Santos, *Balaiada;* Assunção, "Elite Politics"; Paolo, *Cabanagem;* Chasteen, "Cabanos"; Cleary, " 'Lost.' "

17. M. J. M. Carvalho, "Encontro"; idem, "Hegemony," 204–11.

18. F. F. Mendes, "Tributo," 166–99; Meznar, "Ranks," 337–47.

19. MG, *Relatório* (1850), table 14.

20. Assunção, "Elite Politics," 3, 21–22, 24–25, 28–30.

21. Kraay, "Reconsidering," 29–30; Meznar, "Ranks," 347–50.

22. Prado Júnior, *Colonial Background*, 362.

23. Cleary, " 'Lost Altogether' " 112–13, 115–16, 120–21, 134.

24. J. G., *Ligeiras considerações*, 9, 15, 17–18.

25. M. J. M. Carvalho, "Cavalcantis"; Ribeiro, " 'Pés-de-chumbo,' " 147, 159.

26. Kraay, " 'Shelter,' " 641–43.

27. Koster, *Travels*, 2:182–83. See also Leite, *Pernambuco, 1817*, 171–72.

28. M. J. M. Carvalho, "Revisitando," 75–76; Quintas, *Revolução*, 121, 125–27.

29. Leite, *Pernambuco, 1824*, 71, 101–2, 129, 132–35; M. J. M. Carvalho, "Hegemony," 66–68, 83. On Mundurucu, see Chacon, ed., *Confederação*, 40–41; speech, Venâncio Henriques de Rezende, 6 July, *ACD* (1839), 2:97.

30. On the proliferation of black and mulatto militia units in colonial Minas Gerais (and elsewhere), see Russell-Wood, *Black Man*, 85–92.

31. Mott, *Escravidão*, 13; M. D. Graham, *Journal*, 170; Debret, *Viagem*, 2:237. See also J. H. Rodrigues, *Independência*, 3:74, 80, 89–90.

32. For typical examples of this approach, see J. B. Magalhães, *Evolução*; Barroso, *História*; Hayes, *Armed Nation*; Sodré, *História*.

33. R. Graham, *Patronage*; I. R. Mattos, *Tempo*; Uricoechea, *Patrimonial Foundations*; J. M. Carvalho, *Construção*.

34. E. V. Costa, *Brazilian Empire*, 59–61, 76–77.

35. Langley, *Americas*, 108–10. See also Helg, "Limits," 1; Hanger, "Conflicting Loyalties," 193–94.

36. R. Graham, "Free African Brazilians," 42.

37. Vinson III, "Bearing," 437.

38. Whitehead, "Carib Ethnic Soldiering"; Enloe, *Ethnic Soldiers* and *Police*; Peers, " 'Habitual Nobility.' "

39. Degler, *Neither Black nor White*, 177–78; 275–81; Marx, *Making*; Butler, *Freedoms*; Helg, *Our Rightful Share*; idem, "Race."

40. E. V. Costa, *Brazilian Empire*, chap. 9; Andrews, *Blacks*, 7–10; Freyre, *Masters*, xiii–xv.

BIBLIOGRAPHY

Archives

Arquivo Histórico do Exército (AHE)
  Fés de Ofício (FO)
  Reconhecimentos de Cadetes (RC)
  Requerimentos (RQ)
Arquivo do Instituto Geográfico e Histórico da Bahia (AIGHB)
Arquivo do Instituto Histórico e Geográfico Brasileiro (AIHGB)
Arquivo Municipal da Cidade do Salvador (AM)
Arquivo Nacional (AN)
  Seção de Arquivos Particulares (SAP)
  Seção do Poder Executivo (SPE)
    Grupo de Identificação de Fundos Internos (GIFI)
Arquivo Público do Estado da Bahia (APEB)
  Seção de Arquivo Colonial e Provincial
  Seção Judiciária (SJ)
    Inventários e Testamentos (IT)
    Livros de Registro de Testamentos (LRT)
Biblioteca Nacional (BN)
  Seção de Manuscritos (SM)
    Documentos Biográficos (DB)

Newspapers

Rio de Janeiro
  Aurora Fluminense. 1831.

O Homem de Cor. 1833.
Jornal do Commercio. 1837–1838.
Salvador
    O Acoute dos Déspotas. 1832.
    O Alabama. 1870.
    Aurora da Bahia. 1838–1839.
    O Bahiano. 1828–1831.
    Campeão Brazileiro. 1830.
    O Censor. 1837.
    O Commercio. 1842–1847.
    O Constitucional. 1822.
    O Constitucional. 1832.
    Correio Brasiliense. 1839.
    Correio Mercantil. 1836–1849.
    O Defensor do Povo. 1835–1836.
    O Democrata. 1833–1836.
    O Descobridor de Verdades. 1832.
    Diario Constitucional. 1822.
    Diario Constitucional. 1832.
    Diario da Bahia. 1833–1838.
    Escudo da Constituição Brasileira. 1831.
    O Espectador. 1845.
    O Farol. 1828–1832.
    O Fiscal. 1848.
    Gazeta Commercial da Bahia. 1833–1843.
    Gazeta da Bahia. 1830–1836.
    O Genio Federal. 1834.
    Grito da Razão. 1824–1825.
    O Guaycurú. 1844–1848.
    Idade d'Ouro do Brazil. 1811–1823.
    O Imparcial Brasileiro. 1829–1830.
    O Investigador Brasileiro. 1831–1832.
    A Luz Bahiana. 1837.
    O Mensageiro da Bahia. 1832.
    O Mercantil. 1845–1848.
    Nova Sentinella da Liberdade. 1831.
    O Novo Bahiano. 1833.
    Novo Diario da Bahia. 1837–1838.
    O Novo Sete de Setembro. 1837–1838.
    O Orgão da Lei. 1832.
    O Portacollo. 1832.
    O Precursor Federal. 1832.

O Século. 1848–1850.
Semanário Cívico. 1822.
Sentinela da Liberdade. 1831.
O Sete de Novembro. 1837.
A Tolerância. 1849.

Published Primary and Secondary Sources

Aguiar, Antonio Augusto da Costa. *Vida do Marquez de Barbacena*. Rio, 1896.

Alden, Dauril. *Royal Government in Colonial Brazil, with Special Reference to the Administration of the Marquis of Lavradio, Viceroy, 1769–1779*. Berkeley, 1968.

Algranti, Leila Mezan. *O feitor ausente: estudos sobre a escravidão urbana no Rio de Janeiro, 1808–1822*. Petrópolis, 1988.

Almanach para a Cidade da Bahia, anno 1812. Reprint. Salvador, 1973.

Almanach para o anno de 1845. Salvador, [1844].

Almeida, Manuel Antônio de. *Memórias de um sargento de milícias*. 16th ed. Belo Horizonte, 1977.

Almeida, Miguel Calmon du Pin e. "Resposta justificada de . . . a declaração franca que faz o General Labatut." *RIGHB* 65 (1939): 63–124.

Amaral, Antonio José. *Indicador da legislação militar em vigor no exército do império do Brasil organizado e dedicado a S. M. I. pelo. . . .* 2d ed. 3 vols. Rio, 1870–1872.

Amaral, Braz H. do. *História da independência na Bahia*. 2d ed. Salvador, 1957.

Andrade, Laércio Caldeira de. "O Cel. Felisberto Gomes Caldeira e a Independência da Bahia: o Coronel José Bonifácio Caldeira de Andrade e suas 'memórias.'" In *Anais do 1.o Congresso de História da Bahia*. Vol. 3, pp. 213–34. Salvador, 1952.

Andrade, Maria José de Souza. *A mão de obra escrava em Salvador, 1811–1860*. São Paulo, 1988.

Andrews, George Reid. "The Afro-Argentine Officers of Buenos Aires Province, 1800–1860." *Journal of Negro History* 64, no. 2 (1979): 85–100.

———. *The Afro-Argentines of Buenos Aires, 1800–1900*. Madison, 1980.

———. *Blacks and Whites in São Paulo, Brazil, 1888–1988*. Madison, 1991.

Anna, Timothy E. *Forging Mexico, 1821–1835*. Lincoln, 1998.

Aras, Lina Maria Brandão de. "A Santa Federação Imperial: Bahia, 1831–1833." Ph.D. diss., Universidade de São Paulo, 1995.

Araujo, Ubiratan Castro de. "La politique et l'économique dans une société esclavagiste: Bahia, 1820 à 1889." Ph.D. diss., Université de Paris, Sorbonne (Paris IV), 1992.

Archer, Christon I. *The Army in Bourbon Mexico, 1760–1810*. Albuquerque, 1977.

Arnizau, José Joaquim de. "Memoria topographica, historica, commercial e politica da Villa de Cachoeira da provincia da Bahia." *RIHGB* 25, no. 1 (1862): 127–42.

Assunção, Matthias Röhrig. "Elite Politics and Popular Rebellion in the Construction of Post-colonial Order: The Case of Maranhão, Brazil (1820–41)." *JLAS* 31 (1999): 1–38.

Aufderheide, Patricia Ann. "Order and Violence: Social Deviance and Social Control in Brazil, 1780–1840." Ph.D. diss., University of Minnesota, 1976.

Augel, Moema Parente. *Visitantes estrangeiras na Bahia oitocentista.* São Paulo, 1980.

"Auto de devassa do levantamento e sedição intentados na Bahia em 1798." *AAPEB* 35–36 (1959): 1–633.

Azevedo, Carmem Lúcia de, et al. *Fiscais e meirinhos: a administração no Brasil colonial.* Rio, 1985.

Azevedo, Célia Marinho de. *Onda negra, medo branco: o negro livre no imaginário das elites—século XIX.* Rio, 1987.

Azevedo, Thales de. *Povoamento da cidade do Salvador.* 3d ed. Salvador, 1969.

Bahia. *Collecção das leis e resoluções da Provincia da Bahia.* 1835–1850.

———. Arquivo Público do Estado. *Publicações do Archivo do Estado da Bahia.* 6 vols. Salvador, 1937–1948.

———. Arquivo Público do Estado. *Guia de fontes para a história da escravidão negra na Bahia.* Salvador, 1988.

———. President. *Relatório.* 1823, 1828, 1830–1871.

Barbacena, Felisberto Caldeira Brant Pontes, Marquês de. *Economia açucareira do Brasil no século XIX: cartas,* ed. Carmem Vargas. Rio, 1976.

Barickman, B. J. *A Bahian Counterpoint: Sugar, Tobacco, and Slavery in the Recôncavo.* Stanford, 1998.

———. " 'A Bit of Land, Which They Call *Roça:*' Slave Provision Grounds in the Bahian Recôncavo, 1780–1860." *HAHR* 74 (1994): 649–87.

———. "As cores do escravismo: escravistas 'pretos,' 'pardos,' e 'cabras' no Recôncavo baiano, 1835." *População e Família* 2, no. 2 (1999): 7–62.

———. " 'Tame Indians,' 'Wild Heathens,' and Settlers in Southern Bahia in the Late Eighteenth and Early Nineteenth Centuries." *TAm* 51 (1995): 325–68.

Barman, Roderick. *Brazil: The Forging of a Nation, 1798–1852.* Stanford, 1988.

Barretto, Domingos Alvares Muniz. *Indice militar de todas as leis, alvarás, cartas régias, decretos, resoluções, estatutos, e editaes promulgadas desde o anno de 1752 até o anno de 1810.* Rio, 1810.

Barreto, João de Deus Noronha Menna. *Os Menna Barreto: seis gerações de soldados, 1769–1950.* Rio, n.d.

Barros, F. Borges de. "A margem da história da Bahia." *AAPEB* 23 (1934): 3–584.

Barroso, Gustavo. *História militar do Brasil.* São Paulo, 1935.

Baud, Jean Chrétien. "De herinneringen van . . . aan de reis van Z. M. Oorlogsbrik 'De Vlieg' naar Brazilië, 1807–1808." In *De Reis van Z. M. "De Vlieg," commandant Willem Kreekel, naar Brazilië, 1807–1808,* ed. H. J. de Graaf. Vol. 1, pp. 173–214. The Hague, 1975.

Beattie, Peter M. "The House, the Street, and the Barracks: Reform and Honorable Masculine Social Space in Brazil, 1864–1945." *HAHR* 76 (1996): 439–74.

———. "Transforming Enlisted Army Service in Brazil, 1864–1940: Penal Servitude versus Conscription and Changing Conceptions of Honor, Race, and Nation." Ph.D. diss., University of Miami, 1994.

Bebiano, Rui. "Mecanismos disciplinares no exército português (séculos XVII–XVIII)." In *Arqueologia do estado: primeiras jornadas sobre formas de organização e exercício dos poderes na Europa do Sul, séculos XIII–XVIII*. Vol. 2, pp. 1041–58. Lisbon, 1988.

Beresford, William Carr, Viscount. *Regulamento e instrucçoes para disciplina e exercicio dos corpos de infantaria dos exercitos de Sua Magestade Fidelissima feito por ordem do mesmo senhor.* . . . Rio, 1820.

Bethell, Leslie. "The Independence of Brazil." In *Brazil: Empire and Republic, 1822–1930*, ed. Bethell, pp. 3–42. Cambridge, 1989.

Bethell, Leslie, and José Murilo de Carvalho. "1822–1850." In *Brazil: Empire and Republic, 1822–1930*, ed. Bethell, pp. 45–112. Cambridge, 1989.

Beyer, Gustavo. "Ligeiras notas de viagem do Rio de Janeiro á capitania de S. Paulo, no Brasil, no verão de 1813, com algumas notícias sobre a cidade da Bahia . . . ," trans. Alberto Löfgren. *Revista do Instituto Historico e Geographico de São Paulo* 12 (1907): 275–311.

Bieber, Judy. *Power, Patronage, and Political Violence: Statebuilding on a Brazilian Frontier, 1822–1889*. Lincoln, 1999.

———. "Postmodern Ethnographer in the Backlands: An Imperial Bureaucrat's Perceptions of Post-Independence Brazil." *Latin American Research Review* 33 (1998): 37–72.

Bittencourt, Anna Ribeira de Goes. *Longos serões do campo.* 2 vols. Rio, 1992.

Bolivar, Manoel Bernardino. *Breves considerações concernantes á lei da pranxa,—ou da chibata perante a medecina.* Salvador, 1853.

Booker, Jackie R. "Needed but Unwanted: Black Militiamen in Veracruz, Mexico, 1760–1810." *The Historian* 55, no. 2 (1993): 259–76.

Borges, Dain. *The Family in Bahia, Brazil, 1870–1945.* Stanford, 1992.

Boxer, Charles R. *Race Relations in the Portuguese Empire.* Oxford, 1963.

Brading, David A. *The First America: The Spanish Monarchy, Creole Patriots, and the Liberal State, 1492–1867.* Cambridge, 1991.

Brazil. Arquivo Nacional. *A Junta Governativa da Bahia e a independência.* Rio, 1973.

———. *Organizações e programas ministeriais: regime parlamentar no Império.* 2d ed. Rio, 1962.

Brazil. Câmara dos Deputados. *Anais da Câmara dos Deputados.* 1826–1850.

Brazil. Conselho Supremo Militar e de Justiça. *Colleção de provisões do Conselho Supremo Militar e de Justiça do imperio do Brasil de 1823–1856.* . . . Rio, 1861.

Brazil. Ministro da Justiça. *Collecção das leis do Império do Brazil, 1809–1850.*

————. *Relatório* [Title Varies]. 1831–1854.

Brazil. Ministro da Guerra. *Almanak* [Title Varies]. 1844, 1848–1849, 1851–1860.

————. *Relatório* [Title Varies]. 1828–1872.

Brazil. Ministério das Relações Exteriores. *Archivo diplomático da independência.* 6 vols. Rio, 1922–1925.

Brazil. Senado. *Anais do Senado.* 1826–1850.

Brelin, Johan. *De passagem pelo Brasil e Portugal em 1756*, trans. Carlos Perição de Almeida. Lisbon, 1955.

Britto, Eduardo A. de Caldas. "Levantes de pretos na Bahia." *RIGHB* 10 (1903): 69–84.

Brown, Alexandra Kelly. " 'On the Vanguard of Civilization': Slavery, the Police, and Conflicts between Public and Private Power in Salvador da Bahia, Brazil, 1835–1888." Ph.D. diss., University of Texas at Austin, 1998.

Brubaker, W. Rogers. *Citizenship and Nationhood in France and Germany.* Cambridge, 1992.

Bueno, José Antonio Pimenta. *Direito publico brasileiro e análise da constituição do império.* 1857. Brasília, 1978.

Bulcão Sobrinho, Antonio de Araujo de Aragão. "A Bahia nas Cortes de Lisboa de 1821." *RIHGB* 226 (1955): 231–60.

————. *Famílias bahianas.* 3 vols. Salvador, 1945–1946.

————. "Famílias bahianas: Villas-boas." *Revista do Instituto Genealógico da Bahia* 4 (1948): 21–59.

————. "Titulares Bahianos." *Revista do Instituto Genealógico da Bahia* 2 (1946): 26–40; 3 (1948): 55–58.

Burkholder, Mark A., and D. S. Chandler. *From Impotence to Authority: The Spanish Crown and American Audiencias, 1687–1808.* Columbia, 1977.

Burroughs, Peter. "Crime and Punishment in the British Army, 1815–1870." *English Historical Review* 100 (1985): 545–71.

————. "Tackling Army Desertion in British North America." *Canadian Historical Review* 61, no. 1 (1980): 28–68.

Bushnell, David. *Reform and Reaction in the Platine Provinces, 1810–1852.* Gainesville, 1983.

Cahill, David. "Colour by Numbers: Racial and Ethnic Categories in the Viceroyalty of Peru, 1532–1824." *JLAS* 26 (1994): 325–46.

Caldas, José Antonio. *Noticia geral de toda esta capitania da Bahia desde o seu descobrimento até o presente ano de 1759.* Reprint. Salvador, 1951.

Calmon, Pedro. "Um general da independência sul-americana: quem era Labatut. . . . " *RIGHB* 59 (1933): 65–71.

————. "Ladislau dos Santos Titára." *RIGHB* 86 (1976–1977): 159–83.

Calogeras, João Pandiá. *O Marquez de Barbacena.* 2d ed. São Paulo, 1936.

Campbell, Leon G. *The Military and Society in Colonial Peru, 1750–1810.* Philadelphia, 1978.

Campos, J[oão] da Silva. "Crônicas bahianas do século XIX." *AAPEB* 25 (1937): 295–65.

———. *Fortificações da Bahia.* Rio, 1940.

———. "Tradições bahianas." *RIGHB* 56 (1930): 353–57.

Cardoso, Manuel. "Azeredo Coutinho and the Intellectual Ferment of His Times." In *Conflict and Continuity in Brazilian Society,* ed. Henry H. Keith and S. F. Edwards, 148–83. Columbia, 1969.

———. "The Lay Brotherhoods of Colonial Bahia." *Catholic Historical Review* 33, no. 1 (1947): 12–30.

Carneiro, M. Tucci. *Preconceito racial: Portugal e Brasil-Colônia.* 2d ed. São Paulo, 1988.

Carrot, Georges. *La Garde Nationale, 1789–1871.* Toulouse, [1979].

Carvalho, José Murilo de. *A construção da ordem: a elite política imperial.* Rio, 1980.

———. *Desenvolvimiento de la ciudadanía en Brasil.* Mexico, 1995.

———. "As forças armadas na Primeira República: o poder destabilizador." In *História geral da civilização brasileira.* Tomo 3, ed. Boris Fausto. Vol. 2, pp. 181–234. São Paulo, 1977.

———. "Introdução." In *Bernardo Pereira de Vasconcelos,* ed. Carvalho, 9–34. São Paulo, 1999.

———. *Teatro de sombras: a política imperial.* São Paulo and Rio, 1988.

Carvalho, Marcus Joaquim Maciel de. "Cavalcantis e cavalgados: a formação das alianças políticas em Pernambuco, 1817–1824." *Revista Brasileira de História* 18, no. 36 (1998), http://www.scielo.br (18 June 1999).

———. "O encontro da 'soldadesca desenfreada' com os 'cidadãos de cor mais levianos' no Recife em 1831." *Clio* (Recife) 18 (1998): 109–37.

———. "Hegemony and Rebellion in Pernambuco (Brazil), 1821–1835." Ph.D. diss., University of Illinois at Urbana–Champaign, 1989.

———. "Revisitando uma quartelada: os aparelhos repressivos e a questão social em 1817." *Debates de História Regional* (Maceió) 1 (1992): 69–81.

Carvalho, Wenceslau Freire de. *Promptuario dos processos militares. . . .* 2d ed. Rio, 1887.

Castro, Celso. *Os militares e a república: um estudo sobre cultura e ação política.* Rio, 1995.

Castro, Hebe Maria Mattos de. *Das cores do silêncio: os significados da liberdade no sudeste escravista, Brasil, século XIX.* Rio, 1995.

———. *Ao sul da história: lavradores pobres na crise do trabalho escravo.* São Paulo, 1987.

Castro, Jeanne Berrance de. "A Guarda Nacional." *História geral da civilização brasileira.* Tomo 2, ed. Sérgio Buarque de Holanda. 4th ed. Vol. 2, pp. 274–98. São Paulo, 1985.

———. *A milícia cidadã: a Guarda Nacional de 1831 a 1850.* São Paulo, 1977.

Castro, Paulo Pereira. "A 'Experiência Republicana,' 1831–1840." *História geral da civilização brasileira*. Tomo 2, ed. Sérgio Buarque de Holanda. Vol. 2, pp. 9–67. São Paulo, 1964.

———."Política e administração de 1840 a 1848." *História geral da civilização brasileira*. Tomo 2, ed. Sérgio Buarque de Holanda. 4th ed. Vol. 2, pp. 509–40. São Paulo, 1964.

Castro, Renato Berbert de. *A primeira imprensa da Bahia e suas publicações: Tipografia de Manuel Antonio da Silva Serva, 1811–1819*. Salvador, 1968.

———. *A tipografia imperial e nacional da Bahia: Cachoeira, 1823—Salvador, 1831*. São Paulo, 1984.

———. *Os vice-presidentes da província da Bahia*. Salvador, 1978.

"Catálogo de documentos sôbre a Bahia existentes na Biblioteca Nacional." *ABN* 68 (1949): 1–431.

"Catálogo dos jornaes bahianos." *RIGHB* 21–22 (1899): 409–20, 549–79.

Cavalcanti, Zélia. "O processo de independência na Bahia." In *1822: dimensões*, ed. Carlos Guilherme Mota, 231–50. São Paulo, 1972.

Chacon, Vamireh, ed. *Da Confedereção do Equador à Grã-Colômbia (1796–1830): escritos políticos e manifesto de Mundurucu*. Brasília, 1983.

Chalhoub, Sidney. *Visões da liberdade: uma história das últimas décadas da escravidão na Corte*. São Paulo, 1990.

Chambers, Sarah. *From Subjects to Citizens: Honor, Gender, and Politics in Arequipa, Peru, 1780–1854*. University Park, 1999.

Chance, John K. *Race and Class in Colonial Oaxaca*. Stanford, 1978.

Chance, John K., and William B. Taylor. "Estate and Class in a Colonial City: Oaxaca in 1792." *Comparative Studies in Society and History* 19, no. 4 (1977): 454–87.

Chasteen, John Charles. "Cabanos and Farrapos: Brazilian Nativism in Regional Perspective, 1822–1850." *Locus* 7, no. 1 (1994): 31–46.

"Chronica dos acontecimentos da Bahia, 1809–1828." *AAPEB* 26 (1938): 49–95.

Cidade, Francisco de Paula. *Cadetes e alunos militares através dos tempos (1878–1932)*. Rio, 1961.

———. *Síntese de tres séculos de literatura militar brasileira*. Rio, 1959.

———. "O soldado de 1827 (ninharias de história, relativos aos soldados da Guerra Cisplatina)." *Revista Militar Brasileira* 17, no. 1 (1927): 1–70.

Cleary, David. " 'Lost Altogether to the Civilized World': Race and The *Cabanagem* in Northern Brazil, 1750 to 1850." *Comparative Studies in Society and History* 40, no. 1 (1998): 109–35.

Coelho, Edmundo Campos. *Em busca de identidade: o exército e a política na sociedade brasileira*. Rio, 1976.

Coffman, Edward M. *The Old Army: A Portrait of the American Army in Peacetime, 1784–1898*. New York, 1986.

Collier, Simon. *Ideas and Politics of Chilean Independence, 1808–1833*. Cambridge, 1967.

Conrad, Robert Edgar. *World of Sorrow: The African Slave Trade to Brazil.* Baton Rouge, 1986.

Conrad, Robert Edgar, ed. *Children of God's Fire: A Documentary History of Slavery in Brazil.* Princeton, 1983.

Cope, R. Douglas. *The Limits of Racial Domination: Plebeian Society in Colonial Mexico City, 1660–1720.* Madison, 1994.

"Cópia do recurso, e addendo ao mesmo que ás soberanas cortes de Portugal dirigem mil e cincoenta e dois constitucionaes. . . ." *RIGHB* 58 (1932):295–317.

"Correspondência passiva do Senador José Martiniano de Alencar." *ABN* 86 (1966): 7–468.

Corrigan, Philip, and Derek Sayer. *The Great Arch: English State Formation as Cultural Revolution.* Oxford, 1985.

Corvisier, André. *L'armée française de la fin du XVIIe siècle au ministère de Choiseul: le soldat.* 2 vols. Paris, 1964.

———. *Armies and Societies in Europe, 1494–1789,* trans. Abigail T. Siddall. Bloomington, 1979.

Corvisier, André, ed. *A Dictionary of Military History and the Art of War,* ed. John Childs, trans. Chris Turner. Oxford, 1994.

Costa, Afonso. "Genealogia baiana." *RIHGB* 191 (1946): 3–279.

Costa, Avelino Jesus da. "População da cidade da Baía em 1775." In *Actas do V Coloquio Internacional de Estudos Luso-Brasileiros.* Vol. 1, pp. 191–274. Coimbra, 1964.

Costa, Emília Viotti da. *The Brazilian Empire: Myths and Histories.* Rev. ed. Chapel Hill, 2000.

Costa, Samuel Guimarães da. *Formação democrática do exército brasileiro (pequena tentativa de interpretação social).* Rio, 1957.

Costa, Verissimo Antonio Ferreira da. *Collecção systematica das leis militares de Portugal. . . .* 4 vols. Lisbon, 1816.

Cunha, Manuela Carneiro da. *Negros, estrangeiros: os escravos libertos e sua volta à Africa.* São Paulo, 1985.

———. "Silences of the Law: Customary Law and Positive Law on the Manumission of Slaves in 19th-Century Brazil." *History and Anthropology* 1, no. 2 (1985): 427–43.

Cunha, Pedro Octávio Carneiro da. "A fundação de um império liberal." *História geral da civilização brasileira.* Tomo 2, ed. Sérgio Buarque de Holanda. Vol. 1, pp. 135–78, 238–62, 379–404. São Paulo, 1962.

Cunha, Rui Vieira da. *Estudo da nobreza brasileira.* 2 vols. Rio, 1966.

DaMatta, Roberto. *A casa e a rua: espaço, cidadania, mulher, e morte no Brasil.* São Paulo, 1985.

———. *Carnavals, Roques, and Heroes: An Interpretation of the Brazilian Dilemma,* trans. John Drury. Notre Dame, 1991.

Davis, Natalie Zemon. *Fiction in the Archives: Pardon Tales and Their Tellers in Sixteenth-Century France.* Stanford, 1987.

Davis, F. James. *Who Is Black? One Nation's Definition.* University Park, 1991.

Deák, István. *Beyond Nationalism: A Social and Political History of the Habsburg Office Corps, 1848–1918.* New York, 1990.

Dean, Warren. "Latifundia and Land Policy in Nineteenth-Century Brazil." *HAHR* 51 (1971): 606–25.

Debret, Jean-Baptiste. *Viagem pitoresca e histórica ao Brasil,* trans. Sergio Milliet. 3 vols. in 2. São Paulo, 1972.

"Defeza do General Labatut, sobre a sua conduta. . . ." *AAPEB* 10 (1923):97–138.

Degler, Carl N. *Neither Black nor White: Slavery and Race Relations in Brazil and the United States.* Madison, 1971.

Delson, Roberta M. "The Beginnings of Professionalization in the Brazilian Military: The Eighteenth-Century Corps of Engineers." *TAm* 51 (1995): 555–74.

DePalo, William A., Jr. *The Mexican National Army, 1822–1852.* College Station, 1997.

Deschamps Chapeaux, Pedro. *Los batallones de pardos y morenos libres.* Havana, 1976.

Dias, Maria Odila Silva. "Ideologia liberal e construção do estado no Brasil." *Anais do Museu Paulista* 30 (1980–1981): 211–25.

———. "A interiorização da metrópole (1808–1853)." In *1822: dimensões,* ed. Carlos Guilherme Mota, 160–84. São Paulo, 1972.

———. "Sociabilidades sem história: votantes pobres no império, 1824–1881." In *Historiografia brasileira em perspectiva,* ed. Marcos Cezar Freitas, 57–72. São Paulo, 1998.

Dinwiddy, J. R. "The Early Nineteenth-Century Campaign against Flogging in the Army." *English Historical Review* 97 (1982): 308–31.

"Documentos da Independencia." *AAPEB* 12 (1924): 65–75.

"Documentos historicos sobre a emancipação politica da Bahia." *RIGHB* 4 (1895): 127–40; 5 (1895): 281–97; 6 (1895): 375–94; 9 (1896): 341–50; 12 (1897): 175–86; 13 (1897): 433–50; 14 (1897): 547–69; 15 (1898): 123–44; 17 (1898): 351–76; 18 (1898): 554–85.

"Documentos para a historia da independência do Brasil." *AAPEB* 27 (1941): 1–181.

"Documentos sobre a independência." *AAPEB* 10 (1923): 5–161.

Dores, Manoel Moreira da Paixão. "Diario do capelão da esquadra imperial comandada por Lord Cochrane. . . ." *RIGHB* 67 (1941): 3–85.

Dória, Francisco Antonio, and Jorge Ricardo de Almeida Fonseca. "Marechal José Inácio Acciaiuoli: um potentado baiano do início do século XIX." *RIGHB* 90 (1992): 133–42.

Downing, Brian M. *The Military Revolution and Political Change: Origins of Democracy and Autocracy in Early Modern Europe.* Princeton, 1992.

Dudley, William Sheldon. "Professionalisation and Politicisation As Motivational Factors in the Brazilian Army Coup of 15 November 1889." *JLAS* 8 (1976): 101–25.

———. "Institutional Sources of Officer Discontent in the Brazilian Army, 1870–1889." *HAHR* 55 (1975): 44–65.

———. "Reform and Radicalism in the Brazilian Army, 1870–1889." Ph.D. diss., Columbia University, 1972.

Eltis, David. *Economic Growth and the Ending of the Transatlantic Slave Trade.* New York, 1987.

Enloe, Cynthia. *Ethnic Soldiers: State Security in Divided Societies.* Athens, 1980.

———. *Police, Military, and Ethnicity: Foundations of State Power.* New Brunswick, 1980.

Falcão, Edgard de Cerqueira. *Fortes coloniais da cidade do Salvador.* Rio, 1942.

Faoro, Raymundo. *Os donos do poder: formação do patronato político brasileiro.* 5th ed. 2 vols. Porto Alegre, 1979.

Faria, Maria Auxiliadora. "A Guarda Nacional em Minas Gerais (1831–1873)." *Revista Brasileira de Estudos Políticos* 49 (1979): 145–99.

Faria, Sheila de Castro. *A colônia em movimento: fortuna e família no cotidiano colonial.* Rio, 1998.

Fernandes, Florestan. *A revolução burguesa no Brasil: ensaio de interpretação sociológica.* Rio, 1975.

———. *The Negro in Brazilian Society,* ed. Phyllis B. Evelyth, trans. J. D. Skiles, A. Brunel, and A. Rothwell. New York, 1971.

Ferraz, Aydano do Couto. "O escravo negro na revolução da independência da Baía." *Revista do Arquivo Municipal* (São Paulo) 5, no. 56 (1939): 195–202.

Fields, Barbara Jeanne. "Slavery, Race and Ideology in the United States of America." *New Left Review* 181 (1990): 95–118.

Fitz-Roy, Robert. *Narrative of the Surveying Voyages of His Majesty's Ships Adventure and Beagle, between the Years 1826 and 1836....* 3 vols. London, 1839.

Flexor, Maria Helena Ochi. *Oficiais mecânicos na cidade do Salvador.* Salvador, 1974.

Flory, Thomas. *Judge and Jury in Imperial Brazil, 1808–1871: Social Control and Political Stability in the New State.* Austin, 1981.

———. "Race and Social Control in Independent Brazil." *JLAS* 9 (1977): 199–224.

Fonseca, Walter. *Fonseca: uma família e uma história.* São Paulo, 1982.

Forrest, Alan I. *Conscripts and Deserters: The Army and French Society during the Revolution and Empire.* New York, 1989.

———. "Citizenship and Military Service." In *The French Revolution and the Meaning of Citizenship,* ed. Renée Waldinger, Philip Dawson, and Isser Woloch, 152–65. Westport, 1993.

Foucault, Michel. *Discipline and Punish: The Birth of the Prison,* trans. Alan Sheridan. New York, 1979.

Fraga Filho, Walter. *Mendigos, moleques e vadios na Bahia do século XIX.* São Paulo and Salvador, 1996.

Fragoso, João Luís Ribeiro. *Homens de grossa aventura: acumulação e hierarquia na praça mercantil do Rio de Janeiro (1790–1830)* Rio, 1992.

França, António d'Oliveira Pinto da, ed. *Cartas baianas, 1821–1824: subsídios para o estudo dos problemas da opção na independência brasileira.* São Paulo, 1980.

Freitas, Daniel Gomes de. "Narrativa dos successos da Sabinada." Bahia. Arquivo Público do Estado da Bahia. *Publicações do Archivo do Estado da Bahia.* Vol. 1, pp. 261–333. Salvador, 1937.

Freyre, Gilberto. *The Masters and the Slaves: A Study in the Development of Brazilian Civilization,* trans. Samuel Putnam. 2d ed. Berkeley, 1986.

Garcia, Manoel Corrêia. *História da independência da Bahia.* Salvador, 1900.

Garcia, Paulo. *Cipriano Barata ou a liberdade acima de tudo.* Rio, 1997.

Genovese, Eugene D. *Roll, Jordan, Roll: The World the Slaves Made.* New York, 1976.

Geyer, Michael. "The Past as Future: The German Officer Corps as Profession." In *German Professions, 1800–1950,* ed. Geoffrey Cocks and Konrad H. Jarausch, 183–212. New York, 1990.

Gilbert, Arther N. "Military and Civilian Justice in Eighteenth-Century England: An Assessment," *Journal of British Studies* 17, no. 2 (1978): 41–65.

———. "Why Men Deserted from the Eighteenth-Century British Army." *Armed Forces and Society* 6 (1980): 553–67.

Girard, Louis. *La Garde Nationale, 1814–1871.* Paris, 1964.

Goffman, Erving. *Asylums: Essays on the Social Situation of Mental Patients and Other Inmates.* Garden City, 1961.

Gómez Pérez, María del Carmen. *El sistema defensivo americano: siglo XVIII.* Madrid, 1992.

Gorender, Jacob. *A escravidão reabilitada.* São Paulo, 1990.

Graden, Dale T. "An Act 'Even of Public Security': Slave Resistance, Social Tensions, and the End of the International Slave Trade to Brazil, 1835–1856." *HAHR* 76 (1996): 249–82.

———. " 'This City Has Too Many Slaves Joined Together': The Abolitionist Crisis in Salvador, Bahia, Brazil, 1848–1856." In *The African Diaspora,* ed. Alusine Jallah and Stephen E. Maizlish, 134–52. College Station, 1996.

Graham, Maria Dundas. *Journal of a Voyage to Brazil and Residence There, during Part of the Years 1821, 1822, 1823.* 1824. Reprint. New York, 1969.

Graham, Richard. "Free African Brazilians and the State in Slavery Times." In *Racial Politics in Contemporary Brazil,* ed. Michael Hanchard, 30–58. Durham, 1999.

———. *Patronage and Politics in Nineteenth-Century Brazil.* Stanford, 1990.

Graham, Sandra Lauderdale. *House and Street: The Domestic World of Servants and Masters in Nineteenth-Century Rio de Janeiro.* Cambridge, 1988.

Great Britain. Public Record Office. Foreign Office 13. "General Correspondence before 1906: Brazil." vols. 12–270, 1825–1849 (microfilm).

Guardino, Peter F. *Peasants, Politics, and the Formation of Mexico's National State: Guerrero, 1800–1857.* Stanford, 1996.

Hacker, Barton C. "Women and Military Institutions in Early Modern Europe: A Reconnaissance." *Signs* 6 (1981): 643–71.

Hale, Charles. *Mexican Liberalism in the Age of Mora, 1821–1853*. New Haven, 1968.

Halperin Donghi, Tulio. *The Aftermath of Revolution in Latin America*, trans. Josephine de Bunsen. New York, 1973.

———. "Revolutionary Mobilization in Buenos Aires, 1806–1815." *Past and Present* 40 (1968): 84–107.

Hamnett, Brian. "Process and Pattern: A Reexamination of the Ibero-American Independence Movements, 1808–1826." *JLAS* 29 (1997): 279–328.

Hanger, Kimberly. "Conflicting Loyalties: The French Revolution and Free People of Color in Spanish New Orleans." In *A Turbulent Time: The French Revolution and the Greater Caribbean*, ed. David Barry Gaspar and David Geggus, 178–203. Bloomington, 1997.

———. "A Privilege and Honor to Serve: The Free Black Militia of Spanish New Orleans." *Military History of the Southwest* 21 (1991): 59–86.

Harding, Rachel Elizabeth. *A Refuge in Thunder: Candomblé and the Alternative Spaces of Blackness*. Bloomington, 2000.

Haring, Clarence. H. *Empire in Brazil: A New World Experiment with Monarchy*. New York, 1958.

Harris, Marvin. *Patterns of Race in the Americas*. New York, 1964.

Harris, Marvin et al. "A Reply to Telles." *Social Forces* 73 (1995): 1613–14.

———. "Who are the Whites? Imposed Census Categories and the Racial Demography of Brazil." *Social Forces* 72 (1993): 451–62.

Hartnagel, Timothy F. "Absent without Leave: A Study of the Military Offender." *Journal of Political and Military Sociology* 2, no. 2 (1974): 205–20.

Hatch, Nathan O. "Introduction: The Professions in a Democratic Culture." In *The Professions in American History*, ed. Nathan O. Hatch, 1–13. Notre Dame, 1988.

Hay, Douglas. "Property, Authority and the Criminal Law." In *Albion's Fatal Tree: Crime and Society in Eighteenth-Century England*, ed. Hay et al., 17–63. New York, 1975.

Hayes, Robert Ames. *The Armed Nation: The Brazilian Corporate Mystique*. Tempe, 1989.

Helg, Aline. "The Limits of Equality: Free People of Colour and Slaves during the First Independence of Cartagena, Colombia, 1810–15." *Slavery and Abolition* 20, no. 2 (1999): 1–30.

———. "Race and Black Mobilization in Colonial and Early Independent Cuba: A Comparative Perspective." *Ethnohistory* 44, no. 1 (1997): 53–74.

———. *Our Rightful Share: The Afro-Cuban Struggle for Equality, 1886–1912*. Chapel Hill, 1995.

Henderson, William Darryl. *Cohesion, The Human Element in Combat: Leadership and Societal Influence in the Armies of the Soviet Union, the United States, North Vietnam, and Israel*. Washington, 1985.

Hernández Ponce, Roberto. "La Guardia Nacional de Chile: apuntes sobre su orígen y organizaciones, 1808–1848." *Historia* (Santiago) 19 (1984): 53–113.

Higgs, David. "Unbelief and Politics in Rio de Janeiro during the 1790s." *LBR* 21, no. 1 (1984): 13–34.

Hobsbawm, Eric. *The Age of Revolution: Europe, 1789–1848.* Cleveland, 1962.

Hoetink, H[armannus]. *Two Variants in Caribbean Race Relations: A Contribution to the Sociology of Segmented Societies,* trans. Eva M. Hooykaas. London, 1967.

Holanda, Sérgio Buarque de. "A herança colonial—sua desagregação." *História geral da civilização brasileira.* Tomo 2, ed. Sérgio Buarque de Holanda. Vol. 1, pp. 9–39. São Paulo, 1962.

Holloway, Thomas H. *Policing Rio de Janeiro: Repression and Resistance in a 19th-Century City.* Stanford, 1993.

Holmes, Richard. *Firing Line.* London, 1985.

Howard, Philip A. *Changing History: Afro-Cuban Cabildos and Societies of Color in the Nineteenth Century.* Baton Rouge, 1998.

Huell, Quirinus Maurits Rudolph ver. "Mijne Eerste Zeereis." In *De Reis van Z. M. "De Vlieg," commandant Willem Kreekel, naar Brazilië, 1807–1808,* ed. H. J. de Graaf. Vol. 2, pp. 43–367. The Hague, 1976.

Hughes, Daniel J. *The King's Finest: A Social and Bureaucratic Profile of Prussia's General Officers, 1871–1914.* New York, 1987.

Huntington, Samuel P. *The Soldier and the State: The Theory and Politics of Civil-Military Relations.* New York, 1957.

Iglésias, Francisco. "Vida Política, 1848–1866." *História geral da civilização brasileira.* Tomo 2, ed. Sérgio Buarque de Holanda. 4th ed. Vol. 3, pp. 1–112. São Paulo, 1982.

"A Inconfidencia da Bahia em 1798 (continuação)." *ABN* 45 (1922–1923): 3–421.

"A Inconfidencia da Bahia em 1798: devassas e sequestros." *ABN* 43–44 (1920–1921): 83–225.

"Independencia, anno de 1822." *AAPEB* 13 (1925): 55–64.

"Inventário de Pedro Labatut." *RIGHB* 54 (1928): 195–201.

"Inventario dos documentos relativos ao Brasil existentes no Archivo de Marinha e Ultamar por Eduardo de Castro e Almeida (Bahia)." *ABN* 34 (1912): 1–644; 36 (1914): 1–665; 37 (1915): 1–668.

J. G. *Ligeiras considerações sobre as verdadeiras causas do desgosto e depreciamento das fileiras.* Rio, 1871.

J. J. do C. M. *Carta do compadre do Rio S. Francisco do norte, ao filho do compadro do Rio de Janeiro. . . .* Rio, 1821.

Jackson, Robert H. "Race/Caste and the Creation and Meaning of Identity in Colonial Spanish America." *Revista de Indias* 203 (1995): 149–73.

Jancsó, István. *Na Bahia, contra o império: história do ensaio de sedição de 1798.* São Paulo and Salvador, 1996.

———. "A sedução da liberdade: cotidiano e contestação política no final do século XVIII." In *História da vida privada no Brasil*, ed. Fernando A. Novais. Vol. 1, pp. 388–437. São Paulo, 1997.

Janotti, Maria de Lourdes Mônaco. *A Balaiada*. São Paulo, 1987.

Janowitz, Morris. *The Professional Soldier: A Social and Political Portrait*. New York, 1970.

Joseph, Gilbert M., and Daniel Nugent, eds. *Everyday Forms of State Formation: Revolution and the Negotiation of Rule in Modern Mexico*. Durham, 1994.

Joseph, Nathan. *Uniforms and Nonuniforms: Communication through Clothing*. New York, 1986.

Karasch, Mary C. *Slave Life in Rio de Janeiro, 1808–1850*. Princeton, 1987.

Kaxangá João da Virgem Maria. *Oração d'acção de graças pela feliz restituição à pátria dos seus denodados filhos marciaes. . . .* Salvador, 1831.

Keith, G[eorge] M[onant]. *A Voyage to South America, and the Cape of Good Hope; in His Majesty's Gun Brig The Protector, commanded by. . . .* London, 1810.

Kennedy, John Norman. "Bahian Elites, 1750–1822." *HAHR* 53 (1973): 415–39.

Kindersley, Mrs. Nathaniel [Mary Molesworth]. *Letters from the Island of Teneriffe, Brazil, the Cape of Good Hope, and the East Indies*. London, 1777.

Kinsbruner, Jay. *Independence in Spanish America: Civil Wars, Revolutions, and Underdevelopment*. Albuquerque, 1994.

Klein, Herbert S. "The Colored Militia of Cuba, 1568–1868." *Caribbean Studies* 6, no. 2 (1966): 17–27.

Koster, Henry. *Travels in Brazil in the Years from 1809, to 1815*. 2 vols. Philadelphia, 1817.

Kraay, Hendrik. " 'As Terrifying as Unexpected:' The Bahian Sabinada, 1837–1838." *HAHR* 72 (1992): 501–27.

———. "Reconsidering Recruitment in Imperial Brazil." *TAm* 55 (1998): 1–33.

———. " 'The Shelter of the Uniform:' The Brazilian Army and Runaway Slaves, 1800–1888." *Journal of Social History* 29 (1996): 637–57.

———. "Soldiers, Officers, and Society: The Army in Bahia, Brazil, 1808–1889." Ph.D. diss., University of Texas at Austin, 1995.

Kuethe, Allan J. *Cuba, 1753–1815: Crown, Military, and Society*. Knoxville, 1986.

———. *Military Reform and Society in New Granada, 1773–1808*. Gainesville, 1978.

Kuznesof, Elizabeth Anne. "Clans, the Militia, and Territorial Government: The Articulation of Kinship with Polity in Eighteenth-Century São Paulo." In *Social Fabric and Spatial Structure in Colonial Latin America*, ed. David J. Robinson, 118–226. Ann Arbor, 1979.

Labatut, Pedro. "Declaração franca que faz o General Labatut de sua conducta em quanto commandou o Exercito Imperial e Pacificador. . . ." *RIGHB* 65 (1939): 45–61.

Lago, Laurênio. *Brigadeiros e generais de D. João VI e D. Pedro I no Brasil: dados biográficos, 1808–1831*. Rio, 1938.

———. *Os generais do exército brasileiro de 1860 a 1889*. Rio, 1942.

Langley, Lester D. *The Americas in the Age of Revolution, 1750–1850.* New Haven, 1996.

Lavradio, Marquês de. *Cartas da Bahia, 1768–1769.* Rio, 1972.

Leite, Glacyra Lazzari. *Pernambuco 1817: estruturas e comportamentos sociais.* Recife, 1988.

———. *Pernambuco 1824: a Confederação do Equador.* Recife, 1989.

Lenharo, Alcir. *As tropas da moderação: o abastecimento da Corte na formação política do Brasil, 1808–1842.* São Paulo, 1979.

Leonzo, Nanci. "As companhias de ordenanças na capitania de São Paulo: das origens ao governo do Morgado de Matheus." *Coleção Museu Paulista* 6 (1977): 123–239.

———. "Defesa militar e controle social na Capitania de São Paulo: as milícias." Ph.D. diss., Universidade de São Paulo, 1979.

Levine, Robert M. *Pernambuco in the Brazilian Federation, 1889–1937.* Stanford, 1978.

———. *Vale of Tears: Revisiting the Canudos Massacre in Northeastern Brazil, 1893–1897.* Berkeley, 1992.

Lewin, Linda. *Politics and Parentela in Paraíba: A Case Study of Family-Based Oligarchy in Brazil.* Princeton, 1987.

———. "Who Was 'O Grande Romano'? Genealogical Purity, the Indian 'Past,' and Whiteness in Brazil's Northeast Backlands, 1750–1900." *Journal of Latin American Lore* 19 (1996): 129–79.

Lindley, Thomas. *Narrative of a Voyage to Brazil, Terminating in the Seizure of a British Vessel . . . and a Description of the City and Provinces of St. Salvador and Porto Seguro.* London, 1805.

Lindoso, Dirceu. *A utopia armada: rebeliões de pobres nas matas do tombo real (1832–1850).* Rio, 1983.

Liss, Peggy. *Transatlantic Empires: The Network of Trade and Revolution, 1713–1826.* Baltimore, 1982.

Littlepage, Glenn E., and Leon Rappoport. "Factors Affecting Military AWOL Decisions." *Journal of Political and Military Sociology* 5, no. 1 (1977): 117–25.

López Alves, Fernando. *State Formation and Democracy in Latin America, 1810–1900.* Durham, 2000.

Loriga, Sabina. *Soldats: un laboratoire disciplinaire, l'armée piédmontese au XVIIIe siècle.* Paris, 1991.

Love, Joseph L. *Rio Grande do Sul and Brazilian Regionalism, 1882–1930.* Stanford, 1971.

———. *São Paulo in the Brazilian Federation, 1889–1937.* Stanford, 1980.

Lovell, Peggy A., and Charles H. Wood. "Skin Color, Racial Identity, and Life Chances in Brazil." *Latin American Perspectives* 25, no. 3 (1998): 90–109.

Lugar, Catherine. "The Merchant Community of Salvador, Bahia, 1780–1823." Ph.D. diss., State University of New York, Stony Brook, 1980.

———. "The Portuguese Tobacco Trade and Tobacco Growers of Bahia in the Late

Colonial Period." In *Essays Concerning the Socioeconomic History of Brazil and Portuguese India*, ed. Dauril Alden and Warren Dean, 26–70. Gainesville, 1977.

Lynch, John. *The Spanish American Revolutions, 1808–1826*. 2d ed. New York, 1986.

Lyra, Maria de Lourdes Viana. *A utopia do poderoso império—Portugal e Brasil: os bastidores da política, 1798–1822*. Rio, 1994.

Macaulay, Neill. *Dom Pedro: The Struggle for Liberty in Brazil and Portugal, 1798–1834*. Durham, 1986.

Magalhães, João Batista. *A evolução militar do Brasil (anotações para a história)*. Rio, 1958.

Malerba, Jurandir. *Os brancos da lei: liberalismo, escravidão e mentalidade patriarcal no império do Brasil*. Maringá, 1994.

Malheiro, Agostinho Marques Perdigão. *A escravidão no Brasil: ensaio histório-juridico-social*. 3 vols. Rio, 1866–1867.

Mallon, Florencia E. *Peasant and Nation: The Making of Postcolonial Mexico and Peru*. Berkeley, 1995.

Manobra das peças ligeiras de campanha . . . ordenada pelo governo á Companhia de Voluntarios de Artilharia a Cavallo do Principe D. Pedro. Salvador, [1811].

Marchena Fernández, Juan. *Ejéricto y milicias en el mundo colonial americano*. Madrid, 1992.

———. *La institución militar en Cartagena de Indias en el siglo XVIII*. Seville, 1982.

———. *Oficiales y soldados en el ejército de America*. Seville, 1983.

———. "The Social World of the Military in Peru and New Granada: The Colonial Oligarchies in Conflict, 1750–1810." In *Reform and Insurrection in Bourbon New Granada and Peru*, ed. John R. Fisher, Allan J. Kuethe, and Anthony McFarlane, 54–95. Baton Rouge, 1990.

Marchena Fernández, Juan, and María del Carmen Gómez Pérez. *La vida de guarnición en las ciudades americanas de la Ilustración*. Madrid, 1992.

Marjoribanks, Alexander. *Travels in South and North America*. London, 1853.

Marshall, T. H., and Tom Bottomore. *Citizenship and Social Class*. London, 1992.

Marx, Anthony W. *Making Race and Nation: A Comparison of the United States, South Africa, and Brazil*. Cambridge, 1997.

Mattos, Raimundo José da Cunha. *Repertório da legislação militar, actualmente em vigor no exercito e armada do Imperio do Brazil*. 3 vols. Rio, 1834–1842.

Mattos, Ilmar Rohloff de. *O tempo saquarema*. São Paulo, 1987.

Mattoso, Kátia M. de Queirós. *Bahia: a cidade do Salvador e seu mercado no século XIX*. São Paulo, 1978.

———. *Bahia, século XIX: uma província no império*. Rio, 1992.

———. "Conjoncture et société au Brésil à la fin du XVIIIe siécle: prix et salaires à la veille da le Révolution des Alfaiates—Bahia, 1798." *Cahiers des Amériques Latines* 5 (1970): 33–53.

———. "A família e o direito no Brasil no século XIX: subsídios jurídicos para os estudos em história social." *AAPEB* 44 (1979): 217–44.

———. *Presença francesa no movimento democrático baiano de 1798.* Salvador, 1969.

———. *To Be a Slave in Brazil, 1550–1888,* trans. Arthur Goldhammer. New Brunswick, 1986.

Mattoso, Kátia M. de Queirós, ed. "Albert Roussin: testemunha das lutas pela independência na Bahia (1822)." *AAPEB* 41 (1973): 116–66.

———. "O consulado francês na Bahia em 1824." *AAPEB* 39 (1970): 149–221.

Maximiliano. Príncipe de Wied-Neuwied. *Viagem ao Brasil,* trans. Edgar Süssekind de Mendonça and Flávio Poppe de Figueredo. 2d ed. São Paulo, 1958.

Maxwell, Kenneth R. *Conflicts and Conspiracies: Brazil and Portugal, 1750–1808.* Cambridge, 1973.

———. "The Generation of the 1790s and the Idea of Luso-Brazilian Empire." In *Colonial Roots of Modern Brazil,* ed. Dauril Alden, 107–44. Berkeley, 1973.

———. *Pombal: Paradox of the Enlightenment.* Cambridge, 1995.

McAlister, Lyle N. *The "Fuero Militar" in New Spain, 1764–1800.* 1957. Reprint. Westport, 1974.

McBeth, Michael Charles. "The Brazilian Army and Its Role in the Abdication of Pedro I." *LBR* 15, no. 1 (1978): 117–29.

———. "Brazilian Generals, 1822–1865: A Statistical Survey of Their Careers." *TAm* 44 (1987): 125–41.

———. "The Brazilian Recruit during the First Empire: Slave or Soldier?" In *Essays Concerning the Socioeconomic History of Brazil and Portuguese India,* ed. Dauril Alden and Warren Dean, 71–86. Gainesville, 1977.

———. "The Politicians vs. the Generals: The Decline of the Brazilian Army during the First Empire, 1822–1831." Ph.D. diss., University of Washington, 1972.

McCann, Frank D. "The Formative Period of Twentieth-Century Brazilian Army Thought, 1900–1922." *HAHR* 64 (1984): 737–65.

———. "The Nation in Arms: Obligatory Military Service during the Old Republic." In *Essays Concerning the Socioeconomic History of Brazil and Portuguese India,* ed. Dauril Alden and Warren Dean, 211–43. Gainesville, 1977.

McNeill, William H. *Keeping Together in Time: Dance and Drill in Human History.* Cambridge, 1995.

Meisel, Seth J. "War, Economy, and Society in Post-Independence Córdoba, Argentina." Ph.D. diss., Stanford University, 1998.

Mello, José Antônio Gonsalves de. *Henrique Dias, governador dos crioulos, negros e mulatos do Brasil.* Recife, 1988.

"Memoria descriptiva dos attentados da facção demagógica na provincia da Bahia contendo a narração circunstanciada da rebelião de 25 de outubro de 1824...." *RIHGB* 34 (1867): 233–355.

Mendes, Fábio Faria. "A economia moral do recrutamento militar no império brasileiro." *Revista Brasileira de Ciências Sociais* 13, no. 38 (1998), http://www.scielo.br (20 April 2000).

———. "A 'Lei da Cumbuca': a revolta contra o sorteio militar." *Estudos Históricos* 13, no. 24 (1999): 267–93.

———. "O tributo de sangue: recrutamento militar e construção do estado no Brasil imperial." Ph.D. diss., IUPERJ, 1997.

Mendes, Luís António de Oliveira. "Discurso preliminar historico, introdutivo com natureza de descripção economico da comarca e cidade da Bahia." *ABN* 27 (1905): 283–348.

Metcalf, Alida C. *Family and Frontier in Colonial Brazil: Santana de Parnaiba, 1580–1822.* Berkeley, 1992.

Meznar, Joan E. "The Ranks of the Poor: Military Service and Social Differentiation in Northeast Brazil, 1830–1875." *HAHR* 72 (1992): 335–51.

Miller, Joseph Calder. *Way of Death: Merchant Capitalism and the Angolan Slave Trade, 1730–1830.* Madison, 1988.

Miller, Gary M. "Status and Loyalty of Regular Army Officers in Late-Colonial Venezuela." *HAHR* 66 (1986): 667–96.

Miranda, Hypolito Cassiano de. "Noticia biographica do Coronel Ignacio Accioli de Cerqueira e Silva." In Ignacio Acioli de Cerqueira e Silva. *Memorias historicas e politicas da provincia da Bahia...,* ed. Braz do Amaral. Vol. 1, pp. vii–xxvii. Salvador, 1919.

Monteiro, Jonathas da Costa Rego. *Exército brasileiro: estudo sobre a organisação dos corpos de tropa a partir dos tempos coloniaes até 1934....* Rio, 1938.

Monteiro, Candido Pereira. *Consultas do Conselho de Estado relativamente a negocios do Ministerio da Guerra desde o anno de 1843 a 1866....* Rio, 1872.

Morel, Marco. "Entre paixão e martírio: Cipriano Barata e os mecanismos de liderança política no Brasil império." In *O estado como vocação: idéias e práticas políticas no Brasil oitocentista,* ed. Maria Emília Prado, 111–31. Rio, 1999.

Mörner, Magnus. *Region and State in Latin America's Past.* Baltimore, 1993.

Morton, F. W. O. "The Conservative Revolution of Independence: Economy, Society and Politics in Bahia, 1790–1840." D.Phil. thesis, Oxford University, 1974.

———. "Growth and Innovation: The Bahian Sugar Industry, 1790–1860." *Canadian Journal of Latin American and Caribbean Studies* 5, no. 10 (1980): 37–54.

———. "The Military and Society in Bahia, 1800–1821." *JLAS* 7 (1975): 249–69.

Mosher, Jeffrey Carl. "Pernambuco and the Construction of the Brazilian Nation-State, 1831–1850." Ph.D. diss., University of Florida, 1996.

Mota, Carlos Guilherme. *Atitudes de inovação no Brasil, 1789–1801.* Lisbon, [1971].

———. *Nordeste 1817: estruturas e argumentos.* São Paulo, 1972.

Mott, Luiz R. B. *Escravidão, homosexualidade e demonologia.* São Paulo, 1988.

———. *Sergipe del Rey: população, economia e sociedade.* Aracajú, 1986.

Motta, Jehovah. *Formação do oficial do exército (currículos e regimes na Academia Militar, 1810–1944).* Rio, 1976.

Mulvey, Patricia A. "Black Brothers and Sisters: Membership in the Lay Brotherhoods of Colonial Brazil." *LBR* 17, no. 2 (1980): 253–79.

Myerly, Scott Hughes. *British Military Spectacle: From the Napoleonic Wars through the Crimea.* Cambridge, 1996.

Nabuco, Joaquim. *Um estadista do império.* Rio, 1975.

Nascimento, Ana Amélia Vieira do. *Dez frequesias da cidade do Salvador: aspectos sociais e urbanos do século XIX*. Salvador, 1986.

Navarro, Luiz Thomaz de. "Itinerario da viagem que fez por terra da Bahia ao Rio de Janeiro. . . ." *RIHGB* 7 (1845): 433–68.

Nazzari, Muriel. "Vanishing Indians: The Social Construction of Race in Colonial São Paulo." *TAm* 57 (April 2001): 497–524.

Needell, Jeffrey D. *A Tropical Belle Epoque: Elite Culture and Society in Turn-of-the-Century Rio de Janeiro*. Cambridge, 1987.

Neeser, Herman. "Ensaio de um resumo cronológico-biográfico sobre Pedro Labatut, marechal de campo do exército brasileiro." *RIGHB* 68 (1942): 173–206.

Neves, Guilherme Pereira das. "Del imperio luso-brasileño al imperio del Brasil (1789–1822). In *De los imperios a las naciones: Iberoamérica*, ed. Antonio Annino, Luís Costa Leiva, and François-Xavier Guerra, 169–93. Zaragoja, 1994.

Neves, Erivaldo Fagundes. *Uma comunidade sertaneja da sesmaria ao minifúndio (um estudo de história regional e local)*. Salvador and Feira de Santana, 1998.

Nishida, Mieko. "From Ethnicity to Race and Gender: Transformations of Black Lay Sodalities in Salvador, Brazil." *Journal of Social History* 32 (1998): 329–48.

———. "Manumission and Ethnicity in Urban Slavery: Salvador, Brazil, 1808–1888." *HAHR* 73 (1993): 361–91.

Nobrega, Bernardino Ferreira. *Fac-simile da primeira e unica edição da memoria historica sobre as victorias alcançadas pelos itaparicanos no decurso [da] campanha da Bahia*, ed. Pirajá da Silva. Salvador, 1923.

Novais, Fernando A. *Portugal e Brasil na crise do antigo sistema colonial (1777–1808)*. 2d ed. São Paulo, 1981.

Novais, Fernando A., and Carlos Guilherme Mota. *A independência política do Brasil*. 2d ed. São Paulo, 1996.

"Novos documentos sobre Labatut." *RIGHB* 65 (1939): 125–30.

Oliveira, Cecília Helena de Salles. *A independência e a construção do império, 1750–1824*. São Paulo, 1995.

Oliveira, Maria Inês Côrtes de. *O liberto: o seu mundo e os outros, Salvador, 1790–1890*. São Paulo, 1988.

———. "Viver e morrer no meio dos seus: nações e comunidades africanas na Bahia do século XIX." *Revista USP* 28 (1995–1996): 174–93.

Omi, Michael, and Howard Winant. *Racial Formation in the United States from the 1960s to the 1990s*. 2d ed. New York, 1994.

Palmer, R. R. *The Age of the Democratic Revolution*. 2 vols. Princeton, 1959–1964.

Pang, Eul-Soo. *Bahia in the First Brazilian Republic: Coronelismo and Oligarchies*. Gainesville, 1979.

———. *In Pursuit of Honor and Power: Noblemen of the Southern Cross in Nineteenth-Century Brazil*. Tuscaloosa, 1988.

Pang, Eul-Soo, and Ron L. Seckinger. "The Mandarins of Imperial Brazil." *Comparative Studies in Society and History* 14, no. 2 (1972): 215–44.

Paolo, Pasquale di. *Cabanagem: a revolução popular da Amazônia.* 2d ed. Belém, 1986.

Parker, David S. *The Idea of the Middle Class: White-Collar Workers and Peruvian Society, 1900–1950.* University Park, 1998.

Paula, Eurípedes Simões de. "A organização do exército brasileiro." *História geral da civilização brasileira.* Tomo 2, ed. Sérgio Buarque de Holanda. Vol. 1, pp. 265–77. São Paulo, 1962.

Peard, Julyan G. *Race, Place, and Medicine: The Idea of the Tropics in Nineteenth-Century Brazilian Medicine.* Durham, 1999.

Pedro II, Emperor of Brazil. *Diário da viagem ao norte do Brasil.* Salvador, 1959.

Peers, Douglas M. " 'The Habitual Nobility of Being': British Officers and the Social Construction of the Bengal Army in the Early Nineteenth-Century." *Modern Asian Studies* 25, no. 3 (1991): 545–69.

Peregalli, Enrique. *Recrutamento militar no Brasil colonial.* Campinas, 1986.

Pinho, José Wanderley de Araújo. "A Bahia—1808–1856." *História geral da civilização brasileira,* ed. Sérgio Buarque de Holanda. São Paulo: Difusão Européia do Livro, 1964, tomo 2, vol. 2, pp. 242–311.

———. *Cotegipe e seu tempo: primeira phase, 1815–1867.* São Paulo, 1937.

———. "Pesquizas sobre o Marques de Barbacena: alguns inéditos." *RIGHB* 76 (1950–1951): 64–98.

Pondé, Francisco de Paula e Azevedo. *Organisação e administração do Ministério da Guerra no império.* Brasília and Rio, 1986.

Prado Júnior, Caio. *The Colonial Background of Modern Brazil,* trans. Suzette Macedo. Berkeley, 1969.

Querino, Manoel Raimundo. *A Bahia de outrora.* Salvador, 1955.

———. *Costumes africanos no Brasil.* 2d ed. Recife, 1988.

Quintas, Amaro. *A revolução de 1817.* 2d ed. Rio, 1985.

Ramos, Donald. "Social Revolution Frustrated: The Conspiracy of the Tailors in Bahia, 1798." *LBR* 13, no. 1 (1976): 74–90.

Rebello, Domingos José Antonio. "Corographia ou abreviada historia geographica do imperio do Brasil, coordinada, acrescentada, e dedicada á Casa Pia e Collegio dos Orfãos de S. Joaquim desta cidade." *RIGHB* 55 (1929): 5–235.

Rebello, Henrique Jorge. "Memoria e consideração sobre a população do Brasil." *RIHGB* 30, no. 1 (1867): 5–42.

Rebouças, Antonio Pereira. *Recordações da vida patriotica do advogado. . . .* Rio, 1879.

———. "Recordações patrioticas, 1821–1822." *RIGHB* 48 (1923): 455–506.

Redlich, Fritz. *The German Military Enterpriser and His Work Force: A Study in European Economic and Social History.* 2 vols. Wiesbaden, 1964–1965.

"Registro de correspondência do Conselho Interino com o Brigadeiro em Chefe do Exército Pacificador Pedro Labatut e as Juntas Provisórias de Governo das províncias do Brasil." *AAPEB* 41 (1973): 7–115.

Reis, João José. "A elite baiana face os movimentos sociais: Bahia, 1824–1840." *Revista de História* 54, no. 108 (1976): 341–84.

———. *A morte é uma festa: ritos fúnebres e revolta popular no Brasil do século XIX.* São Paulo, 1991.

———. "Recôncavo rebelde: revoltas escravas nos engenhos baianos." *Afro-Asia* 15 (1992): 100–26.

———. " 'The Revolution of the *Ganhadores*': Urban Labour, Ethnicity and the African Strike of 1857 in Bahia, Brazil." *JLAS* 29 (1997): 355–93.

———. *Slave Rebellion in Brazil: The Muslim Uprising of 1835 in Bahia*, trans. Arthur Brakel. Baltimore, 1993.

Reis, João José, and Eduardo Silva. *Negociação e conflito: a resistência negra no Brasil escravista.* São Paulo, 1989.

Ribeiro, Gladys Sabina. " 'Pés de chumbo' e 'garrafeiros': conflitos e tensões nas ruas do Rio de Janeiro no primeiro reinado (1822–1831)." *Revista Brasileira de História* 12, no. 23–24 (1991–1992): 141–65.

Rodrigues, José Honório. *Independência: revolução e contra-revolução.* 5 vols. Rio, 1975.

Rodrigues, Antonio Edmilson Martins, Francisco José Calazans Falcon, and Margarida de Souza Neves. *A Guarda Nacional no Rio de Janeiro, 1831–1918.* Rio, 1981.

Rodríguez Molas, Ricardo. *Historia social del gaucho.* Buenos Aires, 1968.

Rodríguez O., Jaime E. *The Independence of Spanish America.* Cambridge, 1998.

Roediger, David R. *The Wages of Whiteness: Race and the Making of the American Working Class.* New York, 1991.

Roniger, Luis. *Hierarchy and Trust in Modern Mexico and Brazil.* New York, 1990.

Rouquié, Alain. *The Military and the State in Latin America*, trans. Paul E. Sigmund. Berkeley, 1987.

Rugendas, João Maurício [Johann Moritz]. *Viagem pitoresca através do Brasil*, trans. Sérgio Milliet. 8th ed. Belo Horizonte, 1979.

Russell-Wood, A. J. R. "Black and Mulatto Brotherhoods in Colonial Brazil: A Study in Collective Behavior." *HAHR* 54 (1994): 567–602.

———. *The Black Man in Freedom and Slavery in Colonial Brazil.* London, 1982.

———. "Colonial Brazil." In *Neither Slave nor Free: Freedmen of African Descent in the Slave Societies of the New World*, ed. David W. Cohen and Jack P. Greene, 84–133. Baltimore, 1972.

———. "Ports of Colonial Brazil." In *Atlantic Port Cities: Economy, Culture, and Society in the Atlantic World, 1690–1850*, ed. Franklin W. Knight and Peggy K. Liss, 196–289. Knoxville, 1991.

———. "Preconditions and Precipitants of the Independence Movement in Portuguese America." In *From Colony to Nation: Essays on the Independence of Brazil*, ed. Russell-Wood, 3–40. Baltimore, 1975.

————. "Prestige, Power, and Piety in Colonial Brazil: The Third Orders of Salvador."
HAHR 69 (1989): 61–89.

Ruy, Affonso. *Dossier do Marechal Pedro Labatut.* Rio, 1960.

————. *História da câmara municipal da cidade do Salvador.* 2d ed. Salvador, 1996.

————. *A primeira revolução social brasileira (1798).* 2d ed. São Paulo, 1978.

"A Sabinada nas cartas de Barreto Pedroso a Rebouças." *ABN* 88 (1968): 207–18.

Salas, Elizabeth. *Soldaderas in the Mexican Military: Myth and History.* Austin, 1990.

Sales de Bohigas, Nuria. "Esclavos y reclutas en sudamerica, 1816–1826." In *Sobre esclavos, reclutas y mercaderes de quintos,* ed. Sales de Bohigas, 59–135. Barcelona, 1974.

————. "Some Opinions on Exemption from Military Service in Nineteenth-Century Europe." *Comparative Studies in Society and History* 10, no. 3 (1967–1968): 261–89.

Salles, Fritz Teixeira de. *Associações religiosas do ciclo do ouro.* Belo Horizonte, 1963.

Salvatore, Ricardo. "Autocratic State and Labor Control in the Argentine Pampas: Buenos Aires, 1829–1852." *Peasant Studies* 18, no. 4 (1991): 251–74.

————. "Reclutamiento militar, disciplinamiento y proletarización en la era de Rosas." *Boletín del Instituto de Historia Argentina y Americana "Dr. E. Ravignani."* 3d ser., no. 5 (1992): 25–47.

Sampaio, Antonio Manoel da Silveira. *Instrucções para o uso dos officiaes do exército nacional, e imperial nos processos de conselhos de guerra.* Rio, 1824.

Santoni, Pedro. "The Failure of Mobilization: The Civic Militia of Mexico in 1846." *Mexican Studies/Estudios Mexicanos* 12, no. 2 (1996): 169–94.

————. "A Fear of the People: The Civic Militia of Mexico in 1845." *HAHR* 68 (1988): 269–88.

Santos, Francisco Ruas. *Coleção bibliografia militar.* Rio, 1960.

Santos, Maria Januária Vilela. *A Balaiada e a insurreição de escravos no Maranhão.* São Paulo, 1983.

Schaumburg-Lippe, William, Count of. *Regulamento para o exercício, e disciplina dos regimentos de infantaria dos exércitos de S. M. Fidelissima.* Libson, 1794.

————. *Schriften und Briefe,* ed. Curd Ochwadt. 2 vols. Frankfurt, 1977.

————. *Regulamento para o exercício, e disciplina dos regimentos de cavallaria dos exércitos de Sua Magestade Fidelissima.* Lisbon, 1789.

Schulz, John. *O exército na política: origens da intervenção militar, 1850–1894.* São Paulo, 1994.

Schwarcz, Lília Moritz. *O espetáculo das raças: cientistas, instituições e questão racial no Brasil, 1870–1930.* São Paulo, 1995.

————. *Retrato em branco e negro: jornais, escravos e cidadãos em São Paulo no final do século XIX.* São Paulo, 1987.

Schwartz, Stuart B. "Colonial Identities and the 'Sociedad de Castas.' " *Colonial Latin American Review* 4, no. 1 (1995): 185–201.

————. "The Colonial Past: Conceptualizing Post-*Dependentista* Brazil." In *Colonial Legacies: The Problem of Persistence in Latin American History*, ed. Jeremy Adelman, 175–92. New York, 1999.

————. "The Formation of a Colonial Identity in Brazil." In *Colonial Identities in the Atlantic World, 1500–1800*, ed. Nicholas Canny and Anthony Pagden, 15–50. Princeton, 1987.

————. *Slaves, Peasants, and Rebels: Reconsidering Brazilian Slavery*. Urbana, 1992.

————. *Sovereignty and Society in Colonial Brazil: The High Court of Bahia and Its Judges, 1609–1751*. Berkeley, 1973.

————. *Sugar Plantations in the Formation of Brazilian Society: Bahia, 1550–1835*. Cambridge, 1985.

Schwarz, Roberto. *Misplaced Ideas: Essays on Brazilian Culture*, ed. John Gledson. London, 1992.

Scott, James C. *Domination and the Arts of Resistance: Hidden Transcripts*. New Haven, 1992.

————. *Weapons of the Weak: Everyday Forms of Peasant Resistance*. New Haven, 1985.

Seed, Patricia. "Social Dynamics of Race: Mexico City, 1753." *HAHR* 62 (1982): 559–606.

Sena, Consuelo Pondé de. *A imprensa reacionária na independência*: Sentinella Bahiense. Salvador, 1983.

Serrano Ortega, José Antonio. *El contingente de sangre: los gobiernos estatales y departmentales y los métodos de reclutamiento del ejército permanente mexicano, 1824–1844*. Mexico, 1993.

Silva, Alfredo Pretextato Maciel da. *Os generais do exército brasileiro de 1822 a 1889 (traços biográficos)*. 2d ed. 2 vols. Rio, 1940.

Silva, Eduardo da. *Prince of the People: The Life and Times of a Brazilian Free Man of Colour*, trans. Moyra Ashford. London, 1993.

Silva, Evaristo Ladislau e. *Recordações-biographicas do Coronel João Ladislau de Figuerêdo e Mello*. Salvador, 1866.

Silva, Ignacio Acioli de Cerqueira e. *Memorias historicas e politicas da provincia da Bahia...*, ed. Braz do Amaral. 6 vols. Salvador, 1919–1940.

Silva, Manoel Joaquim do Nascimento e. *Consultas do conselho sobre negócios relativos ao Ministério da Guerra...* 1842–1866. Rio, 1884.

————. *Synopsis da legislação militar brasileira até 1874 cujo conhecimento mais interessa aos empregados do Ministério da Guerra*. 2 vols. Rio, 1874.

Silva, Maria Beatriz Nizza da. "Family and Property in Colonial Brazil." *Portuguese Studies* 7 (1991): 61–77.

————. *História da família no Brasil colonial*. Rio, 1998.

————. *A primeira gazeta da Bahia*: Idade de Ouro do Brasil. São Paulo, 1978.

————. "Repercussões do movimento constitucional português de 1820 na Bahia e no Rio de Janeiro." *AAPEB* 51 (1994): 181–89.

Silva, Pirajá da. "Brigadeiro Antonio de Souza Lima (o Lima de Itaparica)." In Bernardino Ferreira Nobrega. *Fac-simile da primeira e unica edição da memoria historica sobre as victorias alcançadas pelos itaparicanos no decurso [da] campanha da Bahia,* ed. Pirajá da Silva, xli–lviii. Salvador, 1923.

Silva, Pirajá da, Bernardino J. de Souza, and C. Muller. "Guerra da independencia na Bahia: os Encouraçados do Pedrão e o Padre Brayner." *RIGHB* 48 (1923): 373–418.

Simas Filho, Américo. "A cidade do Salvador antes e depois da Independência." In *Ciclo de conferências sobre o sesquicentenário da independência na Bahia em 1973,* 99–115. Salvador, 1977.

Sims, Harold Dana. *The Expulsion of Mexico's Spaniards, 1821–1836.* Pittsburgh, 1990.

Skelley, Alan Ramsey. *The Victorian Army at Home: The Recruitment and Terms and Conditions of the British Regular.* London, 1977.

Skelton, William B. *An American Profession of Arms: The Army Officer Corps, 1784–1861.* Lawrence, 1992.

Skidmore, Thomas E. *Black into White: Race and Nationality in Brazilian Thought.* New York, 1974.

Skocpol, Theda. "Bringing the State Back In: Strategies of Analysis in Current Research." In *Bringing the State Back In,* ed. Peter B. Evans, Dietrich Rueschemeyer, and Theda Skocpol, 1–36. Cambridge, 1985.

Slatta, Richard W. *Gauchos and the Vanishing Frontier.* Lincoln, 1983.

Smallman, Shawn C. "Military Terror and Silence in Brazil, 1910–1945." *Canadian Journal of Latin American and Caribbean Studies* 24, no. 47 (1999): 5–27.

Smith, Leonard Vinson. *Between Mutiny and Obedience: The Case of the French Fifth Infantry Division of World War I.* Princeton, 1994.

———. "The Disciplinary Dilemma of French Military Justice, September 1914–April 1917: The Case of the 5.e Division d'Infanterie." *Journal of Military History* 55, no. 1 (1991): 47–68.

Socolow, Susan Migden. *The Bureaucrats of Buenos Aires, 1769–1810: Amor al Real Servicio.* Durham, 1987.

Sodré, Nelson Werneck. *História militar do Brasil.* Rio, 1965.

Soisa, Francisco Manoel Soares de. *Generalidades medicas acerca do recrutamento.* Rio, 1845.

Souza, Adriana Barreto de. *O exército na consolidação do império: um estudo sobre a política militar conservadora.* Rio, 1999.

Souza, Antonio Loureiro de. *Bahianos ilustres, 1564–1925.* 2d ed. Salvador, 1973.

———. "Visconde do Rio Vermelho: os nobres do Rio Vermelho." *Revista do Instituto Genealógico da Bahia* 18 (1972): 221–27.

Souza, Antônio Moniz de. "Viagens e observações de hum brasileiro, que desejando ser util a sua patria se dedicou a estudar os usos e costumes de seus patrícios e os tres reinos da natureza em varios lugares e sertões do Brasil." *RIGHB* 72 (1945): 3–119.

———. "Breve noticia sobre a revolução do Brazil em 1821 nas provincias da Bahia, Sergipe e Alagoas. . . ." *RIGHB* 72 (1945): 120–31.

Souza, Iara Lis Carvalho. *Pátria coroada: o Brasil como corpo político autônomo, 1780–1831.* São Paulo, 1998.

Souza, J. A. Soares de. "O Brasil e o Prata até 1828." *História geral da civilização brasileira.* Tomo 2, ed. Sérgio Buarque de Holanda. Vol. 1, pp. 300–28. São Paulo, 1962.

Souza, Paulo Cesar. *A Sabinada: a revolta separatista da Bahia, 1837.* São Paulo, 1987.

Spitzer, Leo. *Lives in Between: Assimilation and Marginality in Austria, Brazil, and West Africa, 1780–1945.* Cambridge, 1989.

Spix, Johann Baptist von, and Carl Friedrich Philipp von Martius. *Viagem pelo Brasil, 1817–1820.* 3 vols., trans. Lúcia Furquim Lahmeyer. Belo Horizonte and São Paulo, 1981.

Stein, Stanley J., and Barbara H. *The Colonial Heritage of Latin America: Essays on Economic Dependence in Perspective.* New York, 1970.

Stepan, Alfred C. *The Military in Politics: Changing Patterns in Brazil.* Princeton, 1971.

Steppler, G. A. "British Military Law, Discipline, and the Conduct of Regimental Courts-Martial in the Late Eighteenth Century." *English Historical Review* 102 (1987): 859–86.

Stone, Lawrence. *The Crisis of the Aristocracy, 1558–1641.* Abridged ed. Oxford, 1967.

Szuchman, Mark D. *Order, Family, and Community in Buenos Aires, 1810–1860.* Stanford, 1988.

Tannenbaum, Frank. *Slave and Citizen: The Negro in the Americas.* New York, 1946.

Taunay, Hippolyte, and Ferdinand Dénis. *Le Brésil, ou histoire, moeurs, usages et coutumes des habitants de ce royaume.* 5 vols. Paris, 1822.

Tavares, Luís Henrique Dias. "Cipriano José Barata de Almeida." *Revista de Historia de America* 101 (1986): 133–44.

———. *História da Bahia.* Salvador, 1974.

———. *História da sedição intentada na Bahia em 1798.* São Paulo, 1975.

———. *A independência do Brasil na Bahia.* 2d ed. Rio, 1982.

———. *O levante dos Periquitos.* Salvador, 1990.

———. "O processo contra 'O Guaycurú.'" *RIGHB* 81 (1957): 45–48.

Taylor, William B. "Between Global Process and Local Knowledge: An Inquiry into Early Latin American Social History, 1500–1900." In *Rethinking the Past: The Worlds of Social History,* ed. Olivier Zunz, 115–90. Chapel Hill, 1985.

Telles, Edward. "Who are the Morenos?" *Social Forces* 73 (1995): 1609–11.

Thompson, E. P. *The Making of the English Working Class.* New York, 1966.

Thomson, Guy P. C. "Los indios y el servicio militar en el Mexico decimonónico

¿leva o ciudadanía?" In *Indio, nación y comunidad en el México del siglo XIX*, ed. Antonio Escobar Ohmstede, 207–51. Mexico, 1993.

Thurner, Mark. *From Two Republics to One Divided: Contradictions of Postcolonial Nation-Making in Andean Peru*. Durham, 1997.

Tilly, Charles. *Coercion, Capital, and European States*. Cambridge, 1990.

———. "Reflections on the History of European State-Making." In *The Formation of National States in Western Europe*, ed. Tilly, 3–83. Princeton, 1975.

———. "War Making and State Making as Organized Crime." In *Bringing the State Back In*, ed. Peter B. Evans, Dietrich Rueschemeyer, and Theda Skocpol, 169–91. Cambridge, 1985.

Titara, Ladislau dos Santos. *Auditor brasileiro ou manual geral dos conselhos, testamentos e inventários militares para o uso dos officiaes do exército do império do Brasil*. 3d ed. Rio Grande, 1855.

———. *Complemento do auditor brasileiro ou manual geral dos conselhos, testamentos e inventários militares*. 2d ed. Rio Grande, 1856.

———. *Memórias do grande exército aliado libertador do sul da América, na guerra de 1851 a 1852 e dos acontecimentos mais notáveis que a precederam*. 2d ed. Rio, 1950.

———. *Paraguassú: epopéia da guerra da independência na Bahia*. São Paulo, 1973.

Torres, Mário. "Uma família de generais." *RIGHB* 69 (1943): 253–325.

Torres, Theodorico Lopes Gentil. *Ministros da Guerra do Brasil, 1808–1945*. Rio, 1946.

Tranajura, Maria Cristina Fraga. "José Antônio da Silva Castro: um herói injustiçado." *RIGHB* 83 (1962–1967): 123–37.

Turnbull, John. *A Voyage Round the World in the Years 1800, 1801, 1803, and 1804, in Which the Author Visited Madeira, the Brazils. . . .* 2d ed. London, 1813.

Turner, Bryan S. *Citizenship and Capitalism: The Debate over Reformism*. London, 1986.

Turner, Bryan S, ed. *Citizenship and Social Theory*. London, 1993.

Uribe-Uran, Victor M. *Honorable Lives: Lawyers, Family, and Politics in Colombia, 1780–1850*. Pittsburgh, 2000.

Uricoechea, Fernando. *The Patrimonial Foundations of the Brazilian Bureaucratic State*. Berkeley, 1980.

United States. National Archives and Records Service. "Despatches from U.S. Consuls in St. Salvador, Brazil, 1808–1849." Microcopy T-432.

Val, Nilo. "Formação do exército brasileiro e sua evolução no século XIX." *Congresso Internacional de História da América, 1922*. Vol. 7, pp. 619–81. Rio, 1928.

Van Young, Eric. *Mexico's Regions: Comparative History and Development*. San Diego, 1992.

Vargas, Mark A. "The Military Justice System and the Use of Illegal Punishments as Causes of Desertion in the U.S. Army, 1821–1835." *Journal of Military History* 55, no. 1 (1991): 1–19.

Verger, Pierre. *Fluxo e refluxo do tráfico de escravos entre o golfo do Benin e a Bahia de Todos os Santos dos séculos XVII a XIX*, trans. Tasso Gadzanis. 3d ed. São Paulo, 1987.

Veterano, Um. *A estatua equestre: opusculo-politico-historico sobre factos da Independencia do Brazil. . . .* Salvador, 1862.

Viana, Hildegardes. *Antigamente era assim.* Rio, 1994.

Vianna Filho, Luiz. *A Sabinada (a república bahiana de 1837).* Rio, 1938.

Vilhena, Luiz dos Santos. *Recopilação de noticias soteropolitanas e brasilicas. . . .* 2 vols. Salvador, 1921.

Vinson III, Ben. "Bearing Arms for His Imperial Majesty: The Free-Colored Militia in Colonial Mexico." Ph.D. diss., Columbia University, 1998.

———. "Free Colored Voices: Issues of Representation and Racial Identity in the Colonial Mexican Militia." *Journal of Negro History* 80, no. 4 (1995): 170–82.

———. "Race and Badge: The Free Colored Militia in Colonial Mexico." *TAm* 56 (2000): 471–96.

Voelz, Peter M[ichael]. *Slave and Soldier: The Military Impact of Blacks in the Colonial Americas.* New York, 1993.

Wagley, Charles. "On the Concept of Social Race in the Americas." In *Contemporary Cultures and Societies of Latin America*, ed. Dwight B. Heath and Richard N. Adams, 531–45. New York, 1965.

Waldinger, Renée, Philip Dawson, and Isser Woloch, eds. *The French Revolution and the Meaning of Citizenship.* Westport, 1993.

Walker, Charles F. *Smoldering Ashes: Cuzco and the Creation of Republican Peru, 1780–1840.* Durham, 1999.

Wetherell, James. *Brazil: Stray Notes from Bahia: Being Extracts from Letters, &c., during a Residence of Fifteen Years*, ed. William Hadfield. Liverpool, 1860.

Whitehead, Neil Lancelot. "Carib Ethnic Soldiering in Venezuela, the Guianas, and the Antilles, 1492–1820." *Ethnohistory* 37, no. 4 (1990): 357–85.

Wildberger, Arnold. *Os presidentes da província da Bahia, efetivos e interinos, 1824–1889.* Salvador, 1949.

Williamson, Joel. *New People: Miscegenation and Mulattoes in the United States.* New York, 1984.

Wimmer, Linda. "African Producers, European Merchants, Indigenous Consumers: Brazilian Tobacco in the Canadian Fur Trade." Ph.D. diss., University of Minnesota, 1996.

Winant, Howard. *Racial Conditions: Politics, Theory, Comparisons.* Minneapolis, 1994.

Wirth, John D. *Minas Gerais in the Brazilian Federation, 1889–1937.* Stanford, 1977.

Wirtschafter, Elise Kimerling. *From Serf to Russian Soldier.* Princeton, 1990.

INDEX

In this index an "f" after a number indicates a continuation on the next page, and an "ff" indicates a continuation on the next two pages. *Passim* is used for a cluster of references in close sequence.

Individuals are indexed under the last name by which they are referred to in the text, as outlined in the Note on Currency, Military Ranks, Orthography, and Names. In addition, all individuals are indexed under their last surname, with a cross-reference when necessary.